A Man Apart

A Man Apart

The Journal of Nicholas Cresswell 1774–1781

EDITED AND WITH AN INTRODUCTION
BY
HAROLD B. GILL JR.
AND
GEORGE M. CURTIS, III

LEXINGTON BOOKS

A division of
ROWMAN & LITTLEFIELD PUBLISHERS, INC.
Lanham • Boulder • New York • Toronto • Plymouth, UK

LEXINGTON BOOKS

A division of Rowman & Littlefield Publishers, Inc.
A wholly owned subsidiary of The Rowman & Littlefield Publishing Group, Inc.
4501 Forbes Boulevard, Suite 200
Lanham, MD 20706

Estover Road
Plymouth PL6 7PY
United Kingdom

British Library Cataloguing in Publication Information Available

Library of Congress Cataloging-in-Publication Data

Cresswell, Nicholas, 1750–1804.
  A man apart the journal of Nicholas Cresswell, 1774–1781 / edited and with an
introduction by Harold B. Gill, Jr. and George M. Curtis, III.
    p. cm.
  Includes bibliographical references.
  ISBN-13: 978-0-7391-2847-3 (cloth : alk. paper)
  ISBN-10: 0-7391-2847-7 (cloth : alk. paper)
  ISBN-13: 978-0-7391-2848-0 (pbk. : alk. paper)
  ISBN-10: 0-7391-2848-5 (pbk. : alk. paper)
  ISBN-13: 978-0-7391-3440-5 (electronic)
  ISBN-10: 0-7391-3440-X (electronic)
  1. United States—Description and travel—Early works to 1800. 2. United States—
Social life and customs—1775–1783. 3. Cresswell, Nicholas, 1750–1804—Travel—
United States. I. Gill, Harold B. II. Curtis, George M., 1935– III. Title.
  E163.C783 2009
  973.3—dc22   2008046793

Printed in the United States of America

♾™ The paper used in this publication meets the minimum requirements of American
National Standard for Information Sciences—Permanence of Paper for Printed Library
Materials, ANSI/NISO Z39.48–1992.

Contents

Acknowledgments

We thank the Colonial Williamsburg Foundation for granting us permission to publish this new edition of Nicholas Cresswell's journal. The original manuscript has been in their collections for many years. The late Edwin M. Riley, former director of research at Colonial Williamsburg intended to edit the journal himself but because of ill health was unable to undertake the job. We were fortunate that he passed the job on to us.

Thanks as well to the editor, Bernard W. Sheehan, of the *Indiana Magazine of History* for having published our essay, "A Man Apart: Nicholas Cresswell's American Odyssey, 1774-1777," *Indiana Magazine of History*, vol. XCVI, No. 2 (June 2000): 169-90, which forms the foundation for our introduction.

Too many libraries, library staffs, and individuals have been helpful to name them all. We won't try because we would probably not mention all.

Introduction

The American Odyssey of Nicholas Cresswell of Derbyshire, England, began with bright promise. On March 1, 1774, just weeks after his twenty-fourth birthday, as a fitting christening and accompaniment for the commencement of his venture, he began a journal. He had come "to a determined resolution to go into America." He never recorded his real reasons for his desire to travel to America but writes that he had "private reasons, that rather obliges me to leave home, not altogether on my own account." He later says that his friends are "utterly unacquainted with my true reasons for taking this surprizeing whim, as they call it." His "private reasons" for traveling to America was to eventually settle there permanently. Cresswell believed that if he confided the reason to his friends and family, they would probably prevent the trip. Cresswell emphasized that this decision was neither superficial nor novel. Since "almost from my infancy" he had thought much about "going to America." After serious "studying and deliberating," he decided that no time was "more suitable than the present" for a journey to Virginia, for "I like the situation of that Colony the best." He offered no clue as to how he heard about the "situation" of Virginia.[1] He counted on his fortunate place in a Derbyshire gentry family for assurances of financial support as well as useful social and business connections.

However well conceived these private plans were, Cresswell could not anticipate the accidents of time and place. Unintentionally, his quest for personal economic independence away from home ran headlong into the onset of the American Revolution. Cresswell's journal, originally intended to serve as an enduring reminder of a successful business venture, instead became a bitter narrative of an outsider trapped in the American march toward independence.

For years after he stopped his note taking, Cresswell's journal lay dormant. Then in 1928 one of his descendants, Samuel Thornely, published an unannotated version that had softened Cresswell's opinions and actions. During its seventy-five year lifetime, the printed journal has served as a popular source for historians of the American Revolution. No one has yet told Cresswell's story, however. This is a fate not unlike that of many diaries, published and unpublished. Useful as these intimate sources have been for the commentary that they yield for historians, the stories themselves remain largely untold, and so the narrators have remained largely invisible.

Cresswell's history offers a scintillating window into the complex world of the American Revolution. Furthermore, given the significance of Cresswell's 1775 travels west to present-day Harrodsburg, Kentucky, his journal proves a fitting addition to the literature of the Ohio Valley. It is the vibrant and multilayered story of a complex and energetic man caught up in powerful events that threatened to overwhelm him and defeat his most cherished hopes and dreams. His view of the time continues to stand in defiance of much of what historians have said about the course of events, for Cresswell, even after all these years, steadfastly fails to fit easily into historical pigeonholes. He was not a Loyalist in the accepted understanding of this word, for he was technically an English visitor, not an American colonist. He most certainly was not an apologist for the British ministry as his actions in the American West clearly attest and his commentary upon the occasion of his departing from America confirm. More important than all this was his growing affection for certain parts of America, particularly the lower Shenandoah Valley and the west. Throughout his three years in America, save for periods of illness or intemperance driven by despair, Cresswell wrote with vividness of the new people, the remarkable country, and the disarray of empire. The journal reveals that he struggled with the challenge of American liberty that these new people and new places presented to him. As much as he yearned to stay, he could not bring himself to accept the Patriot cause. Feisty and argumentative to a fault, he laced his journal with an ironic dismissal of political passion, American style. Overall, Cresswell's history was not a story of accomplishment. The journal that he started with such a flourish of confidence in 1774 became a sad and troubled record of failures, one venture after another spoiled by what he viewed as an almost tragic American descent into chaos.

Cresswell's original plan possessed the virtues of uncomplicated ambition and candor. Although his decision faced determined opposition from his family and friends, he was "resolved to brave them all and follow my own inclination for once." This was not to be a normal grand tour for the sake of cultural gratification. Instead, Cresswell viewed his American experience as a mission with specific objectives. He was seeking a future where he could "live much better and make greater improvement in America" than he believed was likely if he remained at home. In his opening journal entry, Cresswell made it clear that he would maintain in America that style of life that he had enjoyed in England. He intended to remain "in the farming way as that is the business I have been brought up to." He was confident that he knew the business well, and his initial plan was straightforward reflection of it. Once his parents granted him their reluctant permission, Cresswell expected that his father would extend sufficient credit to finance his trip. If, after a careful survey of the Virginia country, he believed the conditions suitable, the venturer planned "to return immediately and endeavour to prevail upon my Friends to give me something to begin the world with." Thus armed with development credit, he would start up his Virginia agricultural business. Unknown to Cresswell, during the month he was preparing to set out for America, Parliament was putting the final touches on the

Boston Port Act, the first of five legislative assertions of imperial authority soon
to earn the American sobriquet of the Intolerable Acts. Taken as a group, these
acts of Parliament would have an impact upon nearly everything Cresswell did,
the irony of which would not be entirely lost on him during his darkest hours of
disappointment.

Cresswell sailed from Liverpool on Saturday, April 9, 1774, as one of several passengers aboard the *Molly*.[2] After thirty-six days with several stretches of
foul weather, stormy enough to wreak havoc with the rigging on two different
occasions, the ship came abreast of Cape Henry, Virginia. Cresswell first set
foot ashore in America on May 17 at the village of Urbanna, situated on the
lower reaches of the Rappahannock River in Middlesex County, Virginia. His
first intended destination was Alexandria. It was here that James Kirk lived, a
man who had grown up in Cresswell's neighborhood. Kirk had entered into
mercantile business in Alexandria and Leesburg and was also involved in land
investments.[3] As so many others before him had done, Cresswell sought out
someone familiar, a connection that he believed was "absolutely necessary." In
Kirk he hoped to find someone whose knowledge of the country would benefit
him in his own search.

As soon as he arrived, Cresswell commenced his commentary about American agriculture, the magnet for the Virginia venture in the first place. Initially,
what he observed in the tidewater of Virginia and Maryland appeared to sustain
the negative views that he had learned while still in England. He arrived believing that the land was "good and the price very low." From this fact he concluded
that agriculture "must be in its infant state," which his first impressions seemed
to confirm. The labor-intensive nature of tobacco cultivation drew his notice.
Cresswell, not yet two weeks in the colonies, concluded "agriculture is in a very
poor state. In short they know very little about Farming. Tobacco and Indian-
corn is all they make and some little wheat." He was just as dismissive of wheat
culture. He complained about the planting, the yields, and the reaping, hardly
containing his private glee with the prospect of competing with such locals. He
did confess to an admiration of the final product, however. Having seen the flour
from George Washington's mill, Cresswell confessed that it was "as good flour
as I ever saw."

Late in 1774, Cresswell finally found the land that appealed to him. From
Kirk's home in Alexandria, Cresswell toured "the back country" of Berkeley
and Frederick counties. "I am exceedingly pleased with these two Counties, and
am determined to settle in one of them, if ever these times are settled, here is
every encouragement." He was not drawn to the tobacco culture of the Tidewater and remarked with some sense of relief that "little tobacco is made" in these
counties. The country seemed perfect for livestock and wheat culture. The land
"will produce any sort of grain, the average of Wheat is about 12 Bushels to the
Acre but it is not half plowed, and manure of any sort is never used." Furthermore, "meadow may be made with little trouble. And the range for stock is
unlimited." These conditions, he added, were very different from home.

Cresswell proceeded without interruption, save one. What came to be known as the American Revolution intruded, incidentally at first, but more and more in time. The first mention that Cresswell entered in his journal was on May 30, 1774, about two weeks after his arrival in America. The occasion was a dinner at Colonel Richard Harrison's home in Nanjemoy, Maryland. Cresswell's entry was sharp: "Nothing talked of but the Blockade of Boston Harbor the people seem much exasperated at the proceedings of the Ministry and talk as if they were determined to dispute the matter with the Sword." Despite the criticism, Cresswell would return several times to Harrison's home finding him "a very intelligent man." Furthermore, Harrison became a welcome guide for Cresswell, introducing him to the social side of America and taking "pleasure in communicating the Customs and manner of his countrymen." Cresswell never did reveal a critical interest in politics. With neither learning nor experience in the art of government, his reactions to the American Revolution represented a perspective contrary to that of the various American founders.

A sea voyage to Barbados and illness had occupied much of Cresswell's time and energy during the fateful summer of 1774. During the first revolutionary convention held in Williamsburg during August, he was abroad. So it was not until the end of October that he returned to the subject of American resistance. By this time the first Continental Congress had met, and both the Virginia Association and its continental counterpart were deeply engaged in serious political and economic conflict.

During this political, social, and legal maelstrom, Cresswell once again took up his quest for Virginia land in the fall of 1774. By the end of October, he had settled all of the accounts from his Barbados venture, concluding that he would have to make yet another call upon his father's credit, electing to be debtor to his father rather than to some American. Cresswell had now come to the simple conclusion that "everything here is in the utmost confusion." All financial transactions had become chancy since "Committees are appointed to inspect into the Characters and Conduct of every tradesman to prevent them Selling Tea, or buying British manufactures." Seeing only the consequences of such investigations, Cresswell found committee actions offensive and dangerously destructive. He noted that some merchants had been "Tared [sic] and Feathered." Just as frightening, Cresswell noted that others "had their property burned and destroyed by the populace." In a voice that resembled the views of Virginia loyalists, he railed against the destructiveness of people suddenly released from the law. Such behavior suggested, "everything is ripe for Rebellion." Cresswell saw no virtue in breaking the law to sustain actions both irregular in their origin and unequal in their effects.

As worried as these observations left him, Cresswell concluded that "for my own part, did I not think this affair wou'd be over in the spring I wou'd immediately return home." This became the deciding moment for Cresswell's American voyage. His initial reading of the American Revolution persuaded him to remain. He confided in his journal some of the reasons behind his decision, reasons which reflected a distinctive perspective. He felt that he could not return home empty-handed and be "laughed at by all my friends." More importantly, "if I return now and matters are settled they [his mother and father] will never consent to my leaving England again." He did not at this point, nor would he in the darker days to come, ever second guess his initial resolve for independence from his own family.

The resolve may explain why in October 1774 Cresswell classified the American resistance as a "quarrel." In his view, the American side of the squabble lacked any real substance. "The presbyterian Rascals [of New England] has had address sufficient to make the other Colony's come into their Scheme." If "Independence" were the objective of the people of Massachusetts, then "salutary and speedy measures" of Parliament would remedy the "hubbub."[4] Until the colonial world returned to normal, however, Cresswell faced immediate financial demands. To wait out the "quarrel," he decided that he must find work. Kirk, promising support, encouraged him to stay on and to take a "Tour of the back country" in the interim. Cresswell accepted his offer, "determined not to return til I can do it with credit without these Rascals do perswade the Colonies into a Rebellion."

The English visitor attempted unsuccessfully to find his way through the colonial political culture. Not only did Cresswell express disdain for Whigs, but he decried many of the king's friends as well. Cresswell chose to remain an outsider, and it was not long before he realized that the consequences of this could spell defeat for everything he had originally hoped to accomplish. In trying to forestall the looming disaster, he opted for plans that under any other circumstances would have been considered chimerical. As time went on, Cresswell's journal entries came to acknowledge the central importance of a "quarrel" that had grown into a "Rebellion." Throughout, Cresswell's commentaries continued to reveal a person who remained a man apart, a person who neither endorsed the patriotism of a growing "bulk" of Americans nor became active in the affairs of the Loyalists.

This is not to suggest that Cresswell discontinued his commerce with different people. His journal abounds with references that amount to a who's who of the American Revolution, including major and minor players on both sides. Historically, one of the ongoing mysteries of Cresswell's narrative has been this juxtaposition of adversaries. He was not averse to characterizing, sometimes at considerable length, notables whom he had not met but knew by reputation. Cresswell's journal entries were a mirror of his public behavior. His belligerence, amply fueled by the confidence of his youth, got him into private and public trouble almost immediately. For one who believed that the differences between the Americans and Parliament were best understood as a passing "quarrel," he displayed little knowledge of the underlying causes of the dispute and no patience for what he viewed as truculence on the part of the Americans.

On the contrary, Nicholas Cresswell arrived in America with a chip on his shoulder. Initially he was hypercritical of Tidewater agriculture, and he was quick to characterize American political opposition as beyond the pale. It is not at all surprising that the locals responded in kind. Cresswell's argumentativeness was not confined to private conversation. Rather, he was willing to enter into political disputes at any public tavern, places where some local residents may have considered him a guest in their country. The often drunken nature of these sessions promoted misunderstanding and irritation in an already tumultuous political climate. In tones that suggested anything but surprise, Cresswell, in a February 1775 entry, announced that a Maryland Committee of Safety was considering whether "to take me up for a Spy." Given that he had spent but a few weeks visiting Maryland and that February was early for the formation of committees in Maryland and Virginia, Cresswell's behavior was indicative of a person to all appearances hell-bent on public confrontation on the most sensitive political issues.

Cresswell's nonchalant reaction to the investigation of the Maryland Committee of Safety came in part from his knowledge that he would soon be far removed from its reach. In January 1775, not a month after he had first determined to weather the political storm, he decided to go into the American West. On January 6, Kirk informed Cresswell of land interest in "the Illinois country." An initial business offer came with attractive options. Cresswell could take over one third of Kirk's original share "at the first cost," or he could acquire 5,000 acres of his choice if he agreed to go to the place and survey it for them, thus presumably firming their claim. His second option was to take a third of the whole claim of Kirk and his partner, William Sidebotham of Bladensburg, Maryland, upon his return from the survey.[5]

Admitting that he was "not much acquainted with the situation of this country," Cresswell set out to investigate this striking proposition. It had been his immediate good fortune to meet "two Gentlemen" who had lived in the Illinois country for some time. From them he learned that at the conjunction of the Ohio and Mississippi Rivers, "1000 Miles from New Orleans, and 2000 Miles from this place," the land was "exceeding rich." Cresswell also reported that he was assured this country possessed mineral wealth in copper and lead. One further advantage was that there were "very few inhabitants and those French." Cresswell accepted the offer on certain conditions. If his benefactors would "use their interest to procure me Surveyors Warrant," Cresswell believed that such a situation might be "worth some Hundreds a Year, exclusive of the opportunities a surveyor has, of taking up lands for himself." So the promise of the 5,000 acres suddenly became more than a fallback position. Knowing that he could do "nothing here till times are settled," Cresswell figured to be back in Virginia in time to return to England in September 1775, by then secured well enough so that he would not be retuning home "a Beggar."

Cresswell began his venture at a most inopportune moment. After the 1763 Treaty of Paris that ended the French and Indian War vested in Great Britain all the French territory in North America, the American West entered into a complex and confusing time of rapid change. Suddenly gone was the triangular competition between the French, English, and Americans for western lands and trade. Gone too were the triangular approaches to and negotiations with the American Indians. This vast new domain presented Great Britain with administrative and political challenges that added significantly to the burdens of governing a suddenly newly expanded empire. The cost of the war to acquire it and daunting prospect of governing it led the king and Parliament into new administrative considerations, many of which quickly came to be viewed by Americans as materially restrictive and constitutionally iniquitous. As the economic, political, and constitutional contest between Great Britain and the American colonies deepened during the years following the French and Indian War, the adversaries battled one another in the American West in distinctive ways. The central issue was not commercial regulation or taxation as it was in the East. It was land. Specifically, it was the land west of the mountains where French claims had been quieted and only American Indians stood in possession. It was into this territory that Cresswell planned to venture.

The Illinois Company was a departure from traditional American colonial land companies. This new company, born in the years after the French and Indian War, was a child of growing imperial confusion. It was part of the explosion of land companies after Great Britain secured the West. People formed new corporate combinations rapidly during the postwar years in order to possess these vast and potentially profitable new lands. The Illinois Company and its successor, the Illinois-Wabash Company, were products of plotting on the part of a group of speculative people of different political interests to create an extensive, corporate land base in what was then the far Northwest, the Illinois country. But the means this group used to acquire title to the land were unique, almost revolutionary.

Historically, title to western lands had passed from Indians to the colonial or military representatives of the crown. Following the French and Indian War, the Crown and Parliament sought to bring order to the administration of their new American domain by establishing a royal monopoly in Indian affairs. From the Proclamation of 1763 to the Quebec Act of 1774, Privy Council orders, instructions to royal governors, and parliamentary actions articulated an intention to rationalize and centralize western land purchase and settlement. The constituent elements included such features as the firm establishment of territories reserved for Indians, close supervision of Indian trade, surveys and sales in advance of actual settlement, regularized and centralized control of land grants, and stipulations for royal revenues in the form of quitrents. These policies were intended to be more than a temporary restraining order for settlement. They substantiated an imperial declaration of policy towards all corporate venturers and mercantilists in land, including royal governors, who might harbor large and extralegal ambitions for western lands. These policies, taken all together, spelled out a new mercantilist design for the American West, similar to the British designs for its commercial empire.

Contrary to the spirit and letter of these western policies, certain American adventurers with their English allies set about to acquire extensive grants by negotiating directly with different Indian tribes, in effect, sidestepping the government and the new royal interest. A special few of these new adventurers in the aftermath of the settlement of 1763 were engaged in a most inventive reading of a 1757 legal opinion by Lord Camden and Charles Yorke regarding a petition from the East India Company. Certain American merchants in confidential association with various crown officials determined that they could, as private operators, proceed outside of the official orbit of the Crown without any political or legal restraint, thus becoming speculators in the original sense of the word.[6] This, of course, was in direct violation of law and policy that stated that all transfers must be in the king's name and for the king's purposes, regulations that invited political favor-seeking. But the Illinois Company's guiding partner, William Murray, armed with the power of attorney from the Gratz brothers in Philadelphia, proceeded west nevertheless. In July 1773, he completed negotiations with Indians for the purchase of two tracts of land north of the Ohio River in the Illinois country, one of which was situated at the confluence of the Mississippi and Ohio rivers. By mid-April 1774, just days before the outbreak of violence in the west, the conflict that would be remembered as "Dunmore's War." Murray and his partners contacted, of all people, the governor of Virginia, John Murray, the Earl of Dunmore, who was also William Murray's kinsman, and presented him with a petition seeking his official support of their claim.[7]

This contact was a brilliant move. Dunmore's history and ambition revealed why: previous association with John Connolly and George Croghan; his private and unauthorized investments in western lands; his political aggressiveness that would prompt the Virginia war against the Shawnees later in 1774; and his powerful political and family connections in England. All suggesting that he stood ready to read and interpret both his instructions and the new parliamentary mandates with a distinctive imperial vision. Once Dunmore agreed to forward the Illinois Company petition along with some personal supporting comments, the die was cast. It would not be long before other backers, including the governor of Maryland, members of the Carroll family, and several Baltimore merchants, joined this formidable corporation of interests.[8] An added convenience for these adventurers was Virginia's charter claim to jurisdiction over the territory in question. The ironic element in this claim, which the governor knew well, was that imperial policy since 1763 was intended to quiet this Virginia charter claim.

Dunmore did not sit long on the Illinois Company's petition. On May 16, he wrote a long defense of the entire enterprise to the Earl of Dartmouth, secretary of state for the American colonies. This letter would earn him the strongest rebuke from the king and serve as a lasting revelation of just how out of step the Crown remained regarding the fate of the American West. For his part, Cresswell could not have chosen a more fateful western business enterprise. Dunmore started his letter by acknowledging that the Illinois Company petition was most unusual. It sought recognition for a tract "near this Colony" that was purchased from the Indians, a transaction in violation of statutory and royal precedents firmly in place for over fifteen years yet one for which there could in the governor's view be "no doubt of the validity of their title." Immediately Dunmore attempted to mask this disingenuous remark with the appealing promise that company partners were firm in their intention to "comply with the same rules and regulations with respect to Quitrents that all the other Inhabitants of the Colony are governed by."[9] Thus began a remarkable correspondence. Punctuated by the dissolution of the House of Burgesses and Dunmore's campaign against the Shawnees, the letters between the governor and the secretary of state before the end of 1774 included Dunmore's thoroughgoing analysis of the crisis of the British Empire and his recommendations for Crown and Parliament.

Dunmore's focus was on allegiance. He believed the home government was losing the loyalty of the Americans in what everyone ought to realize was a battle for the future of the American West and the future course of the British empire. In his lengthy December analysis of the deteriorating American situation, Dunmore outlined the progress of the Revolution in Williamsburg, Virginia, but this appeared only after an extended discussion of the West. His discussion was neither framed in formal legal terms nor was it an economic interpretation. Rather, Dunmore saw the dissolution of the empire reflected in the mounting unwillingness of men to attach themselves to an increasingly distant crown. In the strongest terms he attempted to disabuse Dartmouth and others in England of any residual faith that they might still harbor in the timeworn notions of perpetual allegiance. In short, Virginians, particularly those in the West, valued their individual liberty more than their connections to the Crown and any resulting control of political or economic interest that such traditional mercantilist connections wrought. The bonds of empire were quickly loosening.[10]

Dunmore had acquired an American vision of space. He opined that the English would either adopt this new view of reality or suffer the inevitable consequences, namely the loss of its newly acquired territories north of the Ohio. This new vision had obliterated past realities. No longer were the traditional ways of producing and controlling wealth applicable. The government, Dunmore argued, would be unable to restrain Americans from moving into the West. "Nothing (so fond as the Americans are of Migration) can stop the Concourse of People that actually begin to draw towards them [the western lands]." Any Crown or Parliament attempts "would have the direct contrary tendency, by forcing the people to adopt a form of Government of their own." Dunmore proceeded to describe just such a venture where people moved west without permission "in a manner tributary to the Indians," and "to all intents and purposes erected themselves into though an inconsiderable yet a separate state." The precedent was clear and acted as a summons to "all the dissatisfied of every other Government." More important, it set a usable example "of forming Governments distinct from and independent of His Majestys Authority."[11]

In light of this crisis, Dunmore urged that the Crown recognition of the Illinois Company petition would send a powerful signal, at once a remedy for the present disorder and an announcement for future development. Recognition would "preserve the peace and order of the back countries." Actually Dunmore was suggesting something stronger than preserving the peace, for he had the temerity to assert that Crown policy had attracted "all the disorderly and unruly People of the Colonies." Traditional ways of doing business in the American West simply were not working. In his estimation, British directives were the cause of the disarray. So Dunmore advised that the Crown endorse private development of the West, a clear reversal of political policy. Dartmouth, citing the Crown's displeasure with such an audacious recommendation, ordered Dunmore to adhere strictly to established plans and to cease his advisories, particularly when they took on the appearance of having openly contradicted the Crown.[12] Late in December after his western campaign, Dunmore replied, unconvinced and unrepentant. He reported that he believed it his official duty to report "matters as they really are." He reiterated that the distance from the home government weakened American allegiance. The situation in the West made this reality even more critical. Dunmore believed that it was imperative that the British authorities recognize that the Americans were different. Americans in the West, according to Dunmore, "do not conceive that Government has any right to forbid their possession of a vast tract of Country, either uninhabited, or which serves only as a Shelter to few Scattered Tribes of Indians." If policy makers in Great Britain refused to recognize this powerful reality they would lose the country to an unrestrainable people incited by "their avidity and restlessness." Dunmore believed that this was critical in understanding the connection between the people and this new land. "Wandering about seems engrafted in their nature," he claimed; such people would not be stopped by artificial barriers imposed at some remote place by a state that the Americans viewed as irrelevant at best. Dunmore conveyed with clarity the need to develop a policy of freeing up the marketplace of western land to people who had already asserted a preemptive claim to it. The American Revolution, however, made immaterial these recommendations for the British empire in the West.[13]

By the time that Cresswell agreed to join the Illinois Company as surveyor, the political situation in the American colonies generally and in Virginia specifically had become deeply confused. Instead of a peaceable occupation of the West, a new version of the three-sided competition for empire that so recently had engaged the Indians, the English, and the French emerged with the Americans substituting for the vanquished French. Whatever political alliances Dunmore had forged in the Virginia legislature as a result of the 1774 war against the Shawnees evaporated in the heat of Virginia's Revolution. In the process, Virginians with important western interests moved quickly to dissociate themselves from the governor. One manifestation of this development was the new legislature's assertion of exclusive control of Virginia's land claims in the West, thus eliminating critical executive prerogatives as well as giving official recognition to certain land companies and excluding those that had fallen out of political favor. In this way the Illinois Company quickly became a casualty of Virginia's Revolution. In January 1775, Cresswell, resolute in his belief that the dispute between home and colonies was soon to be resolved, did not foresee the legal and political chaos that these now hollow land company pretensions would work in the West.

In addition, people informed Cresswell that this western venture would present him with special risks. He doggedly discounted these practical warnings, deciding precipitously to proceed on his mission. His journal remains troublesomely silent about whether he understood the complexities of what faced him as he turned west. Adding to this uneasy quality was Cresswell's willingness to start out almost single-handed. To start, he had to learn the rudiments of surveying, a craft for which his agricultural background was most helpful. He explained that he found running lines "very easy in the Woods from what it is in enclosed lands." Cresswell soon learned that springtime was best for traveling down the Ohio River, timing that was confirmed early in March by a Mr. Finley, a veteran of the Illinois country, who urged him to wait until the "Latter end of April, then to go down the Ohio River with the Flood." Quick to accept this advice, Cresswell at last turned to the task of finding someone to go with him. Initially he was in some doubt, stating as late as March 1 that "there will some difficulty in perswadeing any one to go with me in this place."

It did prove difficult. Cresswell, turning to the most reliable sources he had, took the better part of the month of March and the start of April searching for a suitable guide and companion for his voyage. Friends suggested that Edward Snickers was the best person for finding a capable and reliable guide and supplied Cresswell with a letter of introduction.[14] On April 3, he visited Snickers home but had to content himself with discussing his situation with a relative who recommended George Rice for the job. Cresswell's friend, Gibbs, confirmed this choice, complimenting Rice as "an honest man and a Good hunter." As it would turn out, Gibbs had supplied better than Cresswell could handle, for not only would Rice prove to be an accomplished companion for this western venture, but in time he would also assert his allegiance to the American cause. Their political disagreements would precipitate a terrible rift that would eventually play a central role in ending Cresswell's western project. Initially, however, Cresswell and Rice came to an agreement; Rice accepted an offer of "500 acres" of land, presumably within the grant tract. After a few last-minute purchases and the acquisition of a few more letters of introduction to "several Gentlemen in the neighborhood of Fort Pitt," Cresswell departed from Winchester, Virginia, in the company of his new partner on April 5, 1775.

Following the advice of his local consultants, Cresswell traveled west prepared to trade with the Native Americans, all in the belief that he could "carry out some Silver trinkets and Barter with the Indians for Furs and probably do something more than bear my expenses." Fortunately for him, the silversmiths in Alexandria were adept in providing him with the "trinkets" according to the advice of one already experienced in this trade. Cresswell believed he was well prepared for his voyage. He was armed with the permission to carry out surveys. He knew that at a minimum he could "take the 5000 Acres for going to view the land at my own expense." Furthermore, he held out for the right of first refusal of Kirk's and Sidebotham's share. Unschooled in the history of the western land companies with their troubled legacy of political and cultural unrest and insensitive to the growing political crisis of the American Revolution, Cresswell forged ahead into the wilderness.

His great voyage took Cresswell into a strange new world that fascinated him, eliciting journal comments different from all that had transpired in his previous American adventure. From the outset, the way and pace of travel were new and demanding on him. The second day out, Rice led Cresswell about thirty miles, "over barren hills and bad ways." That night the temperature dropped below freezing, and Cresswell marvels at "going to sleep in the open air, no other covering then the Heaven's and our blankets." The going continued to be rough, revealing a landscape Cresswell often found forbidding and "dismal." Within a few days, he was making geographic and cartographic observations, noting specific mountains, the westward flow of rivers, and the destruction caused by a major tornado.

By April 10 the travelers had come upon the Great Meadow, and Cresswell began his observations of the battle sites of the 1754 and 1755 Washington and Braddock campaigns. Even though the Appalachian Mountains "piled one on top of another with some narrow valleys between them," Cresswell found the land in these valleys "rich and very thinly inhabited." The road they traveled was "very indifferent," but even so, "loaded wagons frequently cross it in the summer." As they proceeded, they found that "every necessary of life is very dear here, provisions in particular." The cause was clear; the scarcity was "occasioned by the Indian War [Dunmore's War] last Summer. Grain is not to be got for money." Cresswell came to view the consequences of this war as significant in his voyage. Initially it was a question of provision. Other consequences would appear in time as he proceeded farther west.

Captain William Douglass, who had accompanied Rice and Cresswell during the first two days before separating on April 6, rejoined them on April 11 and guided Cresswell to the home of John Stephenson.[15] Known as "a great Indian warrior," Stephenson recommended that the company stop in his neighborhood and build the canoes for the journey west, arguing that provisions would be easier to obtain at his place than at Fort Pitt. Rice, who had friends and family in the vicinity, agreed, and Cresswell, seeing how adept Rice was at building canoes, readily accepted "his management." Rice estimated that the construction begun on April 13 would take two weeks. Stephenson's home on the Youghiogheney River served as Cresswell's launching place to the West. Once the journey began, the final party took three days to reach the Monongahela River after which it took less than two days for the final approach to Fort Pitt.

Instead of remaining at Stephenson's, Cresswell decided to accompany Douglass to Fort Pitt by land, arriving on the evening of April 16. Earlier that day, he toured the battlefield where General Braddock "was defeated by the French and Indians on the 9th of July 1755." He was impressed by the presence of "great numbers of Bones," where most of the skulls were either broken or pierced in such a way as to suggest that the injuries were caused by "a Pipe Tommahauk." Cresswell noted that his guide claimed that the Indians left no Englishman alive, a chilling vision of a very different kind of warfare for the newcomer. At the very moment he was witnessing these scenes, Americans and the British had fired at one another in anger. In Lexington and Concord a new war had begun that would blast all of Cresswell's hopes and plans.

The three-day visit to Fort Pitt included meetings with a variety of people for whom Cresswell's Virginia friends had written letters of introduction. Principal among these people was the commandant, Major John Connolly. Cresswell's characterization of Connolly suggests that the interview had not proceeded in the manner that Cresswell had wished, for he found the commandant "a haughty imperious man." Given Connolly's association with Governor Dunmore in the frontier war of the previous summer, the commandant was a source of information vital to Cresswell as he prepared for his western venture. Connolly's military and diplomatic intelligence regarding the western Indians was critical for Cresswell and others who traveled with him. Furthermore, Cresswell was on Illinois Company business, and Connolly's connections with Governor Dunmore made this meeting necessary. Despite their less than amicable meeting, the English traveler secured useful information for his assault on the Ohio River.

After a couple of side trips to see Indian traders, Cresswell returned to his canoes, which were in the final stages of completion. During the last few days before departure, Cresswell's work pace quickened. He spent many hours completing his final provisioning. Most importantly he negotiated a new agreement with Rice. During Cresswell's absence, Rice had "joined some other people" who were building canoes for a trip of "about 600 miles down the river." To accommodate this new arrangement, Cresswell agreed to wait "at the Kentucky River ten days." This adjustment to the original contract was made in the presence of Douglass. Since leaving Winchester, Douglass had spent more and more time with Cresswell and now proposed a bargain that Cresswell found most appealing. Douglass offered to finance half of all Cresswell's expense down the Ohio and back for one half of any land Cresswell might "purchase." Two days later Cresswell agreed, clearly distinguishing in his journal the five-thousand-acre grant that was part of the original Kirk proposition and "anything to do as a surveyor," acknowledging only that he agreed that Douglass could have "one half of any land I may purchase." Adding to his sense of good fortune was Douglass's willingness to grant him a five-year moratorium on interest on the unpaid principal. With a certain smugness, Cresswell concluded that "I have now a prospect of making money without advancing any." So situated, he embarked April 28 upon his western voyage.

During the five days that it took to reach Fort Pitt, the company attained its final complement. The newcomers were bound for Kentucky "to take up land." Among them was James Nourse, "an English gentleman," who, like so many others after 1774, was on his way to Kentucky to enter claims for military service in the French and Indian War. He immediately befriended Cresswell with the offer of sharing "one half of his tent," a gesture Cresswell found "very agreeable."[16] On the third day out, the new company was detained by rain and, taking advantage of the opportunity, "settled our accounts concerning vessels and provisions."

From this moment on, Cresswell became part of the new wave seeking land in the new West. Cresswell's journal reports this phenomenon by listing the variety of people going west: American, Irish, English, German, black, white—in short, all sorts. William Murray and others would champion Cresswell as an ideal agent and participant in the opening of new lands. He was just the sort of person Dunmore had in mind for the Illinois Company: a gentleman venturer who could bring order and proper land management to the West. From the beginning, Cresswell acted the part. He set himself apart from most of his traveling companions, save Nourse, who was not intending to settle in Kentucky, and George Rogers Clark, who joined the company for almost three weeks, a man Cresswell found interesting both for his knowledge of Indian medicine and for his good behavior.

The same could not be said for his relations with Rice, which went steadily downhill. After three weeks on the river, Cresswell was convinced that Rice had no intention of going beyond Kentucky. For this, Cresswell labeled him "a great coward," loose words that bespoke rising anger. In time, anger and confusion dominated much of the company's everyday proceedings. Notices of "great quarreling" began to appear more and more frequently in the journal's narrative. His association with Rice deteriorated to the point that on May 27 Cresswell thought that Rice tried to pick a fight so that violence would nullify their contract. Privately Cresswell vowed "not to give the first affront," a vow shattered two days later when they went toe to toe. Nourse interceded and according to Cresswell prevented what would have been a deadly fight. Nourse scolded both parties, claiming that "neither would have discredited a Billingsgate education." Nourse noted that afterwards Rice "drew in" confirming Cresswell's assessment that the fight "effectually" ended their relationship.[17] On such an unfortunate personal note Cresswell's plans for the Illinois Company came to an end.

Once the company reached the Kentucky River and elected to start the arduous ascent towards the landing close to Harrodsburg, unraveling accelerated. The company had floated down the Ohio when it was at flood stage, taking three weeks to reach the Kentucky. It would require fourteen hard days to pull the canoes 125 miles up the Kentucky River. At first a few of the men started to drift away quietly. Then as the company approached its destination, the land seekers decamped more rapidly, a few stealing from the much-reduced company stores as they left. By June 8, those who remained divided up the rest of the stores. Cresswell realized that everyone who remained was interested in Kentucky lands, not in some uncertain venture in the Illinois country.

The loss of Rice not only put an immediate stop to Cresswell's great western venture, but also left Cresswell with the prospect of finding a way back. He did not have to wait long. That very same afternoon a company bound for Fort Pitt offered him a place. Cresswell opted to join this "ragged Crewe," much as he despaired of "their lookes." Interestingly, Nourse offered Cresswell the chance to go with him. Cresswell declined, for Nourse "intends to go over land." With his inventory of Indian trade goods still intact, Cresswell could not afford such an invitation, as welcome as it was, coming from one who had treated him "with the greatest civility" and whom he had come to respect.

The return to Fort Pitt, punctuated by Indian scares and bickering among the members of the company, took four long weeks of hard work even though the river was now well past its time of flood. The combination of time, accident, and natural conditions had taken their toll on Cresswell's equipment and his patience. Interestingly, he seemed to thrive physically, never mentioning the sort of complaints that had plagued him earlier in Virginia. Despite the failure of his mission, Cresswell embraced the American West. Once back in Fort Pitt, he whiled away more than a month before he agreed to return to the Ohio country with an Indian trader, all in the presumptive hope of salvaging some of the costs of his voyage. In desperation for a loan to tide him over, he at last turned to John Anderson, a veteran of the Indian trade and the only person in town he had not approached for help. Anderson did more than just offer a loan; he agreed to accompany him into the Indian country, serving as both an interpreter and guide.

Once west of Fort Pitt, Anderson led Cresswell through the Ohio Indian country, visiting various sites including several Moravian missions. On August 29 while at the native town of Old Hundy, Cresswell took the sister of his Mohawk host as a temporary wife, whom he called Nancy. She would accompany him until he left Fort Pitt for his return to Virginia on October 2. During the second venture into the American West, Cresswell was able to sell all of his goods, receiving furs in exchange, even though in the end he believed that he was a loser upon the whole. Anderson's association was altogether pleasant, a friendship Cresswell hoped to sustain, promising upon his departure to keep up a correspondence. His departure from Nancy was emotional. He added that, despite what "conscientious people might think," a temporary wife was a necessity for facilitating travel and trade in the Indian country. During this account of the six-week western trading venture, Cresswell's journal conveyed a keen sense of interest and happiness from all that happened earlier. If he was concerned about his own financial and political future, the narrative from the Ohio country did not convey it. On the contrary, he seemed reluctant to return east. In 1777, during the final months of his American stay, he would recall his earlier time, wondering seriously whether or not he should take up this life once again, expressing a certain longing for the places, the people, and new ways of life he found so affecting during the summer of 1775.

Only much later would Cresswell reveal some of the political reasons why he did not hurry back to Virginia. In March 1775 he had written "to all my friends in England and freely declared my sentiments upon the present Rebellion. Those letters never reached their intended destination. Instead they fell into the hands of the Alexandria Committee of Safety. When Cresswell returned at the end of October of that year, the committee was ready for him. In his estimation the committee was prepared for him to be "Arraign'd, Tried, and Condemned and the sentence nearly put in execution before I knew anything about it." Until April 1777, when he made good on his second attempt to escape from America, Cresswell spent much of his time and energy fending off the inquisitive Americans. He complained bitterly that he was trapped between the rock of his independence and the hard place of the American Revolution: "I am now in a disagreeable situation. If I enter into any sort of business I must be Obliged to enter into the service of these Rascals and fight against my Friends and Country if called upon. On the other hand I am not permitted to depart the Continent and have nothing if I am fortunate enough to escape the jail. I will live as cheap as I can and hope for better times." In this straightforward, albeit anguished, statement of what he considered to be his options, Cresswell rendered a prophetic foreshadowing.

The coming eighteen months became for Cresswell a trial period during which he suffered from forced inactivity; considered heading back to the West; attempted to escape the country through New York; considered alternately joining the American and the British armies; and finally concluded that the American Revolution had became a tragic moment. What he witnessed in the East dashed his earlier hopes for a peaceful settlement between the American colonists and the British authorities. As he learned more about the warfare in New England and the military presence in different American cities, Cresswell concluded that "this cannot be redressing grievances, it is open Rebellion and I am convinced if Great Britain does not send more men here and subdue them soon they will declare independence." Upon rendering this conclusion, Cresswell became determined to escape. From October 1775 on, Cresswell's journal became a different narrative, one devoted to the story of his personal ordeal with the American Revolution. During the long months of forced confinement, he turned more and more to questioning the people and events around him, puzzling over the causes and consequences of these troubled times. His distress took a toll on his health. Although free from sickness when he was in the West, his bouts of illness resumed in Virginia, confining him on several occasions for weeks at a time. Also, and more frightening to him, he began to drink more heavily and more often, sometimes for days on end. During the early months of 1776, the journal went silent for weeks as Cresswell lurched between self-inflicted "merry" inebriation and sickness.

On July 19, 1777, after a series of adventures brought him to New York, Cresswell departed from America safely on board H.M.S. *Edward.* Although relieved to be away from the terrible war, he was saddened by what he saw in "this cursed Rebellion." During the weeks before he left, he took time to review his history in America and to comment on the geographical, political, and economic conditions in various states. This analysis served as a fitting end to an adventure launched with hope and concluded in discord. To the very end he sustained his anger that "the artifices of a few designing Villains" had corrupted "honest, well meaning people" so that they relinquished "the invaluable blessing of Peace, the sweet enjoyment of real and happy Liberty." At the same time Cresswell steadfastly refused to sing the virtues of Great Britain, a tune so common in the voices of many Loyalists. During the months following his western venture, he came to view much of British imperial policy as well as military commands of such people as William Howe as deeply flawed policies that neither inspired nor deserved allegiance. Looking at both sides, then, Cresswell concluded that in "the short space of three years, the Villainous arts of a few and the obstinacy of the many, on this side of the water added to the complicated blunders, cowardice, and knavery of some of our blind Guides in England has totally ruined this country."

Over time, Cresswell came to believe that the American Revolution was a tragic history of legal and social degradation, the ruination of individual liberty. The American people had become "like the Dog in the Fable, [they had] quit the substance for an empty shadow." For vain promises of unattainable freedoms, Americans had submitted themselves to "all the dreadful horrors of war, poverty and wretchedness." Everything seemed to confirm this view. From his Virginia experience Cresswell saw only a "Country turn'd Topsy Turvy changed from an Earthly Paradice, to a Hell, upon Terra Firma."

The American world that he had known when he arrived, "this once happy country," was coming apart, including religion. By October 1776 Cresswell lamented that "religion is almost forgot, or most basely neglected." Not only was religion "at a stand," but "the retailers of politicks," particularly the Presbyterian clergy, were active in successfully politicizing the pulpit. Cresswell noted that it was "one of the followers of Whitfield," a low-ranking officer in the Virginia militia, a "violent persecuting scoundrell, who was the principal culprit in staging a 'great riot' in Leesburg between the English prisoners and the 'Yankeys'[sic]." In the name of "Independence," Americans insisted upon choosing their leaders "from the most violent part of the people." These men, "in general very fond of using their usurped authority without mercy," held the law in contempt and were ready to use force to compel allegiance. The accused faced imprisonment, loss of property, and a threat of death, all without the slightest pretense of due process of the law. Cresswell asserted that this clash between political coercion and the popular will to sustain traditional liberties might serve as the undoing of the American rebellion, for "these unhappy wretches are as much divided as it is possible to be without actually drawing the sword against one another." The Congress was largely responsible for the discord, for they "under the fallacious pretence of nursing the tender plant, Liberty, which was said to thrive so well in American soil, have actually tore it up by the very root." This free fall into ruin pained Cresswell, who viewed the physical and moral destruction of America as a sign of the depravity of unchecked human action, a Hobbesian world of ungoverned license mistaken for freedom. Cresswell's only remaining hope was that Americans would somehow summon the courage to "awake from their delirium and refuse further to submit to the new tyranny."

Acknowledging that he knew little of the history and people of New England, Cresswell prided himself in having learned much about the people and place south of New York. These Americans he found to be "the most hospitable people on Earth." Manners reflected a charitable disposition, manifest in both the education of the young and the social habits of adults. He emphasized that if children possessed "any genius tis not cramped in their infancy, by being overawed by their parents." This tended to foster individuals who were "good-natured, familiar, and agreeable on the whole." He noted as well the population explosion and asserted that both immigration and natural increase were twin causes. Cresswell believed that the consequences of growth made America quite different from England. In America, in part because economic prospects were so good and the availability of land was so immediate, people married earlier. Nothing he saw during his stay persuaded him that his first negative impressions of American agriculture were in error. Americans were certainly handy—the men were universal mechanics, carpenters, saddlers, and coopers. Still Americans were very indifferent farmers. In concluding his retrospective, Cresswell prayed for a people and a country that he would never be able to call his own.

> This is a Paradice on Earth, for women the Epicure's Elysium, and the very Center of Freedom and Hospitality. But in the short space of three Years—Tis become the Theater of War, the Country of Distraction, and the Seat of Slavery, Confusion and Lawless Oppression. May the Almighty of his infinite goodness and mercy Reunite and Reestablish them in their former happy and flourishing situation.

The West was for Cresswell the heartland of this American "Paradice." But political circumstances had prevented his attaining a place there. Living on the frontier for several months had been an exhilarating experience for him. However, Cresswell needed more stability than the West in 1775 could offer, a reality he understood even as he bemoaned his lost opportunity in the land of America's future. The Revolution nullified the best-laid plans of both Dunmore and Cresswell. As they departed from the American scene, their ideas of private development of the West went into eclipse as well, for Americans in the Continental Congress very soon replicated British policy regarding the prohibition of Indian land sales to private companies.

Cresswell's voyage home was uneventful and devoid of the anticipation he expressed during his voyage to America. His impending return was a cause not of delight but the occasion for "such an unusual damp upon my spirits that I am more dead than alive." He confided that rather than hurrying ashore, he "had rather stay on board," a most revealing commentary upon his unfortunate and conflicted history in America. England now appeared diminished. Even the historic artery of commerce, the Thames, had become "a narrow crooked river." The people he saw in London appeared sadly uninformed about the situation in America, half of them appearing to him as "Rebels in their Hearts," a sure sign that Great Britain's cause was in jeopardy. Given all of the debts that he had incurred, he dreaded confronting his father, controller of his credit. Failing at the last minute to secure a commission with Lord Dunmore, Cresswell arrived back at Edale on September 24, 1777. His mother was "overjoyed" to see him; his father, who departed in what struck his son to be intentional haste to a local fair, "remembered to order me to sheare or bind corn tomorrow." So on this minor note his three-year odyssey to America came to a close. At the very end of his journal, he entered a vow to stay home at least until "April next, and behave in such a manner as not to give any just offence. I call this waiting the chapter of accidents—something unforeseen may happen." The extraordinary journal of Nicholas Cresswell ceased four years later with one final entry for April 21,

1781, announcing his marriage, prompting him to conclude, "my rambling is now at an end."

The Manuscript Journal

The original manuscript journal is in the John D. Rockefeller, Jr. Library at the Colonial Williamsburg Foundation. Cresswell's journal is contained in four notebooks written in a neat typical 18th century hand. The books, measuring about 4¼ by 6 inches, are hinged at the top. The surviving copy was made by Cresswell, probably soon after his return to England. He evidently kept notes in a small note book, measuring about 4 by 5 inches. Several pages from these notebooks survived. They were inserted in the final copy. There can be no doubt that Cresswell made the final version—both the rough notes and final copy are in the same hand. One can see how he expanded the notes in the final version of the journal. A page of the rough notes is transcribed below with the corresponding entries from the final journal:

> Remarks, Friday Febry 10, '75
> Left mr. Tollivers got to Horatio Dade's.
> Frost on the ground.
> 11th Got to Mr. Alexanders
> Snow on the ground.
> 12th At Do. Snow and Frost
> 13 Left Do got to Nanjemoy. fine weather but Snow
> 14 Rode abt with Capt Knox Dined at the Trap Frost but fair weather.

Final version:

> February 10, 1775
> The Land is pretty good in this neighbourhood and produced a great deal of Wheat. Saw a Machine for thrashing wheat with horses. After dinner went to Mr. Horatio Dades in Stafford County.
> 11th Got to Mr. Alexanders.
> 12th At Mr Alexanders, the wind is too Fresh, Cant cross the River. This is a most abominable Cold house and bad fire.
> 13 Got to Nanjemoy in the evening. This jaunt has only cost me 5 s Vir Curry. The people are remarkable Hospitable, are affronted if you dont call at their house. If you are a perfect stranger
> 14th 15th 16th 17th and 18th Very busy with Captn Knox in runing the Courses of his Plantation and jaunting about in the neighborhood. I understand the Committee are going to take me up for a Spy. I will save them the trouble by decamping immediately. The Committees Act as Justices, if any person is found to be Inimical to the Liberties of America, they give them over to the mobility to punish as they think proper, and it is seldom they come of without Taring and Feathering. It was much as a persons life was worth to speak disre-

fully of the Congress. The people are arming and training in every place. They are all Liberty Mad.

These entries show that he fleshed out his notes when he transcribed them later on and may account for some mistakes and inaccuracies. The change in tense in the third sentence from the end also suggests he wrote the final version at a later date.

Editorial Decisions

We have made every effort to make the transcription as accurate as possible. We have silently added punctuation where it was obvious and corrected what was clearly a slip of the pen. We have not attempted to correct Cresswell's misspellings except in cases where the meaning was unclear. We have attempted to follow the guidelines described in the *Harvard Guide to American History* (1955), p. 98. We have bought superior letters down to the line and expanded abbreviations where necessary for clear meaning. We have left Cresswell's page headings only if they denoted a change of date or place.

We have been unable to identify every individual mentioned in the journal usually because of the lack of specificity.

Beginning on November 7, 1776, Cresswell occasionally inserted some initials such as "O K. F." "O P. E." and others at the end of the journal entries. We have not been able to decipher his meaning.

The newspapers with the title *Virginia Gazette* were all published in Williamsburg, Virginia. At times there were more than one paper with that title published in Williamsburg at the same time. In those cases the publisher is indicated in the notes.

Notes

1. Cresswell, "Journal," entry for March 1, 1774. He may have studied such books as *The Present State of the British Empire* (London, 1768) or *The Present State of North America* (London, 1755), or possibly letters from Virginians praising the colony.

2. Cresswell, "Journal," entries for March 1 and April 9, 1774. The sailing of the *Molly* was reported in *Williamson's Liverpool Advertiser, And Mercantile Chronicle*, April 15, 1774. Its arrival in Virginia was reported in *Virginia Gazette* (Purdie) on May 19, 1774.

3. James Kirk arrived in Virginia sometime before 1762. A prominent merchant in Alexandria, he signed the Fairfax nonimportation association in 1770 and was a member of the Fairfax County committee of safety from 1774 to 1775. He was appointed to the Commission of Peace for Loudoun County in 1777 and was elected mayor of Alexandria in 1785. Robert A. Rutland, ed., *The Papers of George Mason, 1725-1792*, vol. 1 (Chapel Hill, N. C.: University of North Carolina Press, 1970), lxiii; *Virginia Gazette*, August 4, 1774; *Virginia Journal & Alexandria Advertiser*, February 17, 1785. Loudoun County Court Order Book G, 1776-1783, 47 (Microfilm at the Library of Virginia, Richmond). All county court record books cited hereafter are on microfilm at the Library of Virginia, Richmond.

4. Cresswell "Journal" entry for October 4, 1774. Presbyterian ministers did indeed sway public opinion in favor of colonial resistance. Charles Inglis, Anglican rector in New York City, wrote that he knew of no Presbyterian minister "who did not, by preaching and every effort in their power, promote all the measures of Congress, however extravagant. Quoted in John G. Staudt, "Suffolk County," in *The Other New York: The American Revolution beyond New York City, 1763-1787*, Joseph S. Tiedemann and Eugene R. Fingehut, eds. (Albany, N. Y.: State University of New York Press, 2005), 65.

5. For a discussion of land companies see Shaw Livermore, *Early American Land Companies: Their Influence on Corporate Development* (New York, 1968).

6. Robert A. Williams, Jr., *The American Indian in Western Legal Thought: The Discourses of Conquest* (New York, 1990), 275-80.

7. For the background of Dunmore's War see Jack M. Sosin, "The British Indian Department and Dunmore's War," *Virginia Magazine of History and Biography*, 74 (January 1966): 34-50.

8. Thomas Perkins Abernethy, *Western Lands and the American Revolution* (New York: Russell & Russell, Inc., 1959), 122.

9. Dunmore to the Earl of Dartmouth, Williamsburg, Va., May 16, 1774. Public Record Office, London, CO 5/1352, 71-75 (Microfilm in the John D. Rockefeller Library, Colonial Williamsburg). Interestingly, Dunmore wrote John Stuart, Indian agent for the Southern Department, on April 5, 1776: "I receive Accounts from the Back Parts of this Colony that notwithstanding the Kings Proclamation and Regulations of this Government a Sett [*sic*] of People are endeavouring to make a Purchase from the Indians of a Considerable Tract of Land to the South and West of our last Established Boundary line, which I think you would do well to prevent by giving Directions to Mr. Cameron to represent the Impropriety of it to the Indians and to use every means in his power to deterr [*sic*] them from entering into any Bargain with our People in such an Irregular Manner." Dunmore to Stuart, April 5, 1774, Enclosed with Dunmore's letter to Dartmouth, December 24, 1774. PRO CO 5/1353, 40-41. Hereafter all PRO records cited are on microfilm

at the John D. Rockefeller, Jr. Library, Colonial Williamsburg Foundation, Williamsburg, Virginia.

10. Dunmore to the Earl of Dartmouth, December 24, 1774, CO5/1353, 7-39, (Public Record Office, London).

11. Dunmore to Dartmouth, May 16, 1774, CO5/1352, 71-75, (Public Record Office).

12. Dartmouth to Dunmore, September 8, 1774, CO5/1352, 114-115, (Public Record Office).

13. Dunmore to Dartmouth, December 24, 1774, CO5/1353, 7-39, (Public Record Office).

14. Edward Snicker's home, "Springfield," was in Frederick County, Virginia. Donald Jackson, ed. *The Diaries of George Washington*, vol. 2 (Charlottesville, Va.: University Press of Virginia, 1977), 173. In June 1776 he was appointed to the commission of the peace of Frederick County and later was accused of "fraud against the Public." H. R. McIlwaine, ed. *Journals of the Council of the State of Virginia*, vol. 1 (Richmond, Va.:Virginia State Library, 1931), 46, 428.

15. William Douglass (d. 1783) was a resident of Loudoun County, Virginia, and was appointed sheriff of that county in 1777. Loudoun County Court Will Book C, 1783-1788, 15; Court Order Book F, 1773-1776, 18; and Court Order Book G, 1776-1783, 218.

16. James Nourse kept a journal of the voyage, but the original was lost. A typescript survives in the Durrett Collection at the University of Chicago and was published as James Nourse, "A Journey to Kentucky," *Journal of American History*, 19 (1925): 121-38, 251-60, 351-64.

17. Nourse, "Journey to Kentucky," 251.

Chapter I
To Risk the American World
March 1, 1774 to April 30, 1775

Journal of Nicholas Cresswell
of
Edale in Derbyshire
England[1]
Commenced March 1st 1774
Continued to April 30th 1775

Edale Tuesday March 1st 1774

I have been Studying and Deliberating for a long time how to shape my course in the world and am this Day come to a determined resolution to go into America be the consequence what it will I am certain to meet with every possible obstruction from my Parents and Friends but I am resolved to brave them all and follow my own inclination for once. From the best accounts I have been able to get and from my own Idea of the country am sensible a person with a small fortune may live much better and make greater improvements in America then he can possible do in England. Especially in the Farming way as that is the business I have been brought up to, have made it my study to enquire more particularly about it.

The land I am told, is good and the price very low. Consequently Agriculture must be in its infant state.

The Climate must be good on some part of the Continent for it is all climates in extent. I have allmost from my infancy entertained some thought of going to America at some period of my life and none is more suitable then the present. Supposeing I had no inclination to go to America I have a number of Cogent and Substantial tho private reasons, that rather obliges me to leave home, not alltogether on my own account, But in hopes it will be for the future peace and quietness of those for whom I shall allways have the greates[t] esteem

Therefore I am determined to make a Voyage to Virginia as I like the situation of that Colony the best. If I like the Country to return immediatly and endeavour to prevail upon my Friends to give me something to begin the world with. I shall by this Voyage, be better able to judge what will suit the Country or wheather the Country will please me well enough to fix my future residence in it or not. Admit I do not approve of it. It will be a means of settleing me on this side the Atlantic, not only that, but I am in hopes it will have its good tendencys in other respects to those I leave behind. If this last purpose is efected I shall be happy—if neither Misserable.

Intend to get Mr. James Carrington[2] to speak to my Father about it and break the way a little. I am sorry I dare not do it myself. I believe he may have some influence with my Father If any one has.

1

Determined to keep a dayly and impartial Journal from this day. By which I hope to square my future Conduct.

2d Went to Mr Carringtons to get him to interceed with my Father in my behalf. He with some reluctance promises to come tomorrow. I confess I have no great opinion of his oratorial abillities, but believe he will be honest and do me every service in his power, as he finds I am resolutely bent upon it.

Edale Thursday March 3d 1774

This evening Mr Carrington come and by his aid and assistance got the consent of my Father to go into America. I believe it is with very great reluctance he grants it. I am sorry he will not converce with me on the subject but am determined to persevere.

4th and 5th Employed at home, I have found a great deal of Difficulty to get the consent of my Mother, In short all my Friends thinks me mad, for attempting to go abroad. But they are utterly unacquainted with my true reasons for takeing this surprizeing whim, as they call it.

6th Sunday Went to the Chapel.

7th My Father contrary to my expectations went to Mr Hall to get a Letter of introduction to Mr Latham of Liverpool. Intend to set out for Liverpool tomorrow.[3]

Warrington Tuesday March 7th [8th] 1774

Set out for Liverpool. Dined at Manchester. Lodged at Warrington the Sign of the Nag's Head.

9th Got to Liverpool. Dined at the Goolden Fleece.[4] After dinner waited on Mr. Latham, who went with me to look at several Ships that are bound for Virginia. None pleases me so well as the Ship Molly[5] which is bound for the Rappahannock River in Virginia in a fortnight She is to Sail. The Capt whose name is Parry is not in town but expected tomorrow.[6] Spent the evening at the Fleece with Mr. Latham.

10th Drank Tea at Mr. Lathams after Tea met with Tom Middleton who went with me to Capt. Parry's, agree'd with him for my passage for 10 Guineas, And am to be in Liverpool by the last of the Month. Spent the evening at Tom Middletons.[7]

Manchester Friday March 11th 1774

Left Liverpool Dined at Warrington. From Warrington in Co[mpany] with Mr. Whitaker to Manchester. Suped and spent the evening at Mr. Greatrixes with Sam Jackson. Lodged at the Swan.

12th Left Manchester. Dined at Stockport At Chapelinlefrith, Ordered Edward Ford to make me some Cloaths. Got home in the evening Found my Brothers Tom, Ralph, and Joe ill of the Measles.

13th Sunday. In the forenoon went to Chapel. I believe the Parson made a Sermon on purpose for me. His text was taken from the parable of the Prodigal Son. It is very strange that these Sons of the Clergy cannot forbear middling in other peoples affairs. After Dinner went to Castleton[8] to return Mr. Hall thanks for the trouble he has taken in my behalf.

Edale Monday March 14th 1774
And 15th At home employed in preparing things ready for my Voyage. My Father has scarcely spoke to me since I came from Liverpool. this is very disagreeable, but I must submit to it, tho it is of great disadvantage to me as I do not know what he will give me cannot tell how to act with any degree of propriety.
16th Went to Smadale Bradwell and Hope.[9] Drank Tea at Mr. Robinsons.
17th At Home
18th Went to the Newsmithy for directions to James Kirk in Virginia.[10] It will be absolutely necessary to have some acquaintance on the other side the Atlantic or I cannot possible get so good a knowledg of the Country as I could wish.

Wakefield Saturday March 19th 1774
This morning my Father gave me 12 Guineas and desired me to set out for Wakefield, which I did immediately Dined at Mottram with my Aunt Drank Coffee at Peniston. Got to Wakefield late in the evening.
20th Sunday. Went to Church in the forenoon. After dinner went to Chapeltown to Mr. Ellises.
21st After breakfast Mr Ellis gave me this advice, Allways to put my trust and Confidence in God, To do Justice to every one, To act with Honor and Honesty in all my dealings, and that these rules strictly adhered to, will support me in any troubles or adversities that may happen to me. This Sincear and Friendly advice, I will endeavour to follow as far as the Frailty of human Nature will admit.

Ughill
Dined at Sheffield with Mr Furnis. Bought some Hardware of Messrs Broomheads and a small quantity of Mr. Furnis.[11] Very merry with Mr. Furnis and Mr. Magnel at the Rose and Crown. Got to Ughill late in the evening, all the Family in bed.
22d Breakfasted at Ughill. Got home to dinner. In the evening John Briddock[12] brought my Chest home the sight of it affected my Father the most of any thing I have yet seen. I believe he is most heartily vexed and very uneasy at my proceedings. Am sorry for it. What I do proceeds from good motives. And I will persevere.

Edale Wednesday March 23rd 1[774]
In the forenoon employed in packing up my Cloaths. This has cost my Mother many tears. After dinner went to Chapelinlefrith to put up my other Cloths and see my Chest in the Waggon for Liverpool. Spent the evening with Doctor Green. From him I understand that people in general thinks that I am Non Compus Mentus. Some attributes the reason of my going to one thing, some to

another but they are most of them far wide of the real Cause. Got home late in the evening.
24th At home settleing my affairs ready for my departure. A disagreeable business. I wish I was gone.

Milnthrop Friday March 25th 1774
Set out for Milnthrop At Hope my horse fell sick. Borrowed one of Jacob Hall and proceeded, got to Milnthrop late in the evening.
26th Dined with Mr. Perkin at the Rose and Crown in Sheffield, pay'd Messrs Broomheads for the goods I had bought of them. Miss Perkin gave me a Letter to her Cousin in Barbados Got home very late in the evening.
27th Sunday Went to the Chapel in the forenoon. Mr. Bray,[13] John Bore,[14] John Hadfield[15] and Michael Bradbury came to bid me farewell. John Hadfield wants to send his son a long with me but I will not be connected with any person whatever.

Edale Monday March 28th 1774
Went to Castleton to bid Mr Hall adieu Widdow Hall made me a compliment of a pair of Stockings, Am at a Loss to know what is her motive for it. Spent the evening with Mr. Bray, Jacob Hall, John Hadfield and Michael Bradbury at the Castle. Find Bradbury to be an Insinuating, Lying, Backbiteing scoundrel am sorry I ever had any connections with him. But will avoid such acquaintance for the future.
29th Received a Letter from Tom Middleton which informs me the Ship Sails on Friday next. Employed in settleing my private affairs and preparing every thing ready for my Voyage. Intend to set out for Liverpool on Thursday.

Edale Wednesday March 30th 1774
This day I have been taking leave of my Friends. Very disagreeable employ indeed. They all are or pretend to be Very uneasy at my going away. Some of them that I least expected, sheeds tears plentifully, but wheather they are real or affected they are the best judge. Drank Tea with my Grandmother the good Old Lady is very uneasy. She tels me it is the last time she expected to see me in this life. Went and bid farewell to my worthy Friend Mr Champion,[16] who gave me every good advice that lay in his power, in a very Sincear and affecting manner. I am very sorry to part with this most valuable Friend. My Mother and all the Family very uneasy this has been a disagreeable evening. Rendered more so by the behavior of — [sic]

Warrington Thursday March 31st 1774
Early this morning my Father gave me what he thought proper, And I set out for Liverpool. The parting with my Friends has been one of the most affecting scenes I have ever yet experienced. Plenty of Tears on all sides, but this is nothing more than what is usual on the like occasions. My Brother Richard overtook me at the Chapalinlefrith and insists on going with me to Liverpool.

Called at Stockport to see Nat. Pickford, but he has got a Girl with Child and will not be seen. Dined at Mrs Dixons in Manchester. From there to Warrington in Co with Sam Jackson, Charles Graterix, and my Brother. After supper went to see the Wax work and spent the evening very merryly.

Liverpool Friday April 1st 1774
Got to Liverpool before Dinner found my Chest and goods at Mr. Lathams. Captn. Parry informs me the ship will not sail this week.
2nd. Employed in buying things necessary for my Voyage, Sam Jackson and I Dined at Mr. Lathams.
3rd. Sunday. Spent the evening at the Fleece with Mr. Edmund Baker of Litton.
4th. This morning my Brother set out for home with Mr. Baker, Suped and spent the evening at Mr. Sykeses, with Sam Jackson, Greattrex, and a Captn. May. All of us very merry. Intend to go to Mr. Sykes to get acquainted with Navigation if they [sic] Ship does not Sail nex[t] week.[17] It will be much better than Idleing about in the manner I do at present.

Liverpool Tuesday April 5th 1774
This morning Sam Jackson and Greaterix set out for Manchester, And I entered at Mr. Sykes school. In the evening the Burrous, Captn. Bostock from Guinea,[18] come into the Dock, went on Board to see Bob Middleton who is Steward of her, but he was so disguised with dirt and sickness I did not know him indeed I never saw such a scene of Sickness and Confusion before. The Captn. could scarcely stand and several of the men not able to get out of their Hammocks. As a remarkable instance of the Guinea Sailors being accustomed to Mortallity. A Gentleman came on board to enquire for a passenger from Jaimaica. D—m my Blood, says one of the Sailors, He is dead three weeks ago, But we have pul'd his Guts out and stored away on the Ballast below, With a great deal of indifference.

Liverpool Wednesday April 6th 1774
I am pursueing a desperate design at least it appears so in the eyes of all my Friends. In short I have not one friend in the world, to my knowledge, that approves of my proceedings. Mr. Champion excepted. Therefore I ought to act with the greatest caution and prudence. I have a number of Difficulties to encounter. Brought up to no business and allmost ignorant of the ways of the world, the deceits and Knavery of mankind in general. More particularly the part of the world to which I am bound, My education very slender In a Distant Country, No friend that I dare trust to advise with. And little money to support me, A certainty of loosing a considerable part of my dependence at home.
All these things added together, are not sufficient to counterballance a Natural impulse, and the uneasiness of mind I have laboured under at certain periods when at home. What I have undertaken is with a good design, not to wrong or defraud any one, But with this view to be a benefit to myself and service to my friends. What will be the consequences is in the hands of the disposer of all

things and the womb of time to bring forth. As I engage in it voluntary From honest and generous motives, I am reconciled to my Fate, be it what it will. If I am fortunate I make no doubt but my friends will say that I have acted prudently and wisely to persevere.

If I am unsuccessfull not only my friends, but every Rattlescull will condemn me, put on a wise countenance and say they knew my plan would never answer was too well at home, of a restless rambling disposition And possible in the height of their profound penetration, Tax me with extravagance and dissipation, without makeing the least allowance for the common vicissitudes of life. To avoid these imputations it is necessary to lay down short rules, to govern and direct my proceedings. First To act Honestly and pay my debts as far as I am able, as an efectual means of procureing Credit when I may want it. Mem. Never to contract any debts that I can possibly avoid.

Secondly, Not to be over Hasty in makeing any purchase or engageing with any one for any length of time Til I have considered the Temper and disposition of the people, The Climate, Their trade and Commerce, The fertillity of the soil, with the nature, quallity and quantity of the produce, Their form of Government and Colonial or Provincial Polity. Thirdly. If I like the Country to return as soon as I have made what observations I think necessary and endeavour to go out on a better footing and live as fugally as I can with decency. These general rules observed may be of great use to me. Spent the evening with Mr. James Longsdon at the Fleece.

Liverpool Thursday April 7th 1774
Find Navigation is not so hard to learn as I at first immagined. Spent the evening with Mr. Longsdon, who gave me a pattern Book and desires me to do some business for him, but will avoid all connection in the Forreign trade.
8th. Orders to be on Board tomorrow morning by Seven O'Clock. Bought me a Sea Bed pay'd Captn. Parry for my passage. Got my chest and things on Board. Understand we are to have three other passengers but do not know who they are. Spent the afternoon on Mount Pleasant with Mr. Oaks of Sheffield. Wrote to Gustavus Bradford.[19] got every thing ready for going as soon as the wind serves.

Ship Molly towards America April 9th 74
This morning got up very early and wrote to my Father. Got on Board about Nine O'Clock Set Sail with a fair wind and Tide in our favour in the afternoon Calm and pleasant came to an Anchor off Ormshead. We are Four passengers but dont as yet know the others. All of us very merry at supper tho I believe most of us Young Sailors are rather squemish at Eight in the evening A Breeze spring up hove up the Anchor, About 10 Saw the Skerry Lighthouse.
10th. Sunday. Last night in attempting to get into my Hammock the hook at the foot gave way and had like to have broke my bones with the fall to the no small diversion of my fellow passengers. The Hammock is a large pice of Canvas suspended to the roof of the Cabbin at each end with cords.

Ship Molly towards America April 11, 74
Fine pleasant weather. In the afternoon saw Bardsey Island on the Welsh Coast and Carmarthen Bay.[20] Yesterday it Blew fresh and I was very sick but today I am something better. Sleeping in a Hammock is very agreeable tho very different from from [sic] a Bed on Shore.
12th. Slept pretty well last night. This morning made St. Davids Head the NE promontory of Wales. Fine pleasant Breezes much better of my sickness at least I am as well as the rest of the passengers. Saw the Rocks, called the Bishop and Clarks at Night St. Davids Head Bore W 8 Legues.
13th. Saw Ireland about 12 Leagues Dist. Fine pleasant weather Believe I have got over my sickness.

Ship Molly towards America April 14th 74
Fresh Gales and a large Rolling Sea. Broke our Fore Top Gallant Yard. Took our Departure from Holy Head in Latd 53°°23" North Longd 4°°40" West. Got Clear of the Channel with the wind at NEt. Find I am much deceiv'd, very sick all day.
15th. A Fair wind and pleasant Drank a Quart of Sea water which Operated both ways very plentifully and did me great service. Spoke a Brig from Leghorn bound to Bristol.
16th. Fair wind and pleasant weather. Our passengers are the Revd John Baldwin his Brother Thos Baldwin from Chester, bound to Bermudas as they say for the benefit of their Health. But it seems a little strange that they should come a Board under fictitious names. The other is a certain Capt. Alexander Knox a Scotchman bound to Maryland.[21] This evening drank our Sweethearts in a large Can of Grog. It is a custom at Sea on Saturday nights. Very sick indeed.

Ship Molly towards America April 17th 1774
Sunday and we haveing a Parson on Board expected prayers. But instead of Praying he amused himself with reading a Treatise on the Scurvy, while most of the Sailors were reading in their Common prayer Books. I find these men not such an unprincipaled set of beings as they are represented to be. It is true they swear most horridly in general, but when they pray, which I believe is very seldom, they do it heartily. Pleasant weather and good wind. Pretty free from sickness.
18th. and 19th. A fine N.Et Breez and pleasant weather. Begin to be hungry which they tel me is a sign that the sickness is going off. This is certainly one of the most disagreeable sicknesses in Nature Continually Sick at the Stomack Diziness in the Head and Listlesness with a loathing to all sorts of food.
Ship Molly towards America April 20th 1774
Pleasant and a fine wind. Paid forfeit one Bottle of Rum for going aloft.
21st. Fine weather and Light Breeze. Saw a large Fleet of Porpuses playing about the Vessel some of them appeared to be 10 Ft. long but we catcht none of them.

22nd. Pleasant weather. Spoke a Brig from Lisbon. Dined on Stock Fish and Potatoes. This Fish is cured in the Frost without salt, before it is boiled they beat it with Iron hammers against the Anchor Stock to soften it. A general dish on Fridays and is reaconed a great dellicacy, but to me it is none for I hate the smell of it. Saw Corvo one of the Western Islands bearing S.S.E.½ E Distance about 14 Leagues pritty well over my sickness the Sea begins to be agreeable.

Ship Molly towards America April 23rd 1774
Fine pleasant Breeze this morning, But this evening blow's hard and I am sick.
24th Sunday. Hard Gales from the Easward the Ship rolls and pitches the worst I have yet experienced, Very often the waves broke over the Long boat. Broke our Mizzen Yard.[22] Very sick, Messrs Baldin's in the same condition.
25th. More moderate today, But still blows hard.
26th. Strong Gales and a high Sea. The first thing that I saw after I got upon Deck Was the Carpenter tumbling from one side of the Deck to the other in a great Sea we had Ship[e]d in which he lost his Hat and Wig Saw him soon after and asked him what he had done with them D—m My eyes says he they are gone to David Jones Locker. This is a common saying when anything goes overboard. Very Sick.

Ship Molly towards America April 27th 1774
Strong Gales all day my sickness continues so bad that I cou'd almost wish myself ashore again.
28th. Fine pleasant Breese and smooth water. Took a Drink of Sea water which operated very well, and gave me a good appetite. Mr. Baldwin caught a Fish called Portugeeze Man of War it is about 9 Inches Long and appears like a bladder upon the water allways swiming upon the top. I believe it never goes under water. Of a Transparent Blue Colour. The part that appears like a bladder serves as a Sail. The body is like a bunch of red worsted with a long tail, the [one] that Mr. Baldwin caught was 16 Foot long and no thicker than a Straw. If you touch the tail or body it causes a sensation, the same as if you had touched a Nettle.

Ship Molly towards America April 29th 1774
Fresh Breeses with Rain.
30th Fresh Gales from the Eastward and Cloudy weather.

Sunday May 1st 1774
Light Breese and Clear weather. Evening Calm. No prayers today.
2nd. Pleasant weather with light showers of Rain.
3rd. First part of the day Strong Gales with Rain. Saw a Ship to windward. Evening very heavy Rain with Thunder & Lightening.
4th. Light airs with Clear hot weather. The Thermometer to 73 Degrees. Expect to make the Land in a Week. evening Calm.
5th. Pleasant weather but Foul wind.

6th. Fresh Gales, But contrary. With cloudy Hazy Rainy weather. Saw a Ship to Windward.

Ship Molly towards America May 7th 1774
Foul wind with Cloudy weather, Lightning and Rain.
8th. Sunday. Pleasant weather but a foul wind. Spoke a Brig from Georgia bound to Lisbon. No prayers to day.
9th. Sultry Hazy weather. Saw several Grampuses. They appear to be very large and throw the water a great height into the air, it is said from their nostrils. At six this evening the wind came to the Eastward.
10th. Light winds but a great swell from the North With Sultry Hazy weather.
11th. Pleasant weather and a fair wind.
12th. Cloudy hazy weather but fair wind.
13th. A Fair wind with Hazy Cloudy weather. at Six in the evening Hove the Lead and struck Ground in 25 Fathom water, Sandy bottom. But see no Land.

Ship Molly Chesapeak Bay May 14, 1774
At 10 O'Clock this morning made the Land from the Masthead. At 2 afternoon A Breast of Cape Henry from which we see Cape Charles ENE about 18 Miles distant got a Pilot on Board the Land appears low and sandy covered with Pines.[23] Wrote to my Father by a Ship bound to London. At 7 this evening came on a Gust of Thunder Lightning and Rain from the NWt. Obliged to let go our Anchor in 6 Fathom water at the tail of the Horse Shoe.[24] It is a Custom with all Passengers to pay a bottle of Rum to the Sailors as soon as they make the Land. We agreeable to that custom have pay'd ours, and I believe every man aboard (The Capt, Passengers and first Mate excepted) are drunk Swearing and Fighting Like mad men. Blowing very hard. Thundering very loud and Lightning so strong and Quick that I can see to write without Candle.

Ship Molly Chesapeak Bay May 15th 1774
Sunday. At 5 this morning weighed Anchor with a Fresh Breese and Cloudy weather. At Noon Clear and pleasant. The Land appears from the Masthead to be level and covered with Lofty Pines. A great number of Rivers empty themselves into the Bay. Can count Nineteen Sail of Vessels and see the Land on very side. This is one of the finest prospects I have ever seen. What makes it more agreeable, not seeing land before these 27 Days. At 7 in the evening Calm, let go our Anchor off Windmill Point.[25]
16th A head wind and we have got an indifferent Pilot. the Captn does not think it prudent to moove. Still at Anchor. Captn Received a Letter from Liverpool that informs him the two Baldwins are in debt at home and Obliged to go abroad.

Urbanna, Rappahannock River[26] Virginia May 17th, 1774
Contrary wind our Ship at Anchor. Captn Parry, Captn Knox, Messrs Baldwin and I went a shore in the Pilot Boat Landed at this place. After a passage of

Thirty Eight Days from Liverpool.[27] This is a small Village pleasantly situated on a Creek of the same name. The Custom House for the Rappahannock River, and Tobacco warehouses for the County are kept here. Messrs Baldwin went to the house of a Merchant whom they had Letters of introduction to. Knox and I stay'd at the Inn.

18th. At Urbanna Waiting for the Ship took a walk into the Country, find the Land sandy and Barren to all appear[ances], but it produces excellent Garden stuff, Green Peas are in plenty. Intend to keep a Diary for the future.

Urbanna Rappahannock River Virginia May 19, 1774

This day the Ship came up Captn Knox and I hired a Boat to carry us to Nanjemoy on Potowmeck River About 10 Miles from Alexandria which place I intend to go to as soon as possible.

Went up to Deep Creek and got our Baggage on Board the Boat. Parted with Messrs Baldwins, who are bound to Norfolk in Virginia. Got down to Urbanna but so late at Night obliged to sleep in the Boat all night.

20th Left Urbanna about 8 in the morning our Boat mand with three Negroes. At 2 in the afternoon got into the mouth of Potowmack River which is about 12 Miles wide. A Great number of pleasant seats on the Banks of the River.[28] At 10 in the evening came to an Anchor in Majotack Creek.

Nanjemoy Maryland. May 21st 1774

Early this morning Weighed and stood over to Ladlors Ferry[29] in Maryland where we got Breakfast at the Ferry house After Breakfast got underway again but run the Boat aground on a sand bank in the River where we stuck 2 Hours but by Lashing the Canoe to the Masthead and filling her with stones Keeled the Vessel on one side and got her off. Arived at Nanjemoy in the afternoon Captn Knox Brother has a House here but he is not at home. He introduced me to his Brothers partner Mr. Baily who behaves very civilly to me and insists that I shall stay a week with him.[30] Dont intend staying any longer then I can get a passage to Alexandria.

Nanjemoy Maryland May 22, 1774

Sunday This is a small Village of about five houses. All Planters except Knox and Bailey who keep a Store (What they call stores in this country are Shops in England[)]. In the afternoon drank Tea with Captn Knox and Mr Wallace (Knox and Baylies Clerk) at Colonel Harrisons.[31] Captn Knox introduced [me] to every house in the Village. The people are remarkably civil and obliging, appear to live very well and exceeding happy.

23d Capt Knox and I went to Mrs Marsden[32] a Widdow Lady in the neighbourhood. Got some very indifferent Strawberries and Cherry's.

24th Dined on Board a Scotch Ship called the Jenny. Captn McLeash Master.[33]

Nanjemoy Maryland May 25th 1774
Saw them plant Tobacco. The Land is first hoed into small round hills about the size of Mole-hils. And about 4000 of them in an Acre. The plants are something like small Cabbage plants they only make a hole with their finger or a small stick and put them in, one in each hill. Two Negroes will plant three Acres in one day.[34] Small Blisters are broke out all over my body attended with an intollerable itching. They call it the Prickley heat and say it is very wholesome. It may be so, for anything I can tel but it is very troublesome.
26th Waiting for an opportunity to go to Alexandria by water, but I believe Captn Knox does everything in his power to disappoint me for fear I shoud go a way. Drank Tea at Mrs Leftwiches.[35]

Nanjemoy Maryland May 27th 74
Dined on Board the Jenny. McLeash. It is true we had excellent Porter and Wine, but had our stomach's been of a Squemish nature, they wou'd have been disobliged at their Scotch Cleanliness.
28th The Land here is Level sandy and Barren in general except where it is mixed with Oyster shels which renders it very fertile. Agriculture is in a very poor state. In short they know very little about Farming, Tobacco and Indian-corn is all they make and some little wheat. All done by Negroes. The Tobacco is all worked with Hoes, the Indian-corn with Plows but of a bad sort and without a Colter the furrow they make is not more then 2 Inches deep and does little more than kill the weeds. Land sells upon an average here at about three Dollars pr Acre, Thirteen Shillings and six pence Sterling.

Nanjemoy Maryland May 29th 74
Sunday. Capt Knox went to Bulo[36] in Virginia to see his brother. Here is no Church within 14 or 15 Miles of the place. Mr. Bayley and I went to see a Negro Ball, Sundays being the only days these poor Creatures have to themselves, they generally meet together and amuse themselves with Dancing to the Banjor. This Musical instrument (if it may be so called) is made of a Gourd something in immitation of a Guitar with only four strings and play'd with the fingers in the same manner. Some of them sing to it which is very droll musick indeed,
In their songs they generally relate the usage they have received from their Masters or Mistresses, in a very Satirical stile and manner.
Their poetry is like the Music Rude and uncultivated. Their Dancing is most violent exercise, but so irregular and Grotesque, I am not able to describe it. They all appear to be exceedingly happy at these merry makings and seem as if they had forgot or were not sensible of their misserable condition.
30th Dined at Colnl Harrisons. Nothing talked of but the Blockade of Boston Harbor the people seem much exasperated at the proceedings of the Ministry and talk as if they were determined to dispute the matter with the Sword.[37]
31st Waiting for a Passage to Alexandria but cant meet with an opportunity. This is doing nothing.

Nanjemoy Maryland June 1st 1774

Waiting with a great deal of impatience for a passage to Alexandria. I am informed that the Land is much better the higher you go up the River. If it is not, I will not settle in this part of the Country.

2d Spent the afternoon at Colonel Harrisons find him a very inteligent man and seems to take a pleasure in communicating the Customs and manners of his countrymen. Captn Knox returned to Nanjemoy this evening and gave me an invitation to go with him to Annapolis, which I intend to accept.

3d Hired a horse and crossd Nanjemoy Creek. Got to Porttobacco in the evening. This is a small town situated at the head of a Creek of the same name. The County Courts are held here and a Warehouse for the inspection of Tobacco. Several Scotch Factors are settled here.

Marlbro Maryland June 4th 1774

Left Port Tobacco in Co with Mr John Creig a Scotch Merchant, Doctor Gustavus Richard Brown[38] and Captn Knox. Dined at Piscataway a small town 16 Miles from Porttobacco. Our victuals badly Drest and sour Madeira Wine at 7/6 pr Bottle. From Piscataway to Marlbro[39] 16 Miles. Saw the quarter of a Negro man chained to a Tree for murdering his overseer. Land in general appears barron and thinly inhabited some places Sandy and others a Sort of Stiff Clay but plenty of fine Orchards, and I observe they generally plant a Peach Orchard on the worst Land. They had a Frost on the 9th of May, which has killed a great number of Trees the woods for a Mile together seems dead and withered.[40]

Annapolis, Maryland June 5th 74

Sunday. Left Marlbro early this morning Crossed Patuxen River at Mount Pleasant Ferry. Some good Land after this River. breakfasted at Rollins a Publick house, but in this Country called Ordinaries, and indeed they have not their name for nothing. For they are ordinary enough, have had either Bacon or Chickens every meal since I came into the Country. If I still continue in this way shall be grown over with Bristles or Feathers. From Rollins to London town on South River. This is a Small pleasant place at the head of the Bay, but no great trade. Crossed the South River and got to Annapolis to Dinner. 22 Miles from Marlbro. Land very indifferent from London town to Annapolis.

Annapolis Maryland June 6th 74

This is the Capital town or rather City in the Province and the seat of the Governor, Situated at the Head of Chesapeak Bay. It is not very large or populous. But regularly built and some of them good buildings. They are now building an Ellegant State House of Brick, Which is to be covered with Copper.[41] A place of very little trade, Chiefly supported by the meeting of the Provincial Assembly. Here is a Great number of people collected together to get Bills of Credit out of the Provincal Loan Office. A considerable sum in Four,

Three, Two, One, Two thirds, One third, and one Ninth of a Dollar Bills, is struck in these Bills of Credit by an Act of the Provincial Assembly.

An Office is opened and the money devided into Lots of 1000 Dollars each. Any Person a resident in the Province may take up a Thousand Dollars. If he has an Estate in the Province of twice the Value and clear of Entail or Mortgage which Estate he Mortgages to the Office as security for the money, which he has at 4 pr Cent for Ten Years, and then the Bills are called into the Office again. It is Death to Sell or Mortgage an Estate that is Mortgaged to this Office til the expiration of the time and in default of paying the intr[est] the Treasurer of the Loan office has a rig[ht] to sell the whole estate and appropriate the whole of the money to the Province use. These Bills are a Lawfull tender and the greatest part of the business is done with this sort of money.

Not only in this Province, But, every Province, and Colony on the Continent have large sums of this kind of money, Issued by their different House of Assembly. I suppose the Credit of these Bills must be indisputable, If one may be allowed to judge from the number of people that applys for them. It appears to me that there is a scarcity of Cash amongst the people of all ranks here. They Game high, Spend freely, and Dress exceeding Gay. But I observe they seldom show any money, it is all Tobacco Notes. Great number of Scotch tradesmen here, but very few English. Provisions are as dear here, as in England. Mutton and Beef at 6d pr lb. A Violent pain in my Head this evening.

Piscataway, Maryland June 7th 1774

This morning Captn Knox and I left Annapolis. Dined at Marlbro. Lodged at Piscataway. A most violent pain in my Head attended with a high Fever, Obliged to stop and rest myselfe at several houses on the road. Captn Knox behaves exceeding kindly to me.

8th Got to Port Tobacco with great difficulty. Captn Knox insists on me applying to Docr Brown. I have taken his advice, and he tel[ls] me it is a Fever with some cussed physical name, he has give me some Slops and I am now going to bed very Ill.

9th Find myselfe no better, However the Doctor has give me more physic. Got to Nanjemoy. Allmost dead with Pain and Fatigue, added to the excessive heat which caused me to faint twice.

Nanjemoy Maryland June 10th 1774

11th, 12th, 13th, 14th and 15th. Very ill. Confined to my room. This is the first day I have been able to stir out of it. I am much reduced and very weak but my Spirits are good and I hope in God I shall get better. Captn Knox, Mr. Bayley, and the whole Neighbourhood behaves with the greatest kindness to me, some of them has attended me constantly all the time.

17th Much better, The Doctor tels me I am out of all danger. But advices me to take some physic to clear my body, and to drink a little more Rum then I did before I was sick. In short I believe it was being too abstemious that brought this sickness upon me at first, By drinking water.

18th Able to walk about the house. It is such excessive Hot weather or I shou'd mend faster.

Nanjemoy Maryland Sunday June 19, 1774
Dined at a Certain Mr Hambletons Suped and spent the evening at Mrs Leftwiches with some young Ladys from Virginia. After supper the Co amused themselves with several deverting plays. This seems very strange to me, But I believe it is common in this Country. Find myself much better to day, Hope I shall be able to go to Alexandria next week.

20th Gathering strength very fast, the Doctor sent me a Box of Pills with directions to take two at Night and two in a Morning these are the last I intend to take. Dined at Mr Leftwiches. After went over to Virginia with some Young Ladys but retur'd in the evening.

21st And 22d Taking the Pills the Doctor gave me but they dont seem to work, only cause a bad taste in my mouth. Will take three this evening.

Nanjemoy Maryland June 23d 1774
This morning took 4 Pills which has caused a Violent pain in my bowels all day attended with a constant thrist, and a very bad taste in my mouth. But affects me no other way. Colnl Harrison sent me a Huming Bird. This is supposed to be one of the sma[ll]est Birds that is known. It is Green on its Back its Neck and Breast of a Beautifull Azure, The Belly and thighs are of a Whiteish Colour. It has a Long Beak about the thickness of a Needle which it Darts into the Flowers and extracts the Honey upon which it lives. It weighs [Blank] They are only seen in the Summer time their nests are very rarely found and are looked upon as a great curiossity.

Nanjemoy Maryland June 24th 1774
Much worse. My throat and Tongue much swell'd. Have sent for the Doctor. Confined to my Bed, Am affraid that I am poysoned with his confounded Pills. A continual thirst but these people will not let me drink.

25th Captn Knox sent an express for the Doctor who came about Eight this morning. After he had examined the Pills he came with a Truely phisical face to the Bed side and felt my Pulse. Begun to beg my pardon for the mistake he said his prentice had inadvertently commited by sending me strong Mercurial Pills, in the room of Cooling ones. I immediately gave him as hard a blow as I could with my Fist over the Face, And would have given him a good triming had I been able.

This discomposed his physical Muscles a good deal, and made him contract them into a most Formidable Frown, But did not attempt to resent it, Beg'd I would moderate my passion follow his directions and in a short time I should be well again. I believed myselfe poyson'd and grew desperate abused him most unmercifully. However he left me some Brimstone and Salts, which I took immediately after he was gone, which worked very well and has given me a great deal of ease. Tho I am still full of pain, and much swell'd, Spiting and

Slavering like a Mad Dog. My teeth loose and mouth very sore. I believe I have little to trust too but the strength of my Constitution for my life. Much difficulty to write but if I happen to Die I hope this will appear against the Rascal.

Nanjemoy Maryland June 26th 1774

This morning took a Dose of Brimstone. Lay in Bed all day and Sweat abundantly. This has made me very weak and fainty. Doctor came to enquire after me but did not come into the room. Much easier.

27th A great deal better but much relaxed and very weak Able to sit up most part of the day.

28th And 29th Mending very fast. Able to walk about the room. The swelling gone away, My Throat got well but my mouth is very sore, which I wash every two hours with Vinegar. I understand the Doctor sends every day to enquire how I do. Had it not been for the extrordinary care of Captn Knox I must certainly have died.

30th Took a Dose of Salts. Able to walk into the yard.

Nanjemoy, Maryland July 1st 1774

And 2d. Continue mending, but very slowly.

3rd. Sunday. Rode out with Mr Wallace to Collonel Taylors Plantation. It is only two miles, but I find it has Fatigued me too much.

4th. Went to see them Reap Wheat. The greatest slovens I ever saw, believe that one fourth part is left on the Field uncut. Some of them Mow's it with sticks fixed on the Scythe in parrallel lines to lay the Grain streight. These makes worse havock, then the Reapers.[42] The Grain is but indifferent and their crop very light, seldom that they get Seven Bushel from an Acre. But they put it into the ground in such a slovenly manner without any Manure it is a Wonder that they get any.

Nanjemoy, Maryland. July 5th 1774

Took another Doce of Salts which I hope will be the last I shall have occasion to take at this time. Find myselfe pretty well, Free from pain, but very weak and much reduced, my Cloaths hangs about me like a Skelleton. The Doctor has never come in my sight since I struck him. Intend to go and pay the Rascal tomorrow.

6th. Went to see the Doctor, who (contrary to my expectation) Treated me with the greates[t] kindness and acknowledges that he had given me just cause of complaint tho inadvertently. And absolutely refused being pay'd till I am quite recovered. I understand their Doctors bills in this Country are very extravagant. Returned to Nanjemoy much Fatigued.

Nanjemoy, Maryland. July 7th 1774

Took my passage on board a small Schooner bound to Alexandria. Captn Knox and Mr Bayley pressed me to stay a week longer and get a little stronger before I attempt to moove [sic]. I think I am able to go to Alexandria as it is only 100 miles by water. I am und[er] infinite, Obligations to these worthy people every possible care has been taken of me in my late illness, had I been their Brother more tenderness cou'd not have been used for my recovery. They absolutly refuse takeing anything for my Board so that I must remain under obligations to them which I am affraid it will never be in my power to repay. Calm in the evening. the Captn and I went a Shore, to what they call a Reaping Frolic. This is a Harvest Feast. The people very merry Danceing without either Shoes, or Stockings and the girls without Stays but I cannot partake of the Diversion.

Potowmeck River. July 8th 1774
Contrary wind. Come too an Anchor off Maryland Point. Went a shore and Dined at Captn Harrisons[43] had a very genteel dinner but the Captn is a Violent opposer of the Government. Got on Board in the evening. Fair wind got up to Colonel George Washingtons came to an Anchor in the Creek. Here is a small Insect which appears in the Night like sparks of Fire every time it extends its wings there is something of a Luminous nature on the Body, just under the wing which only seen when it extends them, only decernable in the night. And is called the Fire Fly. A great number of pleasant Houses along the River both on the Virginia and Maryland side. All Tobacco Planters some of them People of considerable property. This River parts the Province of Maryland and Colony of Virginia.

Potowmeck River. July 9th 1774
Waiting for a load of Flour from Colnl Washingtons Mill.[44] I am now got pretty well but weak and feeble.
10th. Sunday. Went to see the Mill. It is a very compleat one. Dressing and Bolting mills the same as in England with a pair of Collogne, and a pair of French Stones. And make as good flour as I ever saw. Land much better here then it is lower down the River.
11th. Got our Cargo on board, Weighed and got up to Alexandria about three OClock. After dinner waited on Mr Kirk with my letters. He seems to be very glad to see me gives me great encouragement and insists on me makeing his house my home as long as I stay here. Got my Baggage Ashore.

Alexandria, Virginia. July 12th 1774
Viewing the Town, which is lay'd off in Square [sic] of an Acre each, Streets 80 Feet wide several good Brick Buildings and when it is compleated according to the plan w[ill] be a Beautifull and Regular town. Their Chief trade is Wheat, Flour, and Tobacco. Mr Kirk tells me they exported 100,000 Bushels of Wheat and 14,000 Barrels of Flour, from this Port the last Year. Here is as good Wheat as I ever saw, brought to this market from the back Country. I am told the land is very good about Eighty miles to the Westward of this town. I have told Mr Kirk of my scheme he approves of it, And advises me to take a Tour into the back Country as soon as I am able to travel on horseback. Promises to give me every assistance that lyes in his power. In the afternoon introduced me to Captn

William Buddiecombe[45] a Gentleman from Liverpool and several other gentlemen in town. Am very glad to find him so well esteemed amongst the people.

13th. I begin to gather strength very fast. find this an agreeable place.

14th. An Election for Burgesses in town (there Elections are annual) There was three Candidates. The Poll was over in about two hours and conducted with great order and regularity. The members Colnl George Washington and Major Bro[ad]water.[46] The Candidates gave the populace a Hogshead of Toddy (what we call pun[ch] in England.

In the evening the returned Members gave a Ball to the Freeholders and Gentlemen of the town. This was conducted with great Harmony, Coffee and Chocolate, but no Tea, this Herb is in disgrace amongst them at present, I have been seized with a Violent Gripeing pain in my bowels and obliged to leave the room very early it still continues. I am affraid of a relapse.

15th I have had a most violent pain in my Bowels all night and a very severe Lax some Symptoms of the Flux. If it happens to proove the Flux I am certain to Die. Mr. Kirk & the Doctor advises me take a short Voyage to Sea as the only method of reestablish my health. I have wrote to my Father informing him that I have drawn upon him for Thirty pounds. I am not able to go to Sea without a Supply of money. This money I believe will pay my Funeral expences.

Alexandria Virginia July 16th 1774

17th and 18th Confined to my room. Sick of the Bloody Flux. I am in a most misserable condition, so weak I can scarcely get a cross the room and afflicted with a most excrutiateing pain in my bowels. I believe my Death is approaching very fast. I am wholly resigned to the will of Heaven and submit to my fate without repineing My Conscience does not accuse me with any wicked or unpardonable crimes, therefore I hope to find mercy in the sight of a Just and merciful God. I have not yet drawn a Bill upon my Father, and if it pleases God to take me out of the world, I have effects sufficient to bury me deacently. If I Die I hope Mr Kirk will send this Book home. He behaves to me like a parent, and hope he will not refuse the request of a Dieing man.

Alexandria Virginia July 19th 1774

The virulence of my disorder begins to abate. I find myself surprizeingly better today. Am singularly obliged to Mr Kirk for his great care of me, he advises me to go to Sea as soon as possible. I believe I will take his advise, and go the first Vessel that goes out of port if I am obliged to be carry'd aboard.

20th Able to walk about the house. But I appear more like a Skelleton than a man. Agreed with a Certain Capt. Speak to go to Barbadoes in a small Schooner. Sold my hardware to Mr Kirk of whom I bought 33 Ba[rre]lls Sea Bread which intend to take as a venture. Got my Bread a Board, and if the wind answers we sail tomorrow. A Certain Mr Dundass advises me to drink Port Wine. Am Affraid I have drank too much.

Schooner John Potowmeck River July 21st

Slept very well and undisturbed last night. Find myself pretty well only weak. Early this morning the Captn sent for my Chest and Bed. About 9 OClock I went on Board the Schooner John,[47] Francis Speake Master bound for Barbados. Fell down to the mouth of Broad Creek where we came to an Anchor.

22nd Slept very well last night. I believe the Flux has entirely left me. Fell down with the Tide to Stumpneck Point. The Captn went a Shore and Bought us some Stock. Much fatigued with the motion of the Vessel, scarce able to stand.

23d Able to walk the Quarter Deck. Fell down to Ceder Point. A severe Gust of Thunder lightning and the Largest Hailstones I ever saw and the hardest. Like pieces of Ice cut some of the peoples Faces til the Blood came. Mr. Richard Brooks another passenger came on Board. He is an Invalid.

Schooner John Potowmeck River July 24, 74

Sunday. Fell down to the Maryland Office Went A Shore with the Captn to Clear out his Vessel. Lodged Ashore at the office the Gentleman refuses to do any business on Sunday.

25th Fell down to St Marys River. Went A Shore with the Captn to the Office, All Vessels are obliged to Clear out at both Offices. I am now perfectly well but very weak.

26th At Anchor with a Contrary wind. About noon a Pilot Boat came along side to invite the Captn to A Barbicue. I went with him and have been highly diverted. These Barbicues are Hogs, roasted whole, this was under a large Tree. A great number of Young people met together with a Fiddle and Banjor Play'd by two Negroes with Plenty of Toddy which both Men and Weomen [sic] seems to [be] very fond of. I believe they have Danced and drunk till there is Few Sober people amongst them. I am sorry I was not able to join them. Got on Board late.

Schooner John St Mary's River July 27th 74

Still at Anchor with a Contrary wind. After Dinner went a Shore and bought some Stock. In attempting to get A Board again, was very neare oversetting the Boat, obliged to Lodge A Shore at Mr Miles Herberts.[48] People chiefly Roman Chatholics.

28th Got on Board before five OClock this morning Weighed, and got into the Bay. Calm obliged to come to an Anchor.

29th Early this morning Got underway with the wind at N. N. Wt and stood down the Bay with an easy Breese. I am now able to walk the Deck for an hour together.

30th At 10 this morning a Breast Cape Henry Lat 37°°=00" North Longd 75°°=24" West from whence we take our Departure.

31st Sunday. This morning the Captn kiled a Jew Fish with the gig. It weighted 74 lb and measured 5 Feet long something like a Cod eat very well. Fair Wind and pleasant.

Schooner John Towards Barbados August 1st 1774
Squally weather, with Calms.
2nd and 3rd Squally weather and a heavy rolling Sea. Begin to be Sea sick.
4th and 5th Yesterday a[t] A. M. Begun to blow very hard from the N. W. Before 2 P. M. It hauled round Eastwarly to the S. W. when we was oblidged to Lay her Too under her close Reefd F. S. At 10 P. M. Oblidged to Furl the F. S. and Scud under Bare poles. At 12 P. M. Broke the Tiller, and gave all up for lost. Expecting the Vessel to Founder before we cou'd Rigg another. About 2 A. M. got a new Tiller the weather begun to moderate. But our Vessel made a great deal of Water. At 8 A. M. Set the F. S. and Jibb. still blowing very hard and Monstrous Sea At 6 P. M. Set the Mainsail more moderate But a very great Sea. Very Sick this two days

Schooner John towards Barbadoes Augt 6th 74
Fine pleasant weather. This is very agreeable after such rough Sea.
7th Sunday. Pleasant weather and Light winds. Crossed several Rippling currents, about 100 Yards broad. Seting to the S. W. What they are our Captn is neither Sailor or philosopher sufficient to determine. At 10 P. M. Hove Too for fear of the Rocks of Bermudas.
8th and 9th. Cloudy, Hazy weather with Saualls [sic] of Rain. Wee are now in the Horse Latitudes. The Sailors as posses'd with a notion that it is Impossible to cross them without Rain and Squally weather. I am now (Thanks to the Almighty) as well as ever I was in my life only weak, but I have a good stomack and hope I shall recover my strength shortly.

Schooner John towards Barbados Augt 10th 1774
Squally with Rain contrary wind.
11th, 12th and 13th. Light Breeses an[d] Hot weather. Calm this evening and heavy Rain.
14th. Sunday. Quite Calm and smooth water the people bathed in the Sea. They had not been on board half an hour before A Shark came a Longside. Wee bated a hook but he woud not take it Appeared to be about Ten Foot long of a Brown Coloure, There was a Pilot Fish with it, This is a beautifull Fish, About a Foot long, Variagated with Stripes of Black and White, quite round the Body. Generally accompany the Sharks.
15th Light winds with Clear Hot weather.
16th Morning Light Breeses. This evening blows Fresh and has carry'd away our Main Croggik Yard.[49]

Schooner John towards Barbados Augt 17th 1774
Pleasant weather but hot. We have been in the Trade winds ever since we Cross'd the Tropick. They allways blow from N. E. to S. E. but generally to the Northw'd of East.
18th Saw Three Tropic Birds, they appear to be about the size of Rooks but Milk white with Long Feathers in the Tail of a very singular appearance.

19th Moderate Breeses and pleasant weather Catched a Dolphin. This is one of the most Beautifull Fishes I ever saw. About three Foot long, Adorned with every Colour of the Rainbow. After it is taken out of the water, it changes it's Colour every instant til it dies, when it is of a Light Blue inclineing to a purple. The Flesh is very white but eats dry.

Schooner John towards Barbados Augt 20th
Pleasant weather but excessive Hot.
21st and 22nd Strong Gales of wind and Hazy weather. Pay'd a Bottle of Rum for my Footing in the Tropic. I ought to have pay'd it according to custom, when we cross'd the Tropic of Cancer. But I believe the people had forgot.
23rd and 24th. Fresh Breeses and Cloudy weather.
25th. Fresh Breeses with Squally Hazy weather. Saw Five Land Birds about the size of Ducks, of a Brown Colour, I belive [sic] they all them Boobies. By my Reckoning Barbados Bears, S. S. Wt. Distance 102 Leagues, At Meridian.
26th. Fresh Breeses, with showers of Rain and Hazy weather. At M. Saw a Sail standing to Eastward.

Schooner John towards Barbados Aug 27th 1774
Light winds and Calms Saw a great number of Boobies.
28th Sunday. Light winds with Clear and Hot weather. Took a Dose of Salts Not had a Stool for Fifteen Days. I have enjoyed as good a state of Health all the time as ever I did in my Life. Could eat and sleep very well. But a continual bad taste in my mouth.
29th. Fresh Breeses and Clear weather. At M. in the Latd of Barbados the Captn is A Shore by his Reckoning. I want 10 Leagues. Saw a great number of Land Birds And something floted a Longside, which we suppose to be the Body of a Man.

Schooner John towards Barbados Augt 30th 1774
Fine pleasant weather. At M.[50] made the Island from the masthead Distant about 5 Leagues. At 3 P. M. Abreast the N. Et End of the Island and one of the beautifu[l]est prospects I ever saw. High Land like one entire Garden interspersed with Gentlemens Houses and Windmils in a Delightfull manner At 9 P. M. Abrest Bridgetown. Lay'd Her too till morning.
31st. At 8 this morning run into Carlisle Bay and came to an Anchor in eight Fathom Water. A Passage of 41 Days from Alexandria. More'd Ship, and went A Shore with the Captn to Bridge Town Dined with Mr Charles Willing[51] the Merchant that the Vessel was consigned to. Slept on Board.

Bridge Town Barbados September 1st 1774
Went A shore and saw my Bread Landed. Have attempted to sell it but find I cannot get first cost such quantities are arived from Philadelphia. Have Stored it with Mr Willing in hopes the price may rise a little before we sail. Dined at Mr Willings, who appears to be a Genteel man. Gave me a general invitation to his

house. Agree'd with Captn Speake to live on Board find it too expensive for me to live a Shore. They ask Half a Joehannes pr week for Board. Excessive hot.

2nd. By accident met with Mr Thos Blacket[52] a Relation of Mr Perkins, who invited me to Speights Town where Mr Perkins is. Dined with Mr Hazlewood.[53] After dinner went to Speights Town in one of the Market Boats found Mr Perkin ill in Bed Lodged at Mr. Blackets.

Speights Town Barbados Septmbr 3d 74
Last night it Blew a Hurricane Drove several Ships from the moreings. And has continued Raining all day.

4th Sunday. Early this morning Bathed in the Sea, which is very refreshing in this hot Climate. After Breakfast vewed [sic] the town. It is small, and dirty, has a pretty Church but very little frequented the People amuse themselves with Shooting on Sundays. In the evening went with Mr Perkin to see Mr Kids Plantation. The Sugar works and Rum Distillery are very expensive. The juice of the Cane is expre[sse]d between two Iron rollers which are turned by the wind and then Boiled into Sugar or made into Rum. The Cane is planted in Hills, is ripe about Christmas. It's preasent [sic] appearance is like large Sedge grass. It is all tended by Negro Slaves with Hoes, never use Plows.

Bridge Town Barbados. September 5th 74
Some prospect of selling my Bread to a little proffit, but the person is not at home. Went to Bridge Town in the Market Boat. Dined a Board A Shore with the Captn in the evening.

5th. No prospect of selling or Bartering here to any advantage must go to Speigs'town.

6th. After dinner went to Speighst [sic] Town. Called at Hole Town. This is a small Village with a Church.[54] This evening as Mr. Perkin and I walked along the Shore was attacked with Shower of Stones from a Mangeneel Grove by some Negroes but was not hurt. Thes[e] Negroes are very rude in the night to people unarmed. Lodged at Mr. Blackets. Gave Mr Perkin the Knives his Uncle had sent him and the letter from Miss R.

Bridge Town Barbados Septm 8th 1774
Cannot sell my Bread at Speighs Town got to Bridge Town to dinner. Most intolerably Hot.

9th. Sold part of my Bread but cannot get the first cost, the other part I have exchanged for Cotton, this Article sell well in Virginia, hope to make up my loss by it.

10th. Got my Cotton on Board. Wrote home and to Sam Jackson put the Letters on Board a Ship for London.

11th. Sunday. Took a Ride with Mr. Iffil[55] one of Mr Willings Clarks to his Fathers about 10 Miles from Bridge Town. The road is very bad and Rocky where it is level the land appears very rich a Fine Black Mould. But I am in a new world I know neither Bush or Produce. Dined on a Roasted Kid And Lodged at Mr Iffils.

Bridge Town Barbados September 12th 1774
Got to Town to Dinner very well pleased with my jaunt.
13th. Went a shore and saw a Cargo of Slaves landed. One of the most shocking sights I ever saw. About 400 Men, Women, and Children, Brought from their native Country deprived of their Liberty and themselves and posterity become the property of cruel strangers without a probabillity of ever enjoying the Blessing of Freedom again, Or a right of complaining be their sufferings ever so great. The Idea is Horrid and the Practice unjust. They were all naked except a small piece of Blue Cloath about a Foot broad to cover their nakedness and appear much dejected. Suped and spent the evening at Mr. James Bruces.

Bridge Town, Barbados. September 14th 1774
Captn Thos Bragg[56] & Richard Rous Dotin Esqr[57] A Merchant in town dined on Board. In the evening went A Shore with them to the Jews Synagogue.[58] To see one of their Grand Festivals called the opening of the Five Books of Moses. The ceremony was begun before we got there they was just Bringing out the Books under canapys of Green Silk something like Umbrellas adorned with small Bells of Gold or Brass they caryed them into the middle of the Congregation Where the Rabby or Chief Priest made a Long and Loud talk in Hebrew. He had a long Black Gown like a Surplus and a Large Fur Cap with Venerable long Beard. The Jews worship Standing and their Hats on with a Long piece of White Silk or Fine Linen (according to the persons circumstances) like a Towel with the ends tied together they put their Arms through it and the loose part lies across their back. They appear to perform their Religious Ceremonies with great Solemnity. The Build[ing] is very neat and Ellegantly finished within. Spent the evening at Captn Braggs in Co with Eight Young Lady's, very merry.
15th Went a Shore and Dined at the Five Bits Tavern, what they call a Bit is half a Pistereen or Six pence sterling. This is one of the cheapest Taverns in town. I believe there is only two other houses that you can get dinner or anything to eat.

Captn Bragg, Mr Dotin and Four other Gentlemen Suped and spent the evening on Board the Schooner.

Bridge Town Barbados September 16th 1774
This Island is one of the most Windward or Easward of the West India Islands situated in Latd 12°°=58" North Longd 58°°=50" West. About 20 Miles long and 12 Broad Contain[ing] about 20000 White Inhabitants, and 90,000 Blacks. Exports about 20,000 Hhds of Sugar and 6000 Hhds of Rum Annually. They are supplyed with the greatest part of their provisions from the Colonies, and all their Staves and Lumber comes from there with Horses and Livestock of all kinds. In excha for which They give Rum, Sugar and Cotton but very little of the last article. It is a high Rockey Island and Reckoned the most healthy Island in

the West Indies, I suppose there is one Eighths part of the land too Rockey for Cultivation.

The roads are very bad, It is nothing uncomon to see twelve Yoke of Oxen to draw one Hhd of Sugar but their Cattle are very small. Their chief Produce is Sugar Indigo, Pimento and Cotton. The Pimento grows on large Trees like small Berries the Cotton on Small Bushes which they plant annually. The Indigo is planted in the same manner. Here is great variety of Fruits, Pine Apples, Bananas, a Fruit like a Large Bean Pod very sweet. Plantains something in the same shape these when roasted are a good substitute for Bread. Alligeta Pear, Or Vegetable marrow, this is exactly the shape of a Pear but has a large stone in it. the flesh has the taste and appearance of real Marrow. These all grows on Trees, except the Pine Apple.

Tammarinds Grows on very large trees the Bodys of the trees are full of pricks like a Brier, Shaddocks are a large Fruit like an Orange but much larger. Limes in plenty—Oranges and Lemmons are very indifferent here, Guavas are a small fruit something like a Lime but has a sickley taste they make a fine Jelly from them. Mamme Apples are larger then an Orange with a Stone in them the flesh has the appearance of a Carrot and eats something like it. The Mangineel Apple has the Smell and appearance of an English apple, but small, grows on large trees Generally along the Sea Shore, they are Rank poison I am told that one apple is sufficient to kill 20 people. this poison is of such a Malignant nature that a single drop of Rain or Dew that falls from the tree unto your Skin will immediatly raise a blister. Neither Fruit or Wood is of any use that I can learn. The Cabbage tree is very beautifull, Grows very lofty the Bark of a Fine Green and remarkable smooth, the Fruit is good pickled as Cabbage but does not appear like it on the tree.

The Coco Tree grows to an amazeing height some of them 80 Foot with only a Tuft of Leaves at top. The Fruit grows at the root of the leaves, as some are ripe others is blossoming so that they are never without Fruit. It is surprizeing with what agillity the Negroes climb these trees. Here is a number other Fruits I am not acquainted with. Yams are like our potatoes but much larger.

This is the Chief Town in the Island and was pretty large. But a Great part of it was burned down in the year 1766, and is not yet rebuilt. Here is a Good Church Dedd to St Michael with an Organ the Church Yard is planted round with Coco Trees which make a pretty appearance. The houses are built of Stone but no Fire places in them only in the Kitchen, the Heat of the Climate rende[rs] that unnecessary only for Cooking. Indeed it wou'd be insupportable was it not for the Sea breese which blows all Day. And from the Land in the Night. All the S. E. part of the Island is Fortified with Batteries the Windward part of the Island is fortified by nature. No Garrison or Soldiers here only the Militia which are well deciplined to keep the Negroes in Awe.

The Planters are in general Rich, but a set of Dissipateing Abandoned and Cruel people, Few even of the Maried ones, but they keep a Mulatto or Black Girl in the house or at Lodgings, for certain purposes. The women are not killing

Beauties, nor very engageing in their conversation but some of them has large Fortunes which covers a multitude of imperfections. The Brittish nation famed for humanity suffers it to be tarnished by their Creolian Subjects. the Cruelty exercised upon the Negroes is at once shocking to Humanity and a disgrace to human nature. For the most trifleing faults, sometimes for meer whim's (of their Masters) these poor wretches are ty'd up and whiped most unmercifully. I have seen them tied up and floged with a twisted piece of Cow Skin till there was very little signs of Life then get a dozen with an Ebony sprout which is like a Bri[ar?] this Lacerates the Skin and Flesh This lets out the bruised blood, or it wou'd mortify and kill them. some of them dies under the severity of these Barbarities, others whose spirits are too great to submit to the insults and abuses they receive put an end to their own lives. If a person kils a Slave he only pays his value as a Fine. It is not a Hanging matter. Certainly these Poor Beings meets with some better place on the other side the Grave for they have a Hell on earth. It appears that they are sensible of this. if one may judge from their behaviour at their funerals. Instead of weeping and wailing, They are Danceing and Singing and appear be the happyest Mortals on earth. Went with Mr and Mrs Dottin to see the Funeral of Mr Stephenson a Capital Merchant in Town. Most part of the men were Drunk. No tears shed but by Mulatto Girls. Spent the evening at Captn Braggs.

17th Dined at Mr Willings, got all our Cargo on Board. Drank Tea at Mr Dotins who is desireous of keeping a correspondence with me. At 8 in the Evening Weighed anchor and stood out of the Bay With a Stout Breese at E. N. E.[59]

Schooner John towards Virginia Septr 18th 74
Fresh Breeses and Clear weather. Saw Martinico it appears high land. At 8 P. M. Saw a Rainbow by moon light.

19th Fres[h] Breeses at 2 P. M. Saw Monseratat 4 P. M. A Breast Desseada Latd 16°°=20" North Longd 60°°=10" West from whence we take our departure. Sea sick.

20th 21st 22nd 23rd And 24th Pleasant weather but a great deal of Thunder and Lightning.

25th Pleasant weather but a foul wind and more Lightning, but no Thunder.

26th 27th 28th 29th and 30th Moderate Breeses and pleasant weather. Mr Brook, the other passenger, I dont expect to live till morning, the Captn has treated him most barbarously. The Captn and I has quarreled about it. Mem, To give him a drubing when I get a Shore.

Schooner John towards Virginia Octor 1st 1774
Fine pleasant weather. Saw the Body of a man flote alongside. Calm this evening.

2nd Sunday Pleasant weather. Mr Brook begins to mend a little but is in a most Shocking condition.

3d A remarkable Whirlwind this morning which put the Vessel about in a Minuit and then fell Calm for 2 Hours. At 4 P. M. Blew very hard at N. E. Obliged to Lay the Vessel Too under Her Fore Sail.

4th By our Reckoning we are pretty near Cape Hatteras. Still Lying Too under Refd F. Sail. Blowing very hard At N. E. Shiped several heavy Seas. One of which has carryed away our Starboard Quarter Rail with thre [sic] Baggs of Cotton two of them belongs to me. This is all my venture, I am now a Beggar. This is a stroke of fortune I can bad[ly] bear at present but must submit. Blows very hard and a great sea.

Schooner John towards Virginia Octr 5th 1774
At 4 A. M. The wind came to the Southward made Sail under Fore Sail and Jibb. Have been obliged to eat raw meat the last two days. Very uneasy but must submit to the Frown of Fortune. Catched a Dolphin, in his belly found a Fish of a peculiar shape. It was about 2 Inches long something like a Frog but neither Fins or Feet of a whitish colour and covered over with small priccles like a Hedghog. Saw a number of Flying Fish one of them light on board the Vessel. Shaped like a Trout and about that size. the Shoulder fins are long and thin with these it is able to fly as long as the fins keep wet and then the[y] dip in the Sea. By this method they elude the Dolphin which preys upon them.

Schooner John towards Virginia October 6th 1774
Pleasant Breeses and Clear weather.

7th Fine weather at 8 P. M. Hove the Lead got Ground in 15 Fathom Sandy Bottom.

8th At 8 this morning got abreast Cape Henry with Fine Breese. At 7 P. M. came to an Anchor off the Tanjeir Islands.[60]

9th Sunday. Calm, deverted ourselves with catching Crabs.

10th Last night it came to blow and obliged us to Bear away for the Rappahannock River. Came to an Anchor in Fleets Bay.[61] Went A Shore with the Mate to buy stock in the Character of a Sailor, and have been highly diveted with the Frolic.

11th Went a Shore to Colnl Fleets who gives us very bad accounts of their proceedings in the Colonies nothing but War is talked of. Captn Batson of the Brig, Two Betsys Dined with us.[62] Fair wind this evening got out of the River.

Schooner John St. Mary's River October 12th 1774
Came to an Anchor in St Mary's. Went a Shore with the Captn. Pleasant weather.

13th Got up to Cedar point. The Captn gone to Port Tobacco for Orders.

14th At Anchor. The Captn returnd this evening.

15th Got into Port Tobacco Creek. The Vessel is to discharge her Cargo here.

16th Sunday Went to Port Tobacco Church. Dined in town. Nothing talked of but War with England. After Dinner caled at Doctor Browns who proffers to send a Boy and Horse with me to Alexandria. Obliged to lodge at a little House along Shore cou'd not get on board this evening. J. H.

17th. Company on board spent the evening very merrily.

18th. Sent Mr Knox Some Sweetmeats and Coconuts by the Captn who is gone to Nanjemoy. Left the Vessel and went to Doctor Browns.

Alexandria Virginia October 19th 1774

This morning settled with the Doctor who has charged me 14 Guineas, and has the impudence to tell me it is very cheap. I was obliged to comply with it, and gave him an order on Mr Kirk.

Got Horses and a Boy from him. Dined at Piscataway. Arived at Alexandria in the evening. Mr Kirk condoles with me in my misfortune. But seems very glad to see me return in good health. He tells me that he never expected to see me alive again and had defered writing home till the Vessel arived supposing that it wou'd bring news of my death.

20th 21st and 22nd Settling my accounts which will not turn out to my satisfaction.

23rd Sunday. Went to Church and heard a very indifferent Sermon.

Alexandria Virginia October 24th 1774

This morning, Ballanced my accounts and find myself in debt to Mr Kirk £47.10.2 Virginia Currency without one sixpence in my Pocket. I am under the Disagreeable Necessity of Drawing on my Father for £50=00 Sterling. I have no orders for this but as I have not wantonly squandered away what he gave me, think it better to trust to his paternal regard then be in debt without a prospect of paying this gives me much uneasiness but Necessity, absolute necessity, compels me to it. Every thing here is in the utmost confusion, Committees are appointed to inspect into the Caharacters [sic] and Conduct of every tradesman to prevent them Selling Tea, or buying British Manufactures.[63]

Some of them has been Tared and Feathered others had their property Burned and destroyed by the populace. Independent Companies are raiseing in every County on the Continent appointed adjutants and train their men as if they was on the Eve of a War.[64] A General Congress of the different Colonies met at Philadelphia on the 5th of last month are still siting, but their business is a profound Secret. Subscription are raiseing in every Colony on the Continent for the relief of the people of Boston. The King is openly Cursed and his authority set at defyance. In short every thing is ripe for Rebellion.

The New Englanders by their Canting whineing Insinuateing Tricks have perswaded the rest of the Colonies that the Government is going to make absolute slaves of them.

This I believe never was intended but the prebyterian Rascals has had address sufficient to make the other Colony's come into their Sche[me]. By everything that I can understand, in the different Co I have been in, that Independence is what the Massachusets people aims at. But am not in the least doubt but the Government will take such salutary and speedy measures, as will entirely Frustrate their abominable intentions. I am affraid it will be some time before this hubbub is settled and their is nothing to be done now. All trade is allmost at a stand every one seems to be at a loss in what manner to proceed. For my own part, did I not think this affair wo'd be over in the spring I wou'd immediately return home.

But I am very unwilling to return in a worse Condition then I was when I came out and be laughed at by all my friends. If I return now and matters are settled they will never consent to my leaveing England again, And I am very sensible from what I have allready seen of the Country that I can with a small sum make a very pretty fortune here, in a little time if I am any ways fortunate As a Farmer. Mr Kirk advises me to stay till spring and take a Tour in the back Country gives me every possible encouragement and offers me every assistance in his power. I will take his advice, Am determined not to return til I can do it with credit without these Rascals do perswade the Colonies into a Rebellion.

Alexandria Virginia October 25th 1774

This day agree'd with Mrs Fleming to Dine at her house every day at 1s p Day Vir[ginia] Currency I Breakfast and sup at Mr Kirks must live as cheap as possible.

26th and 27th Exceedingly uneasy in mind. I do not know what to do or in what manner to proceed for the best.

28th Suped and spent the evening with Mr William Horner a Merchant from Liverpoole.

29th The Schooner Arived got my Chest A Shore and payd £20 Vir Currency for my passage.

30 Sunday Went to Church a pretty Brick Building and large Congregation but an indifferent Parson.

31st Mr Kirk to make my time agreeable but find myself very Low spirit'd. Drank Coffee at Captn Sandfords.

Alexandria Virginia November 1st 1774

This evening went to the Tavern to hear the Resolves of the Continental Congress read A petition to the Throne and an address to the people of Great Britain.[65] Both of them full of Duplicity and false representation. I look upon them as insults to the understanding and Dignity of the British Sovereign and people. Am in hopes their petitions will never be granted. I am sorry to see them so well received by the people and their sentiments so universally adopted, it is a plain proof that the seeds of rebellion are allready sown and have taken very deep root, but am in hopes they will be eradicated next summer. I am obliged to act the Hypocrite and extol these proceedings as the wisest productions of any assembly on Earth. But in my heart I Despise them and look upon them with contempt.

Alexandria Virginia November 2d 1774

Writing to my Friends at home. Obliged to put the best side outwards and appear a little Whigifyed as I expect my letters will be oppened before they get to England.

3rd Saw the Independent Company exercise. The Effigy of Lord North was Shot at, then carried in great parade into the town and burned.

4th And 5th Wrote to Mr Champion. It is very hard that I cannot write my real sentiments.

6th Sunday Went to a Presbyterian meeting these are a set of Rebellious scoundrels nothing but Political discourses instead of Religious Lectures.

7th Drew a Bill upon my Father for £50 Str. in favor of Mr Kirk payable at Messrs Greaves Lofters & Brightmores to Messrs Broomheads Forty days after sight. I hope it will be duly honored or I am for ever ruined. The Thought makes makes [sic] me misserable.

Alexandria Virginia November 8th 1774

Wrote to my Father. But dare not inform him what my intentions are in staying here.

9th 10th 11th and 12th Exceedingly uneasy and low spirited. Mr Kirk gives me some hope of geting a Commission for purchaseing Wheat.

13th Sunday Went to Church. But wont go any more to hear their Political Sermons. Captn Buddecombs Brig Sailed to day, by her I sent my Letters and a Box with some Sweetmeats and Coconuts to my Friends.

14th 15th And 16th Exceedingly unhappy.

17th Went on some business for Mr Kirk to Bladensburg in Maryland about 20 Miles from Alexandria. This is a Little town of considerable trade but the Land about it is sandy and Barren returned in the evening.

Alexandria Virginia November 18th 1774

Drank Coffee at Colnl John Carliles a Gentleman from Carlisle in England.[66]

19th 20th 21st 22nd 23rd And 24th Waiting in expectation of geting a Wheat Commission but am disappointed. Great quantity's of this Article is brought down from the back Country in Waggons, To this place as good wheat as I ever saw in England and sells from 2/9 to 4/6 Sterling, pr Bushel, it is sent to the Eastern markets. Great quantity's of Flour is likewise brought from there, but this is generally sent to the West Indies, And sometimes to Lisbon and up the Streights. I am doing nothing here Am determined to take a Tour immediatly.

25th Hired a Horse and intend to set out for Berkley County tomorrow.

Mosses Ordinary[67] Loudon County Virginia Novr 26 1774

Left Alexandria in Co with Capt Buddecomb. Got to this place in the evening about 20 Miles from Alexandria. Land pretty level but not very good, either Stiff Brown Clay or Sand.

27th Sunday Got to Leesburg 40 Miles from Alexandria. The Land begins to grow better. A Gravelly soil and Produces good Wheat but the roads are very bad Cut to pieces with the Waggons, number of them we have met to day. Their method of mending the roads is with poles about 10 Foot long layd across the road close together they stick fast in the mud and make an excellent Causeway. Very thinly peopled along the road allmost all Woods. Only one publick house between this place and Alexandria.

Leesburg Loudon County Virginia. Novbr 28th 1774
Viewing the town. It is regularly lay'd off in Squares, but very indifferenly built and few inhabitants and little trade tho very advantageouly situated for it at the Conjunction of the great Roads from the North part of the Continent to the South and the East and West Lodge at Mr Moffit[68] Mr Kirks partner in a Store which he has here.
29th Went with Captn Buddecomb about 10 Miles into the Country. Find the Land Stoney intermixed with Spar but brings good Wheat.
30th This being the Anneversary of St Andrew the Titular St of the Scotch, Was invited to spend the evening with Captn William Douglass[69] and a number of other Scotch Gents have been Genteelly treated and am now gone to bed Drunk. This is the first time.

Leesburg, Loudon County Virginia Decbr 1st 1774
Sick with my last nights Debauch.
2nd And 3rd Went to several places in the neighbourhood of the town. The Land is pretty good but is monopolized, and consequently thinly inhabited. Gravelly soil in general.
4th Sunday Went to a Methodist meeting.[70] This Sect are scattered in every place, and has got considerable footing here Owing to the great negligence of the Church Parsons.
5th Set out in Co with Captn Buddecomb and Mr Moffit. Crossed the Blue Ridge. This a High Barren Mountain, produceing nothing but Pines. It Runs North and South through Virginia and Maryland, Carolina's and Pensylvania. Crossed the Shanandoe River on the West side of the Mountain. Here is some of the Finest Land I have ever seen. This is called Keys Ferry.[71] Got to Whitheringtons Mill Lodged at a Poor house. The Land is exceeding fine From the Shando River to this place 80 Miles From Alexandria.

Frederick County Virginia December 6th 1774
Went from the Mill to a place called Hopewell, a fine Plantation belonging to Mr Jacob Hite.[72] Here is some of the Finest Land I ever saw either for the Plow or pasture. Got to Mr Wm Gibbs[73] an acquaintance of Mr Kirks. We have traveled over some as fine land to day for about 25 Miles as I wou'd wish to see. Limestone in general. Abounds with Shumack, Wallnut and Locust trees which are certain indications that the Lands are rich, pretty level, it is Rocky in some places, but affords excellent pasturage and well watered, Produces good Wheat and Barley. The people appears to be more industerous in this part of the Country then they are on the other side of the Blueridge.

Frederick County Virginia Decembr 7th 74

Went to Winchester. It is one of the largest towns I have seen in the Colony, the capital of this County. Regularly Layd out in Squares the Buildings are of limestone, Two Churches, one English and one Dutch but the Dutch Church is not finished.[74] General Braddock built a Stockade Fort here, in the Year 1755. But it is now demolished. Saw Four Indian Chiefs of the Shawneess Nation Who have been at War with the Virginians this Summer, but have made peace with them, and are sending these people to Williamsburg as Hostages.[75]

They are tall, manly, well shaped men, of a Copper Colour with Black Hair, Quick pierceing Eyes and good features. They have rings of Silver in their nose and bobs to them which hangs over their uper lip. Their ears are cut from the tip, two thirds of the way round and the piece extended with Brass wire till it touches their Shoulders in this part they hang a thin Silver plate, wrought in Flourishes, about 3 Inches diameter, with plates of Silver round their arms and in the Hair which is all cut of except a Long Lock on the top of the head, they are in whitemens mens dress excep[t] Breeches which they refuse to wear, instead of which they have a girdle round them with a piece of Cloath drawn through their Legs and turned over the girdle and appear like a short apron before and behind. All the Hair is puled from their eye brows and eye lashes and their Face painted in different parts with Vermillion. They walk remarkable straight and cut a Grotesque appearance in this mixed dress. Got to Mr Gibbs in the evening.

Frederick County Virginia December 8th 1774

Confined in the House today with Rain.

9th Rideing about the neighbourhood with Mr Gibbs. Find the land good, the Country Healthy and a good Neighbourhood. I am exceedingly pleased with these two Counties, and am determined to settle in one of them, If ever these times are settled, here is every encouragement. Land is purchased at 30 Shillings this Currency pr Acre, that is 26 Shillings Sterling. It will produce any sort of Grain, the average of Wheat is about 12 Bushels to the Acre but it is not half plowed, and manure of any sort is ever used. Meadows may be made with little trouble. And the range for stock is unlimited. Horses sell amazeingly high, and Fat Cattle of All sorts. When Lean are bought very cheap. The Farmers here are little acquainted with Feeding cattle. Indeed they are too Lazy. Publick Taxes are very trifleing. Little Tobacco is made in the Counties of Frederick and Berkly.

Leesburg Loudon County, Virginia December 10th 1774

This morning left Mr Gibbs, who has behaved with the greatest civillity and gave me a pressing invitation to come and spend part of the winter with him. Crossed the Shanandoe River at the Fording place a little above the Ferry. Dined at Pursleys Ordinary on the East side of the Blue Ridge.[76] Got to Leesburg in the evening. Well pleased with my journey.

11th Sunday But no Prayers.

12th Court day A great number of Litgious suits the people seems to be fond of Law. Nothing uncommon then to bring suit against a person for a Book debt, and trade with him on an open account at the same time. To be arrested for debt is no scandal here.

13th Saw the Independent Co exercise. A raged crew.

14th Returned to Alexandria in Company with Capt. Buddecomb and Mr. Maye [Mosse?]

Alexandria Virginia December 15th 1774
Nothing but Committees and Politicks which puts everything in confusion.

16th 17th 18th 19th And 20th Exceeding Cold Frosty and bad weather the winter is now set in and more severe then ever I felt it [in] England. Cannot get any sort of employ to get a liveing, must be obliged to winter here and live as cheap as I can in hopes that the differences between the Mother Country and the Colonies will be settled in the Spring.

21st 22nd 23rd And 24th Great quantities of Hogs Kiled in town they salt the Pork and export it to the West Indies, And makes a considerable Branch of commerce. Sells at 13/6 pr Hundred.

25th Christmas Day But little regarded, here.

26th 27th 28th 29th 30th And 31st. Mr Kirk Captn Buddecomb and I have spent as merrily as can be expected considering the times. This year ends with confusion. But am in hopes the ensueing one will put an end to the Quarrel.

Alexandria Virginia January 1st 1775
Sunday. The Parson is Drunk and cant perform the Duties of his Office. This is the first day of the New Year, which seems to be bigg with matters of great consequence. I have spent the last to little purpose. But am in hopes things will answer better this.

2nd 3rd And 4th Amused myselfe with Shooting Wild Geese and Ducks. Here is incredible numbers in the River. Likewise Swans. It is said they come from the Lakes.

5th This being my Birthday Mr Kirk Captn Buddecomb, Mr Wm Sydebotham[77] and Mr Fleming, All of them Englishmen, Spent the evening with me. All of us very merry and good company. Mr Sydebotham comes from Marple Bridge.

Alexandria Virginia January 6th 1775
Mr Kirk and Mr Sydebotham have got share in a large purchase of Land in the Illionois Country. And have offered me one third part of it at the first cost if I chuse to accept it, or they will give me 5000 Acres to go and take a view of it for them and to be left to my Choice, to take the third of their share at my return. They tel me their influence is pretty considerable with A great many of the other Proprietors and they will endeavour to get me a Surveyors Warrant. As I am not much acquainted with the situation of this country they have given me their Deeds to peruse, and I am to give them my Answer in a Week. I have just reced an invitation ticket to a Ball this evening.

Alexandria Virginia. January 7th 1775

Last night I went to the Ball. It seems this is one of their annual Balls supported in the following manner -- A Large rich Cake is provided and cut into small pieces and handed round to the Company who at the same time draws a ticket out of a Hat with something merry wrote on it. He that draws the King has the Honour of treating the Company with a Ball the next year which generally costs him Six or Seven pound. The Lady that draws the Queen has the trouble of makeing the Cake. There was about 37 Ladys Dressed and Powdered to the life, some of them very handsom, and as much Vanity as is necessary. All of them fond of Danceing. But I do not think they perform it with the greatest elleganse. Betwixt the Country Dances they have What I call everlasting Jiggs.

A Couple gets up, and begins to dance a Jig (to some Negro tune) others comes and cuts them out, these dances allways last as long as the Fiddler can play. This is social but I think it looks more like a Bacchanalian dance then one in a polite Assembly. Old Women, Young Wifes with young Children in the Lap, Widows, Maids, and Girls come promsciously to these Assemblys which generally continue til morning. A Cold supper, Punch, Wine, Coffee, and Chocolate, But no Tea. This is a forbidden herb. The men Chiefly Scotch and Irish. I went home about Two OClock, but part of the Company stayd got Drunk and had a fight. Spent this evening with Mr Kirk Captn Buddecomb Captn Wroe, and Captn Scot at the Tavern very merry.[78]

Alexandria Virginia January 8th 1775

9th And 10th These three days I have spent in makeing enquireing about the nature and situation of the Land in the Illionois Country. And have fortunately met with two Gentlemen who resided there some time. The Lands are exceeding rich, Produces Tobacco, Indigo and Wheat, Situated at the Conjunction of the Ohio with the Missisippi, Rivers, about 1000 Miles from New Orleans, and 2000 Miles from this place. It likewise abounds with Lead and Mines of Copper. But very few inhabitants and those French. I am told by these Gentlemen that their will be some risque in going down the Ohio River, the Indians often cut the White people off, in their passage down to the Missisippi. Think I have a prospect of makeing it worthwhile and will hazard the passage.

I have agreed to go if Messrs Kirk & Sydebotham will use their intrest to procure me Surveyors Warrant this they have promisd to do and will write to Philadelphia to the Gentlemen who are concerned in the purchase in my b[e]half, Some of the principle People are in England, if I can by any meanes make Friends sufficient to get their interest the place of Surveyor will be worth some Hundreds a Year, exclusive of the opportunities a Surveyor has, of takeing up Lands for himselfe. If that fails 5000 Acres of Land will amply pay me for my trouble of going there. I can do nothing here till times are settled and am in hopes that I can get Bac[k] before September next and go home in the fall. By that time I expect this affair will be settled upon a permanent footing. In short I have no other prospects of makeing up my losses but this, And I can not bear the thoughts of returning a Beggar.

Alexandria Virginia January 11th 1775
Intend to go to Captn Knox at Nanjemoy to get some instructions in Surveying from him.
12th This morning came on Board the Brig Potomeck Captn Wroe, Got a Ground at Roziers Bluff. The sharpest Frost I ever knew. The spittle freeses before it fall to the Deck.
13th Fell down to Cany Island.[79]
14th Got to Checamuxen Went a shore and Dined at Mr Wm Smallwoods[80].
15th Sunday got to Nanjemoy in the Night
16th Captn Knox seems very glad to see me. Introduced me to his Brother, and will give me every instruction that lies in his power.
17th Went over the River to Mr John Alexanders.[81] Dined there. Returned in the evening.
18th 19th 20th And 21st Industerously employed with Captn Knox in Surveying a Track of Land.

Nanjemoy Maryland Sunday January 22nd 1775
Dined at Mrs Marsdens on a roasted Swan. The Flesh appears black but eats very well.
23rd Went with Captn Robert Knox to a Plantation of his called Thornsgut,[82] in our Return Dined at a Publick house called the Trap after dinner went to Ignatius Ryans,[83] and Danced most part of the night with some young Ladys.
24th Most part of this day at Mr Ryans got to Nanjemoy in the evening.
25th This morning saw a Negro Quarter of Mrs Marsdens burned down. In the evening went on Board a Brig called the Renfrew Capt. James Somerville with Captn Knox. Both got Drunk.
26th Sick with my last nights debauch.
27th 28th 29th 30th And 31st Employed in drawing plats and practiceing the different branches of Surveying. Find it very easy in the Woods from what it is in enclosed lands.

Stafford County, Virginia February 1st 1775
Left Nanjemoy in Co with Captn Alexander Knox. Lodged at Mr Richard Fouxes.
2nd Traveled over some hilly Broken bad land about 14 Miles. Lodged at Pilchards Ordinary.
3rd Got Breakfast at a Plantation of Captn Knox in Acquire County.[84] In the evening got to another Plantation of his in Stafford County.
4th Dined at Captn Innises, and spent the Afternoon in Co with two agreeable Lady's!
5th Sunday Dined at Mr Bailey Washingtons.[85]
6th Drank Coffee at Captn Innises. The Land in this neighbourhood is sandy and poor. Obliged to dung their Tobacco grounds, Sells at 35 Shi Currency pr Acre.
7th Dined at Mr. John Rauls'es,[86] an Englishman.

8th Left Buloe Crossed the Rappahannock River. Lodged at Fredericksburg.

Fredericksburg Virginia. February 9th 1775
This is a pretty large town, situated at the falls of the River on the West Bank. The River is Navigable for Vessels of considerable burthen up to the town. Great quantities of Tobacco is Ship'd from this place. Saw the Independent Company exercise they make a poor appearance. Dined with Mr William Horner. After dinner crossed the River and went to Mr John Tolivers.
10th The Land is pretty good in this neighbourhood and produces a great deal of Wheat. Saw a Machine for thrashing wheat with horses. After dinner went to Mr Horatio Dades in Stafford County.[87]
11th Got to Mr John Alexanders.
12th At Mr Alexanders, the wind is too Fresh. Cant cross the River. This is a most abominable Cold house and bad fire.

Nanjemoy Maryland February 13, 1775
Got to Nanjemoy in the evening. This jaunt has only cost me 5 s Vir Curry. The people are remarkably Hospitable, are affronted if you dont call at their house. If you are a perfect stranger.
14th 15th 16th 17th And 18th Very busy with Captn Knox in runing the Courses of his Plantation and jaunting about in the neighborhood. I understand the Committee are going to take me up for a Spy. I will save them the trouble by decamping immediately. The Committees Act as Justices, if any person is found to be Inimical to the Liberties of America, they give them over to the mobility to punish as they think proper, and it is seldom they come of without Taring and Feathering. It is as much as a persons life is worth to speak disrespectfully of the Congress. The people are arming and training in every place. They are all Liberty Mad.

Nanjemoy Maryland February 20th 1775
Left Capt Knoxes who has treated me with the greatest kindness and Civillity. Went to Captn Fouxes, spent an agreeable evening with the Miss Fouxes, who Sing and play very well upon the Spinet.
21st Went to Doctor Browns, at Port Tobacco.
22nd Left Doctor Browns and went to Mr Frank Marsdens,[88] Found My old fellow Traveler Mr Brooks, very well, contrary to expectation.
23rd And 24th At Mr Marsdens, Shooting Wild Geese and Ducks, of which here is increditable numbers. I am told 60 Ducks have been kild at one shot.
25th Mr Brooks sent his Boy and horses with me to Alexandria. He is exceedingly grateful for the assistance I gave him in his passage from Barbados. Mustering in every Village they will all be Soldiers by and by. Confusion to them alltogether.

Alexandria Virginia Sunday February 26th 1775
No Letters from home I am affraid none will arive while the times are in such

confusion. The Rascals seize all Forreign Letters.

27th Mr Kirk informs me he has received Letters from Philadelphia and assures me of a Surveyors deputation admit I can get the consent of the Gentlemen proprietors at home. I am determined to risque this, and my life. Have confirmed the bargain for to take the 5000 Acres for going to view the land at my own expence, and the firs[t] refu[sal] of the third of Mr Kirk and Sydebothams share. I can carry out some Silver trinkets and Barter with the Indians for Furs and probably do something more then bear my expences. As I can get what Credit I please.

28th This is the last day Tea is allowed to be drank on the Continent, By an Act of Congress. The Lady's seem very sad about it.

Alexandria Virginia March 1st 1775

Mr Finley[89] a Gentleman who has been at the Illionois advices me not to set out til the Latter end of April, then to go down the Ohio River with the Flood. I believe there will be some difficulty in perswadeing any one to go with me in this place.

2nd 3rd 4th 5th 6th 7th 8th And 9th These eight days have made it my business to find out a person proper to go with me, but can find none that are willing to undertake the journey. I intend to go to Mr Gibbs, as the likelyest place to get a man for my purpose.

10th 11th 12th 13th 14th 15th And 16th Employed in prepareing for my journey. Got some Silver trinkits made by a Silver smith in town by the directions of Mr Finley who has been an Indian Trader, and has given me some general instructions concerning the trade.

Alexandria Virginia. March 17th 1775

Went to a Ball made by the Irish Gentry in Commemoration of St Patrick the Titular St of the Irish. Conducted with great decorum. Just going to Bed at two OClock in the morning.

18th This day the Gentlemen, and Mechanic Independent Companies, Reviewd by Colnl George Washington. All of them in Uniform. The Gentlemen Blue and Buff. The Mechanics Red and Blue, In all about 150 Men and make a formidable appearance.[90]

19th Sunday But the Parson is too Lazy to preach.

20th And 21st Prepareing for my journey Got my silver ware packed up in as sma[ll] Compas as possible. Mr Finley advises me to trade with a party of Dellawars that are settled on the Ouabash River[91] For Bever Skins. Mr Finly gave me letter of Credit to Mr Richard Winstone at Kaskasky Villiage Illionois.

Alexandria Virginia March 22nd 1775

This day a certain Richard Taylor from Tidswell Came to town with a quantity of Rum. Spent the evening at Mr Kirks, Sensible industerous man.

23rd Bought me a Gun, Powder and Lead.

24th Mr Henly, Mr Caul and Mr Richard Harrison spent the evening at Mr Kirks. A dispute arose (about politics) between Mr Kirk and Captn Buddecomb they differed in sentiments and abused each other most unmercifully. It is most absurd for individuals to quarrel about state affairs. Both of them remain Obstinate.

25th Wrote to my Father. Intend to set out for Mr Gibbs tomorrow. Mr Kirk and the Captn refuse to be reconciled. Memd never to enter into Political disputes with Mr Kirk. He has rebellous principles.

Leesburg Loudon County Virginia March 26th 1775

Sunday Left Alexandria in Company with Capt Buddecomb. Dined at Mosses Ordinary got to Leesburg in the evening.

27th Went with Captn Buddecomb to Mr Canby[92] who informs me Mr Edward Snickers[93] is the likeliest person to get me a guide. Gave me a Letter of Introduction to Mr Snickers.

28th Captn Buddecomb set out for Alexandria and intends to go to England the first opportunity. This gentleman has allways behaved to me with the greatest civillity and kindness but think him rather too much of a Sycophant.

29th Went to looke at a Silver mine, saw some appearance of metal but dont know what it is.

30th And 31st At Leesburg waiting for my Gun and goods comeing from Alexandria. The Peach Orchards are in full Blossom and make a beautifull appearance.

Leesburg Loudon County Virginia April 1, 1775

Wrote to Mr Kirk and Captn Buddecomb

2nd Sunday But no Parson, it is a shame to suffer these people to neglect their duty in the manner they do.

3rd Got my things from Alexandria. Hired a Horse for £4 curr from Mr Moffit to carry me to Fort Pitt.[94] Left Leesburg. Crossed the Blue Ridge at Snickers Gap B. O. B. Dined at Mr Snickers but he is not at home but his Soninlaw gave me a letter to a Certain George Rice whom he recommends as a proper person to go with me.[95] Crossd the Shanandoe River Got to Vinchester. Land is very rich from the River to the town. All Limestone well wattered and very level. I am sorry it is not in my power to Settle here. Winchester is about 80 Miles from Alexandria.

Winchester Frederick County, Virginia April 4th 1775

Met with Mr Gibbs, and George Rice. Mr Gibbs recommends him as an honest-man and a Good hunter. Agreed to give him 500 Acres of Land to go with me. He is going to his Brothers near Fort Pitt with two horses and intends to set out tomorrow. this is very lucky. Bought some Blankets, Gun powder, Lead, Flints, Camp Kettle, Frying pan and Tomhawk, with several other necessaries. Got Letters of introduction to several Gentlemen in the Neighbourhood of Fort Pitt, from Mr John Neville.[96] Gave my Boots and Spurs to the care of Mr Gibbs till my return, must weare Leggings these are pieces of Coarse woollen Cloth wraped round the leg and tied below the Knee with a string, to prevent the Snakes biting you.

Winchester, Virginia April 5th 1775
After dinner, Left Winchester and got to Rinkers Tavern 10 Miles from Winchester.[97] Captn Douglass and Mr Valentine Craford[98] came here this evening they are going to Fort Pitt. Land is good from Winchester to this place.
6th Left Rinkers in Co with Capt Douglass and Mr Craford. Breakfasted at the Dry Tavern a little Dutch house nothing to drink but Whiskey. Crossed the Cape Capon Creek and North Branch of Potowmeck River. Captn Douglass and Mr Craford left us. We have traveled about 30 Miles to day, over Barren hills and bad ways and are now going to Sleep in the open Air no other Covering then the Heaven's and our Blankets, and it is very Cold and Freezes. But we have got a good Fire.

Apalachian Mountain April 7th 1775
Slept very little last night Mr Rice tells me it is because I did not take of my Cloaths. Water Froze in a Kettle about 10 Foot from the fire. Crossed Little Cape Capon Creek and the south mountain which is one entire Rock. Dined at Runnels tavern. Traveled over Barren Hills to Ashby's Fort on Patterson Creek. Camped about 2 Miles to the West of it. About 30 Miles today.
8th Slept very well last night considering the hardness of our bed. Crossed the Knobby mountain. Called at Creigs Tavern for a supply of Rum, then over the Devils hunting ground to Tittles Tavern. This is the worst road I ever saw large Rocks and Boggs. Crossed the Savage mountain and through the Shades of Death.

This is one of the most dismal places I ever saw. The lofty Pines Obscures the Sun, and the thick Laurels are like a Hedge on each side the Road is very narrow and full of large stones and Boggs. I measured a Pine that was blown down 130 ft Long. Camped about 2 Miles West of the Shades. 28 m.
9th Crossed the Little Meadow mountain supposed to be the highest part of the Apalachian or Allegany mountain. The waters begin to fall to the Westward. Crossed the Negro mountain and the Winding Ridge. Crossed the Line between Maryland and Pennsylvania, it is cut through the Woods in a West course, from some part of Delawar Bay about 20 yards wide. it is on the top of the Winding Ridge. Crossed the Youghaganey River at the Bigg Crossings. Camped 2 Miles West of it. Shot some Pheasants which has made a good supper.

Apalachain Mountain. April 10th 1775
Crossed the Fallen Timbers. Occasioned by a violent Gust of wind from the East. The Trees are either tore up by the roots or broke off near the ground, some Oaks 2 Foot diameter are broke off and the top carryed to a considerable distance. Scarcely one tree left standing. I am told it continues 100 Miles in a West course and about a Mile broad. Dined at the great Meadows. A large

Marshey place clear of trees. Saw the Vestages of Fort Necessity, this was a small Picketed Fort built by Colonl Washington in the Year 1754.[99] About a Mile to the Westward of this Fort General Braddock is buried at a small Run. They tel me he was buried in the middle of the road to prevent the Indians diging up his body.

Crossed the Laurel mountain Saw the place where Colonel Dunbar was encamped when he received the news of General Braddocks defeat in 1755. Great quantities of broken Bomb Shells Cannon Bullets and other Military store scattered in the woods. This is called the Laurel mountain from the great quantities of Laurel that grows upon it. A most delightfull Prospect of the country to the westward of it. Called at Gist's Fort. Crossed the Youghagany River at the Stewards Crossings.[100] Got to Zachariah Connels Brother in law to George Rice.[101] Much fatigued this evening. Heavy Rain most part of the day.

West Augusta County, Virginia April 11th
The Apalachian or Allegany Mountain is not one entire Mountain but a number piled one on the top of another with some narrow Valleys between them. The mountains are Barren and Rockey. But the Valleys tho very narrow, are in general Rich, very thinly Inhabited. The road is but very indifferent tho loaded Waggons frequently cross it in the Summer. Here is some excellent land about this place and all the way from the foot of the Mountain.

Every necessary of life is very dear here, provisions in particular occationed by the Indian War last Summer. Grain is not to be got for money. In the evening went to Mr Valentine Crafords with Captn Douglass, with much difficulty have got half a Bushel of Rye for my horse.

West Augusta County Virginia April 12, 1775
Went with Captn Douglass to Captn John Stephensons.[102] This gentleman is a great Indian Warriour, But appears to be a good natured man.
13th Captn Stephenson advices me to build our canoo here provisions are cheaper here then at Fort Pitt. Rice prooves to be a Carpenter and understands the building of them is acquainted here and will undertake to have one finished in a fortnight.
14th This morning, Rice and another man begun to cut down a tree to make a Canoo, have left it entirely to his management. Capt Douglass and Capt Stephenson to the Stewards Crossings to Major Crafords. Returnd to V. Crafords in the evening. Agreed to go with Capt Douglass [to] Fort Pitt tomorrow.

West Augusta County, Virginia. April 15th 1775
Left Mr Crafords in Co with Captn Douglass Crossed Jacobs Creek, and Saweekly Creek Got to Mr John De Camps[103]. Land very rich and Level.
16th Left Mr De Camp's. Traveled over small hills, Woods and dirty roads to Bush Creek called at a Mill where by acting the Irishman, got a feed of Corn for our horses. Cross[ed] Turttle Creek Dined at Myers Ordinary[104] After dinner got

a man to conduct us to the place where General Braddock was defeated by the French and Indians the 9th of July 1755. It is on the Banks of the Mon-in-ga-ha-ley River, found great numbers of Bones both men and horses. The trees are gauled, I suppose by the Artillery.

It appears to me the Front of our Army never extended more then 300 Yards and the greates[t] slaughter seems to have been made within 400 Yards of the River where it is level and full of under wood farther from the River it is hilly and some Rocks where the Enemy woud still have the advantage of the ground. We could not find one whole Skull all them Broke to pieces in the uper part, some of them had holes broke in them about an Inch diameter, suppose it to be done with a Pipe Tommahauk. I am told the wounded were all Massacreed by the Indians. Got to Fort Pitt in the Evening. Land very good but thinly Inhabited. Our Landlord seems to be very uneasy to know where we come from.

Fort Pitt Virginia April 17th 1775
After Breakfast Waited on Major John Connoly Commandant at the Fort to whom I had a Letter of introduction.[105] Find him a Haughty imperious man. In the Afternoon viewing the town and Fort. It is pleasantly situated at the conjunction of the Moningahaley and Allegany Rivers. The Moningahaley on the S. W. And the Allegany on the North side the town. These two Rivers make the Ohio. The town is small about 30 houses the people Chiefly in Indian trade. The Fort is some distance from the town close in the forks of the Rivers. It was built originally by the French deserted by them and the English took possession of it under the Command of General Forbes November 24th 1758.

Beseiged by the Indians but relievd by Colonel Bouquet in August 1763. Deserted and demolished by our troops about three Years ago. But repaired last summer by the Virginians and has now a small Garrison in it. It is a Pentagonal form. Three of the Bastions and two of the Curtains Faced with Brick the rest Picketed. Barracks for a considerable number of men, And there is the remains of a Genteel house for the Governour but now in ruins, as well as the Gardens which are beautifully situated on the Banks of the Allegany well planted with Apple and Peach trees. It is a strong place for Musquetry, but was Cannon to be brought against it, very defenceless several eminences within Cannon Shot. Spent the evening at Mr Cambels an Indian trader in town.[106]

West Augusta County Virginia April 18, 1775
This morning Mr Cambbell informed me that Adam Grant lived about 12 Miles from town. Left Fort Pitt. Dined at Turtle Creek. Escaped drowning very narrowly in crossing Turtle Creek. Got to Adam Grants late in the evening. Great scarcity of every necessary of life in this house but the man is glad to see us, and gives us the best he has got with a heartly welcome. He has got a small tub mill and Land enough but it is of little value in this part of the world. Very heavy Rain all day.

19th Left Adam Grants. Got to Saweekly Creek but it is too high to Ford returned to Mr De Camps. We have been lost several times today. The by roads are only small narrow paths through the woods and in some places not the least appearance of a road.

West Augusta County Virginia April 20th 75

Left Mr De Camp Crossed Jacob Creek and Saweekly Creek. George Rice has joined some other people that are going down the Ohio in assisting them to Build Canoos. They go about 600 Miles down the River and will be ready to set out in Eight or ten days.

21st This day made a full agreement with George Rice to go with me to the Illionois Country on Condition that I will wait for him at the Kentuckey River Ten days. I have agreed to do this and give him 500 Acres of Land for his trouble, this Contract was made before Captn William Douglass who wants to take one half of my purchase paying half my expences in going to the Illionois and comeing back. Am to give him a possitive answer in two days. Wrote to Mr Kirk.

West Augusta County Virginia April 22nd 75

Employed in geting provisions for the Voyage.

23rd Sunday. Went to Major Crafords who gave me an account of the different Rivers on the Ohio and the distances between them.

24th Employed in geting provisions find them very scarce and dear.

25th Agreed to let Captn Douglass have one half of any land I may purchase of Mr Kirk or Mr Sydebotham at the Illionois he is to pay half my expences there, have nothing to do with the Land that Messrs Kirk & Sydebotham gives me, or anything to do as a Surveyor. Wrote to Mr Kirk that will take his share if the times are settled as formerly. Captn Douglass is to advance all the money and I am to pay no interest for Five Years after the money is payed.

    I have now A prospect of makeing money without advanceing any, this suits my Circumstances very well.

West Augusta, Virginia April 26th 75

And 27th Got our Canoos finished and our provisions collected together intend to set out tomorrow.

28th Left part of my Cloaths with Mr Craford till my return. Parted with Captn Douglass by whom I returned the Horse. Launched our Canoo's. One of them we called the Charming Sally the other Charming Polly. They are 30 Foot long and about 20 Inches wide made of Walnut trees, dug out something like a manger. Proceeded down the Youghagany River Obliged to get Pilots to cary the Canoos down the Falls, very bad Navigation full of dangerous Rappids. Camped at Washingtons Bottom, expect the rest of the Company to join us in the morning. I may now bid adieu to Sleeping in Beds or houses for some months.

Yough-a-ga-ny River, Virginia April 29th

This morning we were joined by Mr James Nourse,[107] an English gentleman going down to the Kentuckey River to take up Land in Right of his Brother who is an Officer in the Navy. Mr. Benjamin Johnston[108] and Captn Edmond Taylor,[109] who are going to take up land on the Kentuckey River. Got all our provisions on Board. Mr Norse Captn Taylor, Mr Nourses servant,[110] and me in the Charming Sally, Mr Johnston his servant, George Rice, Captn Taylors Brother and a servant of his[111] in the Charming Polly. Proceeded down the River to the mouth of Saweekly Creek. The navigation very bad, Obliged to push the Canoos over the shoals for two miles together. A great number of Rappids is a very dangerous navigation. Mr Norse insists on me takeing one half of his tent, this is very agreeable.

Yough-a-ga-ny River, Virginia April 30, 1775

This day we have been detained by the Rain. Settled our accounts concerning Vessels and Provisions. The Land from the foot of the Laurel mountain to Fort Pitt is rich beyond conception. Wallnut and Cherry trees grows to an amazeing size. I have seen several three Foot diameter and 40 Foot before they come to a limb. Great plenty of Wild Plumb trees and a Species of the Pimento, these are small Bushes. The soil in general is Black and of a Fat Loamy nature. Coal and Limestone in the same Quarry, I have seen Stratums of Coal 14 Feet thick equal in quality to the English Coal. Land is at a very low rate 1000 Acres might be purchased for £100 Pennsylvania Currency. Very thinly inhabited, the few there is, are in general, great Rascals.

An Account of the Different Currency's

	Half Johanness			Guinea's			Dollars		
	£	S	D	£	S	D	£	S	D
New England	2	8	0	1	8	0	0	6	0
New York	3	4	0	1	17	0	0	8	0
Pennsylvania	3	0	0	1	14	0	0	7	6
Maryland	3	0	0	1	14	0	0	7	6
Virginia	2	8	0	1	8	0	0	6	0
North Carolina	3	4	0	1	17	0	0	8	0
South Carolina	12	12	0	1	1	0	1	11	6

Cream of Tartar, 4 Oz Flaxseed 4 Oz Gum Arrabik. All beaten together and then made up in Ounce Doses. One of these Doses is to be infused in a Quart of warm water, And Drank, in common, As much as You think proper. A little Laxative Electuary should be taken to keep the Body open.[112]

Notes

1. Edale is in the High Peak area in North Derbyshire. D. P. Davies, *A New Historical and Description View of Derbyshire* (Belper, England: S. Mason, 1811), passim.

2. James Carrington was a long-time resident of Edale. He was married in the Parish on April 24, 1746. FamilySearch International Genealogical Index. FamilySearch.com.

3. This was probably Thomas Latham of Highfield Street, Liverpool. He was designated as "Gentleman" in *Gore's Liverpool Directory for the Year 1774*, (Liverpool, J. Gore, 1774), 35.

4. The Golden Fleece was in Dale Street. *Williamson's Liverpool Advertiser, And Mercantile Chronicle*, January 4, 1774.

5. The *Molly* was a 180 ton vessel manned with 18 men and mounting two guns. Register of Passes, 1772-1774, Adm. 7/98, 103. (Public Record Office, London.) Hereft er all PRO records cited are on microfilm in John D. Rockefeller, Jr. Library, Colonial Williamsburg Foundation, Williamsburg, Virginia.

6. Henry Parry, captain of the *Molly*, lived in Clayton's Square in Liverpool. *Gore's Liverpool Directory... 1774*, 44.

7. Thomas Middleton, merchant in Williamson's Square, Liverpool. *Gore's Liverpool Directory... 1774*, 40.

8. Castleton is a village in the High Peaks area of Derbyshire. Davies, *A View of Derbyshire*, passim.

9, Hope is a small village situated on the banks of the Derwent. Davies, *A View of Derbyshire*, passim.

10. James Kirk arrived in Virginia sometime before 1762. He was born in Hayfield, Derbyshire, England in 1743, son of Robert Kirk. A prominent merchant in Alexandria, he signed the Fairfax non-importation association in 1770 and was a member of the Fairfax County committee of safety from 1774 to 1775. He was appointed to the Commission of Peace for Loudoun County in 1777 and was elected mayor of Alexandria in 1785. FamilySearch.com. Robert A. Rutland ed., *The Papers of George Mason, 1725-1792*, vol. 1, (Chapel Hill, N. C.: University of North Carolina Press, 1970), lxiii; *Virginia Gazette* (Williamsburg), August 4, 1774; *Virginia Journal & Alexandria Advertiser*, February 17, 1785; Loudoun County Court Order Book G, 1776-1783, 47 (Microfilm in the Library of Virginia, Richmond). All county court records cited hereafter are on microfilm at the Library of Virginia, Richmond.

11. Cresswell is probably referring to Benjamin and Joseph Broomhead, merchants and manufacturers of cutlery, and John Furniss, scissorsmith, of Sheffield. *A Directory of Sheffield, Including the Manufacaturers in the adjacent Villages.* (Sheffield: Gales & Martin, 1787. Reprint. New York: Da Capo Press, 1969), 52, 59.

12. The Briddock family was present in the Hope area for many generations. A John Briddock of Castleton married Mary Bagshaw on May 12, 1786, in Hope Parish. Hope Parish Marriage Register.freepages.genealogy.rootsweb.com/~dusk/hope_marriages.html #top (accessed April 11, 2008).

13. This was probably William Bray who wrote "A Sketch of a Tour into Derbyshire and Yorkshire, including part of Buckingham, Warwick, Leicester, Nottingham, Bedford, and Hertford-shires." He also wrote an article entitled "Observations on the Indian

method of Picture-Writing" in which he received information from Cresswell. Repton-Priory Deed Transcripts; Tymm Family of Edale, Nicholas Cresswell of Edale and miscellanea. (Derbyshire Record Office, Derby, England.) http://www.a2a.org.uk/search /documentxsl.asp?com=1&i=0&nbKey=2&stylesheet=xsl\A2A_com.xsl&keyword=Nich olas%20Cresswell%20ADJ1%20Edale&properties=0601 (accessed August 13, 2005).

14. John Bore, the son of Robert Bore and Mary Marriot Bore, was born on September 6, 1747, in Ashover, Derbyshire, England. FamilySearch.com. www.familysearch .org/Eng/search/frameset_search.asp?PAGE=ancestorsearchresults.asp (accessed April 10, 2008).

15. This was likely the John Hadfield who married Martha Bradley on July 2, 1750. They were both of Peak Forest. "Parish Register of Peak Forest Chapel," transcribed by Rosemary Lockie, April 1996. www.genuki.org.uk/big/eng/DBY/PeakForest.pftext2.html (accessed August 14, 2005).

16. This was probably Joseph Champion who died in 1784. A resident of Edale, he left money to support a schoolmaster in Hope "for teaching so many poor children living in Hope to read English," as the funds would support. W. S. Porter, *Notes from a Peakland Parish* (Sheffield, England: J. W. Northend, 1923), 51.

17. John Sykes was identified as a schoolmaster in Liverpool who lived on Houghton Street, Liverpool. *Gore's Liverpool Directory...1774*, 54.

18. On April 15, 1773, Capt. Robert Bostock recieved a pass to take the ship *Burrows* of Liverpool to Africa and America. She was a 70 ton ship manned with 30 men and armed with four guns. Register of Passes, 1772-1774, Adm 7/98, 57. (Public Record Office, London.)

19. Probably Gustavus Bradford, worsted stuffmaker, of Bradford, Yorkshire. Bankrupt Certificates held by the Society of Genealogists in London. homepages.rootsweb.ancestry.com/~mwi/bankrupt1.txt (accessed April 11, 2008).

20. Bardsey Island is a small island—1 ¾ miles long—containing about 500 acres. It lies off the Lleyn Peninsular in North Wales. Charles Alfred Matley, "The Geology of Bardsey Island," *Quarterly Journal of the Geological Society*, 69 (1913): 514-29.

21. Alexander Knox was a merchant of Boyd's Hole, Virginia, His brother, Robert Knox, operated a store in partnership with Andrew Baillie in Nanjemoy, Maryland, directly opposite Boyd's Hole. *Virginia Gazette* (Purdie and Dixon) September 3, 1772. William Allason, Ledger G 1768-1769, 27, 60, 190 (Library of Virginia). American Loyalist Claims—Special Agents' Reports on Claims, 1784-1803, 20, T.79/73 (Public Record Office, London.)

22. This must have been a yard on the mizen, the aftermost mast on a square rigged ship. Peter Kemp, *Oxford Companion to Ships and the Sea* (Oxford: Oxford University Press, 1988), 552.

23. Cape Charles and Cape Henry mark the entrance to the Chesapeake Bay.

24. The Horseshoe is a shoal extending from the Lower Peninsula toward the entrance to Chesapeake Bay. John Henry, *A New and Accurate Map of Virginia* (London, 1770).

25. Windmill Point is in Lancaster County at the mouth of the Rappahannock River. Henry, *Map of Virginia*.

26. Urbanna is in Middlesex County on the south side of the Rappahannock.

27. The Williamsburg newspaper reported the arrival of the *Molly* in its May 19th issue. *Virginia Gazette* (Purdie), May 19, 1774.

28. That is, planters' homes.

29. Cresswell probably means Leidler's Ferry in Charles County, Maryland. At this time it was operated by Elizabeth Leidler. *Maryland Gazette* (Annapolis) January 6, 1774.

30. See note 18 above.

31. This was probably Col. Richard Harrison of Charles County, Maryland. Jean B. Lee, *The Price of Nationhood: The American Revolution in Charles County* (New York: W. W. Norton & Co., 1994), 109.

32. This was likely Mary Mastin, widow of Robert Mastin who died in 1769, leaving land on Pope's Creek and several children among them Francis Mastin. Charles County, Maryland, Wills AD No. 5, 1752-1767, 286-90.

33. Cresswell may be mistaken about the name of McLeash's ship. On May 12, 1773, Robert McLeash, captain of the ship *Houston* of Glasgow, received a pass to travel to Virginia. There were several ships named *Jenny* in the Potomac at this time—one belonging to the Glasgow firm of John Glassford & Co. Register of Passes, 1772-1774, Adm 7/98, 60. (Public Record Office, London.) List of Vessels entered inwards into the South Potomac Between the 5th day of January 1774 and the 5th day of April following, T 1/506, (Public Record Office, London).

34. For a discussion of tobacco culture see G. Melvin Herndon, *William Tatham and the Culture of Tobacco* (Coral Gables, Florida: University of Miami Press, 1969), passim.

35. This was probably Mary Leftwich, the widow of Elisha Leftwich. Charles County, Maryland, Accounts 61, 300-304.

36. Beulah was a plantation in Staffford County once owned by John Ralls. It was about twelve miles from Dumfries and seven miles from Acquia Church. George H. S. King, *The Register of Overwharton Parish, Stafford County, Virginia, 1723-1758* (Fredericksburg, Va.: G. H. King, 1961), 196.

37. The Boston Port Act, closing the port of Boston, was known in Virginia by May 19, 1774, when it was published in the *Virginia Gazette*. As a result the House of Burgesses resolved, on May 14th, to declare June 1st as a "Day of Fasting, Humiliation, and Prayer." Governor Dunmore found it necessary to dissolve the House. For a discussion of the effects see George M. Curtis, III, "The Role of the Courts in the Making of the Revolution in Virginia" in James Kirby Martin, ed., *The Human Dimensions of Nation Making: Essays on Colonial and Revolutionary America*, (Madison, Wisc.: The State Historical Society of Wisconsin, 1976), 121-46.

38. Dr. Gustavus Richard Brown (1747-1804), a graduate of the University of Edenburgh in 1768, served on the Maryland Provincial Council in 1774 and the Charles County, Maryland, committee of safety. He was one of the attending physicians at Washington's last illness. Brown lived at "Rose Hill" in Port Tobacco. Rutland, ed., *Papers of George Mason*, I: xxxviii; James Thomas Flexner, *George Washington: Anguish and Farewell (1793-1799)* (Boston: Little, Brown & Co., 1972), 458. Wyndham B. Blanton, *Medicine in Virginia in the Eighteenth Century* (Richmond, Va.: Garrett and Massie, 1931), 300, 311. Maryland Historical Trust, *Inventory of Historic Sites in Calvert County, Charles County and St. Mary's County* (Annapolis, Md.: Maryland Historical Trust, 1980), 58.

39. The town of Upper Marlboro was often called Marlboro.

40. Philip Vickers Fithian, a tutor on a plantation in Northumberland County, Virginia, recorded on May 4, 1774: "Last night & this morning fell a very considerable Snow, so much that I imagine had it not melted after it fell it would have been six inches deep!" The next day he wrote: "Last night very cold; I shall scarce be believed if I say that I saw, handled, & measured Ice this morning two inches thick!" On May 6 he wrote: "The leaves on the Trees are grown black, the Fruit must be past recovery, probably, the

Flax too." Hunter Dickinson Farish, ed., *Journal & Letters of Philip Vickers Fithian 1773-1774: A Plantation Tutor of the Old Dominion*, (Williamsburg, Va.: Colonial Williamsburg, Inc., 1957), 103.

41. In 1769 the Maryland assembly passed an act to build a new State House. William Eddis remarked in 1773: "This work has been carried on with great dispatch, and when completed will at least be equal to any public edifice on the American continent." William Eddis, *Letters from America*, ed. Audrey C. Land, (Cambridge, Mass.: Harvard University Press, 1969), 76.

42. Cresswell is describing the cradled scythes commonly used in the Chesapeake colonies. Wheat was mowed with scythes and if sickles were used it was referred to as reaping. Harold B. Gill, Jr. "Wheat Culture in Colonial Virginia," *Agricultural History*, 52 (1978): 388.

43. This may have been Captain Benjamin Harrison who was commander of the ship *Sally* of Maryland in 1772. Naval Office Returns, South Potomac District, 8 Oct. 1772-5 Jan. 1773. T 1/498. (Public Record Office, London.)

44. Washington's mill was on Dogue Run. Charles W. Stetson, *Washington and His Neighbors* (Richmond, Va.: Garrett and Massie, Inc., 1956), 147-48.

45. William Buddicomb (1727-1802) was born in Bristol, England, and was for a long time master of a vessel trading from Liverpool to America. From 1766 until 1775 his vessel was involved in the Liverpool and Alexandria trade. He died in Liverpool in January 1802. American Loyalist Claims XXXVIII, 11783-1811, T 79/38, 4-6. Plantation Registers, 1765-1773, entries for June 6, 1765 and August 19, 1772, Custom House, Liverpool. (Public Record Office, London.)

46. The *Virginia Gazette* printed the Fairfax Resolves confirming the election of Washington and Charles Broadwater as its "representatives to serve in the general assembly, attend the convention at Williamsburg on the first day of August next." *Virginia Gazette* (Rind), August 4, 1774. Cresswell is mistaken when he says elections were annual. They were held whenever the governor called for them. Charles Broadwater (1722-1806) was born in that part of Stafford County that later became Fairfax County. He served as a justice of the peace for Fairfax from the 1740s to 1803. Besides serving as a burgess from Fairfax he also represented the county in the four Revolutionary Conventions. Sara B. Bearss et al, eds., *Dictionary of Virginia Biography*, vol. 2 (Richmond, Va.: The Library of Virginia, 2001), 244-45.

47. The vessel was a square stern sloop, 50 tons, built in New England in 1769. It was owned by John Eden of Maryland. "A List of all Ships and Vessels which have Cleared Outwards in the Naval Office at the Port of Bridgetown in the Island of Barbadoes between the 5th day of July 1774 and the 10th day of March following." T 64/48. (Public Record Office, London). The Naval Office returns for the South Potomac for July 1774 are missing.

48. This was probably the house of Margaret Herbert of Prince George's County, Maryland. She had a 28 year old son whose name in not given in the census records. Bettie Stirling Carothers, *1776 Census of Maryland* (Westminster, Md.: Family Line Publications, 1992), 139.

49. Cross-jack (pronounced crojerk) is the lower yard on the mizen-mast of a square-rigged ship. Kemp, ed., *The Oxford Companion to Ships and the Sea*, 214. R. C. Allen, *The Rigging of Ships in the Days of the Spritsail Topmast, 1600-1720* (New York: Dover Publications, Inc., 1994), 243.

50. Meridian, that is, noon. Kemp, ed., *The Oxford Companion to Ships and the Sea*, 542.

51. Charles Willing was a prominent merchant in Barbados. He died in 1795. He married Ann Shippen. His obituary appeared in the *Barbados Mercury* on June 3, 1787. He died in Chester County, Pennsylvania on March 22, 1787, and was buried in Christ Church cemetery in Philadelphia. His son, Charles Willing, was a merchant in Philadelphia. James C. Brandow, compiler, *Genealogies of Barbados Families* (Baltimore: Genealogical Publishing Co., 2001), 615. "Extracts from 'The Barbados Mercury,'" *The Journal of the Barbados Museum and Historical Society*, XVII (1950): 110.

52. There was a Thomas Blackett in St. Philip's Parish, Barbados, whose children were baptized in 1732 and 1734. Joanne McRee Sanders, compiler, *Barbados Records: Baptisms, 1637-1800* (Baltimore: Genealogical Publishing Co., 1984), 476, 477.

53. This may have been Richard Haselwood who married Mary Taylor Lucas on August 29, 1775, in St. Michael's Parish. Brandow, compiler, *Genealogies of Barbados Families*, 407.

54. Sometimes called Jamestown, Holetown was a village of about 100 houses in 1700. It was in St. James Parish. Robert H. Schomburgk, *The History of Barbados* (London: Longman, Brown, Green and Longmans, 1848. Reprinted London: Frank Cass & Co., Ltd, 1971), 238-39.

55. Cresswell doesn't give enough information to identify Mr. Iffil. A family of that name was present in Barbados from at least 1700 until 1835 when Benjamin Iffil died at age 60. Brandow, compiler, *Genealogies of Barbados Families*, 35, 182, 674.

56. Thomas Bragg married Mary Grasett on June 10, 1770, in St. Michael, Barbadoes. In January 1775 he was listed as the master of the *Mentor*, a 85 ton bark, bound from Bridgetown to Georgia. "A List of all Ships and Vessels which have Cleared Outwards at the Naval Office at the Port of Bridgetown in the Island of Barbadoes between the 6th day of January 1775 and the 5th day of April following." T 64/48, 1. (Public Record Office, London.) FamilySearch.com.

57. This was likely the son of Thomas and Mary Dotin who was baptized in St. Thomas Parish, Barbados, on May 9, 1737. Sanders, ed., *Barbados Records: Baptisms 1637-1800*, 519.

58. The Synagogue was severely damaged by a hurricane in 1831 so that it was necessary to build a new one. Jews had been present on the island since at least 1628. Schomburgk, *The History of Barbados*, 97.

59. The *John* cleared the Naval Office in Bridgetown on September 17, 1774, with a cargo of sugar and rum bound for Maryland. There is no mention of Cresswell's bales of cotton. T 64/48. (Public Record Office, London.)

60. Tangier Island is in the Cheaspeake Bay about mid-way between the eastern and western shores of Virginia.

61. Fleet's Bay is in Lancaster County at the eastern end of the Northern Neck. John Henry, *A New and Accurate Map of Virginia* (London, 1770).

62. On October 19, 1773, Henry Botson, captain of the Brig *Two Betsys* of Yarmouth, received a pass to go to the Mediterranean. The brig was a 100 ton vessel with a crew of eight. Register of Passes, 1772-1774, Adm 7/98, 79. (Public Record Office, London.)

63. For a discussion of the Virginia committee see Larry Bowman, "The Virginia County Committees of Safety, 1774-1776," *Virginia Magazine of History and Biography*, 79 (1971): 322-37.

64. See William E. White, "The Independent Companies of Virginia, 1774-1775," *Virginia Magazine of History and Biography*, 86 (1978): 149-62.

65. The Congress passed these resolves on October 21 and 26. Worthington Chauncey Ford, ed. *Journals of the Continental Congress*, vol. 1, (Washington, D.C.: Government Printing Office, 1904), 90-101; 115-22.

66. John Carlyle (1720-1780), a native of Carlisle, England, came to Virginia in 1741 and settled in Fairfax County. He was a prominent merchant in Alexandria where he was appointed one of the trustees when the town was chartered in 1749. He married Sarah Fairfax in 1747. W. W. Abbot, ed., "General Edward Braddock in Alexandria: John Carlyle to George Carlyle, 15 August 1755," *Virginia Magazine of History and Biography*, 97 (1989): 205-14.

67. John Moss operated the ordinary on Sugar Land Road, about halfway between Alexandria and Leesburg. Donald Jackson, ed., *Diaries of George Washington*, vol. 3, (Charlottesville, Va.: University Press of Virginia, 1978), 239.

68. Josiah Moffitt later agreed to assist Cresswell in moving his chest to Philadelphia. See entry for November 4, 1776. Moffitt sold lot 23 in Leesburg to James Kirk on November 7, 1775. Loudoun County Court Deed Book L, 1775-1778, 69-72a. All Virginia county court records cited are on microfilm in the Library of Virginia, Richmond.

69. William Douglass (d. 1783), lived at his estate, Garralland, in Loudoun County north of Leesburg. This estate was named for Garralland, Ayrshire, Scotland. He arrived in Virginia about the middle of the eighteenth century. He held several offices in the county including justice of the peace, coroner, and was appointed sheriff of that county in 1777. On May 13, 1777, Douglass presented his commission from the Virginia convention appointing him captain of the Loudoun County militia. Loudoun County Court Will Book C, 1783-1788, 15; Loudoun County Order Book F, 1773-1776, 57; Loudoun County Order Book G, 1776-1783, 42, 47, 218. Harrison Williams, *Legends of Loudoun: An Account of the History and Homes of a Border County of Virginia's Northern Neck* (Richmond, Va.: Garrett and Massie, Inc., 1938), 77-78.

70. Said to be the earliest Methodist meeting house in Virginia, it was built between 1766 and 1770. It stood until 1902. Calder Loth, ed., *The Virginia Landmarks Register*, 4th edition (Charlottesville, Va.: University Press of Virginia, 1999), 274.

71. Keyes Ferry was operated by Humphrrey Keyes who lived on the west bank of the Shenandoah River. W. W. Abbot et al., eds., *Papers of George Washington. Colonial Series*, vol. 10, (Charlottesville, Va.: University Press of Virginia, 1995), 188-89.

72. Jacob Hite was one of the first justices of the peace in Berkeley County appointed in 1772. Benjamin J. Hillman, ed., *Executive Journals of the Council of Colonial Virginia*, vol. 6, (Richmond, Va.: Virginia State Library, 1966), 456. Hite was later killed by the Indians. See below, December 19, 1776. Hopewell was later purchased by General Charles Lee following the advice of Horatio Gates. Charles Lee, *Collections of the New-York Historical Society for the Year 1873: The Lee Papers*, vol. 3, (New York: New-York Historical Society, 1874), 470-74; John Richard Alden, *General Charles Lee: Traitor or Patriot?* (Baton Rouge, La.: Louisiana State University Press, 1951), 52-53; 138.

73. This was probably the William Gibbs who was appointed to the Commission of the Peace for Frederick County on October 19, 1776. Henry R. McIlwaine, ed., *Journals of the Council of the State of Virginia*, vol. 1, (Richmond, Va.: Virginia State Library, 1931), 207.

74. Philip Vickers Fithian, visiting Winchester in May 1775, reported that the "Dutch-Lutheran Church" was on "pleasant Hill North-East from the Town at a Small Distance." He said it was a stone church with a tall steeple. Albion and Dodson, eds., *Philip Vickers Fithian: Journal, 1775-1776*, 13.

75. The four Indians were Wissecapoway, a son of Cornstalk, Chenusaw, Cutenwha, and Newa. Colin G. Calloway, *The American Revolution in Indian Country: Crisis and*

Diversity in Native American Communities (Cambridge, England: Cambridge University Press, 1995), 162-63.

76. Thomas Pursley was granted a license to keep an ordinary at his house in Loudoun County on August 13, 1770. Loudoun County Court Order Book E, 1770-1773.

77. William Sydebotham lived in Bladensburg, Maryland. Richard Graham, Dumfries, to James Hunter, Fredericksburg, August 5, 1776. Walter R. Coakley, compiler, "Calendar of the Hunter Family Manuscripts, 1704-1779 in the University of Virginia."

78. Capt. Scot was likely William Scott who lived in the same house with Kirk and Buddecomb from August 1774 until May 1775. Letter: Wm Scott to Mrs. Jane Buddicom, August 8, 1806. T 79/38. British Public Record Office. Capt. Wroe was George Rowe master of the brig *Potowmack*. W. W. Abbot, ed., *The Papers of George Washington*, Colonial Series, vol. 10 (Charlottesville, Va.: University Press of Virginia, 1995), p. 180.

79. Crane Island was a small islet just upstream from the present site of Gunston Hall. James W. Foster, "Potomac River Maps of 1737 by Robert Brooke and others," *William and Mary Quarterly*, 2nd ser., 18 (Oct., 1938): 412.

80. William Smallwood (1732-1792), native of Maryland, served in the Maryland Assembly in 1761. He was commissioned colonel in January 1776 and raised Smallwood's Maryland Battalion. He was promoted to Brigadier General in October 1776 and to Major General in September 1780. He was elected governor of Maryland in 1785 and served three one-year terms. Mark M. Boatner, *Encyclopedia of the American Revolution*, (New York: David McKay Co., Inc., 1974), 1013-1014.

81. Alexander (b. 1736) served as burgess from Stafford County from the May 1765 session. In 1774 he was elected a delegate to the first Virginia convention. William J. Van Schreeven and Robert L. Scribner, eds., *Revolutionary Virginia: The Road to Independence*, vol. 2, (Charlottesville, Va.: University Press of Virginia, 1975), 346 n. 24.

82. This may have been the property Knox advertised for lease in May 1777. He described it as "pleasantly situated on Patowmack river, about half a mile from Nanjemoy warehouse." *Maryland Gazette*, May 15, 1777.

83. Ryan died in Charles County, Maryland, in 1807. By his will, dated July 20, 1786, he left his wife "all my Church furniture to be disposed of as she may think fit." He also desired the family graveyard be preserved forever. Charles County, Maryland, Will Book A.L, No. 12, 1801-1808, 477-80.

84. Cresswell must mean Aquia Creek which empties into the Potomac River in present day Stafford County, Virginia. There was no Aquia County in Virginia.

85. Bailey Washington (1731-1807) lived in Stafford County at Windsor Forest Plantation on Aquia Creek. King, *Overwharton Parish*, 124.

86. This was probably John Ralls, Sr. (died 1782), who, according to tradition, was from Somerset, England. Jerrilynn Eby, *The Accokeek Iron Works Business Ledger, 1749-1760* (Westminster, Md. Willow Bend Books, 2003), 4.

87. Cresswell probably means the adjoining county of King George. Horatio Dade was a member of the King George County Committee of Safety. Van Schreeven and Scribner, eds., *Revolutionary Virginia: The Road to Independence*, 3: 239.

88. This was probably Francis Mastin, son of Mary and Robert Mastin. See note 32 above.

89. During the 1760s John Finley, an itinerant peddler, traveled throughout the back country. He was instrumental in arousing Daniel Boone's interest in finding the Cumberland Gap. He settled in Alexandria carrying on the trade of a merchant. He died in 1785. Park Rouse, Jr. *The Great Wagon Road* (Richmond, Va.: Dietz Press, 1995), 108. *Virginia Journal & Alexandria Advertiser*, January 13, 1785. Lucien Beckner, "John Finley:

The First Pathfinder of Kentucky," *The Filson Club History Quarterly* 43 (July 1969): 206-215.

90. Cresswell was mistaken about seeing Washington on this day. Washington was in Fredericksburg all day on March 18, 1775. However, Washington did review the Independent Company in Alexandria on February 18, 1775, but Cresswell was in Najemoy on February 18th. Both Washington and Cresswell were in Alexandria on February 28th. Cresswell probably made the mistake in transcribing his notes. Jackson, ed., *Diaries of George Washington*, 3: 309-10, 314.

91. Wabash River.

92. This probably was Samuel Canby, a Quaker merchant in Leesburg. He was there from at least 1773. He moved to Kentucky about 1795. Loudoun County Court Order Book F, 1773-1776, 27. William W. Hinshaw, *Encylopedia of American Quaker Genealogy*, vol. 6, (Ann Arbor, Mich.: Edwards Brothers, Inc., 1936-1950) 480. T 79/80, 119. (Public Record Office, London.)

93. Edward Snickers's home, "Springfield," was in Frederick County. Donald Jackson, ed., *The Diaries of George Washington*, 2: 173. In June 1776 Snickers was appointed to the commission of the peace of Frederick County and later was accused of "fraud against the Public." McIlwaine, ed., *Journals of the Council of the State of Virginia*, 1: 46, 428.

94. The present site of Pittsburgh, Pennsylvania.

95. On September 6, 1774, George Rice produced his commission as lieutenant in the Frederick County militia to the county court. Frederick County Court Order Book 16, 1772-1778, 269. He was later captain in the 11th Virginia Regiment under the command of Brigadier General Daniel Morgan. Bounty Warrant of Pierce Noland, (Library of Virginia).

96. John Neville was appointed as one of the first justices of the peace for Berkeley County in 1772 He was a large land-owner in the vicinity of Pittsburgh. He later served as commandant of Fort Pitt during the first two years of the Revolution. Hillman, ed., *Executive Journals of the Council of Colonial Virginia*, 6: 456. Nicholas B. Wainwright, ed., "Turmoil at Pittsburgh: Diary of Augustine Prevost, 1774," *Pennsylvania Magazine of History and Biography*, 85 (1961): 148 n. 110.

97. Located on the road from Winchester to Cumberland, Maryland, Rinker's Tavern was operated by Casper Rinker, a member of the early German settlers in the area. Jackson, ed. *Diaries of George Washington*, 2: 278.

98. Cresswell probably means Valentine Crawford. Crawford had surveyed land for George Washington. Jackson, ed., *Diaries of George Washington*, 2: 280.

99. Great Meadows, the scene of George Washington's first battle, was purchased by him in 1770. Hugh Cleland, *George Washington in the Ohio Valley* (Pittsburgh, Pa.: University of Pittsburgh Press, 1955), 286.

100. This was Stewart's Crossing on the Youghiogheny River below present-day Connellsville, Pennsylvania. The site was named for William Stewart who settled there in 1753. Jackson, ed., *Diaries of George Washington*, 2: 280.

101. Zachariah Connell, founder of Connellsville, Pennsylvania, was appointed captain of Yohogania County militia in 1776. He died in 1813. Reuben Gold Thwaites and Louise Phelps Kellogg, *Frontier Defense on the Upper Ohio, 1777-1778* (Madison, Wisc.: Historical Society of Wisconsin, 1912), 220.

102. John Stephenson had served in the French and Indian War and settled in the vicinity of the Great Crossing of the Youghiogheny about 1768. He was half-brother of Valentine Crawford. Jackson, ed., *Diaries of Washington*, 2: 280.

103. John De Camp died in 1778 likely as a result of an accident.. He probably operated a tavern at this time. His tavern license was renewed on April 17, 1776. Thaites & Kellogg, eds. *Frontier Defense on the Upper Ohio, 1777-1778*, 252; Boyd Crumrine, ed., *Virginia Court Records in Southwestern Pennsylvania: Records of the District of West Augusta and Ohio and Yohogania Counties, Virginia, 1775-1780.* (Reprint. Baltimore, Md.: Genealogical Publishing Co., Inc., 1974), 29, 145.

104. The widow Myers (Miers) operated a tavern on Turtle Creek about twelve miles above Fort Pitt. John C. Fitzpatrick, *Diaries of George Washington, 1748-1799*, vol. 1, (Boston: Houghton Mifflin Co., 1925) 402.

105. Patrick Henry thought Connolly a "Sensible man" and George Washington found him "a very sensible Intelligent Man." Lord Dunmore appointed Connolly commandant of the Virginia militia in the Pittsburgh area in 1773 and early in 1774 he took over Fort Pitt renaming it Fort Dunmore. The boundaries between Virginia and Pennsylvania in the area of Pittsburgh had long been disputed. Connolly enraged Pennsylvanians with his high-handed actions resulting in a series of arrests and counter-arrests by Virginia and Pennsylvania officials. On June 20, 1775, Connolly was summoned to Lord Dunmore who sent him to Boston with dispatches for General Gage. On his return to Virginia, Dunmore appointed him, with Gage's approval, Lieutenant Colonel on November 5, 1775. Connolly was to raise a regiment of troops and to win the support of the Indians. On his way to Detroit, Connolly was captured and held prisoner by the Americans for five years. Abbot et al. eds., *The Papers of George Washington, Colonial Series,* 9: 98; 10: 43-44. Claim of John Connolly. A. O. 12/54, 27-32. (Public Record Office, London.) John Connolly, "A Narrative of the Transactions, Imprisonment, and Sufferings of John Connolly, An American Loyalist and Lieut. Col. in His Majesty's Service," *Pennsylvania Magazine of History and Biography*, 12 (1888): 310-24, 407-20; 13 (1889): 61-70, 153-67, 281-91.

106. This was probably John Campbell. See entry for May 2, 1775, below.

107. James Nourse (1731-1784), born in Herefordshire, England, lived at Piedmont in Berkeley County, Virginia. In 1753 he married Sarah Fouace in London and moved with his wife and nine children to Virginia in 1769. He accompanied Cresswell on his trip down the Ohio and his journal of the trip survives in typescript, the original being lost. Jackson, ed., *Diaries of Washington*, 3: 13. Maria Catharine Lyle, *James Nourse and his Descendants*, (Lexington, Ky.: Transylvania Printing Co., 1879), 8-10. James Nourse, "Journey to Kentucky in 1775," *The Journal of American History*, XIX, (1925): 121-39, 251-60, 351-64.

108. Johnston had been town clerk of Fredericksburg, Virginia. By 1782 he was living on Chartiers Creek in Pennsylvania. In 1783 he succeeded William Crawford as surveyor of Yohogania County. W. W. Abbot et al., eds., *The Papers of George Washington*, Colonial Series, vol. 10 (Charlottesville, Va.: University Press of Virginia, 1995), 59.

109. Edmund Taylor was appointed captain in the Frederick County, Virginia, militia on September 6, 1774. Frederick County Court Order Book 16, 1772-1778, 369.

110. Nourse's servant was Tom Ruby. Nourse, "Journey," *The Journal of American History*, XIX (1925): 122-23, 128.

111. This was Reubin Taylor and his servant George Noland. Nourse, "Journey," 128.

112. As a reminder Cresswell must have inserted this remedy that he found useful for some unspecified ailment.

Chapter 2
In the West
April 30, 1775 to November 9, 1775

Journal of Nicholas Cresswell
of
Edale near Chapelinlefrith
Derbyshire, in England

Continued from Vol 1st April 30th 1775
To November 9th 1775

Yough-a-ga-ney, River, Monday 1st May 1775
After breakfast, left Saweekly and stood down the River, crossed several Fish-pots—these fishpots are made by throwing up the small stones and gravel something like a mill ware, beginning at the side of the River and proceeding in a Diagonal line till they meet in the middle of the stream where they fix a thing like the body of a Cart, contracted where the water flows in just to admit the fish, but so contrived as to prevent their return or escape.

Got over the shoales by hauling our canoos—fell into the Mon-in-ga-ha-ley about noon. Eat our diner at Magees Fort this is a stockade fort built the last summer.

Mon-in-ga-ha-ley River Monday 1st May 1775
This River is about 100 Yards broad at its Conflux with the Yough-a-ganey and has continued its bredth—upon the banks of this river (where they are high and broken) I observed stratums of leaves about a foot thick, twenty foot below the surface of the earth, they appeared to be sound and not concreted together, much like those that are drove together by winds in autumn.

—fell down a little below Braddocks field where we Camped in a heavy shower of rain,[1]—one of our company shot a wild Turkey which made us an excellent supper.

Mon-in-ga-ha-ley River Tuesday 2nd May 1775
Proceeded down the River our Canoos are so heavy loaded that we are in great danger of overseting the water is within three inches of the Gunnel which aded to the exceeding crankness of our vessel makes me uneasy.

—Called at Fort Pitt and bought some necessaries such as Lead, Flints, & some Silver trinkits to barter with the Indians. Dined at Mr John Campbells[2]—After diner proceeded down the Ohio River passed McKeys Island, it is about a mile long and belongs to Captn Alexander McKey Superintendent of Indian affairs[3]—Camped at the lower end of Montures Islands three fine Islands belonging to John Monture a half Indian.[4] The Land exceedingly rich.

Ohio River, Wednesday 3rd May 1775

This morning Mr Robert Bell & one Harrison[5] left us to go to their plantations in this Neighbourhood. They had come with us from Youghaganey River and been very serviceable in instructing us how to navigate our little barks. Proceeded down the River passed Loggs Town (an old Indian town but now deserted) it is on the W. side then Bigg Beaver Creek, on the W. then little Bever Creek on the W,[6] neither of them so large but they may be forded in dry weather. A little before dark stoped at a Farmers house to bake bread. Agreed to lash our vessels together and floate all night. The River is very high and rappid suppose we can floate two miles in an Hour.

Ohio River Thursday 4th May 1775

In the morning found ourselves opposite Yellow Creek[7] on the W.—very heavy rain for several hours—Very few inhabitants not a house to be seen in 40 Miles, tho the land is exceeding rich, in general—The River is exceedingly crooked full of small Islands and rappid, if their is high land on one side there is allways a rich level bottom on the opposite shore.

Got to Wheeling Creek, Fort Fincastle[8] on the East side of the River. This is a Quadrangular Picketed Fort on a little hill beside the River, built last Summer by Lord Dunmore—a small garison in it, here we took into our Co a Captn George Clark.[9]

Lashed our Canoos together and drifted all Night stoped at Grave Creek[10] about 2 in the morning.

Ohio River Friday 5th May 1775

Got up very early and went to v[i]ew the Grave it bear's East of the River, about a mile from it, and above the mouth of the Creek. The great Grave is a round hill something like a sugar loaf, about 300 feet in circumference at bottom 100 feet high and about 60 feet Diameter at top where it form's a sort of irregular Bason. It has several large trees upon it but I could not find any signs of Brick or Stone on it, seems to have been a trench about it. there is other two hills about 50 yards from this but not much larger then a Charcoal pit and much in that shape, with other Antique Vestiges, some appears to have been works of Defence but very irregular.

All these Hills appear to have been made by human art, but by whom, in what age, or for what use I leve it for more able Antiquarians to determine. The Indian tradition is that there was a great Battle fought here and a many great Warriors kild these mounts were raised to perpetuate their memory the truth of this I will not pretend too assert. Proceeded down the River entertained with a number of Delightfull prospects in their native wild yet truly beautifull. Pass'd several Creeks and small Islands—few inhabitants but rich land—Got to the head of the Long reach where we have a view of the River for 15 Miles.[11] Drifted all night.

Ohio River Saturday 6th May 1775
Found ourselves opposite Muddy Creek the heavy Rain obliged us to take shelter in a lone house and stay all night.

7th This morning Captn Clark (whom I find is an intelligent man) showed me a root that the Indians call pocoon, good for the bite of a Rattle Snake, the root is to be mashed and applyed to the wound a decoction made of the leaves which the patient drinks. The root exceedingly red the Indians use it to paint themselves with at sometimes. Left Muddy Ck passed two small Islands to the Bigg tree Island so called from the number of large trees upon it.

Went ashore on the Bigg tree Island and measured a large Sycamore tree it was 51 feet 4 Inches in Circumference one foot from the ground and 46 Foot Circumference five feet from the ground and I suppose it would have measured that twenty feet high—their is several large trees but I believe this this [sic] exceeds the rest. One of the Co caught a large Catfish which made a most delitious pot of Soup. past the Muskengum River[12] on the W. Fine land between that and the little Muskingum—passed the Little Kanhawa River on the East. Barren Land about the mouth of it. Stoped to cook our super at Fort Gower—a little picketed Fort Built las[t] summer but now deserted at the mouth of Hokhokin[13] on the W. Drifted all night.

Ohio River, Monday 8th May 1775
Heavy rain this morning, which obliged us to make a sort of Awning with our tent Cloth and Blankets. Got round the Horseshoe, a large Curve of about 4 Miles made by the River in the form of a horseshoe from whence it takes its name.[14] Here is excellent land—passed a number of small Islands—River continues rappid—Camped about 4 Miles below the Horseshoe where we met with some people who gave us very bad encouragment, say that the Indians are broke out again and kild four men on the Kentuckey River.

My courageous companions spirits begin to droop.

Ohio River, Tuesday 9th May 1775
Proceeded down the River—passed four Islands—About noon got to the mouth of the Great Kanhaway, or Conhauway River. Here is a large pi[c]keted fort called Fort Blair, built the last summer by Colnl Andrew Lewis, who entirely defeated the Shawannee Indians about a mile from it, in August 1774[15] —it is now garrisoned with 100 men under Captn Russel,[16] who invited us to dine whith [sic] him, and treated us as well as his situation wou'd admit. Confirms the account we heard yesterday.[17]

My companions exceedingly fearful and I am far from being easy, but am determined to proceed as far as any one will keep me company. Drifted all night.

Ohio River, Wednesday 10th May 1775
Found ourselves opposite Guiandot Creek on the East Side the River. Rowed hard and got to Sandy Creek to breakfast, where we found Captn Charles Smith

encamped with 22 men.[18] He was takeing up land as we are now out of the inhabitants. Intend to stay here for Captn Lee.[19]

11th Employed in washing our linen, and mending our Cloaths.

12th This day held a council wheather we shou'd proceed or turn back, after much Altercation our Co determin'd to persevere tho I believe they are a set of Damed cowards. With much perswation prevailed upon them to let me endeavour to make our Vessels more safe and commodious. This has been a most arduous task to Efect, so difficult is it to beat these people out of there own Course when it is for their safety.

Ohio River Saturday 13th May 1775

Camp at the mouth of Sandy Creek. Employed in fixing our Canno's together by two beames, one athwart the heads the other at the stern seting the Canoos about one foot apart. In the middle of the aftermost piece I fixed a strong pin, on that hung the Rudder made something like an Oar, but bent down towards the water and projected about two feet astern of the Vessel rigged her out with four Oars & called her the Union. Some of our Co laughs at it and declares She will not answer the Helm. But it pleases me well and hope it will deceive them.

Ohio River Sunday 14th May 1775

Camp at the mouth of Sandy Creek. This morning very wet—after breakfast Mr Edmund Taylor and I entered into discourse on politics which ended in high words. Taylor threatned to Tar & Feather me. Obliged to pocket the affront. Find I shall be torifyed if I hold any further Confab with these red hot Libertymen. Memd. Taylors usage to be remembered.

15th Left Sandy Creek. Captn Lee not arived. Find our Vessel answer well and give universal satisfaction to the Co. one of the Co Shot a Turtle which made us an excellent supper. Land good and level in General. All of us strangers to the River. Drift all night but keep watch spell & spell about.

Ohio River Tuesday May 16, 1775

Passed the mouth of the Siato River in the night. This river is on the N. W. side. Stoped to cook our breakfast on a small gravelly Island where we found plenty of Turtle eggs with which we made pancakes equal in goodness to those made with hens eggs, it must be people of a nicer taste then me that can distinguish the difference. These animals come out of the water and lay their eggs in the sand to be hatched by the Sun. They are white but smaller then those of a hen and perfectly round with a tough skin instead of a shell the inside has all the appearance like that of a Fowls egg generally find about Twenty together about 2 Inches below the surface.

—after breakfast attempted to fix a sail in our Vessel but the wind soon blew up the River which rendered it useless. Passed several Creeks and Islands but unknown to us. This evening Mr Rice & I went ashore and each of us kild a wild Turkey which made us an excellent supper. Drifted all night.

17th This morning did not know where we were, or wheather we had passed the mouth of any River in the night. I believe our watch had slept most of the night. Fell down to a Creek by the description Mr Johnston had from his brother we take it to be Bracken Creek.[20]

Stoped at Brakens Creek and went a hunting (as they call it here) Mr Rice, Johnston, and I went together in a short time Mr Rice fired at a Buffaloe. Johnston and I went to him and found him standing behind a tree loading his Gun and the beast lay'd down about 100 yds from him as soon as he was ready we fired at him again upon which he got up and run about a quarter of a mile where our dogs bayed Him till we came up and shot him. It was a large Bull from his breast to the top of his shoulder measured 3 feet from his nose to his tail 9 feet 6 Inches, black and short hornes all before his shoulders long hair, from that to the tail as short as a mouse. I am certain he would have weigh'd a Thousand Camped a little below the Creek.

Ohio River Thursday May 18th 1775
All hands employed in cureing our Buffaloe meat, which is done in a peculiar manner—the meat is first cut from the bones in thin slices like beef stakes then four forked sticks is stuck in the ground in a square form and small sticks layed on these forks in the form of a gridiron about three feet from the ground, the meat is lay'd on this and a slow fire put under it, and turned till it is drye. This is called Jirking meat. I believe it is an Indian method of perserveing meat it answers very well where Salt is not to be had, and will keep a long time if it be secured from the wet the lean parts eats very dry. The Buffaloe flesh difers little from beef —only ranker taste. Hot weather.

Ohio River Friday May 19th 1775
Proceeded down the River passed the mouth of the little Miamme River on the N. W. And Salt River or Licking Creek, on the S. E. Saw an Elk and a Bear cross the River but could not get a shot at them. Got to the mouth of the Great Miamme River on the N. W. it is about 100 yds wide at the mouth and appears to be pritty gentle current, stoped to Cook and take a view of the land on the S. E. side of the Ohio River it is a little hilly but rich beyond Conception. Wild Clover what they here call wild Oates and Wild Rye in such plenty it might be mown and would turn out a good crop. The great quantity of Grass makes it disagreeable walking. The land is thin of Timber and little underwood. drifted all night.

Ohio River Saturday May 20th 1775
In the morning in doubt wheather we had passed Ellephant Bone lick or not went a shore at a small Creek on the S. W. side in quest of it but in vain believe we are too low down the River according to our Charts, begun to rain about noon, floated down the River till night when we mored to a stump in the midle of the stream. Some of our company are in a panic about the Indians again. Shot at a Panther this afternoon but mised him.

Hot weather with Thunder.

Ohio River Sunday May 21st 1775
Proceeded down the River about noon got to the mouth of the Kentuckey River
on the S. E. side. The Ohio is about three quarters of a mile wide here—the
Kentuckey is about 130 yards wide at the mouth and continued its width about
two miles when we camped in a Beechey bottom.[21] Our Co in great feare of the
Indians some of them insisted on sleeping without fire after a long contest it was
agreed to put the fire out when we went to sleep, but I believe it was not done,
whatever my companions may be I am not uneasy. I suppose it is because I do
not know the danger of our situation. Rainy Weather.

Kentuckey River, Monday May 22nd 1775
Notwithstanding the danger of our situation last night I slept sound and
undisturbed, tho some of the Co was kept in perpetual alarm by the barking of
the dogs and their own feares. This morning held a council to consult our
present safety when after many Pro's and Con's, it was determined to keep two
men on each side the River as scouts, the rest to work up the Vessel and relieve
each other by turns. It hapened to be my turn to walk as a scout but found it
disagreeable clambering over gullies and wadeing amongst the weeds as high as
my head in some places and raining all the forenoon. Saw several Buffaloe traks
and a flock of Paroquets. At noon went aboard and rowed till night—find the
current here as pritty strong. Camped on a hill in a Beech thicket all hands well
tired and D—d cross. One of the scouts kiled a Deer.

Kentuckey River Tuesday May 23rd 1775
Proceeded up the River, found several Rapids which obliged us to get out and
haule our Vessel up with ropes. the Current stronger then Yesterday. Saw
several roades that crossed the River which they tel me are made by the
Buffaloes going from one lick to another. (These Licks are Brackish or salt
springs which the Buffaloes are fond of) With hard labour suppose we have
come twenty miles today.

No signs of Indians. Camped on a stoney hill neare a Buffaloe Lick, saw
several of them and kiled two Calves & a Bull. Limestone impregnated with
shells. Large Beech bottoms but our scouts inform me the Land is better a
distance from the River. Believe G. Rice does not intend to go down the Ohio
which will be a great disappointment to me.

Kentuckey River, Wednesday, May 24th
Proceeded up the River find the navigation worse more rappids and strong
Current. Surrounded 30 Buffaloes as they was crossing the River, shot two
young Heifers, and caught two Calves alive whose ears we marked and turnd
them out again. About noon Captn Michael Cresap[22] met us, informed us it is
100 Miles to Harwoods landing—the place our Co intends to take up lands. No
danger of the Indians.

Captn Clark left us and went with Captn Cresap. Clark always behaved well while he stayed with us.

Land in general covered with Beech. Limestone in large flags. Few rivulets emties [sic] into the River, or few springs to be seen, which makes me suppose the Country is badly watered.

Camped at a place where the Buffaloes cross the River—in the night was alarmed with a plunging in the River, in a little time Mr Johnston (who slept on board) called out for help we run to his assistance with our Arms and to our great Mortification and surprize found one of our Canoos that had all our flour on board sunk, and would have been inevitably lost, had it not been fixt to the other.

We immediately hauled our shattered Vessel to the shore and Landed our things tho grea[t]ly damaged. It was done by the Buffaloes crossing the River from that side where the Vessel was mored. Fortunate for Mr Johnston he slept in that Canoo next the shore the Buffaloes jumped over him, into the other and split it about fourteen foot. Mr Nourse & Mr Taylors servants usually slept on board, but had by mistake brought their Blankets on shore this evening and were too lazy to go on board again or probably they had both been kiled.

Kentuckey River, Thursday May 25th 1775

Repairing our Vessel by puting in knees and Calking her with the bark of the white Elm pounded to a paste, which is tough and Glutinous something like Birdlime answers the purpose very well. Some of the Co shot a Buffaloe Bull, saw several cross the River while we was at work. Two Canoos full of men past us down the River going to Fort Pitt. Am convinced Rice will not go with me, find he is a great coward. On inspection find our Flour is much damaged obliged to come to an allowance of a Pint a man pr day. had we come to this resolution sooner it would have been better. Great quarreling among the Co.

Kentuckey River, Friday May 26th 1775

Proceeded up the River. Met 2 Canoos bound to Redstone. Shot an old Buffaloe Bull that had his eares marked. Passed a bad Rapid which tooke all our force to tow the Vessel up.

Much tormented with Ticks, a small animal like a Sheeplouse but very tough skin, they get on you by walking in the Woods in great numbers, And if you don't take care to pick them off in time they work their heads through the skin and then you may pull the body away but the head will remain in the Skin which is very disagreeable. If they are not removed in a short time they grow like the Ticks on a Dog. Beechey bottoms. Camp at the mouth of Elk horn Creek. Our Co still continues to be Crabed with one another and I believe will be worse as Bread grows scarce.

Kentuckey River, Saturday May 27th 1775

This day got up several smart rapids. Thunder Lightening and Rain. Some high

Rocks and Ceder hils. Find Rice does every thing in his power to quarrel with me am determined not to give the first affront.

28th Sunday. Proceeded up the River. Saw a great many Buffaloes cross the River above us, all hands went a Shore to surround them. I kept on the out side them and shot a fine young Heifer some of the rest shot a Cow and Calf. Our stupid Co will not stay to stay to [sic] Jerk any, tho we are in want of provisions. Camped on a Gravelly Island. Beech bottoms & Ceder hills with few rivulets.

Kentuckey River, Monday May 29th 1775

This morning George Rice (without any provocation) began to abuse me in a most Scurrilous manner threatened to Scalp and Tomhawk me. I was for bestowing a little manual labour upon him, but he flew to his Gun & began to load swearing he would shot me. I did the same and had it not been for the timely interposition of my worthy Friend Mr Nourse, I believe one of us had been kiled. A good deal of abusive Language was give on boath sides, but nothing more. I have expected this for some time. He did it on purpose to get off his engagement to go down the Ohio which it has efectually done—proceeded a little way up the River to a Great Buffaloe Crossing where we intend to kill some meat our provision is almost out.

Kentuckey River, Tuesday May 30th 75

This day Mr Nourse, Mr Taylor & Rice, went to take a view of the Country. Mr Johnston and I took a walk about 3 miles from the River find the Land pritty level a blackish sandy soil Timber chiefly Beech.

In our absence those at Camp caught a large Catfish which measured six Inches between the Eyes, we supposed it woud weight 40 pound.

Dont expect our Co back to night.

31st At the Camp washing and mend[ing] my Cloaths. In the evening Mr Nourse & Co returned and says the Land a distance from the River, is the Levelest, Richest and finest they ever saw but badly watered.

Kentuckey River, Thursday June 1st 75

Proceeded up the River bad navigation many rapids and strong Currents. Saw a Gang of Buffaloes cross the River shot a Bull see some Deer but kiled none. Camped at a place where we found some Corn in a Crib a Gun and some Cloaths, supposed to be left their by some people come to take up land. Rocks, Cedar Hills, and Beech Bottoms.

2nd This day met eight Canoos bound to Redstone & Fort Pitt. Went about 9 Miles and Camped, to hunt, shot at some Buffs but kiled none. Land good weeds as high as a man. Pleasant weather. Our Co continually quarreling but I have the good luck to please them all but Rice, whom I treat with Contempt.

Kentuckey River, Saturday June 3rd 1775

Proceeded up the River till noon when after being wet to the skin we Camped about 10 Miles below Harwoods landing. Another Canoo passed us this day bound to Wheeling. Rocks, Cedar hills & Beech Bottoms.

4th Sunday. Arived at Harwoods Landing in the Evening. Saw a Rattle Snake about 4 feet long. A bark Canoo at the landing. We have been Fourteen days in comeing about 125 Miles. My right foot much swell'd owing to a hurt I got by Bathing in the River. Rockey & Cedar hills, along the banks of the River. My foot very painfull.

Harwoods Landing, Monday June 5th 1775

This is called Harwoods Landing as it is nearest to a new Town that was layed out the last summer by Captn Harwood who gave it the name of Harwoodsburg about 15 Miles from the Landing for which place Mr Nourse, Mr Johnston, Taylor & Rice set out this morning.[23] I would have gone with them but my foot is so bad I am scarcely able to walk applyed a Fomentation of Herbs to asswage the swelling.

Very little to eate and no possibility of geting any flour here, must be without Bread very soon.

Harwoods Landing, Tuesday June 6th 75

Mr Nourse & Co Returned in the Evening gives good accounts of the richness of the land but says it appears to be badly wattered & Light timbered. They lodged in the town. Mr Norse informs me their is about 30 houses in it all built of Loggs and covered with Clapboards but not a nail in the whole Town, inform us that the Indians has kiled four men about nine miles from the town. this has struck such a panic that I could not get any one to go down the Ohio with me on any account. Determined to return by the first opportunity. My foot much better— much provoked at my disappointment.

Harwoods Landing, Wenesday [sic] June 7th 75

My foot much better. All of us that had Guns went a hunting. Rambled over a great hill saw a great deal of fine land but no Game. Mr Johnston left us and went to Harwoodsburg.

8th This day devided our provisions which came to 2 Quarts of flour, half a peck of Indian Corn sprouted as long as my finger, one Gallon of Salt, and about two pound of Bacon pr man. In the afternoon Four men came to the landing who are bound up the River Ohio to Fort Pitt. they tel me that they have some flour are willing to take me in Co determined to go with them but dont much like their lookes. A confoun[d]ed raged Crewe. My foot allmost well.

Harwoods Landing Friday June 9th 75

About three OClock this morning we was alarmed with a great noise in the River. The men I had agree'd to go with was Camped betwixt us and the River. Called to know wheather any of our Co was Crossing the River as they saw two people in a Canoo endeavouring to get to the other shore, on examining we found two of our Co missing, an indentured Servant belonging to Mr Taylor[24] &

another that was come for Mr Johnstons Baggage from Harwood. They had tooke all my flour & Mr Johnstons and about two pound of Gun powder belonging to Johnston but no Gun. the people at the landing threatened to fire on them if they did not return upon which they go a shore and took to their heels.

They had set all the Canoos a drift except that they took with them which luckeyly stuck on a Rock till one of the Co swam across the River and brought her over and my flour which they had got on shore but in their hurry forgot. What can be their motive for runing a way in this wilderness Country I cannot conceive. My new fellow travelers got the Charming Sally from my old Co put our things on board toke leave of Mr Nourse with whom I should have been glad to have returned, but he intends to go over land. This Gentleman has treated me with the greatest Civillity. My new Co Henry Tilling an Englishman, Thos O. Briant an Irish man, John Clifton and Joseph Boassiers, Americans.[25] Stoped about 30 Miles below the Landing at a hunting Camp where we got some Buffalo meat.

Kentuckey River, Saturday June 10th 75

The people at the Camp we lodged at last night give us some Jerked meat. On inspecting our flour find it does not amount, for the whole, to more then 15 pound amongs [sic] 5 people must make no more bread but save our flour for soup. Proceeded down the River. These people behaves very kind to me. I believe here is but two pair of Breeches in the Company one belonging to Mr Tilling the other to my selfe, the rest wears Breech Clouts, Legings and Hunting shirts, which has never been washed only by the Rain since they was made. Our Canoo very Leakey, determined to change her the first opportunity Camped at a Buffaloe road.

Kentuckey River, Sunday, June 11th 1775

This morning kiled a Buffaloe Cow Crossing the River. Fell down to Elkhorn Creek. Camped and Jerked our meat sprinkling it with salt which makes it more pallatable. Found Captn Hancock Lee Camped at Elkhorn, surveying land.[26] This is a new settlement by some Carolina Gentlemen who pretend to have purchased the Land from the Indians but with what truth I cannot pretend to say, as the Indians affirm they have never sold these Lands.

These Gentlemen claims all the Land on the S. W. side of this River to Green River a tract of Land about 200 Miles broad, and I suppose twice as long. They sell it about five pound sterling a Thousand Acres subject to an annual quit rent of five Shillings pr thousand, no quitrents to be paid til the land has been possessed five yeares. It is surprizing what numbers of people has took up Lands on these terms, tho they are generally of the most profligate sort in short it is an Assylum of rascals of all Denominations.

I believe the Land is good in general through the whole track, several salt Springs as I am informed and immence numbers of Buffaloes that frequent them. Buffaloes are a sort of wild cattle but have a large hump on the top of their shoulders all Black and their necks and shoulders covered with long shaggy hair with large bunches of hair growing on their fore thighs, short Horns bending forwards short noses peircing Eyes and bearded like a Goat, in the Summer the hair behind their shoulders is short as that on a horse.

In the winter they are covered with long soft curling hair like wool their tails are short with a bunch of long hair at the end when they run they carry them erect. Some of them will weigh when fat 14 or 15 Hundred and are good eating particularly the hump, which I think makes the finest stakes in the world they feed in large herds and are exceedingly Fierce when wounded. Their sense of smelling is exqusite, if you get to Leeward of them you may go up to them or at least within shot, but if you are to windward they run long before they see you.

They are fond of Salt or Brakish water. Springs of this sort have large roades made to them as large as most publick roades in a populous Country. they eat great quantities of a sort of redish Clay found near Brakish springs I have seen amazeing large holes dug or rather eat by them in this sort of earth, wheather it is impregnated with Saline particles or not, I cannot determine. they do not roare like other Cattle but Grunt like Hoggs. Got a large pine Canoo out of some drift wood with great Labour, but her stern is beat off and several bullet holes in her bottom which we intend to repair tomorrow. Excessive hot.

Kentuckey River, Monday June 12th 1775
Repairing our Canoo by cuting the Stern out of the Charming Sally and puting it into her, Calked her and made her tight believe she will answer very well, boath stiff and light. Went to Captn Lees Camp who treated me very kindly with a Dram of Whiskey and some bread which at this time is a great Luxury with me. Captn Lees brother gave me a Rattlesnake skin about four feet long. Very Hot.
13th Fell down the River to a great Lick where we intend to kill some meat my Co begin to quarrel among themselves but behave well to me.

Kentuckey River Wednesday June 14th 75
Very heavy rain las[t] night which we had no shelter from but a large tree it made us wet lodging. Went to the Lick in the mor[n]ing found no Buffaloes their. determined to go to Grinins Lick. Fell down to Grinins Lick shot at some Buffaloes but kiled none tho I am certain we must have woun[de]d a great number five of us fired at a Herd of two Hundred and odd not more than twenty yards.

This is the largest Lick I ever saw. I suppose here is 50 acres of Land trode by the Buffaloes that their is not a blade of Grass upon it. Increditable numbers comes here to the salt Springs.

Here is a number of salt and Brakish spring[s] in a small compass some of them so strong of the Brime that the Sun forms the Salt round the edge of the Spring. Here was two Dutchmen sent by the proprietors to make an experiment on the water of the strongest spring they had made about a pint of Salt from sixteen Gallons of water. Some of Captn Cresaps people had been Camped here for 4 Days kiling meat but intend to set out for Fort Pitt tomorrow; our Co intend to go with them and trust to providence for provision. I think this a foolish act but will not contradict them. Bought a Buckskin to make mockeysons.

Kentuckey River, Thursday June 15th 1775
Intend to kill some meat at the Ellephant Bone Lick. Proceeded down the River in Co with nine of Captn Cresaps people, our Co is increased to 14 persons and almost as many different nations, two Englishmen, two Irishmen, one Welchman, two Dutchmen, two Virginians, two Marylanders, one Sweed, one African Negro, and a Mulatto. With this Motley Rascallly & Raged Crew I have to travel Six Hundred miles. I expect we shall have a great deal of quarreling but as we are in three Canoos it will be a means to keep them quiet. Got to the Mouth of the River about noon. Proceded up the Ohio where we kiled a Buffaloe and Camped.

Ohio River, Friday June 16th 1775
Very heavy Rain last night which made our lodging uncomfortable. Got under way this morning early with wet Cloaths & Hungry Bellies. Obliged to pole up the River—this is done with poles about 12 Feet long the men stands in the Vessel sets the pole against the bottom of the River and pushes themselves along. It is a Laborious exercise. Fortunatly for me none of our Co can steer with a pole. I am obliged to set and steer with a paddle. Kiled another Buffaloe on the Bank of the River. Our Co quarreled and the Irishman left us and went to Cresaps people but returned to us at the Bone Lick where we Camped.

Ohio River, Saturday June 17th 1775
This morning set out for the Ellephant Bone Lick which is only three miles S. E. of the River however we lost our way and I suppose traveled twenty miles before we found it. Where the bones are found is a large muddy pond a little more then knee deep with a salt spring in it which I suppose preserves the bones sound. Found several bones of a prodigious size I take them to be Ellephants for we found a part of a Tusk about two Foot long, Ivory to all appearances but by length of time was grown yellow and very soft.

All of us striped and went into the pond to grabble for teeth found several. Joseph Bassiers found a jaw tooth which he gave me, it was judged by the Co to weigh 10 pound. I got a shell of a Tusk of Hard and good ivory about eighteen Inches long. Their is a great number of bones in a Bank on the side of this pond of an Enormous size but Decayed and rotten, Ribs 9 Inches broad, Thigh bones 10 Inches Diameter.

What sort of Animals these was is not Clearly known. All the traditionary accounts by the Indians is that they were White Buffaloes that kiled themselves by drinking Salt water.

It appears to me from the shape of their Teeth that they were Grasseaters. Their neither is or ever was, any Ellephants in North or South America that I can learne, Or any Quadruped one tenth part as large as these was. If one may be allowed to judge from the appearance of these bones, which must have been

Considerably larger then they are now. Captn Hancock Lee told me he had found a Tusk here that was Six Foot long very sound but Yellow. These Tusks are Like those brought from the Coast of Africa.

Saw some Buffaloes but kiled none. Several Indian paintings on the trees. Got plenty of Mulberrys very sweet and pleasant fruit but bad for the teeth. One of the Co shot a Deer. The loudest Thunder & Heaviest Rain I ever saw this afternoon. Got to the Camp well wet and most heartily tired. A D—d Irish rascal has broke a piece of my Ellephant tooth, put me in a violent passion can write no more.

18th Left the Bone Lick. Got to the mouth of the Miamme River to diner. Nothing but Jerked meat without Bread. Camped about eight miles above the Miamme.

Ohio River, Monday June 19, 1775
Got underway early this morning. As we sat at Diner saw two Buffalo Bulls crossing the River, when they was about half way over four of us got into a Canoo and attacted them in the River, the rest went along shore to shoot them as soon as they came a shore. The River was wide and we had fine diversion fighting them in the water. The man in the head of the canoo seized one of them by the tail and he towed us about the River for half an hour. We shot him eight times let him get a Shore and he run away. Our comrades a shore very angry with us and they have a great right to be so.

Passed the mouth of the Little Miamme. In great fear of the Indians. Saw a Black Wolfe pursueing a Faun into the River, the Faun we caught but the Wolfe got away. My Co quarrels amongst themselves but behave well to me. Camped late in the Evening.

20th Very Cold last night N. W. wind. Camped early in the evening.

21st Cold in the night. Got up Le Torts Falls this is only a small rappid scarce perceivable when the River is high. Current very strong. Our people weary not able to make more than 20 Miles pr day in general. Camped early.

Ohio River Thursday June 22nd 1775
Proceeded up the River. Strong Current. The River is twenty feet lower now then it was when we went down.

23rd Saw a Bear cross the River but did not get a shot at her. Got up to the Great Buffaloe Lick where we intend to kill some meat as ours is allmost done. All hand much fatigued and the scarcity of provisions makes them very Quarrelsom, they pay some respect to me, and I have hitherto prevented them fighting. Pleasant weather.

Ohio River Saturday June 24th 1775
This morning set out to the Lick without Breakfast. The reason was we had nothing to eat, three of us stayed at the Lick till the afternoon waiting for the Buffaloes but saw none. When our out Hunters came loaded with meat and informed us they had kiled a Buffaloe about five mile off set out and found it,

and loaded ourselves and returned to the Camp but never so much fatigued before. Haveing allready experienced the want of victuals was willing to guard against it for the future.

I believe I have exerted myself more then I can beare, it is judged by the Co that I brought between 70 and 80 pound of meate exclusive of my Gun and Shot pouch, to add to my distress my shoe soles came off and I was obliged to walk bare foot for six miles. Find myselfe very unwell. Shot a pole Cat. One of our Co missing all the rest (except Tilling and myselfe) are for going this evening as they expect he is kiled by the Indians. But I think he has lost himselfe in the Woods. Very arduous task to perswade them to stay as they all expect to be kiled before morning.

Ohio River Sunday June 25th 75
Slept little last night, over Fatigued. This morning our Co are for seting out immediately, confident that the man is kiled. With much importunity prevailed on them to stay till evening, but could not perswade any of them to go seek the man. About Sun down they all prepared for going notwithstan[d]ing all that Mr Tilling and I could say against it, but just as we were going aboard saw the man come along Shore to our great joy.

It had happened as I supposed he lost himselfe in the woods and had rambled all night. If we had left him he must have perished. Very unwell.

Ohio River, Monday, June 26th 75
Proceeded up the River. Passed the mouth of the Sioto River on the N. W. in feare of the Indians. Camped early.
27th Very stiff Current all day. Heavy showers and very Sultry. It is a custom with our Co as soon as it begins to Rain to strip naked and secure their C[l]oathes from the wet, I have attempted it twice today but the drops of rain are so disagreeable to my skin, that it obliged me to put on my Shirt. Kiled a Fawn. Saw a Bear cross the River not coud not get a shot at her. All hands very weary and very crabed.

Ohio River, Wednes[d]ay, June 28th 1775
This morning started early in a very thick fogg, about three miles from our Camp the River was very broad and shallow a long way from the shore on that side we were on, which obliged us to keep out of sight of the shore for deeper waters Opening a point of a Bar saw 4 Canoos full of Indians about two hundred yards a head of us upon which we pushed for the shore but to our great surprize saw six other Canoos full of Indians betwixt us and the shore so that we were entirely surrounded.

Every thing was prepared for an engagement, all our lumber and a great part of our provision was hove over-board. Out of twelve Guns five was rendered unfit for present use by the wet, mine happened to be in good order and I loaded her with an Ounce Bullit and seven swan shot, the Command of our Canoo was given to me we had only two Guns on Boatd fit for use Mr Tillings & mine,

Tom O'Brien in the scuffle let his fall in the River and got her filled with water, he lay down in the bottom of the Canoo, begun to tell his beads and pray & Howl in Irish.

Boassiers Gun was wet and unfit for use. He followed OBriens example, Weeping, praying, and Ave Mary's in abundance at the same time hugging a little wooden crucifix he puled from his bosom most hearty. Jacob Nulen (a Sweed) Commanded a Canoo had three Rifle guns on board. Williams the Welchman Commanded the other with two muskets. We held a short and confused Council, wherein it was determined that Nulen shoud lead the Van, I in the Center, and Wms bring up the Reare.

The Indians had observed our Confusion and lay on their paddles about 30 Yards from shore their was 23 Indians in the six Canoos betwixt us and the shore all them had poles or paddles but our fears had converted them into Guns, these six we determined to attack as the River was shallow if we by accident overset our Canoos we might wade a shore. The Canoos above us with 21 Indians bore down upon is, we made for the shore, I ordered Tom O'Brien to steer the Canoo within ten yards of Nulins Vessel and Boassiers and Cliffton to take their paddles.

Cliffton tho a young Boy behaved with the greatest resolution. Mr Tillings countenance was not in the least changed his behaviour annimated me very much. Boassiers & OBrien lay crying in the bottom of the Canoo and refused to stir. I set the mussel of my gun to O'Briens head threatening to blow his Brains out if he did not immediatly take his paddle, it had the desired effect, he begged for his life, invoked St Patrick, took his paddle and howled most horrible. Dangerous and Desperate as we immagined our situation to be I could not forbear laughing to see the Condition of this poor fellow.

Boassiers pretended to be in a Convulsion fit. Mr Tilling threw several canfull of water in his Face but he refused to stir. I put 4 Pistol Bullets upon the load I allready had in my Gun. I was Determined to give some of them their Quietus. I confess I felt very uneasy. When we got within thirty yards of them some of Nulens Crew haled them and to our great satisfaction they told us they were friends. They had seen our Confusion and laughed at us for our feares.

It prooved to be one Catfish a Dellawar Indian and a party with him going to hunt they had several Squaws or Indian women with them some of them very handsome. We gave them some salt and Tobacco with which they seemed well pleased. Proceeded up the River very merry at the expence of our cowardly companions. Boassiers braggs what he would have done had his Gun been in order. O'Brien says he was not fit for death, all of them makes some excuse or other to hide their Cowardise. Heavy Rain all afternoon. Camped five miles above Sandy Creek. Obliged to sleep upon a logg the ground is so wet and still continues to Rain.

Ohio River, Thursday June 29th 1775
The great Rains has raised the River about four feet last night, causes a strong Current and laborous Navigation. Saw another Canoo with Indians but did not speak them.

Slept on a fallen tree uneasy lodging.
30th Got to the Great Conhaway about noon find the Fort evacuated. Saw some people that are settled about 5 miles above the mouth of the river who informs us that the New Englan[d]ers have had a Battle with the English troops at Boston and kiled seven Thousand. I hope it will proove that the English have kiled seven thousand of the Yankeys.

Ohio River, Saturday July 1st 1775
This morning John Cliffton left us he intends going home by land. He has behaved very well.

Our provisions allmost done, all our hooks and lines broke, all our feet so tender by standing continually wet that it is impossible we can hunt, and the small quantity of provision we have is swarming with maggots our flour expended and this night we have put the last of our Indian Corn to boil (about three half pints sprouted as long as my finger) this we have allways reserved for Sunday Diner with a little Elk fat rendered amongst it and thought it delicious.

Ohio River Sunday July 2nd 1775
Captn Cresaps Co had a mind to keep Sunday but quarreled about it and Wm Connor left them and came to us. They are all on wages and have some provision left. We eat the last mouth full we had this morning except a little stinking Jerked Beef full of maggots.

Proceeded up the River past Hockhockin about noon found a Buffalo Fish about six pound weight that an Eagle had just kiled and brought a shore, made a hearty meal of it. In the Afternoon Boassiers went to our Beef Barrel but found it so bad in a passion hove it over board. Now we have not a morsel to eat. Slept on a Rock with out fire.

Ohio River, Monday July 3rd 1775
Got under way very early this morning not a morsel to eat. Our people quarrel very much but behave to me with great Respect. Camped very late.
4th Got to mouth of the Little Conhaway about noon when I found myself very sick at the Stomach for want of meat, went a shore & got a little Ginseng root and Chewed it which refreshed me exceedingly, in the Evening got to one Doctor Briscoe's[27] Plantation about a mile from the River, it was night when we got their found the house deserted no Corn, Fowls, or meat of any kind.

We all went into the Garden dark as it was, to get Cucumbers, or any thing we could find that wou'd eat, found a Potatoe bed and I eat about a Dozen of them raw and thought them the most delicious food I ever eat in my life. Heavy and constant rain all day—made a fire in the house dried ourselves and went to sleep. Very much Fatiegued.

5th This morning one of the Co went to the Canoo for our Kettle the rest plundered about the plantation and got some young Cabbages, Squashes and Cimbelines.

This medley of Vegetables we boiled alltogether and seasoned it with pepper & Salt made a most Ellegant repast. Proceeded to French Creek where Cresaps people overtook us but wou'd not give us a mouthful of Victuals. Rain all day one of our people sick. I gave half a Dollar for about two Ounces of Bread for him.

6th Got to one Pursleys plantation where we got some Sour milk, but no bread. I dare eat none of it got me Genseng root. This is an excelent Stomatict, went to sleep very Hungry. Our sick man much better.

Ohio River, Friday July 7th 1775

Got to a plantation belonging to one Raus a Dutchman. Bargained with the Old Woman for as much mush as we all could eat (this is hasty puding made of Indian meal) for about two Dollars worth of Gun powder, we had the Corn to Grind on a hand mill and I thought it an age before we had done and the mush made, I suppose we might have eat till we had kiled ourselves before we had satisfyed our Voracious appetite, the old Woman prudently took our Victuals away when we had eat about a Quart apice. Have eat no bread for twenty eight days.

Ohio River, Saturday July 8th 75

This morning one Captn David McClure[28] came here on his way to Wheeling he behaves civilly and offer me a place in his Canoo to Wheeling. Mr Tilling & Boassiers intend to go by land to Redstone. Tilling has allways treated me with the greatest respect & kindness, this poor man was once a Lieutenant in the Train of Artillery but broke at New York for Caneing a Collonell he has took up a good track of land on the Kentuckey. O'Brien & I went with Captn McClure. One of his Co Shot 2 Does plenty of meat and a little bread. Got to Captn Rodgers[29] plantation.

Ohio River, Sunday July 9th 1775

Past Grave Creek, and Juniata Creek. Got to Fort Fincastle in the Evening. No Soldiers here but about 8 men from the neighborhood all drunk and our Co soon got in the same condition. A man had got Whiskey to sell. Captn Cresaps people joined them and in a short time a general engagement begun. I got up into a loft and went to Sleep.

10th Waiting for Captn McClure who is going within a little way of Mr Shepherds[30] with a Horse and will carry my Baggage. Disagreeable Co Fighting and Quarreling.

Fort Fincastle, Tuesday July 11, 1775

Waiting for Captn McClure. Bought a Belt of Wampum from him. Disagreeable situation.

12th Left the Fort and got to Mr David Shepheard. Saw an Allum mine near to Mr Shepheards with a mine of Good Coal in a Limestone Rock. Hired a Horse from one of the neighbours to go to V. Crafords.

13th Left Mr Shepheards rambled thro Woods & Wilds, shot a Rattle Snake which had like to have bite my horse it was about 4 Feet long. Lodged at Catfish Camp.[31] Great scarcity of Provisions.

West Augusta County, Friday July 14th 75

Left Catfish Camp, traveled over a great deal of fine land but very thinly inhabited. Crossed the Moningahaley River at Redstone Fort[32] where I lodged at one Thos Browns.[33] Listing the best Rifle men that can be got to go to Boston under Captn Cresap for the humane purpose of kiling the English Officers.[34] Confusion to the Scoundrels. Here is a number of them here and I believe suspect me being a Spy they ask me so many impertinent questions. Very much Fatigued this day.

West Augusta County, Saturday July 15th 75

Left Redstone Fort and after looseing my [way] several times, Got to Captn Thos Gists.[35] Very kindly treated by Miss Nancy Gist an agreeable Young Woman who informs me that their has been two very severe engagements at Bos[ton] and great numbers kiled on boath sides. [36]

Forgot the part of an Ellephants tusk at the Fort.

16th Sunday. Went to Major Crawfords[37] delivered some Letters I had for him—gives me bad accounts of the Boston Affairs Informs me Lord Dunmore has abdicated the Government of Virginia and gone on Board a man of War.

West Augusta County, Monday July 17th

Left Major Crawfords. Crossed the Youghhaganey River and went to Mr. V. Crafords. In the evening went to Captn Stevensons to what they call a Reaping Frollick usually make a feast when they get done Reaping—very merry.

18th At Mr V. Crafords, Jacobs Creek. These Rascals has wore out all the Cloaths I left here so that I am now reduced to three Ragged Shirts two pair of linen Breeches in the same Condition, A Hunting Shirt and Jacket, with one pair of Stockings.

West Augusta County July 19th 1775

Rode to Captn Gists, returned in the Evening. Intend to stay here a week or two to recover my selfe my late Fatigues has reduced me exceedingly.

20th Very ill of the Gravel felt some symptoms of it for two days but now I am in violent pain.

21st Much worse a total suppression of Urine and most excruciating pain took a Decoction of Roots prescribed by Mr Crafords Houskeeper who uses me with the greatest Care and tenderness.

West Augusta, Saturday July 22nd 75
Something easier—this morning tooke some Tea made of the Roots of a Small Shrub which gave me allmost immediate ease. Miss Grimes came to see me and Cryed most abundantly to see me in so much pain, as She said, but believe she has too much of the Irish in her.
23rd Sunday. Got pretty well again but still continue to take the Tea. Captn Prior Theobald came here to day invites me to his house but don't intend to go.

West Augusta, Monday July 24th 75
Free from all symptoms of the Gravel. Walked about a little but find myselfe weake.
25th Intend to go into the Indian Country as soon as I am able to dispose of the Silver Trinkets I bought for that trade. I believe shall be put to my shifts for Cash to carry me their.
26th Rode up to the Laurel Mountain with some Young Girls to get Huckeleberries. They are the same as our Billberries only grow in Clusters.

West Augusta, Thursday July 27th 75
Went a Shooting and knocked down a Young Turkey. Nothing but Whores and Rogues in this Country.
28th At Mr Crafords. Hot Weather.
29th The Revend Mr Belmain,[38] only Church Minister in this County came here to day intends to give us a Lecture tomorrow.
30th Mr Belmain preached under a large tree. a Polittical discourse.
31st The people here are Liberty mad nothing but War is thought of. Flux begins to rage in the neighbourhood.

West Augusta, Tuesday August 1st 75
Went with Mr Belmain and Captn Stevenson to Major Crafords.
2nd Returned to V. Crafords, intend to go to Fort Pitt the first opportunity. I am now got strong & Healthy.
3rd This morning went with Mr V. Craford & Mr James Berwick[39] a Machester [sic] man to Major Crafords where we stayed all night, bad news from Boston. The English drove to their Ships and great numbers of them kiled. I hope it is a Lye.

West Augusta, Friday August 4th
Agreed to go with Major Craford to Mr John Gibsons[40] an Indian Trader, about 12 Miles below Fort Pitt. He is a man that has great intrest [sic] amongst the Indians. Consequently the best person to direct me how to dispose of my goods to the best advantage.
Mr Berwick lost his watch this evening.
5th At Mr Crafords. Heavy Rain.
6th At Mr Crafords. Heavy Rain for Forty Eight Hours without intermission.

West Augusta, Monday Aust 7th 75
At Mr Crafords, waiting for Major Craford. I believe he is a Dilatorry man and little dependance to be put in him.

8th Very uneasy to wait here doing nothing. Am affraid I shall be too late to return home this fall. Went with Miss Craford & Miss Grimes to John Mintors.[41] When we came to a Small Creek we had to cross the Girls tuck'd up their petticoats above their knees and forded it with the Greatest indifference. Nothing unusual here, tho these are the first people in the Country.

West Augusta, Saturday, Augst 9th
Mr Berwick & I set out this morning to Major Crafords but met him at his Misstresses. This woman is common to Him, his Brother, Half Brother, and his own Son. And his Wifes Sisters Daughter at the same time. A set of Vile brutes. He informs me the Congress has Discarded all the Governors on the Continent and taken all Affairs Civil and Millitary into their management. Independance is what these Scoundrels aims at. Confusion to their Schemes.

West Augusta, Thursday, Aust 10th 75
At Captn Stevensons—instructed his people to make a Stack of Wheat. Farming in a poor uncultivated state here. Captn Stevenson an honest worthy man. Went to V. Crafords in the evening. No prospect of Major Craford going to Gibsons soon. Determined to set out for Fort Pitt on Monday next.

11th Last night Miss G. came to bed to me. A fine blooming Irish Girl. The Flesh overcame the Spirit.

West Augusta, Saturday August 12th 75
No prospect of geting money for Bills upon Mr Kirk here. This evening Captn James Wood arived here from the Indian towns. He had been sent to invite the Indians to a treaty at Fort Pitt to be held on the tenth of September.[42]

The Convention of Virginia had employed him. He says that an English Officer & a French man from Detroit had been at all the Indian towns to peswade the Indians not to go to any Treaty held by the [blank] But tels us his superior Ellogence prevailed and all the different Nations he has been at will certainly attend the Treaty.

West Augusta, Sunday August 13th 75
Mr Berwick was kind enough to let me ride his horse to Fort Pitt where I am to deliver him to a certain Mr John Madison.[43] Left Mr V. Crafords, and with him I left my Watch, K[n]ee Buckles, Breast Buckle, Stock Buckle, and Silver Buttons with a paper directing how I would have them disposed off, If Death shoud happen to [be] my lot, as every one tels me that I run a great risk of being kiled by the Indians. I am not affraid of meeting with bad usage from them. Got to Mr John De Camps at night.

West Augusta, Monday August 14th 75
Left Mr De Camps. Dined at Turtle Creek. Arived at Fort Pitt in the evening
with only two Dollars in my pocket and very shabby Dress. Put up my horse at
the best Inn in Town know the Landlady to be a Tory Sisterinlaw to Major
Connoly.
15th Delivered the horse to Mr Mattison applyed to four people in town to get
Cash for my Bills on Mr Kirk but my appearance prevents my success. Offered
to sell my Silver ware to them but the Rascals knowing my distress will not give
me more than half its value. Exceedingly uneasy.

Fort Pitt, Wednesday, August 16th 75
A great Deal of Co in Town being Committee day. No one willing to supply me
with a little Cash tho I have applyed to every man in Town where their is a
probabillity of geting any. O, the disadvantages of of [sic] a Raged dress. Very
uneasy.
17th Very low Spirited. At super had a political dispute with Mr John Gibbson.
Find him much prejudiced against me by the Malevolent Aspersions of that
double faced Villain B. John[s]ton. No prospect of geting money here. Made my
situation known to the Landlord desireing Credit for my board till the Treaty
when some Gentlemen of my acquaintance will be their and [lose?] me, Told me
he paid ready money for his provision. By the influence of his wife got credit.

Fort Pitt, Friday, August 18th 1775
Never till now, did I put any confidence in Dreams. Last night I went to sleep
with a mind as much confused as a Skein of Silk puled the wrong way. The
behaviour of my landlord had been a principal cause. But find I have a good
Friend in my Landlady, who weres the Breeches. Dreamed that there was a
Friend that would relieve me neare at hand. I woke with a Gleme of hope and
waited on Mr John Anderson the only person in Town that I had omited.[44] He
generously proffered me any Cash I might want, find me a Horse, and go with
me into the Indian Country, serve as an interpreter and Guide. This Gentleman is
an Indian Trader and has business at their Towns.

Tels me he has observed my situation for some days and intended to offer
me his assistance this day had I not spoke to him. Got some money from him to
pay my Landlord when he found I had got a Friend his tone altered and it did not
signify anything if I did not pay him til the Treaty. I made use of his own words
to him. told him as he payed ready mony for his provisions Consequently he
must expect the same from me. His wife abused him a good deal about his
meanness. Called him pittifull Rascals in abundance.

Fort Pitt, Saturday, August 19th 75
Waiting for Mr Anderson. Employed an Indian Woman to make me a pair of
Mockeysons, & Leggings. This evening two of the Pensylvania Delegates to
Treat with the Indians, Arived here Escorted by a party of paltry Light horse,
Colnl Arthur St Clair and Colnl James Willson.[45] Suped and spent the evening

with them. My Landlady remarkable kind to me owing to my Political sentiments agreeing with hers. She is by nature a most Horrid Vixen.
20th Sunday. Waiting for Mr Anderson he is Detained by the Indians comeing to trade.

Fort Pitt, Monday, August 21st 75
Mr Anderson informs me that the Indians are not well pleased at any one going into their Country dressed in a Hunting shirt. Got a Callico Shirt made in the Indian fassion trimed of with Silver Broaches and Arm plates so that I scarcely know myselfe. Crossed the Allegany River and went about two miles and Camped at a small run to be ready to start early in the morning. We had forgot a Tin Kettle in Town I went back for it while Mr Anderson made a fire, returning in the Dark lost my way and got to an Indian Camp where I found two Squaws but they could [not] speak English, by sines made them understand what I wanted and they put me right.

Indian Country, Tuesday, August 22nd 75
A very heavy Fogg this morning. We had got two Bottles of Rum, two Loaves of Bread, and a Bacon Ham a long with us. Agreed to take a Dram to prevent us catching the Fever and Ague. But Drank rather too much, and most stupidly forgot our provisions. Got to Loggs Town, about noon, crossed the River & went to Mr John Gibbson Lodged their, but would not make our wants known for feare of being laughed at. We crossed the River in a Canoo made of Hickery Bark stretched open with sticks.

Indian Country, Wednesday, August 23rd 75
Proceeded on our journey—but not one morsel of provision. Crossed Great Bever Creek at Captn White Eyes house this an Indian Warrior of the Dellaware Nation.[46] Camped at Little Bever Creek with three Indian Squaws and a man. Nothing to eat but Berry's such as we found in the woods. Find Mr Anderson a good hearty Companion. One of the Indian Squaws invited me to sleep with her, but I pretended to be sick. I have no mind to engage such a Tawney Brib [?], she was very kind and brought me some plums she got in the Woods.

Indian Country Thursday, August 24th 75
Parted with the Indians. Met Captn Killbuck[47] an Indian Warrior. Camped at White Oak run. Got plenty of Red plums & Wild Cherries which is our only food.
25th Very Heavy Rain all day. Lost our Horses, but an Indian brought them to us in the Evening for which we gave him a pair of Leggings. Breakfasted, Dined and Suped on plums and Wild Cherry's. Here is wild plums in great abundance about the size of our common white plums in England—some Red others White and very well flavored. The Cherrys are small and black very sweet and grows in Bunches like Currans.

Indian Country, Saturday August 26th 1775

Set out early this morning traveled very hard till noon when we pased through the largest plum tree Thicket I ever saw I believe it was a mile long nothing but plum & Cherry trees. Kiled a Rattlesnake. Just as the Sun went down we stoped to get our Supper on some Dear Berry's, a small Berry something like a Goosberry. Mr Anderson had done [sic] before me and said he would ride on about two miles to a small run where he intended to Camp, as soon as I had got sufficient.

I mounted my Horse and followed him til I came to a place where the road forked. I tooke the path that I supposed he had gone and rode til it began to be dark when I immagined myselfe to be wrong, and there was not a possibility of me finding my way back in the night. Determined to stay where I was til morning. I had no sooner lighted from my horse, but I discovered the glimmering of a Fire about four Hundred Yards from me. This rejoiced me exceedingly supposeing it was Mr Anderson.

When I got there to my great Disappointment and surprise, found Three Indian women and a little Boy. I believe they was as much surprised as I was. None of them could speak English and I cou'd not speak Indian. alighted and marked the path I had come, and that I had left, on the ground with the end of my stick, made a small channel in the earth which I poured full of water, layed some fire by the side of it, and then lay'd myselfe down by the side of the fire repeating the name of Anderson which I soon understood they knew.

The youngest Girl immediately unsaddled my Horse unstoped the Bell Hoppled him & Turned him out, then spread my Blankets at the fire and made signes for me to sit down. The oldest made me a little hash of dried Vennison and Bears Oil which eat very well but neither Bread or Salt. After supper they made signes I must go to sleep, then they held a consulation for some time which made me very uneasy, the two Oldest women and the Boy lay down on the opposite side of the Fire and some distance.

The youngest (she that had took so much pains with my horse) came and placed herselfe very near me. I begun to think she had some Amorous design upon me. In about half an hour she begun to creep nearer me and pull my Blanket. I found what she wanted, and lifted it up. She immediately came to me and made me as happy as it was in her power to do.

She was young, Handsom & Healthy, Fine regular Features & Fine Eyes had she not painted them with Red before she came to Bed. And I suppose answers as well as My Lady in the Dark.

Indian Country, Sunday, August 27th 75

This morning my Bedfellow went into the woods and caught her horse and mine, Saddled them, put my Blankets on the Saddle, and prepared every thing ready Seemingly with a great deal of good nature. Absolutely refused my Assistance. The Old woman got me some Dryed Venison for Breakfast.

When I took my leave returned them thanks as well as I could by signs, My Bedfellow was my guide and conducted me through the woods, where was no sign of a road, or without me knowing certainly whither I was going. She often mentioned John Anderson talked a great deal in Indian. I attempted to speak Indian which diverted her exceedingly. In about an hour She brought me to Mr Andersons Camp, who had been very uneasy at my absence and employed an Indian to seek me. I gave my Dulcinea a Match coat with which she seemed very well pleased. Proceeded on our journey and about noon got to an Indian Town called Whale-hak-tup-pake, or the Town with a good Spring.[48] On the banks of the Muskingham, and inhabited by Dellawar Indians.

Christianized under the Moravian Sect, it is a pretty town consisting of about Sixty houses built of Loggs and covered with Clapboards. It is regularly layed out in three spacious streets which meet in the Center where there is a large meeting house built of Loggs Sixty foot square covered with Shingles, Glass in the windows and a Bell, a good plank floor with two rows of forms. Adorned with some few pieces of Scripture painting but very indifferently executed. All about the Meeting house is keept very clean.

In the Evening went to the meeting. But never was I more astonished in my life. I expected to have seen nothing but Anarchy and Confusion as I have been taught to looke upon these beings with contempt. Instead of that, here is the greatest regularity order, and Decorum, I ever saw in any place of Worship in my life. With that Solemnity of Behaviour and Modest, Religeous deportment would do Honnor to the first religeous Society on earth. And put a Bigot or Enthusiast out of countenance.

The parson was a Dutchman but preached in English. He had an Indian interpreter that explained it to the Indians by sentences. They sing in the Indian language. The men sits on one row of Forms and the women on the Other with the Children in the front each Sex comes in and goes out on their own side the house. The Old men sits on each side the parson. Treated with Tea Coffee & Broiled Bacon at supper the Sugar they make themselves out of the sap of a certain tree. Lodged at white mans house maried to an Indian Woman.[49]

Indian Country, Monday August 28th 75

Left Wale-hak-tup-pake crossed the Muskingham and went to Kanautonhead another pretty Moravian Town but not so large as Wale-hak-tup-pake About eight miles asunder.[50] Crossed Muskingham again and a large plain about 3 miles over without tree or shrub and very level. Saw several Indian Cabins built of Bark.

Got to Newcomers Town about noon this has been a large town but now allmost Deserted, it is on the Muskingham built without any order or regularity. I suppose their is not twenty houses inhabited now.[51]

Crossed the Muskingham again and another large plain. Met several Indians comeing from a Feast Dressed and painted in the grandest manner. Lodged at Whiteeys Town only three houses in it.[52] Kindly treated at a Dutch Blacksmiths who lives with an Indian Squaw. Got a very heaity supper of a sort of Dumplings made of Indian Meal and dryed Huckeleberrys which serves instead of Currants. Dirty people find it impossible to keep myselfe free from Lice. Very Disagreeable companions.[53]

Indian Country, Tuesday August 29th 75
Left Whiteeyes town. Saw the Bones of one Mr Cammel a White man (that had been kiled by the Mingo Indians last summer) lay by the side of the road. Got to Co-a-schoking about noon. It is at the forks of the Muskingham. The Indians have removed from Newcomestown to this place. King Newcomer lives here.[54] Sold part of my goods here to good advantage. Crossed a Branch of Muskingham and went to Old Hundy this is a scattering Indian settlement. Lodged at a Mohawk Indian house who offered me his Sister and Mr Anderson his Daughter to Sleep with us, which we were obliged to accept.

Indian Country, Wednesday August 30th
My bedfellow very fond of me this morning and wants to go with me. Find I must often meet with such encounters as these if I do not take a Squaw to myselfe. She is yound [sic] and sprightly. Tolerable handsome and can speak a little English. Agreeed [sic] to take her. She saddled her horse and went with us to New Hundy about 3 Miles off, where she had several relations who made me very welcom to such as they had. From their to Coashoskin where we lodged. My Squaws Brother made me a Compliment of a Young Wolfe but I coud not take it with me.

Indian Country Thursday Aust 31st 75
At Coashoskin. Mr Anderson could not find his horse. Sold all my goods for Furs. In the afternoon rambled about the Town, Smoaking Tobacco with the Indians and did every thing in my power to make myselfe agreeable to them. Went to see the King he lives in a poor house, as is as poor in dress [as] any of them, no emblems of Royalty or Magesty about him. He is an Old man treated me very kindly called me his good friend and hoped I woud be kind to my Squaw. Gave me a small string of Wampum as a token of Friendship. My Squaw uneasy to see me write so much.

Indian Country, Friday Septr 1st 1775
At Coashoskin. Mr Anderson found his horses. Saw an Indian Dance in which I bore a part, painted by my Squaw in the most Ellegant manner. Divested of all my cloaths, except my Callico Shirt Breechclout, Legings, and Mockesons. A Fire was made which we Danced round with little order whoping and hollowing in a most frightfull manner. I was but a Novice at the deversion and by endeavouring to act as they did, made them a great deal of sport, and ingraciated me much in their esteem.

This is the most violent exercise, to the Adepts in the art I ever saw, no regular figure but violent Distortion of Features, Writhing and twisting the body in the most uncouth and Antic postures immaginable. Their musick is an old Kegg with one head knocked out and covered with a skin and beat with sticks which regulates their time. The men have strings of Deers hoofs tyed round their ancles and knees, and Gourds with shot or pebble stones in them in their hands, which they continually rattle.

The women have Morris bells or Thimbles with holes in the bottom and strung upon a leathern thong tyed round their Ancles, Knees, and Waist. The jingling of these Bells and Thimbles, The rattleing of the Deershoofs & Gourds, Beating of the Drum & Kettle, With the Horrid Yells of the Indians, Renders it the most unharnonious Concert, that human Idea can possibly conceive. It is a favoured Diversion in which I am informed they spend great part of their time in Winter.

Saw an Indian Conjuror dressed in a Coat of Bearskin with a Vizor mask made of wood, frightfull enough to scare the Devil. The Indians believe in Conjuration and Witchcraft.

Left the Town, went about two miles Camped by the side of a run. A young Indian Boy son of one Baubee a Frenchman came after us and insists on going with us to Fort Pitt.[55] Find myselfe very unwell this evening pains in my Head and Back. Nancy seems very uneasy about my wellfare. Afraid of the Ague.

Indian Country, Saturday Sept 2nd 75

Got to White-Eyes Town to breakfast. Saw the Indian Warmarks made by Captn Wingenund a Dellawar Warrior,[56] which Mr Anderson and Captn White Eyes explained to me.[57]

Indian Warmarks

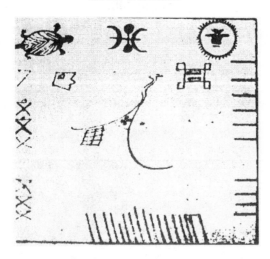

These Hieroglyphic marks are the history of his whole warfare. The rude resemblance of a Turtle on the Lefthand is the emblem by which his Tribe or Nation is known. The Cross and two Halfmoons are the Characters by which he is personally distinguished among his Nation. That figure on the Righthand is the Sun. Those strokes under it signifys the number of times he has been at War. Those at the Bottom signify the number of men he had with him when he made these mark, their leanin[g] to the Left signifies that they have their backs towards the Sun and are bound to the Northward.

Those marks on the Lefthand under the Turtle signify the number of Scalps & Prisoners he has took and of what sex. Those marked thus X [with a bar over it] are Scalps, Thus, X [bar and circle over it] Men prisoners and those marked thus X [with additional marks superimposed on it] Women prisoners. The rough Sketches of Forts in the middle are what he has helped to attack but what their names was I cannot learn. Called at several Indian Villages Crossed the River and Got to Newcomers Town. Very sick Nancy is gone to fetch and [sic] old Indian woman to cure me, as she says, therefore I must lay by my pen.

Indian Country, Sunday, Septr 3rd 1775
Last night, Nancy brought an Indian Squaw which called me her Nelum, i.e. Nephew, which called me her relation as Mr Anderson told me, And behaved very kindly to me, She put her hand on my head for some time then took a small Brown root, out of her pocket and with her knife choped part of it small then mixed it with water, which she gave me to drink, or rather swallow being about a spoonfull, but this I evaded by keeping it in my mouth till I found an opportunity to spit it out. She then took some in her mouth and chewed it and spouted on the top of my head rubing my head well at the same time. Then she unbuttoned my shirt Collar and spouted another mouthfull down my back this was uncomfortable but I bore it with patience. She lent me her Matchcoat and told me to go sleep. Nancy was orderd not to give me any water til morning however I prevailed on the good natured Creature to let me take a Vomit that Mr Anderson had with him as soon as the Old Woman was gone, which has cured me tho the Old woman believes her nostrum did it. Obliged to stay here this day, somebody has stole one of Mr A's Horses.

Indian Country, Monday Septr 4th 75
Saw an Indian Scalp. Heard an Indian play upon a Tin Violin and make tolerable good Musick.

Went to Kanaughtonhead, walked all the way my horse loaded with skins. Camped close by the Town. Nancy's kindness to be remembered.
5th At Kanaughtonhead. Went to the meeting where Devine service was performed in Dutch and English with great Solemnity. This Chapel is much neater than that at Wale-heck-tup-pake.

Adorned with Basketwork in varrious colures all round With a Spinet made by Mr Smith the Parson) and played by an Indian. Drank Tea with Captn White Eyes & Captn Wingenund at an Indian house in Town. This Tea is made of the tops of Ginseng and I think it very like Bohea Tea. The Leaves are put into a tin Canister made water tight, and Boiled till it is dry by this means the juices do not evaporate. N. did not chuse to go into the town but employed herself in makeing me a pair of Mockasons.

Indian Country, Wednesday, Septr 6th 1775

Left Kanaughtonhead. Mr Anderson Bought several Cows there, which he intends to take to Fort Pitt. Camped within two miles of Walehacktuppake.

7th Got to Walehaktuppake to Breakfast. N. refused to go into the Town knowing that the Moravians will not allow any one to cohabit with Indians in their town. Saw an Indian Child Baptized, eight God fathers and four God mothers, cou'd not understand the ceremony as it was performed in Indian.

Indian County, Friday Septr 8th 1775

At Walehacktuppake. Find my body invaded with an Army of small Animals which will be a little troublesome to dislodge. Saw an Indian sweat house. It is built of Logs about eight feet by five and about two foot high, with a small door and covered all over with earth to keep in the steam. The patient creeps into the house wrapped in his Blanket, when his friends put in large Stones red hot and a pail of Water then make up the Door as close as possible, the patient throws the Water upon the hot stones till the house is filled with hot Steam and Vapour. He continues in this little Hell as long as he is able to bear it, when the Door is opened and the patient instantly plunged into the River. This method of treating the Smallpox has been destructive to many of them.

Bought a blanket made of a Buffalo Skin.

9th Left the town. Mr Anderson N. and I went to the Tuscarora town, then got lost in the Woods and rambled til dark when we Camped by the side of a little run. Very merry this Afternoon with our misfortune.[58]

Indian Country, Sunday Septr 10th

Rambled til noon when we found ourselves at Bouquets old Fort now demolished. Went to an Indian Camp where Mr Anderson met with an old Wife of his, who would go with him which he agreed to. We have each of us a Girl, it is an odd way of traveling but we are Obliged to submit to it. Met with Mr Andersons people in the evening Camped by the side of Tuscarora Creek. Saw the Vestige the Tuscarora Old town but now de[serted?].

Indian Country Monday Septr 11th 75

Mr Anderson and I with our Ladies proceeded and left the people to bring the Skins & Cattle which he had purchased. Traveled over a great deal of Bad land. About Sundown Mr A. caled out a panther I looked about and saw it set in a tree about twenty Yards from me Fired at it on horseback and shot it through the neck. it is of a Brown Colure and shaped like a Cat but much larger. It measured Five foot Nine inches from Nose to Tail end. Camped and Skined the panther. This exploit has raised me in N. esteem exceedingly, tho I claim no merrit from it being meerly accidental.

Indian Country, Tuesday, Septr 12th 1775

Our Squaws are very necessary fetching our horses to the Camp and Saddleing them makeing our fire at Night and cooking our victuals, and every other thing they think will please us. Traveled over several barren mountains some of them produces great plenty of wild Grapes. Lodged in an old Indian Camp. Bad water. *13th* Met John Gibbson and an Indian going to hasten the Indians to the Treaty. Dined at Mr Gibbsons. Camped at the mouth of a small run ten miles from Fort Pitt.

Fort Pitt, Thursday Septr 14th
Got to Fort Pitt about noon. Left our Girls among the Indians that are come to the Treaty. Great number of people in Town come to the Treaty.[59]

Terrible news from the Northward but so confused I hope there is little truth in it.
15th Very few of the Indians come in Yet the Commissioners has been waiting for them a week. Shall be obliged to stay here some time to see the Treaty.
16th Got acquainted with Mr Ephraim Douglass an Indian trader find him sensible and an agreeable Companion.[60] N. Finished my Leggings and Mockeysons—very neat ones.

Fort Pitt, Sunday September 17th 75
Here is members of Congress to treat with the Indians. Delegates from the Conventions of Virginia & Pensilvania for that purpose and Commissioners from the Convention of Virginia to settle the accounts of the last Campaign against the Indians. All Colnls, Majors or Captains and very bigg with their own importance.[61] Confound them alltogether. Collonial disputes are very high between Virginia & Pensilvania and if not timely Suppresed will end in Tragical consequences.

Fort Pitt, Monday September 18th 1775
Spent the day in Co with Mr Douglass.
19th No news of the Indians, the Commissioners are afraid they will not come at all.
20th N. uneasy at parting with me obliged to promise her to return in two Moons.
21st Great Commotions among the people about the Boundaries of Pensilvania, Virginians imprisoning the Magistrates in the Pennsylvania Intrest. Expect some lifes will be lost on the occasion.
22nd Begin to be very uneasy to stay her[e] doing nothing but cannot get my affairs settled as the Furs are not yet come.

Fort Pitt, Saturday, September 23rd 75
In the Afternoon with Mr Douglass and some of the Pennsylvania party to see a rejectment served. A disagreeable scene between the partys.
24th Sunday. Nothing but quarreling and fighting in every part of the town.
25th Informed that the Shawnee Indians were at Logstown. Went over the Allegany River with Mr Douglass to get Island Grapes. This is a small Grape

and grows on low vines on the Gravilly beeches and Islands in the River. But the most Delicious Grape I ever eat.

Fort Pitt, Tuesday September 26th

This morning N. informed me that the Indians wou'd come to the Council fire. About noon the Shawnee & Dellaware Indians with one of the Ottawa Chiefs crossed the River in two Canoos about thirty in number. They was met at the River side by the Delegates and Garrison under arms who saluted them with a Volley, which the Indian Warriours returned then proceeded to the Council house. Danceing, Beating the Drum, and Singing the Peace Song, all the way.[62]

When they got to the Council house the Danceing ceased and all tooke their place according to Seniority, and a profound silence ensued for the space of ten minutes. One of their old men then got up and spoke a few words to the Delegates signifying that he hoped they shoud brighten the Chain of Friendship and gave them a small string of white wampum several others spoke and gave Wampum. Then they lighted a pipe and smoaked with every one in the house out of one pipe. The Delegates had an artfull speech prep[are]d for them and adjourned the Business til tomorrow.[63] The Indians seem a little confused.

The following is the Distances from this place to the mouth of the Missisippi River.

Distances from Fort Pitt to the Mouth of the Missisippi[64]

		Miles	Sum	Lattd
Fort Pitt at the head of the Ohio R.				40°21"
To Loggs Town	S. W.	18½	18½	
Bigg Beaver Creek	S. W.	11¾	29¼	
Little·Beaver Creek	S. W.	21¾	42	
Yellow Creek	S. W.	10	52	
Mingo Town	S. W.	18½	70½	
Cross Creek	N. E.	2½	73	
Wheeling Creek, or Fort Fincastle	E.	24¾	98	
Grave Creek	E.	10	108	
To the begining of the long Reach		16	124	
To the end of the long Reach		13	138	
Muskinghum River	W.	23	162	
Little Kanhaway, or Conhaway River	E.	11¾	173¾	
Hockhoking River	W.	13¼	187	
Bigg Kanhaway, or Conhaway River	E.	80	267	
Giandot Creek	E.	42	309	
Big Sandy Creek	E.	13	322	
Siato River	W.	45	367	38°°22"
Big Buffaloe Lick, or Salt Spring Ck	E.	24	391	
A Large Island		20	411	
Little Miamme River	W.	82½	493½	
Licking Creek	E.	8	501½	

Big Miamme River	W.	27½	529	
Elliphant Bone Lick	E.	22½	561½	
Kentuckey River	E.	44	605	
Fall of the Ohio River		78	683	38°°08"
Falls of the Ohio from F Pitt			683	38°°08"
The low Country now begins		155	836	
First of the Five Islands		45	883	
Green River	E.	27	913	
Great Island		58	961	
Ouabash River	W.	40	1001	
Great Cave	W.	62	1063	
Shawana River	E.	33	1096	
Tennesee or Cherakee River	E.	12	1108	
Fort Messier	E.	11	1119	
Mouth of the Ohio River		46	1165	37°°00"
To the Chickasaw hills	E.	210	1374	
To the Mountains		63	1437	
To St Francis River	W.	67	1504	
White River		108	1612	
Arkinsaw River				
Ross's Creek		228	1840	
Yazou's River	E.	65	1905	
To the Grand Gulph		66	1971	
To the Little Gulph		18	1989	
To Collins's		9	1998	
To Fort Natchez		30	2028	
To Point Coupee		153	2181	
To New Orleans		156	2337	
To the Mouth of the Missisippi		96	2433	

Fort Pitt, Wednesday September 27th
The treaty renewed to day when the Ottaway Chief made one of the best speeches I ever heard from any man. Determined to get a Coppy of it if possible. My Landlady informs me that I am likely to be took up for a Spy by the Dellegates.
28th My peltry arived this day which I sold to Mr Anderson, but find I shall be a Looser upon the whole. Determined to leave the town on Monday.
29th The Indians seem displeased at something. Meet in the Council house every day.

Fort Pitt, Saturday September 30th 75
Went over the River and bought a Porcupine Skin of an Indian. It is something like our Hedghog at home only the Quills are longer the Indians die them of various colours and work them on their trinkets. Mr Edward Rice promised me

his horse to carry me to V. Crafords on monday next. Sold my Gun to Mr James Berwick, who gave me a Coppy of the Indian speech. Saw the Indians Dance in the Council house. N. very uneasy she weeps plentifuly. I am unhappy that this Honest Creature has took such a Fancy to me.

Fort Pitt, Sunday, October 1st 1775
Took leave of most of my acquaintances in town. Mr Douglass gave me an Indian Tobacco pouch made of a Mink Skin adorned with porcupine Quills he is desirable of keeping a Correspondence with me which in all probabillity will be for the interest of us boath. I have conceived a great regard for the Indians and realy feel a most sensible regret in parting from them however Contempttible opinion others may entertain of these honest poor Creatures.

If we take an impartial view of an Indians general conduct with all the disadvangages they labour under, at the same time Divest ourselves of prejudice, I believe every honest mans sentiments would be in favor of them. As soon as an Indian comes into the World he is tied with his back to a Board which serves for bed and Cradle and by puting a string through the end of the board next his head is very conveniently conveyed from place to place on his mothers Back.

He is kept in this posture til half a year old, but often plunged in the water in Summer and roled in the Snow in the Winter, he is then set at Liberty to walk as soon as he can. Their youth is never troubled with surly Pedagogues to whip their sences away for they are entirely unacquainted with Letter or Figures the little knowledge they have of past times is handed to them by Hyeroglyphics or Tradition subject to numberless errors and misrepresentations.

Hunting is their diversion as well as support and in this they are initiated early in life. There is established in each Nation a Species of Government which I cannot just now find a name for. It is neither Despotic, Aristocratical or Democratical but rather a compound of the two last their Kings has no more honor or respect payed them then another man, and is Obliged to hunt for his liveing as well as the rest. Except in Council or War [the last two words appear to be scratched out] he has a right to speake first. And if he be an Old man in whose abilillities they can confide his advise is generally observed.

In War he acts as General. When anything of Consequence is to be done the whole nation is Convened at the Council house built for that purpose, every one has a right to speak but it generally left to the Old men to debate the matter, as they pay the greatest attention to the voice of wisdom which experience has confered on the Aged, every thing is conducted with the greatest regularrity & decorum, silence and deliberation, only one speakes at once, and then the most profound silence and attention is observed.

Those famed for Oratory have an opportunity of displaying their tallents to the greatest advantage. They express themselves in a bold Figurative stile, accompanyed with violent gestures tho exceedingly natural and well adapted to what they are saying and are in general as expressive as their words. Their Dress, Attitude, and Firmness of Countenance (when speaking) even to a person ignorant of their language Strikes his mind with something awful and his Ideas with something great and Noble.

The following speech shows they are not wanting in words.

Speech of Shaganaba, the Ottawa Chiefe[65]

Fathers,

From the information of the people at Detroit, With distrust I acceped [sic] your invitation, And measured my way to this Council fire with trembleing feet, Your reception of me, Convinces me of his falshood and the gounlessness [sic] of my fears, Truth and they have long been enemies. My Father and many of our Chiefs have lately tasted of death. The remembrance of that misfortune allmost unmans me, and fills my eyes with teares. Your kind condolence has lightened my Heart of its heavy burden, and shall be transmited to my latest posterity.

Here he gave a sting a White Wampum.

Fathers,

I rejoice to hear this day, what I have heard, And do assure you it shall be faithfully delivered to my Nation. Should you want to speak to me in future I shall joyfully attend, and now thank you for the present invitation. The particular favour shewed me, And the Gun you have given me, for the kindness I shewed your Brother, Young Fields, claims my warmest acknowledgments. I am conscious I did but my duty. He who barely does his duty merits no praise.

If any of your people Visit mine, wheather Curiosity or Business be their Motive, Or if unwillingly compeled by the strong hand of Victor, they shall find the same entertainment your Brother found. You inform me if my people Visit yours they shall meet with an hospitable welcom. My fears are done away I have not one doubt remaining. I will recommend it to my Young men to Visit and get acquainted with yours.

Fathers,

What has passed this day is too deeply engraved on my heart for time ever to erase.

I foretell that the Sunny Rays of this days Peace, shall warm and protect our childrens Children from the storms of misfortune. To confirm it give you my Right hand, That hand which never yet was given, but the Heart consented. That never shed Human blood in peace or spared an Enemy in War, And I assure you of my Friendship with a Tongue which never yet mocked at Truth, since I was of Age to know that Falshood was a Crime.

Here he gave a Belt of Wampum as a token of peace.

I think this speech would do honnor to an Orator of the first magnitude, allowances being made for the beauty's it looses in Translateing. The power of their King is rather perswasive than Coersive. He is rather reverenced as a Father than feared as a King. He has neither Revenue, Officers, or prison or can put any one to death or inflict any corporeal punishment on any of his people. One act of injustice woud pull him from the head of Affairs forever. No hereditary honors or tittles amongst them, an Indian has no method of render himselfe of consequence among his companions but by his superiority of personal qualifications of Body or mind, and are far from being such fools as they generally immagined to be. Though they have not the advantages of learning they by the light of natural reason distinguish Right from Wrong with the greatest exactness. They never mean deceit themselves and detest it in others nor ever place confidence a second time where it has been once abused. Indeed those that have conversed much with the whites have learned several things from them, that the natural honesty of the[m] their nature woud never have thought of in all their trade with the Europeans they are imposed on the grossest manner. Their sensibillity is quick and their passions ungoverned I may say ungovernable and it is not to be wondered at if they make returns in kind whenever it is in their power. It is said they are cruel and babarous and I believe they exercise some Cruelties the thought of which makes human nature shudder, but this to be attributed to their national customs, not to their natural disposition. it is a general opinion with Whitemen that the difference in colure and advantages of education gives them a superiority over these poor people which Heaven and Nature never designed, They are beings endowed with reason and common sense and I make not the least doubt but they are as Valuable in the eyes of their maker as we are, our fellow creatures and in general above our level in many Virtues that give real preheminence, however despicably we think of or injuriously we treat them.

Their persons are tall and remarkable straight of a Copper colure with long black hair regular Features and fine black Eyes. The dress of the men is short white linin or Callico Shirt which comes a little below their hips without buttons at Neck or wrist and in general ruffled, and a great number of small Silver broaches stuck in it. Silver plates about three Inches broad round the wrists of their arms, Silver wheels, in their Ears, which are stretched long enough for the tip of the Ear to touch the shoulder.

Silver rings in their noses, Breechclout, and Mockeysons, With a Matchcoat, that serves them for a bed at night. They cut of their hair except a lock on the crown of the head and go bareheaded, pluck out their Beards.

Their women weare the same sort of shirts as the men and a sort of short petticoat that comes no lower then the knee, Leggings and Mockeysons the same as the men, Weare their hair long Cued down the back in Silver plates if they can afford if not tied in a Club with red gartering no rings in the nose but plenty in the eares.

Both Men and women paints with Vermillion and other colures mixed with Bears Oil and adorns themselves with any tawdry thing they think pretty. Their language is Soft, Copious, and expressive. God in Delawar Walehak-maneta, the Devle, Maneta, Bread, Augh-pone. They cannot curse or swear in their own language (are obliged to the Europeans for that vice[)]. Religion, they have little amongst them and that seems to have something of the Jewish manner in it.

They have some particular dances at the full and change of the Moon, and sometimes pay a sort of adoration to the Sun. At certain periods the Women absent themselves from society for a few days and will not suffer any one to touch a rag of their cloaths or eat with them. Before they join their friends again they wash all their Cloaths and purify every vessel they have made use of with fire. Marriage is little observed as they live together no longer then they can agree. the Woman keeps all the Child[ren]. are absolute slaves to their Husbands. It is very rare for a couple lives all their life together without changing. Polygamy is is [sic] not allowed. They pay great respect to the dead particularly those that have rendered themselves Conspicuous in War.

Their houses are built of Logs or Bark with the fire in the middle, and benches on each side the house which serves for Chairs, Bed, and Table. In Summer they chiefly live in the woods, in Bark tents. Smoke much Tobacco mixed with the leafes of Shumack and is very pleasant, inclined much to Silence except when in Liquor which they are very fond of, and then they are very Loquacious commiting the greatest outrages on each other, the women allways hide all offencive weapons as soon as the men get intoxicated. And it is observed that they never all get drunk together, one of them will keep sober to take care of the rest. Their is upwards of Thirty diferent Nations nearly similar in customs and manner none of them very numerous.

Since Spirituous Liquors was introduced amongst them they have depopulated fast. Smallpox has made terrible havock.

John Monture a half Indian gave me the names of the following Tribes of Indians that he has been in their country

Chic-a-saws}	On the E. side of the Missippy
Cherakees }	and S. E. side of the Ohio
Catawbas }	
Creeks}	
Kus-kus-keighs	Hurons
Wau-we-aughthanees	Ottaw-ways
Py-ank-a-shees	Senekas
Twigh-twies	Mohawks
Pic-a-willanees	Cayugas
Shaw-nees	Onidas
Mingoes	On-on-di-gas
Wiandots	Missis sau-gas
Delawars	I-ro-quois
Poo-ta-wat-ta-mees	Tus-car-ro-ras

These are on the N. W. side of the Ohio on the Lakes.

Ark-in-saws	Kano-a-ti-noe }	Westward of the
Pa-dau-cas	Missauris}	Missisippi River

Am informed that the Delegates intend to examin my papers. I will prevent the Scoundrels if possible.

2nd Settled my affairs with Mr John Anderson. Who has behaved more like a Father then a common acquaintance. Made him a compliment of my Silver Buckles and agreed to keep up a corespondence. Parting with N. was the most affecting thing I have ever experienced since I left home the poor Creature wept most plentifully. However base it may appear to concientious people it [is] absolutly necessary to take a Temporary Wife if they travel amongst the Indians. Left Fort Pitt. Dined at Widdow Myers.[66] Got to Mr John De Camp.

West Augusta Virginia, Tuesday, October 3rd 1775
At Mr John De Camps, who absolutly refuses to let me go away til tomorrow.
4th Left Mr De Camps, lost my way several times, but got to V. Crafords in the evening.
5th At V. Crafords. Performed the part of a Clergyman at the funeral of an Infant. At the Grave the parents and friends, Wept and drank Whiskey alternately. V Craford promised to hire me a horse to carry me over the mountain before I went to Fort Pitt but I believe he never intends to perform.

West Augusta Virginia Friday, October 6th 1775
Went to Captn Gists to see if he coud assist me with a horse. He treated me very kindly but cou'd not furnish me with a horse. Lodged their.
7th Returned to V. Crafords. Find V. wants to take the advantage of my necessity. Experience teaches me adversity is the touchstone [of] friendship.
8th At V. Crafords, very uneasy my Cloaths wore out and my money allmost expended. I have made an unfortunate summers work of it but cannot tax myselfe with extravagance, but with a great deal of imprudence in the choise of my companion Rice.

West Augusta Virginia, Monday, October 9th 1775
In my way to Major Crafords, saw the Vestiges of an Old Fortification. It appears to me that this Country has been inhabited by a race of people superior in Millitary knowledge, to the present Indians. In different parts of the country their is the Vestiges of regular Fortifications, and it is well known the Indians have not the least knowledge of that art. When, or by whom, these places were built, I leave to more able Antiqurians, then I am to determine.

Fortunately for me Zacharia Connel is going over the Mountain tomorrow and will find me a horse to go along with him. returned to V. Crafords.

West Augusta, Virginia, Tuesday, October 10th 1775
Left V. Crafords, whom I believe to be a Scoundrel. Set out with Mr. Z. Connel for Winchester. Lodged at the Great Meadows at one Linches Tavern in Co with Colnl Lee, Colnl Peyton, Colnl Clapham, Colnl Blackburn, Colnl McDonald, and Mr Richard Lee All of them Commissioners from the Virginia Convention, for settling the accounts of the last Indian War.[67] A set of niggarly beings. Great want of beds but I am well content with the Floor & my Blanket.

Allegany Mountain, Wenesday, October 11th 1775
Crossed the Falling Timbers. Yough-a-agany River at the Great Crossing.[68] Laurel mountain. Breakfasted at Rices Tavern. Then over the winding Ridg, Crossed the Maryland line, and Negro Mountain. Lodged at Tumblestones Tavern, on the top of the Allegany mountain.

12th Crossed the little meadow mountain. Shades of Death, and the Savage Mountain. breakfasted at Tittles Tavern. Then to Gregs Tavern, Fort Cumberland now deserted and demolished, on Will's Creek and Potowmeck River. Got to Old Town in Maryland 14 Miles from Fort Cumberland. Lodged at one Rollins Tavern.

From Old Town to Mr Wm Gibbs, Friday October 13th 1775
This is a pretty little town for such an inconvenient situation, some good land about it first settled by [blank] Cresap an Englishman from Skipton in Craven.[69] Crossed the Potowmeck River at the conjunction of the North and South Branches met a Woman with two small Children in great distress on whom I bestowed my last Shirt except that I had on, crossed the Spring Gap mountain and Dined at Rinkers Tavern. Got to Mr Gibbs in the evening. Mr G. not at home. Two young Ladyes there who gaze at me as if I was a wild man of the Woods. Them and my raged Breeches caused me to spend a disagreeable evening.

Piedmont, Berkly County Virginia, Saturday October 14th 1775
Got up early this morning and mended my Breeches with a piece of my Shirtlap. Shaved and made myselfe as deacent as my circumstances woud admit.

After settleing with Mr Connel I had only one penny left. No money to [be] got at Mr Gibbs as he is not at home.

Went to Mr Nourses who makes me welcom and will assist me to Leesburg. *15th* At Mr Nourses, very genteelly entertained. Major Gates Lady[70] here on a Visit who insisted on me going to Church raged as my dress was. Mr Nours [sic] read prayers—no parson.

Leesburg Loudon County Virginia Monday October 16th 1775
Mr [Norse] lent me a horse to Leesburg where I arived in the evening. Lodged at Mr Moffets.
17th Went to Captn Douglasses in Co with Mr Cavan.[71] Captn Douglass agreed to pay one half of the expences I have been at and confirm the bargain, but this I will defer for sometime till their is a probabillity of these disputes being ended.
18th Slept very little last night it being the first night I have slept in a Bed since the 28th of April last. Got a Boy and horse from Captn Douglass to carry me to Alexandria. Returned Mr Nourse's horse by Mr F. Keys.[72] Set out for Alexandria in Co with Mr Charles Little. Dined at Mosses. Lodged at Mr Littles about 5 Miles from Alexdr.[73]

Alexandria, Virginia, Thursday, October 19th 1775
Got to Alexandria to Diner, found Mr Kirk very well, he was glad to see me expected that I was kiled by the Indians. A Letter from my Father dated Sepr 16th 74 which makes me very unhappy with one from Mr Latham of the same date. Every thing is in confusion all exports are stoped and hardly a possibillity of geting home. I have nothing to support me and how to proceed I do not know.

I am in necessity obliged to rely on Mr Kirks kind promises, this is disagreeable but I must submit to it.

Alexandria, Virginia, Friday October 20th 1775
Slept very little last night owing to my agitation of mind. To add to my distress the Moths has eat two suits of my Cloaths to pieces. Nothing but War talked off raising men and making every millitary preparation. A large Army at Boston, another in Cannada, and another at or about Norfolk in Virginia. This cannot be redressing grievances, it is open Rebellion and I am convinced if Great Brittain does not send more men here and subdue them soon they will declare Independance. C. T. M. P.

Alexandria, Virginia, Saturday Octr 21st 75
I am now in a Disagreeable situation if I enter into any sort of business I must be Obliged to enter into the service of these Rascals and fight against my Friends & Country if called upon. On the other hand I Am not permited to depart the Continent and have nothing if I am fortunate enough to escape the jail. I will live as cheap as I can and hope for better times.
22nd Sunday. No Church.
23rd News that Lord Dunmore was comeing up the River with four Thousand men to destroy the town. I am determined to get on Board the King's Ships as soon as possible.[74]

Alexandria, Virginia, October 24th 1775
The inhabitants begin to remoove their most Valuable efects out of town but I think it will proove a fals alarm.
25th Exceedingly uneasy. Mr Kirk does every thing in his power to make me happy.
26th News that Lord Dunmore had landed at Norfolk at [sic] seized 50 Guns and spoiled all the Cannon there.
27th Suped and spent the evening at Captn Ramsays,[75] Great political dispute with him.
28th Mr Kirk went to Leesburg and left me to take care of his house and people. Very unwell this evening.

Alexandria, Virginia, Sunday October 29th 1775
A Violent pain in my breast this morning took a Dose of Salts which has took it away.
30th The people here are ripe for a revolt nothing but Curses and imprecations against England her Fleets, Armys, and Friends. The King is publicly cursed and Rebellion rears her horrid head The people r. his Colony and the Province of Maryland are in general grea[t]ly in debt to the Merchants in England and think a revolt woud pay all.

31st Understand I am suspected of being what they call a Tory (that is a Friend of my Country) and am threatened with Tar, Feathers, Imprisonment and the Devil knows what. Curse the Scoundrels.

Alexandria, Virginia, Wednesday Novbr 1st 1775
News that 300 people on the Eastern shore in Maryland had gone over to Lord Dunmore. The committee took an account of the Flour in town as they apprehend his Lordship will pay them a visit.
2nd Nothing remarkable.
3rd Determined to talk about the times as little as possible and slip away as soon as I can get an opportunity.
4th Captn McCabe came down and brought me a letter from Mr Kirk.[76]
5th Sunday. No preaching the people are too much taken up with the War.

Alexandria, Virginia, Monday, Novr 6th 1775
News that the Kings Ships had burned Falmouth in New Hampshire.[77] Some New England Masters of Vessels that lye here being the Anniversary of the Gunpowder plot, Had the Pope, Lord North, Barnard, Hutchinson and the Devil, burned in Effigy, after Carting them through the town with Drums & Fifes.
7th Nothing remarkable. 0 K. F.
8th Want of employment and my disagreeable situation makes my life misserable something must be done to get a liveing.

Alexandria, Virginia Thursday Novr 9th 75
At diner had a long Dispute with Doctor Jackson about the Origins of the present proceedings. I believe he was employed to draw me into a political dispute. I proceeded with great caution and timerrity. Most of the company agreed that I had the better of the argument. But never so much embarrased in my life. Which convinces me, tho parents take eversomuch pains to inculcate every virtue in the minds of their Children, they commit a great error by treating them too long as meare Children. I can experimentally proove that this System is attended with the worst consequences.

A severe restraint over youth, unless those in whom bad dispossitions are apparent, is the surest method to make blockheads of them, for they are thereby prevented learning to think and by appearing to make little of their opinion, smother every ray of genius, and almost every qualification, they possess and gives them such a diffidence of themselves as will make them appear, though possesed of the best understandings, unpolished clowns. A young allways under the eye of a severe parent and by his rigour restrained from enjoying those amusements, to which Youth are naturally addicted and from which a little indulgence would wean him, no sooner becomes his own master, then hurried on by those gratifications which his imagination has represented so delicious to him and generally plunges into excesses, which in a short time dissipates his fortune, ruins his health, and too often brings him an untimely martyr to his grave. Another ill consequence attending this conduct is that it is impossible to know their dispositions, without allowing them the liberty of acting as they chuse, in things of no material consequence, I mean when they are arived at the age of eighteen or twenty for at that time of life, their passions are just ripening when the bent and turn of their minds their good or bad dispositions will be seen and are easily brought to perfection or in a great measure extinguished. I am led into this train of thoughts by the many embarasments, this System, has frequently lay'd me under at different periods, and am convinced it will be a great obstruction to my future proceedings or advancement in life when I am in Co with people of equal or superior abillities or those of an unconstrained behaviour, tintured with a large share of assureance, my diffidence and timerrity is so great, that it renders me rediculous even when the discourse hapens to turn upon a Topick I understand as well as any of them. Mem) never to enter into Political disputes again till I have more impudenc[e] or am in a free Country.

   0   K. F.

NOTES

1. According to James Nourse, they were about seven miles from Fort Pitt. James Nourse, "Journey to Kentucky in 1775," *The Journal of American History*, 19 (1925): 123.

2. John Campbell was chosen a member of the Committee of Safety for "that part of Augusta County that lies on the west side of the Laurel Hill" on May 16, 1775. On March 4, 1777, he was appointed county lieutenant of Yohogania County, Virginia. He had been a merchant in Pittsburgh since at least 1767. Boyd Crumrine, *History of Washington County, Pennsylvania, with Biographical Sketches of Many of its Pioneers and Prominent Men* (Philadelphia, Pa.: L. H. Everts & Co., 1882), 74. H. R. McIlwaine, ed., *Journals of the Council of State of Virginia*, vol. 1, (Richmond, Va.: Virginia State Library, 1931), 358. Letter from John Campbell, Pittsburgh, October 28, 1768. Correspondence of Baynton, Wharton, & Morgan 1763-1783, (Pennsylvania Historical and Museum Commission, Harrisburg).

3. Alexander McKee, the son of an English trader and a Shawnee, was the British government's principal informant on the Indians of the upper Ohio. He had served in the French and Indian War and Dunmore's War. At this time McKee was deputy to Sir William Johnson, superintendent of Indian Affairs of the Northern District. He died in January 1799. In 1772 he had been appointed a justice of the peace in the newly formed county of Fincastle. Woody Holton, *Forced Founders: Indians, Debtors, Slaves, & the Making of the American Revolution in Virginia* (Chapel Hill, N. C.: University of North Carolina Press, 1999), 14, 24-25. William J. Van Schreeven and Robert L. Scribner, eds., *Revolutionary Virginia: The Road to Independence*, vol. 3, (Charlottesville, Va.: University Press of Virginia, 1977), 154-55, n. 8. Richard White, *The Middle Ground: Indians, Empires, and Republics in the Great Lakes Region, 1650-1815* (Cambridge, England: Cambridge University Press, 1991), 475. Benjamin J. Hillman, *Executive Journals of the Council of Colonial Virginia*, vol. 6, (Richmond, Va.: Virginia State Library, 1966), 505.

4. John Montour was the son of Andrew Montour, the son of a French father and Iroquois mother. Andrew was prominent in Indian-white relations on the frontier. James H. Merrell, *Into the American Woods: Negotiators on the Pennsylvania Frontier*, (New York: W. W. Norton & Co., 1999), 48, 54, 55, 294.

5. This was Benjamin Harrison. Bell and Harrison joined the party on April 29. This was probably the Robert Bell who accompanied George Washington on this trip down the Ohio in 1770. Bell lived near McKee's Island. Nourse, "Journey to Kentucky," *The Journal of American History*, 19 (1925): 123, 124. Donald Jackson, ed., *Diaries of George Washington*, vol. 2 (Charlottesville, Va.: University Press of Virginia, 1976), 294.

6. Little Beaver Creek enters the Ohio about 42 miles from Pittsburgh. Jackson, ed., *Diaries of George Washington*, 2: 282.

7. Yellow Creek enters the Ohio River about fifty miles below Pittsburgh. Nicholas B. Wainwright, ed., "Turmoil at Pittsburgh: Diary of Augustine Prevost, 1774," *Pennsylvania Magazine of History and Biography*, 85 (1961): 147 n. 107.

8. Fort Fincastle was built in the spring of 1774 under the management of Colonels William Crawford, Angus McDonald, and Dorsey Pentecost. It was lately renamed Fort

Henry. Thomas Perkins Abernethy, *Western Lands and the American Revolution* (New York: Russell & Russell, Inc., 1959), 107, 142.

9. George Rogers Clark had recently been hired as an assistant to the surveyor, Hancock Lee. Kenneth P. Bailey, *The Ohio Company of Virginia and the Westward Movement, 1748-1792*, (Glendale, Calif.: The Arthur H. Clark Co., 1939), 275. John Bakeless, *Background to Glory: The Life of George Rogers Clark* (Philadelphia, Pa.: J. B. Lippincott Co., 1957), 30-31. Allan W. Eckert, *That Dark and Bloody River* (New York: Bantam Books, 1996), 98-99.

10. Grave Creek, in Marshall County, West Virginia, took its name from the "Big Grave," a prehistoric Indian Mound in the vicinity. The town of Moundsville is at its junction with the Ohio River twelve miles below Wheeling. Reuben Gold Thwaites and Louise Phelps Kellogg, eds., *Documentary History of Dunmore's War* (Madison, Wisc.: Wisconsin Historical Society, 1905), 36 n. 64. C. W. Butterfield, ed. *Washington-Crawford Letter. Being the Correspondence between George Washington and William Crawford, from 1767 to 1781, concerning Western Lands,* (Cincinnati, Ohio: R. Clarke & Co., 1877), 26 n. 2.

11. The "long reach" is a fairly straight section of the river reaching approximately from Paden City to Raven Rock, West Virginia. It is about 18 or 20 miles long. Jackson, ed., *The Diaries of George Washington,* 2: 283. Thomas Hutchins claimed it was sixteen and a half miles long. Thomas Hutchins, *A Topographical Description of Virginia, Pennsylvania, Maryland, and North Carolina* (London: J. Almon, 1778), 6.

12. The Muskingum River enters the Ohio River from the Ohio side at Marietta. Jackson, ed. *Diaries of Washington,* 2: 283.

13. Fort Gower, named for an English earl, was built in September 1774 by Major William Crawford during Dunmore's War. It was on the east side of the Hockhocking River in what is now Ohio. It served as a base during Dunmore's War. Hockhocking River, now called the Hocking River, enters the Ohio from the west at Hockingport, Ohio. Thaites and Kellogg, *Dunmore's War,* 302. Butterfield, ed. *Washington-Crawford Letters,* 53. Otis K. Rice, *The Allegheny Frontier: West Virginia Beginnings, 1730-1830,* (Lexington, Ky.: University Press of Kentucky, 1970), 86. Hugh Cleland, *George Washington in the Ohio Valley* (Pittsburgh, Pa.: University of Pittsburgh Press, 1955), 258.

14. This is probably what George Washington referred to as the "Great Bend." Jackson, ed., *Diaries of Washington,* II, 283.

15. The battle Cresswell refers to was the Battle of Point Pleasant fought during Dunmore's War. It was a crucial victory for the Virginians and nine days later Lord Dunmore signed a treaty with Chief Cornstalk who gave all of the territory south of the Ohio River to Virginia. Point Pleasant, in present-day West Virginia, is where the Great Kanawha River enters the Ohio. Fort Blair was at Point Pleasant. John E. Selby, *The Revolution in Virginia: 1775-1783* (Williamsburg, Va.: The Colonial Williamsburg Foundation, 1989), 17. Reuben Gold Thwaites and Louise Phelps Kellogg, eds., *The Revolution on the Upper Ohio, 1775-1777* (Madison, Wisc.: Wisconsin Historical Society, 1908), 13.

16. Capt. William Russell was the commandant at Point Pleasant. Thwaites and Kellogg, eds., *The Revolution on the Upper Ohio,* 5-6.

17. James Nourse recorded: "breakfasted and dined with Capt. Russell, Lieut. Shelby, ensigns Roberts and Sharp, all very obliging. Capt. Russell much of the gentleman, here we learnt from Capt. Russell who had been up Sandy Creek to Clinch Settlement, for corn for the fort, that he had certain intelligence that the Indians had killed 4 and wounded 2 men upon Kentuke, the company all resolve to continue there rout[e],

myself undetermined, but having come so far loath to return without my errant." Nourse, "Journey to Kentucky in 1775," *The Journal of American History* 19 (1925): 126-27.

18. This may have been the same Charles Smith who had served in the First Virginia Regiment in 1754 and was entitled to 400 acres. W. W. Abbot, et al., eds., *The Papers of George Washington: Colonial Series*, vol. 9 (Charlottesville, Va.: University Press of Virginia, 1994), 143-46; 460-61.

19. Capt. Hancock Lee. See below entry for June 11, 1775.

20. In Bracken County Kentucky the creek was named for Matthew Bracken who surveyed the area with Hancock Taylor in 1773. He was killed at the Battle of Point Pleasant in 1774. Thwaites & Kellogg, *Dunmore's War*, 120.

21. John Filson described the Kentucky River as "amazingly crooked, upwards of two hundred miles in length, and about one hundred and fifty yards broad." John Filson, *The Discovery, Settlement and Present State of Kentucke* (New York: Corinth Books, 1962, reprint of 1784 edition), 13.

22. The son of Thomas Cresap, Michael was born in Maryland in 1742. He early set up as a trader and in 1772 had a store at Redstone. He came to the Ohio and made improvements on land claimed by George Washington. Commissioned captain by Lord Dunmore in June 1774, he served throughout the campaign. Cresap was accused of murdering the Indian chief Logan's family during that campaign. In the spring of the next year, he enlisted a rifle company of Maryland troops, and joined Washington at Cambridge. He died in October 1775 at New York City and was buried in Trinity Church Yard. Thwaites and Kellogg, *Dunmore's War*, 12. *Dictionary of American Biography*. Kenneth Scott, comp., *Rivington's New York Newspaper: Excerpts from a Loyalist Press, 1773-1783* (New York: New-York Historical Society, 1973), 123. Ewald Gustav Schankirk, "Occupation of New York City by the British," *Pennsylvania Magazine of History and Biography*, 10 (1886): 420.

23. Harrodsburg, also called Harrod Town, was founded on June 16, 1774, by James Harrod and abandoned soon afterwards. It was not reoccupied until March 15, 1775. John E. Kleber, ed., *Kentucky Encyclopedia* (Lexington, Ky.: University Press of Kentucky, 1992), 414.

24. This was George Noland. Nourse, "Journey to Kentucky," *Journal of American History* 19 (1925): 256.

25. John Clifton may have been the same person who patented 98 acres of land on the South Branch of the Potomac River. Hillman, ed., *Executive Journals of the Council of Colonial Virginia*, VI, 476. Joseph Boassiers was Joseph Brashier. Neil Hammon and Richard Taylor, *Virginia's Western War: 1775-1786* (Mechanicsburg, Pa.: Stackpole Books, 2002), 21. The other two men have not been identified.

26. In 1774 the College of William and Mary appointed Hancock Lee deputy surveyor to William Crawford, Surveyor for the Ohio Company. Hancock Lee and his brother, Willis Lee, founded in the town of Leestown on the Kentucky River in June 1775. Lee and Crawford completed the Ohio Company's survey in 1775. In April 1776 Willis Lee was killed by the Indians. Bailey, *The Ohio Company of Virginia and the Westward Movement, 1748-1792*, 324. Kleber, ed., *Kentucky Encyclopedia*, 542. Kenneth P. Bailey, "George Mason: Westerner," *William and Mary Quarterly*, Second series, 23 (1943): 417.

27. This was probably a plantation owned by Dr. John Briscoe (1717-1788) of Berkeley County. He came to the vicinity of Shepherdstown in 1733. He originally settled on land claimed by George Washington but moved to an adjoining tract. He was active in organizing the militia during the Revolution, and at one time acted as surgeon to a company. In 1780 he purchased Piedmont, near Charlestown, from the Nourse family

and lived there until his death in 1788. Danske B. Dandridge, *Historic Shepherdstown* (Charlottesville, Va.: The Michie Co., 1910), 304. Abbot, ed., *The Papers of George Washington, Colonial Series*, 9: 135. Cleland, *George Washington in the Ohio Valley*, 302.

28. David McClure was appointed Lieutenant Colonel of the Ohio County militia on March 4, 1777. On June 30, 1777, he was noted as Colonel David McClure on a receipt from David Shepherd. David Shephard Papers, Draper Manuscripts (Madison, Wisc.: State Historical Society of Wisconsin). McIlwaine, ed., *Journals of the Council of the State of Virginia*, 1: 358.

29. This may have been David Rogers who was appointed county lieutenant of Ohio County on March 4, 1777. McIlwaine, ed., *Journals of the Council of the State of Virginia*, 1, 358.

30. David Shepherd was born in January 1734 and died in 1795. He was the eldest son of Thomas Shepherd of Shepherdstown. David Shepherd settled near Wheeling before 1775. On May 5, 1775, he was appointed to the Committee of Safety for West Augusta and appointed colonel of the Ohio County militia on March 4, 1777. Dandridge, *Historic Shepherdstown*, 346. McIlwaine, ed., *Journals of the Council of the State of Virginia*, 1: 358. Thwaites and Kellogg, eds., *The Revolution on the Upper Ohio, 1775-1777* (Madison, Wisc.: Wisconsin Historical Society, 1908), 196 n. 30. Crumrine, *History of Washington County, Pennsylvania*, 74. *Virginia Gazette* (Pinckney), July 6, 1775.

31. Catfish Camp, named for Catfish, a Delaware Indian, who established a village here. It is now the site of Washington, Pennsylvania. Reuben Gold Thwaites and Louise Phelps Kellogg, ed., *Frontier Defense on the Upper Ohio* (Madison, Wisc.: Wisconsin Historical Society, 1912), 6 n. 7.

32. Redstone Fort was in what is now Fayette County, Pennsylvania. It was at the mouth of Redstone Creek on the Monongahela River, about 37 miles from Pittsburgh. W. W. Abbot, et al., eds., *The Papers of George Washington, Colonial Series*, vol. 10 (Charlottesville, Va.: University Press of Virginia, 1995), 50, 257. Wainwright, ed., "Turmoil at Pittsburgh" *Pennsylvania Magazine of History and Biography*, 85 (1961): 149.

33. Thomas Brown was appointed Lieutenant Colonel of the Yohogania County militia on March 7, 1777. H. R. McIlwaine, ed., *Journals of the Council of the State of Virginia*, 1: 358.

34. This was Michael Cresap who operated a store at Redstone Fort. Wainwright, "Turmoil at Pittsburgh," *Pennsylvania Magazine of History and Biography*, 85: 149. See note 22 above.

35. Thomas Gist arrived on the frontier with his father, Christopher Gist, in the 1750s. After his father's death in 1759, Thomas took over his plantations, which he called Monongahela, at the foot of Laurel Hill, near present-day Mount Braddock, Pennsylvania. Jackson, ed., *Diaries of George Washington*, 2: 289.

36. The engagements referred to were likely the Lexington and Concord affair (April 19) and the Battle of Bunker Hill (June 17). Richard B. Morris, ed., *Encyclopedia of American History* (New York: Harper and Row, Publishers, 1976), 101, 102-104.

37. William Crawford, surveyor and George Washington's agent, lived at Stewart's Crossing on the Youghiogheny River. Valentine Crawford was his brother. Alexander Scott Withers, *Chronicles of Border Warfare*, edited by Reuben Gold Thwaites (Cincinnati, Ohio: The Robert Clarke Co., 1908), 334. Edgar W. Hassler, *A History of Western Pennsylvania during the Revolution* (Pittsburgh, Pa.: J. R. Weldin & Co., 1900), 10.

38. Alexander Belmain (1740-1815) was ordained in England and on Oct. 23, 1772, received £20 towards his passage to Virginia. He came to Virginia as a tutor in the family of Richard Henry Lee and in 1773 he became curate of Augusta Parish, Augusta County,

Virginia. He served as a chaplain in the Virginia line throughout the war. Public Record Office, Treasury: General Accounts, Quarterly, T33/161; Treasury: General Accounts, Auditor's Declarations, T31/284. (Public Record Office, London.) All references to records in the Public Record Office are on microfilm in the John D. Rockefeller, Jr. Library, Colonial Williamsburg Foundation, Williamsburg, Va. Robert G. Albion and Leonidas Dodson, eds., *Philip Vickers Fithian: Journal, 1775-1776* (Princeton, N. J.: Princeton University Press, 1934), 180.

39. James Berwick was appointed ensign in Capt. Neville's company on November 22, 1775. He served as clerk to the West Augusta Committee of Safety in 1775 and 1776. In 1779 he was noted as being Judge of the General Election in Westmoreland County, Pennsylvania. McIlwaine, ed., *Journals of the Council of the State of Virginia*, 1: 32; 2: 482. Robert L. Scribner and Brent Tartar, eds., *Revolutionary Virginia: The Road to Independence* 6: 245, 324, VII, 568, 762. *Pennsylvania Archives*, 6th ser., 11: 405.

40. John Gibson was born in Lancaster County, Pennsylvania in 1746. He served in the French and Indian War under General Forbes. After the war he engaged in the Indian Trade. His Indian wife, Logan's sister, was killed at Yellow Creek. David Jones, who met Gibson in 1773, described him as a man "both of sense and learning." In 1775 he was appointed to the Committee of Safety for "that part of Augusta county that lies on the west side of the Laurel Hill at Pittsburg." Later he was judge of Alleghany County, Pennsylvania, and served as secretary of the Indiana territory. He died in 1822. *Virginia Gazette* (Pinckney) July 6, 1775. Thwaites and Kellogg, *Documentary History of Dunmore's War*, 11, n. 6. David Jones, *A Journal of Two Visits Made to Some Nations of Indians on the West Side of the River Ohio in the Years 1772 and 1773* (New York: Arno Press, 1971. Reprint of the 1774 edition), 63.

41. This may have been the John Minter who commanded a company in William Crawford's expedition against the Wyandots in 1782. E. M. Sanchez-Saavedra, *A Guide to Virginia Military Organization in the American Revolution, 1774-1787*, (Richmond, Va.: Virginia State Library, 1978), 146-47.

42. Wood, one of the commissioners of Virginia appointed to treat with the Indians, was sent on a tour of the Indian towns north of the Ohio to explain the nature of the problem with Britain and to ascertain sentiments and to invite them to Pittsburgh where they would hammer out a treaty with the colonies. James Wood's journal of his trip to the Indians is printed in Thwaites and Kellogg, *The Revolution on the Upper Ohio, 1775-1777*, 34-66. Wood was governor of Virginia, 1796-1799. Solon J. Buck and Elizabeth Hawthorn Buck, *The Planting of Civilization in Western Pennsylvania* (Pittsburgh, Pa.: University of Pittsburgh Press, 1979), 181-82. Emily J. Salmon, ed., *Hornbook of Virginia History* (Richmond, Va.: Virginia State Library, 1983), 77, 160.

43. This was either John Madison, clerk of Augusta, or his son John Madison, Jr. who was later deputy clerk of West Augusta. Scribner and Tartar, eds., *Revolutionary Virginia: The Road to Independence*, 3: 480.

44. John Anderson was appointed a member of the West Augusta County Committee of Safety on May 16, 1775. Scribner and Tartar, eds., *Revolutionary Virginia: The Road to Independence*, 3: 137.

45. Arthur St. Clair (1737-1818) was at this time a colonel of a Pennsylvania militia unit. In January 1776 he was appointed colonel of the 2nd Pennsylvania Battalion. James Wilson (1742-1798), a signer of the Declaration of Independence, was elected colonel of the 4th Battalion of Cumberland County associators and on May 6, 1775, was elected to the Continental Congress. In August and September of 1775 his duties included dealings with the western Indians. He was in Pittsburgh at this time to attend the conference with

the western Indians. Mark M. Boatner, III, *Encyclopedia of the American Revolution* (New York: David McKay Co., Inc., 1974), 956-57; 1212-14.

46. White Eyes' house was on Big Beaver Creek. White Eyes was murdered by American militiamen in 1778. For a discussion of his career see White, *The Middle Ground,* 360-62, 385. R. Douglas Hurt, *The Ohio Frontier: Crucible of the Old Northwest, 1720-1830* (Bloomington, Ind.: Indiana University Press, 1998), 88.

47. A Delaware Indian, Killbuck, or Gelelemind, a grandson of Newcomer, was born in the Lehigh Water Gap sometime in 1737. He moved west with his tribe where he was noted for his friendship with the whites. Killbuck succeeded Netawatwees as chief at Coshocton. He died in 1811. Thwaites and Kellogg, *The Revolution on the Upper Ohio,* 30. Hurt, *The Ohio Frontier: Crucible of the Old Northwest, 1720-1830,* 87. Michael N. McConnell, *A Country Between: The Upper Ohio Valley and its Peoples, 1724-1774* (Lincoln, Nebr.: University of Nebraska Press, 1997), 251-52. Frederick Webb Hodge, ed., *Handbook of American Indians North of Mexico,* vol. 1 (New York: Pageant Books, Inc., 1959), 489.

48. Welhik Thuppeek, or Schoenbrunn, was selected as a townsite by David Zeisberger in 1772. Russell H. Booth, Jr., *The Tuscarawas Valley in Indian Days, 1750-1797* (Cambridge, Ohio: Gomber House Press, 1994), 100-101, 170. Edward G. Williams, ed., "The Journal of Richard Butler, 1775: Continental Congress' Envoy to the Western Indians," *Western Pennsylvania Historical Magazine,* 47 (1964): 156.

49. On August 27, 1775, David Zeisberger recorded in his diary: "We received a packet of congregational newsletters and letters from *Pittsburgh.* They had been in *Lancaster* since spring waiting for transportation." David Zeisberger, *The Moravian Mission Diaries of David Zeisberger, 1772-1781,* trans. Julie Tomberlin Weber, edited by Herman Wellenreuther and Carola Wessel, (University Park, Pa.: Pennsylvania State University Press, 2005), 283.

50. Gnadenhutten. Booth, *Tuscarawas Valley,* 174.

51. Newcomers Town, or Gekelemupechunk, had been the chief town of the Delaware tribe on the Muskigum. In 1771, Zeisberger reported there were about one hundred houses in the town but by 1775 it was nearly deserted. Thwaites and Kellogg, *Dunmore's War,* 36, n. 64; Earl P. Olmstead, *David Zeisberger: A Life among the Indians* (Kent, Ohio: Kent State University Press, 1997), 265-66.

52. White Eyes' Town was in what is now Coshocton County, Ohio. It was about six miles west of Newcomerstown. Williams, ed., "The Journal of Richard Butler, 1775," *Western Pennsylvania Historical Magazine,* 47 (1964): 155, note 3.

53. On this date someone recorded in the Gnadenhutten Diary: "Mr. Anderson came with a gentleman from Pittsburgh, and I received encouraging letters from the beloved Brethren Matthaus, Thrane, and Grube, and also from Europe from the dear Brother Johannes, dated Barby, the 1st of August 1774, containing the printed abridged historical report of the present Evangelical United Brethren under the Augsburg Confession." Quoted in Booth, *The Tuscarawas Valley in Indian Days, 1750-1797,* 176.

54. Newcomer was a very old Delaware chief said to have been born before 1700. He died at Fort Pitt in 1776 while attending a council. He was the grandfather of Killbuck. Williams, "The Journal of Richard Butler, 1775," *Western Pennsylvania Historical Magazine,* 46, 391, note 4.

55. The Indian boy was taken to Williamsburg by Dr. Thomas Walker to be educated at the College of William and Mary. Two years later James Slate, a Williamsburg tailor, was paid for making "Cloathes for Baubee an Indian youth at College." *Virginia Gazette* (D) November 18, 1775. Virginia Treasurer's Office Receipt Books TR 25 and October 9, 1777 – April 4, 1778, 418, (Library of Virginia).

56. Captain Wingenund (d. 1791) was captain of the Wolf clan. Wellenreuther and Wessel, eds., *The Moravian Mission Diaries of David Zeisberger, 1772-1781*, 611.

57. The map, drawn on sugar maple bark by Munsee Wingenund, a Delaware, represents the British forts in and near the Ohio in 1762. James H. Merrill mistakenly credits Cresswell with making the drawing. The drawing pictured by Merrill and McConnell is taken from William Bray, "Observations on the Indian Method of Picture-Writing" *Archaeologia* 6 (1782): 159. Cresswell sent Bray a copy of the "Indian Warmarks in February 1781. Draft letter, Nicholas Cresswell to William Bray, February 4, 1781. Repton Priory deed transcripts; Tymm family of Edale; Nicholas Cresswell of Edale, and miscellanea. Catalogue Reference D6230. Derbyshire Record Office. www.a2a.org.uk/search/documentxsl.asp?com=1&i=0&nbKey=1&stylesheet=xsl\A (Accessed August 13, 2005) McConnell, *A Country Between,* 185; Merrell, *Into the American Woods,* 196.

58. David Zeisberger wrote on this day "With several white people who passed through, we sent letters by way of Pittsburg to Lititz and Bethlehem." Quoted in Booth, *The Tuscarawas Valley in Indian Days, 1750-1797,* 175. Wellenreuther and Wessel, eds., *The Moravian Mission Diaries of David Zeisberger, 1772-1781,* 283-85.

59. William Trent, who arrived in Pittsburgh, reported that on his arrival he "met with Commissioners from the Continental Congress sent to treat with the Indians on behalf of the 13 united Colonies, likewise with Delegates from the Colony of Virginia, to settle the Disputes between that Government and the Shawnise." William Trent, Fort Pitt, October 15, 1775, to unknown. Intercepted Letters, 1770-1782, CO 5/40. (Public Record Office, London.)

60. Ephraim Douglass arrived in Pittsburgh about 1769 where he engaged in the Indian trade with Richard Butler and Devereux Smith. He became fluent enough in Indian languages to act as an interpreter. He was appointed regimental quartermaster to the 8th Pennsylvania Regiment in 1776. He later served as aide-de-camp to General Lincoln. He died in 1833. Clarence M. Burton, *Ephraim Douglass and his Times: A Fragment of History,* (New York: William Abbatt, 1910), 8-9. Francis B. Heitman, *Historical Register of Officers of the Continental Army* (Baltimore, Md.: Genealogical Publishing Co., Inc., 1982), 202.

61. During its last session on June 24, 1775, the House of Burgesses appointed Richard Lee, Francis Peyton, Josias Clapham, Henry Lee, and Thomas Blackburn commissioners to settle the accounts resulting from Dunmore's War of pay of the militia, "of all Provisions, Arms, Ammunition, and other necessaries, furnished the said Militia" for "that part of the County of Augusta which lies Westward of the Allegany Mountains, and for the Provinces of Maryland and Pennsylvania." John P. Kennedy, ed., *Journals of the House of Burgesses, 1773-1776,* vol. 13 (Richmond, Va.: Virginia State Library, 1905), 282-83.

62. The Virginia Indian Commissioners reported on September 26, 1775: "The Shawanese being Arrived the Commissioners received them with Drum and Colours and a Salute of small Arms from the Garrison" and conducted them to the Council House. Scribner and Tartar, eds., *Revolutionary Virginia: The Road to Independence,* IV, 143.

63. The Indian speaker was Cornstalk and Andrew Lewis spoke for the Virginians. Scribner and Tarter, eds. *Revolutionary Virginia: The Road to Independence,* 4: 143-44.

64. This list was probably copied from the calculations made by Thomas Hutchins in 1766 and a Mr. Hooper. David Jones wrote in 1772, "As Mr. Hooper favoured me with the distances of places [along the Ohio River], the calculations are theirs [i.e. Hooper and Hutchins]". Jones, *A Journey of Two Visits Made to Some Nations of Indians on the West Side of the River Ohio,* 21-22, 43. "The distances from Fort Pitt to the Mouth of the Ohio" were taken by Capt. Harry Gordon in 1766 and published in 1776. Pownall, *A*

Topographical Description... of the Middle British Colonies, &c., in North America (London, 1776). Beverly W. Bond, Jr., ed., *The Courses of the Ohio River Taken by Lt. T. Hutchins Anno 1766 and Two Accompanying Maps* (Cincinnati, Ohio: Historical and Philosophical Society of Ohio, 1942), 19-73. In November 1770 George Washington recorded in his diary a list which he said "was taken (by) one Mr. Hutching" that is substantially the same as the list recorded by Cresswell. Washington included a few places that Cresswell did not list but the distances are the same or very close. Washington noted the distance from Fort Pitt to the mouth of the Ohio as 1164 miles while Cresswell recorded 1165. Jackson, ed., *Diaries of George Washington*, 2: 318-19.

65. Shaganaba was the son of the renowned Ottawa chief Pontiac. A shortened and different version of Shaganaba's speech delivered on October 9th is recorded in the Commissioners' Report. The Commissioners' clerk, John Madison, Jr., recorded: "Fathers I thank you that you have Wiped the Tears from my Eyes the Sweat from my body and thoroughly cleansed me [.] I was at first Unwilling I Acknowledge to come to this Treaty from Evil reports I had heard and which I have now found to be falsehoods[.] my father and many other Cheifs [sic] have lately Tasted of Death[.] Accept my hearty thanks for your kind Condolence on that Occasion[.] I Present you my right hand in token that I rejoice to see you United nore [sic] shall my Children be untold of it[.] Accept this String of Wampum as a Pledge of my Sincerity and Freindship[.] my Fathers knew you but Unhappily are no more[.] I have now found the road to your Hospitable Mansions nor shall it be Untrodden by my People in the future." Scribner and Tarter, eds., *Revolutionary Virginia: The Road to Independence,* 4: 182, 183. Thwaites and Kellogg, *Revolution on the Upper Ohio,* 89-90.

66. The widow Myers (Miers) operated a tavern at Turtle Creek above Fort Pitt. Jackson, ed., *Diaries of George Washington*, 2: 280-81.

67. On June 24, 1775, the Virginia House of Burgesses appointed Richard Lee, Francis Peyton, Josias Clapham, Henry Lee, and Thomas Blackburn commissioners to settle the accounts for expenses incurred during Dunmore's War "in that part of County of Augusta which lies to the Westward of the Allegany Mountains, and for the Provinces of Maryland and Pennsylvania." The third Virginia Convention, on August 22, 1775, allowed the men to be absent for the remainder of the session. Kennedy, ed., *Journals of the House of Burgesses, 1773-1776,* 282-83. Scribner and Tartar, eds., *Revolutionary Virginia: The Road to Independence,* 3: 478. David J. Mays, ed., *The Letters and Papers of Edmund Pendleton, 1734-1803,* vol. 1 (Charlottesville, Va.: University Press of Virginia, 1967) 134-35.

68. The Great Crossing on the Youghiogheny River is near present-day Addison, Pennsylvania. Jackson, ed., *The Diaries of George Washington,* 2: 280.

69. Old Town was established by Thomas Cresap who purchased the land in 1740. It is near present-day Green Spring, Maryland. Lois Mulkearn, ed., *George Mercer Papers Relating to the Ohio Company of Virginia* (Pittsburgh, Pa.: University of Pittsburgh Press, 1954), 473.

70. Horatio Gates lived at Traveller's Rest not far from the Nourse family in Berkeley County. He wrote in March 1774: "Since I have been here, I have compleated a Snug little Dwelling, as you will Say when you see it, & a most Spacious Barn, Two things there is no farming without, & thank Heaven all is paid for. I have been Labouriously industrious to do all this, together with the necessary business of The Farm, indeed I lead a Life very different from you Elegant Virginia, as I seldom see Company, Drink little, & never Game." Paul David Nelson, *General Horatio Gates: A Biography* (Baton Rouge, La.: Louisiana State University Press, 1976), 35. Horatio Gates to John Winstone, Travelers Rest, March 15, 1774. (Chicago Historical Society, Miscellaneous Manuscripts.)

Microfilm in John D. Rockefeller, Jr. Library, Colonial Williamsburg Foundation, Williamsburg, Va.

71. This was probably Patrick Cavan who married Sarah Baker in Loudoun County on March 1, 1798. He would become Cresswell's close friend. Cavan and Cresswell witnessed a deed in Loudoun County Court on November 28, 1776. Cavan was appointed one of the trustees of the town of Leesburg in 1787. Mary Alice Mertz, compiler, *Marriages of Loudoun County, Virginia, 1757-1853* (Baltimore, Md.: Genealogical Publishing Co., Inc., 1985), 25. W. W. Hening, ed., *Statutes at Large,* vol. 12 (Richmond, Va.: George Cochran, 1823), 600. Loudoun County Court Deed Book L, 1775-1778, 236-38.

72. Francis Keys was appointed deputy clerk of Loudoun County on May 13, 1777, and on March 9, 1778, he took the oath of an attorney. Loudoun County Court Order Book G, 1776-1783, 42, 75.

73. Charles Little was later a major, probably in the Fairfax militia. Janice L. Abercrombie and Richard Slatten, *Virginia Revolution Publick Claims*, vol. 1 (Athens, Ga.: Iberian Publishing Co., 1992), 339.

74. At his time Dunmore was trying to reassert royal authority in Virginia but did not have the forces necessary. David Syrett, *The Royal Navy in American Waters, 1775-1783* (Hants, England: Scolar Press, 1989), 16-18.

75. This was probably William Ramsay, a member of the Fairfax County committee. Scribner and Tartar, eds., *Revolutionary Virginia: The Road to Independence,* 3: 69.

76. Capt. Henry McCabe was a landholder in Loudoun County and Alexandria. He died in 1780 or 1781. The Harry McCabe and "Mr Henry McCabe" Cresswell mentions on September 18, 1776 and March 17, 1777 respectively are references to Capt. McCabe's son. Loudoun County Court Order Book G, 1776-1783, 384. Abbot, ed., *Papers of George Washington*, Colonial Series, 10: 312-13. Hening, *Statutes at Large*, 10: 488.

77. Falmouth was destroyed on October 18, 1775. Boatner, *Encyclopedia of the American Revolution.* 359-61.

Chapter 3
Trapped by Revolution
November 9, 1775 to September 30, 1776

Journal By Nicholas Cresswell
of
Edale near Chapelinlefrith
Derbyshire, in England
Continued from Vol 2nd, Novbr 9th 1775
To September 30th 1776

Alexandria, Virginia, Friday Novr 10th 1775
This War is caried on by the Americans in the most curious manner. The name of liberty is most vilely prostituted under this sanction the Congress has perswaded the people to believe that paper Bills issued by them is transmuted into Real Gold and Silver after it has received their infallable emblem and Benediction. Their is some few heretics which dispute the Orthodoxy of this doctrine but if it is in the power of prisons and persecution to convince them of their mistaken notions, I believe it will not be wanting. Their emblems and Mottos on their Bills are well addapted

On the 8 Dollar bills their is the figure of an harp, with this motto - Majora minoribus consonant (The greater and smaller ones sound together) On the 4 Dollar bills is impressed, a Wild Boar runing on the spear of the hunter, with this motto, Aut mors, Aut Vita Decora Either death or life is glorious. On the three Dollar bills is drawn an Eagle on the wing pouncing on a Crane, who turns upon his back, and receives the eagle on the point of his long bill, which pierces the eagle's breast, with this motto, Exitus indubio est (The event is uncertain[)]

On the 5 Dollar bills we have a thorny bush which a hand seems attempting to eradicate. The hand seems to bleed, as if pricked by the spines. The motto is, Sustine vel abstine (Which may be rendered, Bear with me, or let me alone, or thus, Either support, or leave me. On the six Dollar bills is the Figure of a Beaver, gnawing a large tree, with this motto, Perseverando, (By perseverence) on the 2 Dollar bills, is the figure of a Hand and flail over sheaves of wheat, with this motto, Tribulatio ditat (Thrashing improves it.)

On the one Dollar bills is the plant Acanthus, sprouting on all sides under a weight placed upon it, with the motto, Dipressa resurgit. Tho' oppressed it rises. The 7 Dollar bills have for their device, a Storm descending from a Black heavy Cloud with this motto, Serenabit—It will clear up. The 30 Dollar bills have a Wreath of Laurel on a marble monument, or Alter, the motto, Si recte facies,—If you act rightly. The Congress have issued Two Million of Dollars in these bills for the support of the present War. It is to be sunk by the sale of Land, in Terra Incognita.

Alexandria, Virginia, Saturday, Novbr 11th
News—Chambly taken.[1]
12th Sunday. Mr Kirk returned home and is well pleased with my management in his absence.
13th Mr V. Craford called to see me, and Lodged with me at Mr Kirks.
14th Nothing remarkable.
15th No prospect of geting home this winter as I am suspected of being a Spy. I am very narrowly watched. Agreed to go to Leesburg to assist Mr Kirks Bookkeeper to settle his books but this must be kept a profound secrcret that I am any ways employed by him tho I receive no wages, only my board, such is the fassion of the times.

Alexandria, Virginia, Thursday, Novbr 16th 75
No news. Hope General How has given them a drubing [which] makes them so quiet.
17th Left Alexandria. Dined at Mosses. Got to Leesburg in the evening. Lodged at Mrs Sorrels,[2] with Mr Cavan.[3]
18th At Leesburg spent the Evening with Captn Douglass, Mr Johnston, Mr J. Booker[4] and Cavan, at a Turkey feast in the neighborhood.
19th Went to Church, or Courthouse which you please, in the forenoon, spent the evening at Mr George Ancram's.[5]
20th Spent the Evening at Captn McCabes great disturbances for want of Salt.
21st Nothing remarkable.

Leesburg, Loudon County, Virginia, Novr 22nd 1775
Find Cavan to be a good natured serious young man and his sentiments agree with mine. Spent the evening at George Johnstons.[6]
23rd Very uneasy Dam the Rascals. Ile think no more of them.
24th News—that St Johns was took and 500 prisoners in it and that Major Connolly was taken in disguise at Frederick town in Maryland.[7]
25th Spent the evening at Captn McCabes in Co with Captn Douglass and Cavan.
26th A methodist meeting in town!
27th Spent the evening at Mr Johnstons with Hugh Nielson & Cavan.
0 P. B.

Leesburg, Loudon County, Virginia, Tuesday Novr 28th 1775
Nothing worth notice.
29th Dined at Captn McCabes, spent the Evening at the store in Co with Captn McCabe & Captn Jo Speake and all of us got drunk.[8]
30th Dined at Captn Douglasses, being the aniversary of St Andrew the Titular Saint of the Scotch, in Co with Captn McCabe, Messrs Cavan, Booker, Johnston, Neilson, & McIntire,[9] we had had one of the best diners I have ever seen in America. Spent an agreeable day but find myself low spirited in short allmost stupid sometimes continually unhappy.

Leesburg, Loudon County, Virginia, Friday Decr 1st 75
Dined at Captn Douglasses, Got to town in the evening which I spent with an honest Quaker, One Matthews. News that Quebeck was taken, by the Rebels but I believe it to be D--d lye.[10]
2nd Nothing remarkable.
3rd Sunday. No preaching in town!
4th Left Leesburg in Co with Mr Matthews and Mr James Booker. Dined at Nolands Ferry[11] where we crossed the Potowmeck and went to Fredericktown in Maryland. This is a smart town a small manufactory of Stockings and Guns. A Dutch Church and an English one, with a poor house and several very good buildings. The inhabitants are chiefly Dutch. It is 25 miles from Leesburg. Lodged at Charltons Tavern.

Leesburg, Loudon County, Friday, Decbr 5th 1775
Went to see Major Connoly, who is prisoner at Fredericktown, but obliged to get one of the Committeemen to go with me, they woud not trust us alone. Found him in good spirits he was bound to Detroit and had one Smith and Cameron with him to raise a Regmt their and meet Lord Dunmore at Alexar in the spring.[12] Left Fredericktown. Dined at Nolands Ferry got to Leesburg at night.!
6th 7th 8th & 9th Nothing remarkable
10th Sunday. Went to Church. spent the evening at Mr Johnstons with the Revd Mr David Griffiths[13] and several Gentlemen.
11th Court day—no business done, every thing in confusion. Wrote to Fort Pitt by V. Craford.

Leesburg, Loudon County, Tuesday, Decbr 12th 75
Nothing remarkable!
13th 14th 15th and 16th Nothing worth mentioning.
17th Went to hear, Bombast, Noise and Nonsense, uttered by a methodist and an Annabaptist preacher. spent the evening at Mr G. Johnstons.
18th 19th 20th and 21st Nothing but lyes in paper.
22nd Spent the evening at Captn McCabes in Co with George West Esqr. Find him a Volatile flighty man.
23rd Very cold day, Freezing and snowing.
24th Went with Captn McCabe to Mr Wests about five miles from town—no news for several days.

Pea Hill, Loudon County, Monday Decbr 25th 1775
Christmas day, which we spent at Mr Wests.
26th After Diner went to Mr Wm Elzeys[14] but returned to Mr Wests at night.
27th The sharpest Frost last night I ever knew, we slept in a very small room and had a large fire it froze the urine in the pot which did not stand more than five foot from the fire.
   Left Pea Hill Mr West treated us with the greatest civillity. Went to town.

28th A methodist meeting in town great numbers of people came in slays. They are something like our sleds.   0
29th No news, an invitation to Captn Douglasses on monday next.
30th Nothing remarkable.

Leesburg, Loudon County, Sunday Decr 31st 1775
This is the last day of the year 1775 which I have spent but very indifferently, in short I have done nothing but wore out my cloaths and Constitution, and according to the present prospect of affairs, the nex[t] Year wears a forbiding aspect. I am here a prisoner at large if I attempt to depart and dont succeed a prison mus[t] be my lot, if I do anything to get a living perhaps I must be obliged to fight against my King & Country which my conscience abhors. I will wait with patience till summer and then risk a passage.

Garralland, Loudon County, Monday Jan 1st 1776
Went to Garralland the seat of Captn Wm Douglass, a great deale of agreeable Co and very merry.[15]
2nd At Garralland, Dancing and playing at Cards. In the evening several of the Co went in quest of a poor Englishman whom they supposed had made Songs, on the Committee, But did not find him.
3rd Went to Leesburg. Spent the Evening at Mr Johnstons.
4th Alarmed with some symtoms of the Itch.
5th This being my birthday, invited Captn McCabe, H. Neilson, Wm Johnston, Mathews, Booker, and my particular Friend P. Cavan to spend the Evening with me. We have kept it up all night and I am at this time very merry.

Leesburg, Loudon County, Virginia Jany 6th 1776
Spent the Evening at Mr Johnstons with our last nights Co. He is going to Camp. All of us got most feloniously Drunk. Captn McCabe, Hugh Neilson and I kept it up all night.
7th Sunday. Went to bed about two O Clock in the afternoon stupidly drunk. Not been in bed or asleep for two nights.
8th My last two days Conduct will not bear reflection. The uneasiness of my mind causes me to drink deeper when in Co to ellevate my spirits. Fatal remedy indeed.
9th 10th 11th 12th and 13th nothing remarkable.

Leesburg, Loudon County, Virginia, Sunday Jany 14th 1776
Went with Captn McCabe to Dine with Mr Mathew Cammel[16] about two miles from Town returned in the evening. No news.
15th Spent the Evening at Captn McCabes with Captn Jos Speake, who gives us certain accounts that Norfolk was burned on the 1st of the present and that there is a Vessel repairing at Alexandria bound for London with passengers. Determined to go down and take a passage tomorrow.

16th Left Leesburg in Co with Captn Speak. Dined at Mosses ordinary. Got to Alexandria. Mr Kirk informs me that the Vessel will not be permited to go to England or Ireland. No hopes of going in her. Mr Kirk advises me to keep my intention of going home a Secret or I am certain to be imprisoned. D--n the Rascals.

Alexandria Virginia, Wednesday January 17th 1776

Drank Coffee at Captn Harpers.[17] Spent the evening at Captn Speaks with Captn F. Speak and Denis Ramsay.[18] Two conceited ignorant Fops. No news, except it be lies.

18th A many of my old acquaintance looks very cool upon me because I will not be as great scoundrels as themselves. 0 K. F.

19th A pamphlet called Commonsense makes a great noise.[19] One of the vilest things that ever was published to the world. Full of false representations, Lies, Calumny, and Treason whose principles are to subvert all Kingly Government and erect an Indepen[d]ent Republic. I believe the Writer to be some Yankey Presbyterian, Member of the Congress. The sentiments are adopted by a great number of people who are indebted to Great Britain.

20th An odd adventure this evening / [?] / Think The Follies of Life are innumerable.

Alexandria, Virginia, Sunday, January 21st 1776

Nothing but Independence talked off.

22nd Nothing remarkable. ! M. 0 K.

23rd Last night the River froze over. Dined at Captn Conways[20] with Mr Buckhanhan. Drank Coffee at Mr Johnes's.

24th Left Alexandria. Dined at Mosses. Got to Leesburg in the Evening. 0 D. G.

25th and 26th Nothing but Indepen[d]ence will go down. The Devil is in the people.

27th This evening Mr Cavan and I salved for the Itch, and got very merry. Curse the disorder.

28th Sunday. Received a Letter from Mr Kirk advising that Lord Dunmore was comeing up the River as soon as the Ice wou'd permit him, and desireing us to send him all the Waggons that we can get. I wish his Lordship a safe Arival ! S.

Leesburg, Loudon County, Monday January 29th 76

All in confusion. The Committee met to chuse Officers for the new Cos that are to be raised. They are 21 in number the first men in the County and had two Bowls of Toddy, but could not find Cash to pay for it. Spent the evening at Captn McCabes.

30th Preparing for the reception of Mr Kirk and his people. Mr Hugh Neilson spent the evening at the store. News, that Quebeck was not taken, but that Montgomery had stormed it; he was kiled and his rabble defeated.

31st Nothing remarkable.

Leesburg Loudon County Virginia, Thursday Feby 1st 1776
Nothing remarkable.
2nd Find our Landlady to be a Thief. Determined to watch her narrowly.
3rd Spent the evening at the Tavern with Messrs Nielson, Booker, & Cavan. Mr Kirks goods arived in town.
4th Sunday. Methodist meeting in town.
5th Spent the evening at the tavern with Mr V. Craford.
6th Went with Mr Craford to Captn Douglasses but returned to town in the evening.
7th This day the town was alarmed with a Horsestealer being pursued through the streets several times. The poor fellow had neither Saddle or Bridle, but got away by swearing he had won the race.

Leesburg Loudon County, Virginia, Thursday Feb 8th
News, That Genrl. Lee was sent with 5000 men to reinforce the Rebbel Army at Quebeck. Spent the evening with Mr B. Call.
9th and 10th Nothing remarkable.
11th Sunday. Went with Mr Cavan & Mr Thos Matthews to a Quaker meeting, about 7 Miles from town. This is one of the most comfortable places of Worship I was ever in, they had two large fires and a Dutch stove. After a long silence and many groanes a Man got up and gave us a short Lecture with great deliberation.
　　　Dined at Mr Jos Janneys[21] one of the Friends. Got to Leesburg at night.

Leesburg Loudon County Virginia Monday Feb 12th 1776
Court day, great confusion, no business done. The populace deters the Magistrates and they in turn are courting the Rabbles favour. Enlisting men for the Rebble Army upon credit their paper money is not yet arived from the Mine. !. S.
13th Mr Kirk Arived in town informs me their is some hopes of a Reconciliation. I wish it may be true. 0 D. P.
14th Some thoughts of attempting to make Nitre out of the floors of Tobacco houses if I can effect it, it will gain me a little favour with the people and assist me in my escape from this hatefull Country. Mentioned it to Mr J. Booker who is wiling to join me.

Leesburg Loudon County Virginiu Thursday, Feb 15th 1776
Spent the evening at Captn McCabes with Mr Kirk & Cavan.
16th Breakfasted at Mr McCreas[22] with Mr Kirk, who advises me to attempt the Nitre. Mr K. returned to Alexandria.
17th Got some earth and fixed tubs as if I was going to make lye, of Ashes, which I intend to let stand two days before I draw it.
18th Dined at Captn Douglasses returned to town in the Evening.
19th Spent the evening at the Tavern with Messrs Nielson, Cavan, Booker, one Doctor McNichols and Doctor McGinnis.[23] A Confounded mad Frollick.

Leesburg Loudon County, Virginia, Tuesday, Feb 20th 76
Very sick with my last nights Debauch. Temperance is a most finished Virtue.
21st Boiled my lye and set it to cool, but am doubtfull of success.
22nd My success is greater then I expected am certain I can bring it to beare after a few trials. Went with Mr Booker and H Nielson to Garralland.
23rd Returned to Leesburg this morning. Mr Cavan went to Collect debts and left me to take care of the store.
24th and 25th Nothing remarkable 0.D.G.
26th A Report that Commissioners are arived at Philadelphia to settle Affairs with the Congress. Mr Cavan returned.

Leesburg Loudon County Virginia Tuesday, Feb 27th
Nothing remarkable.
28th Spent the evening at the store with Captn George Johnston & Mr Jos Janney. Captn Joh[n]ston informs me the[y] kiled 82 of the Kings troops at the great Bridge neare Norfolk, without haveing one man on their side kiled or wounded. this is very strange if it be true.
29th Spent the evening with Captn Johnston. Politics the general Topick, and Indepenence seems to be his favourite Scheme, and I believe it will be declared very soon. Exceeding Cold.
0. M. !. S.

Leesburg Loudon County, Virginia, Friday March 1st 1776
Some talk of a Reconciliation but am affraid it is not well grouned. Very unwell today.
2nd Spent the evening at the tavern in Co Booker, Cavan, Rispes[24] & Doctor McGinnis but was obliged to go home to bed Sick.
3rd Violent pains all over my body some Symptoms of a nervous fever.
4th Applyed to the Doctor who assures me it is a complication of the Nervous Fever and Rheumatism, gave me phisick.
5th 6th 7th 8th 9th 10th 11th 12th 13th 14th 15th 16th 17th 18th and 19th Confined to my room in violent pain. A little better today.
20th Able to walk about my room, this is the first day I have [been] ab[l]e to write since the 4th of the pres.

Leesburg Loudon County, Virginia, Thursday March 21st 1776
Much better but very weak. Takeing a Decoction of the woods. My spirits are good and I hope I shall get over this bout. News that the Great Sanhedrim, the Congress had given the Colonies liberty to trade with all nations but Great Britain and its Islands, And that they had begun to Bombard Boston.
22nd Free from pain, wraped myself up and went to see the general muster of the Malitia in town, about 700 men but few arms—great confusion among th[em].
23rd Am affraid I got cold yesterday violent pain in my Back & head.

Leesburg Loudon County, Virginia, Sunday, March 24, 1776
Confined to my room—the Doctor scolds me and brings more of his Damed No[s]trums.

25th 26th 27th 28th and 29th Confined to my room and greatest part of the time to my bed, unable to help myselfe. I am a little better to day able to walk about the room, but look like the picture of Famine.

30th Something better. News, that the Rebels had defeated the Kings friends under the command of Genrl McDonald at Widow More's Creek in South Carolina—part of Genl Lee's Body guard went through town.

31st News, That the English had evacuated Boston & gone to Sea. Hope it is a lie.

Leesburg Loudon County, Virginia, Monday April 1st 1776
A great deal better but weake, still continue to take the Doctors slop's, and he is for confining me another week to my room. Mr Kirk has wrote several kind letters to me, but Cavans kindness I shall never be able to repay.

2nd Captn McCabe and Mr West came to see me and stayed late, attending on them is of bad consequence to me at this time.

3rd Siting up last night has caused a relaps confound them both.

5th 6th 7th 8th and 9th Confined to my room.

10th Took a Violent sweat last night which has eased me of all pain and restored the use of my limbs. No news.

Leesburg Loudon County, Virginia, Thursday April 11th
Find myself much better. Confound the stupid Blockhead that he coud not prescribe a sweat sooner. I can walk about and eat heartily.

12th Agreed with Mr James Booker to join him in makeing Saltpeetre.[25] He is to find wood, earth, and Negros to work, and a house proper to boil it in. I am to find Boilers, tubs and have the managment of the work and go equal shares in the proffit, And pay him for my board at the Cattail.

Bought a Large kettle and three Rum Hhds to make tubs of and sent them to the place. I shall not be able to go to Sea if I had an opportunity this three months. This will take off all suspision and I can live cheaper then in town admit I make nothing by the business.

Leesburg Loudon County, Virginia, Saturday April 13th 1776
Much better. Rode to the Cattail (about a mile from town) Set four Tubs with earth for Saltpeetre, returned at Night believe my ride has done me good.

14th Sunday. Nothing but Methodist meetings in every part of the town.

15th I am now free from pain but very weak and feeble and not fit for anything. Mr Kirk is comeing here I am determined to go to the Cattail.

16th Prepareing to go to the Cattail Captn Douglass & Captn McCabe came to see me and spent the evening with me.

Cattail Loudon County, Virginia Wednesday April 17th
Left Leesburg. Went to the Cattail. Set my tubs a runing, but think it is to weake.
18th Got my pot fixed to boil the lye and other necessary matters.
19th Began to boil but find I must contrive some method of fixing the Volatile Salts or I shall make very little Nitre.
20th Set the tubs with fresh earth and put about half a bushel of wood ashes in the bottom of each. I am not able to beare much Fatigue.
21st Sunday. Mr Nielson & Mr Cavan came to see me. My hair begins to come off.
22nd A Violent headache, not able to do any thing.

Cattail Loudon County Virginia Tuesday, April 23th 1776
Much better. Boiling lye with the Ashes in it find it answer better then expectation.
24th Dined at Thomson Masons Esqr,[26] riding is of service to me if my strength wou'd bear it.
25th Set more tubs, and one with Ashes alone the Lye I intend to mix.
26th Went to Captn Douglasses returned at night.
27th Mixed the Nitrous Lye and the wood ash lye together which breaks like curds, but makes purer nitre, and more of it.
28th Sunday. Dined with Mr Kirk, who is come to live in Leesburg. He does every thing to encourage me. With great proffessions of friendship.
29th and 30th At Town very unwell.

Cattail Loudon County, Virginia Wednesday May 1st 1776
News. That a fleet fited out by Congress under the command of a certain Esack Hopkins,[27] a Yankey man, had made a Descent on New Providence in the West Indies, and tooke a considerable quantity of Cannon and millitary stores. In their passage back had met with the Glassgow man of War and made her runaway.
2nd Find by mixing the Nitrous Lye with about one third part strong Wood ash lye, fixes the Nitre and prevents its flying off in Air.
3rd Am affraid my partner will be dilatory.
4th Sunday. Experiments tried today but none answers, so well as that on Thursday last which I am determined to pursue.

Cattail Loudon County, Virginia, Sunday May 5th 76
Went to town which was rather more then I can well bear am so weak. Mr Kirk lend me his mare for the Summer. No news.
6th 7th 8th 9th 10th and 11th Employed at home I shall make bread and something more.
12th Went to town returned in the evening.
13th 14th 15th and 16th Employed at home. News that Mr John Goodrich a Merchant in Norfolk was confined in Williamsburg jail with 100 wt of Irons upon him. This is persecution with a witness.[28]

17th This day is appointed by the Great Sanhedrim, to be kept an Holy Fast throughout the Continent.[29] But we have no prayers in Leesburg—the parson is gone into the Army.

Cattail Loudon County, Saturday May 18th 76
Employed at home. No news.
19th Went to town nothing but Methodist preaching, hypocrisy and nonsence.
20th Employed at home.
21st Dined at Mr Kirks. Bespoke some new cloaths, as mine begins to be shabby, and it is absolutely necessary to keep up a genteel appearance, tho I can badly afford it.
22nd and 23rd Employed at home.
24th After I had finished my work for the day was seized with a most violent pain in my Back & Head.
    A Great Riot in town about Torys. Mr Cavan obliged to hide himself.

Cattail Loudon County, Virginia, Saturday May 25th 76
The pain continues but not with such violence as at first.
26th Sunday. Something better, rode to town, got a Vomit from Mr Kirk which I intend to take in the morning.
27th Took the Vomit which has give me some ease at the Stomach.
28th A pain in my head and Feverish have nothing proper to nourish me or any thing to be got. Curse the Country.
29th 30th and 31st Very ill and exceeding[ly] low spirited. Nobody to dress a mouth full of Victuals fit for a Dog to eat.

Cattail, Loudon County Virginia, Saturday, June 1st 1776
Weak and fainty with pain in my limbs.
2nd Sunday. Something better, went to town and Dined with Captn McCabe.
3rd Set 4 Tubs of fresh earth.
4th Dined at Mr Masons, where I saw the part of a Horned Snake skin about 5 foot long. This is the most venomous Snake that is known. It is covered with scales like a fish, Black and white on the Back, the belly white, with a small horn in it's tail like a Cockspur, from whence it takes it's name. It does not crawl on its belly like other snakes but tumbles tail over head and by that meanes strikes it Horne into it's enemy which is of such a Poisonous nature it is instant death. I have been informed by several creditable persons some of them ofers to sweare that if it strikes it[s] horne into a tree in full Leafe it withers and dies in twenty four hours. I never saw this, but have not the least reason to doubt the truth of it. They had cut the head off this snake, they tel me it had small horns, and was about 9 foot long, when they had disabled it, it roared like a Calf. The Rattlesnake is scaly, the Back variegated with Black and Yellow, in an angular manner, the Belly White, the head Black and Green with the brightest Eye I ever saw in any Creature on earth.

It has a power of extending its mouth at pleasure furnished with 4 teeth crooked like a Cats claw with these they bite and introduce the venom which is of a Yellow colour into the wound, they only use them as weapons of defence, as they never mastigate their food but swallow Rabbits and Birds whole, after they have anointed them with their Saliva. Their Rattle is a sort of drye horny substance joined together very curiously, it is said they have an additional one every year. I have seen some with ten of [them], they generally rattle at your approach and are easily avoided. People that travels much in the Woods weare Leggings of coarse woollen Cloath which their teeth cannot get through. Neither them or the Horned Snake propagate by eggs, But bring their young entire, they all disappear in winter. Here is several other Snakes, as the Copper snake very like the Rattle snake but no rattle whose bite is venomous. The Glass snake, the Garter snake and the Black snake, these three last are not hurtfull. The Glass snake if you strike it, it breaks to pieces like Gall.

Cattail Loudon County Virginia, Wednesday June 5th 1776
Went to town, to instruct the workmen how to erect a pump in Mr Kirks Distillery. No news for this week past.
6th Employed at home, very much indisposed.
7th Mr Kirk sent for me to dine with him and proposed me joining him in the Potash makeing, which he perswades me I am capable of manageing, but I declined it as I am determined to leave this county as soon as I can.
8th Employed at home.
9th Went to town in the afternoon. Mr Kirk advises me to take a Decoction of the Woods which he is kind enough to prepare.
10th 11th 12th 13th 14th & 15th Employed at home, and takeing the decoction. Very weake and feeble believe I use too much exercise.

Cattail Loudon County, Virginia Sunday June 16th 1776
Went to town and Dined with Mr Kirk.
17th 18th 19th 20th 21st and 22nd Employed in my business. News that the Yankey Privateers or rather Pirates has taken three Jamaica Ships worth £100,000 D--n the ungratefull double tongued scoundrels, Certainly the Spirit of the Nation will now be roused.
23rd Sunday. Went to town and heard a Methodist Sermon.
24th 25th 26th 27th and 29th [sic] Employed at home—find I can by hard labour make as much as will pay my board. Begin to get strength tho very slowly. No news this week.
30th Sunday. No preaching of any sort. Mr Kirk & the Doctor advises me to bath in cold water every morning.

Cattail Loudon County, Virginia, Monday, July 1st 1776
News. That [blank] Washington had discovered a plot lay'd for his life and that of all the Staff Officers, At New York, one of the Conspirators was hanged and

several of the others confined in Jail.[30] No News of any troops ariveing from England. Made myselfe a Bath.

2nd 3rd 4th 5th and 6th Employed at home—find great benefit from the cold Bath.

7th Sunday. Dined at Mr Kirks in Co with Mr Booker. No news.

8th Directing Mr Kirks people how to make a Hay rick.

9th At Mr Kirks. News that the Sanhedrim had declared the thirteen united Colonies, Free and Independent States. That this was intended by the Northern Colonies from the first I am well convinced, and the two following Letters confirms me in that opinion. [31]

Anonymous letter to the Honbl James Warren, Watertown near Boston
Dear Sir,

In Confidence—I am determined to write freely to you this time—A certain great Fortune and piddleing Genius whose Fame has been loudly trumpeted has given a silly Cast to our whole proceedings. We are between Hawk and Buzzard. We ought to have had in our hands a Month ago the whole Legislative, Executive, and Judicial of the whole Continent and have compleatly Moddelled a Constitution to have raised a Naval Power, and opened all our Ports wide, to have arrested every Friend to Government on the Continent and held them as Hostages for the poor Victims in Boston. And then opened the door as wide as possible for Peace and Reconcilliation. After this they might have petitioned and negotiated and addressed & & &, if they woud. Is all this extravagant. Is it wild. Is it not the soundest Policy?

One Piece of news. Seven Thousand Weight of Powder arived here last night. We shall send along some as soon as we can. But must be patient and frugal.

We are lost in the extensiveness of our Field of business. We have a Continental Treasury to establish, a Paymaster to choose, and a Committee of Correspondence, or Safety, or Accounts, or something I know not what that has confounded us all Day.

Shall I hail you Speaker or Counsellor, or what. What Kind of an Election had you. What Sort of Magistrates do you intend to make.

Will Your new Legislative and Executive feel Bold or irresolute. Will your Judicial Hang and Whip and Fine, and Imprison without Scruples. I want to see our distressed Country once more. Yet I dread the Sight of Devastation.

You observe in you[r] Letter, the Oddity of a great man. He is a queer Creature. But you must love his Dogs, if you love him, and forgive a Thousand Whims for the sake of the Soldier and the Scholar. Philadelphia July 24th 75.
The following is a Letter from Mr John Adams, To his Wife Abigail in which the Letter to Mr Warren was enclosed.

Philadelphia July 24th 1775

My Dear,

It is now allmost three months since I left you, in every Part of which my Anxiety about you and the Children as well as my Country, has been extreme.

The Business I have had upon my Mind has been as great and important as can be intrusted to Man and the Difficulty and Intricacy of it is prodigious. When 50 or 60 Men have a Constitution to form for a great Empire at the same time that they have a Country of fifteen hundred Miles extent to fortify,

Millions to Arm and train, a Naval Power to begin, an extensive Commerce to regulate, numerous Tribes of Indians to negotiate with, a standing Army of Twenty Seven Thousand Men to raise, Pay, Victual and Officer, I realy shall pitty those 50 or 60 Men. I must see you e'er long. Rice has wrote me a good Letter and so has Thaxter for which I thank them both.

    Love to the Children. J. A.

    P. S. I wish I had given you a compleat History from the beginning to the end of the Journey of the behaviour of my Compatriots No mortal tale woud equal it. I will tel you in future, but you shall keep it secret. The Fidgets, the Whims, the Caprice, the Vanity the Superstition, the Irritability of some is enough to ----

    Both these Letters were intercepted by the Kings Officers, and published in Drapers Massachusetts Gazette in August last.

Cattail Loudon County, Virginia, Wednesday July 10th 1776

11th 12th and 13th. Employed at home—still continue the cold Bath and find great benefit from it. This cursed Independence has given me great uneasiness.

14th Sunday. Drank Tea at Mr Kirks.

15th Employed at home.

16th Went to Captn Douglasses returned in the evening.

17th 18th 19th and 20th Employed at home. I am now got allmost strong enough to shoot a Yankeman.

21st Sunday. News that Lord How was arived at New York with a Large Fleet and a numerous Army. God send him good he[alth?].

        0 C. G.

Cattail Loudon County, Virginia, Monday July 22nd 1776

News that the Roebuck was comeing up to Alexandria.[32]

23rd 24th & 25th At home finished the last of my earth and my partner will not cleare out the other Tobacco houses.

26th Dined at Mr Masons, who proffers to give me a Letter of recommendation to the Governor Henry for liberty to go on board the Fleet in the Bay. I have no other choice to get home but this.

27th At Town. A General Muster of the Malitia. Great confusion among them Recruiting parties ofers 10 Dollars advance and 40 s. per month.

        0 C. G.

28th Sunday. At home.

29th 30th and 31st At home employed in refining Salt peeter.

Cattail Loudon County, Virginia, Thursday Aust 1st 1776

Refining Nitre. I have made several experiments but have hit on one that a[n]swers well by puting the crude Nitre into a pot and fluxing it til it has the appearance of milk, then let it cool and put to every pound of Nitre three pints of Water boil it a little and sit to shoot. I[t] makes a beautifull appearance like Icecicles white as Snow and transparant as Glass, from 7½ pound of Crude Nitre

I have got 4½ pound pure. News that Lord Dunmore was drove from Gwinns Island and the Fleet had left the Bay. I am now at a loss again. Determined to go to New York and endeavour to get to the Army.

Cattail Loudon County, Virginia, Friday August 2nd 1776
At home. I am now got pretty healthy again but very uneasy, believe I am one of the most unfortunate dogs on earth intend to go with Mr Cavan to Mr Wm Nielsons.[33]
3rd Went with Cavan to Mr Nielsons about 15 miles from town. He cals this place Scotland and I think it is well named.
4th Sunday. Left Mr Nielsons, Crossed the Blueridge and Shanando River, went to Mr Nourses at Piedmont, Berkly County.
5th Went with Mr & Mrs Nourse to Colnl Saml Washington,[34] Brother to the General drank some Whiskey Grog and came back.
6th Left Mr Nourses. Dined at Mr Fra[n]k Willis,[35] got to Mr Nielsons at night. Mr H. Nielson gave me some Rattlesnake teeth.

Scotland, Loudon County, Virginia, Thursday Aust 7th
At Mr Nielson, who is the most industrious man I have seen in Virginia, but an ugly place to Cultivate.
8th Left Mr Nielsons, got to the Cattail at night.
9th At town. Dined at Mr Kirks.
10th Directing Mr Kirks people how to top the Hayrick. Lodged at Mr Kirk 0.M.N.
11th Sunday. At home. No news this week.
12th 13th 14th 15th 16th and 17th At Home employed in dressing Faunskins. Am Determined to go to New York I must either escape that way or go to jail for Toryism.
18th Sunday. Mr Kirk sent for me to to [sic] ask my advice about a Mare he has sick believe she will die. Am certain she has the maw worms.

Cattail Loudon County, Virginia, Monday Aust 19th 1776
This morning found the Mare dead. My conjecture was right The worms had eat through her maw. Mr Kirk proffers to lend me his horse to New York.
20th Went to Mr Joseph Jenneys. Got a Letter of introduction from him to Messrs Warder & Sons in Philadelphia—returned in the evening.
21st Went to Captn Douglasses setled my affairs with him. Called at Mr Masons who says he will give me letters of recommendation to some of the members of Congress. Dont act fairly by Mr Mason not to let him know my Designs.

Cattail Loudon County Virginia, Thursday Aust 22nd 1776
Settled my affairs with Mr James Kirk and parted with great concern, as he has behaved to me with the greatest respect and kindness, but dare not tell him of my design. Left my chest and Cloaths to the care of my good Friend P. Cavan

who is the only person privy to my intention. I owe nothing to any one but Mr Kirk. His horse I intend to return by Mr Cooper.

23rd Left Leesburg in Co with Mr Alexander Cooper a Storekeeper in town.[36] Called at Mr Masons, who gave me Letters to Messrs Francis Lightfoot Lee, Thos Stone, Thos Jefferson, and John Rodgers Esqr all members of the Congress.[37] Dined at Fred town Mansceyson Creek. Lodged at Bentleys Tavern, Frederick County, Maryland.

York Town, Pennsylvania, Saturday August 24th 1776

Left Bentleys Tavern. Crossd Little Pipe Creek at a Bridg. Breakfasted at Tauney town, small place inhabitants chiefly Dutch. Crossed the Pennsylvania line. Peeter Littles town, very small. Dined at McCallisters or Hannover town, this is a smart little town with a Church chiefly Dutch people.[38] Lodged at Yorktown, the Sign of the Brewhouse, the Landlord is a Dutchman with a confounded hard name and a D--d dirty house. This is a pretty large town some manufactories in Iron, pleasant and well lay'd out, the inhabitants Dutch and Irish. Droll adventure this evening.

Pennsylvania, Sunday, August 25th 1776

Left Yorktown. Breakfasted at the Sign of the Plow, a Dutch house about 3 miles from Y. T. Crossed Susquehanna River at Wrights Ferry. River about 1¼ miles Broad. Dined at Lancaster the Sign of the two Highlandmen, Landlords named Ross.[39] This is a Large town but the situation is disagreeable between two hills, severall good Buildings and some manufactories of Guns and Woollens but no navigation. Four hundred English prisoners here. Crossed Connestogo Creek. Lodged at the Sign of the Duke of Cumberland, the Land lord is a Scotch Irish, Rebel Collonel and his house as dirty as a Hogstye. Land good in general. Farmers Rich and industrious. Irish and Dutch inhabitants.

Pennsylvania, Monday, August 26th 1776

Left the Duke of Cumberland which is one of the dirtiest houses I ever put my Foot in. Breakfasted at the Waggon[40] the Landlord a riggid Irish Presbyterian. Dined at the Cross Keys.[41] Lodged at the Spread Eagle a Clean Dutchmans house.[42] Land broken and hilly but the Farmers seem Rich good stock and their Land well cultivated. Passed 5 Companies going to Camp.

27th Left the Spread Eagle. Crossed Schulkhil Ferry got to Philadelphia to Breakfast. In our journey from Leesburg, I have only seen 3 Signes hanging. The rest is puled down by the soldiers. Makeing my observations. Lodged at the Black horse in Market street.[43]

Philadelphia, Wednesday, August 28th 1776

Viewing the Town. Delivered my letters to Mr Warder who received me very kindly and invited me to dine with him. Introduced me to several Gentlemen of his acquaintance. All Quakers. Spent the Evening at the Signe of the Black horse with Mr Joseph Brewer,[44] Clarke to Mr Jeremiah Warder.[45] Dont like my lodgings full of Irish Colnls, Captns, and Convention men, most them profoundly ignorant and as imperitinent as any Skipkinnel. These are here for the purpose of makeing a new Code of Laws for the Province.

O, Happy people indeed that has such wise [councils?]

Philadelphia, Thursday, August 29, 1776
Viewing the town. Dined at Mr Brewers with Mr Buckhannan, an Irish Gentleman find him a sensible polite man.

In the afternoon met with Phillip Marchington who keeps a pretty large Store here.[46] Spent the evening with him and one Thos Thornbur from Shipton and one Gresswold, a Distiller in town. At the Citty tavern.[47] Thornbur & Gress'd two sensible men, but Marchington is an extravagant Fop. Great preparations for War, and great numbers of Ragged soldiers comes into town.

News that they [sic] English had defeated the [blank] on Long Island and took a Thousand prisoners.

Philadelphia, Friday, August 30th 1776
Mr Buckhanhan went with me to every place of note in town. Dined at Marchingtons Lodgings. Spent the Evening with Messrs Brewer & Buckhahan both Sgink Sdneirf [King's Friends].
31st Waited on Mr Francis Lightfoot Lee and Mr Thos Jefferson with my Letters who behaved with the greatest complaisance and politeness, proffer to get me a pass from the Congress by virtue of which I may travel where I please. Mr Buckhan went with me to the Fishing house on the River Schuylkill about 5 Miles from town. Here is a small collection of Marine and Indian Curiosities, but dont think it a good one.[48] Snuff mill and paper mill. Several Ellegant Country Seates.

Philadelphia, Sunday, September 1st 1776
Went with Mr Brewer and Mr Buckhanhan, by water to see the Fort, Gondolas, and Chevaux-de-Frise or rather the Vis a de Frise about 7 Miles below the citty. The Fort is on a low dirty Island at the conflux of the Schuylklill with the Dellaware, only a shell not finished part of it picketted and three Blockhouses there is Eight 32 pounders well situated to cover the Vis a de Frise. A large Boom across the River. Thirteen Gondolas some carries 4 Guns, some 2 and some one trifleing things rowed with Ores. A Floating Battery which mounts 14 Heavy Cannon very Formidable—in our return dined at Gloster town in New Jersey. Fine view of the Citty from the River. 0. P. E.son

Philadelphia, Monday, September 2nd 76
Waited on Mr Jefferson who gave me a pass wrote by Mr John Hancock, Press of the Congress. Went with P. Marchington to Germantown about 9 Miles from Philadelphia. A long rambleing place a considerable manufactory of Course stockings inhabitants chiefly Dutch. Determined to go to New York and make my escape to the English Army. Marchington will send the horse to

Leesburg. In short I have no other alternative if I stay among the Sleber [Rebels] I mus[t] go the Liaj [jail]. Great numbers, I believe halfe the people in town are, Sgnik Sdreirf, [king's friends]. Some of the people has hung Washington, Putnam, and Mifflin[49] on their Sign Post in publick. 0 P. E.

Philadelphia, Tuesday, September 3rd 1776
This is a Large, Rich, populous and Regular town. The Dellaware River is on the North side the town and Schuylkill River on the South West, Streets run parrallel with the Dellaware River, others in direct lines which form it in Squares—the Streets are Sixty foot wide except Ma[r]ket street which is an Hundred, but the Markethouse is set in the Middle of this street which entirely spoils the beauty of it. They are paved with Brick and kept very cleane, with walks on each side for the foot people.

Well supplyed with pumps, very level and so remarkable streight there is nothing to obstruct your view from one end of the town to the other. Three English Churches, Christ Church, St Pauls, and St Peeters and two Dutch Lutherian Churches, Nine Decenting meeting houses, Two Roman Chapels, Four Quarker meeting houses, and a Sweedish Church. All Neat plain buildings but none of the Ellegant ones. The State house is a good building but does not make a grand appearance. Here all publick business is done. Now the nest of the great and mighty Sanhedrim.

Near this is the New jail a Good and large Stone Building now occupied with, Sgnik Sdneirf. A Handsome Brick Hospital but not Large. Here is a Good Building they call a Bettering House[50] where all Strollers and Disorderly people are confined to labour till they can give a sufficient account of the themselves. Here is a Colledge for the education of Youth, it makes no great appearance, and how it is endowed I cannot tell. The Buildings are Brick very plain, convenient and neat, no very Grand Edifices as the Quakers have the management of public [affairs?]

Here is a large and plentifull Market but chiefly supplyed from the Jerseys. It is a Corporation town Governed by a Mayor 20 Aldermen and Common Council men every thing is kept in the greatest order. Here is Barracks for 7 or 8 Thousand men. They build as fine Ships here as any part of the World and with as great dispatch. Here is Four continental Frigats built here in a few months two of them 111 Foot keel and two 96. As Fine Vessels as I ever saw. I suppose they will be ready for sea in a month—if they can get hands to man them.

This is [one of {marked out}] the mos[t] Regular neat and convenient Cities I ever was in and has made the most rapid progress to its present greatness. 0. P. E.

Spent the day with Mr Buckhannan.

Philadelphia, Wednesday, September 4th 1776
Spent the day with Mr Buckhanhan & Mr Thornbur. Great many Ships lay'd up and unrigged at the warfs. Took my passage in the Stage for New York. Left the Horse in care of Marchington to send him to Leesburg if I dont return in 6 Days.

5th Set out from Philadelphia about 5 OClock this morning in a Vehicele neither Coach nor Waggon but between both, it holds 15 Persons and is not uneasy traveling. Breakfasted at the Wheatsheafe 12 Miles. Crossed Shammony Ferry. Stoped at Bristol[51] a small town opposite Burlington where we changed Horses—20 Miles from Philadelphia.

Cross'd Delaware River at Trenton Ferry. Dined at Trenton this is a small town and very little trade. Through a small town or rather Village called Maidenhead. Lodged at Prince-town this is a neat Little town with a Ellegant College for the education of Youth. I believe there is 60 Rooms in it for the Students each room has two Closets & two beds. A Chapel Library and Schoolroom. Cellars and Storerooms compleat.[52]

Saw the Orrery and electrical Machines. Orrery made by the Famous David Writtenhouse, Electrical Machine and apparatus not compleat. Doctor Wetherspoon Mr.

Lodged at the Sign of Hudebrass.[53]

Newwark, New Jersey, Friday Septr 6th 1776

Left Prince-town—passed thro Kingston. Breakfasted at Brunswick this is a sm[all] tradeing town situated on Rareaton River which is navigable to the town for small Craft. Crossed Rareaton River several pleasant seats along the Banks. Land good. Changed horses at Woodbridge and paid the other half of the fare 11 s. here and 10 s. at Philadelphia. This is a small neat town. Dined at Elizabeth-town, this is a small town of some trade. Lodged at Newark this is nothing more than a Village. Country populous in general but now in distraction. Land along the Rivers good, hills rather poor. Believe one of the Co is a Spye upon my actions.

New York, Saturday, September 7th 1776

Left Newark, Crossed Passihack or Second River, About from that Crossed Hack-in-sack River. Then North River at Powlershook Ferry.[54] River about 1½ Miles wide. Landed in New York, about Nine O'Clock, when one Cullens, an Irish Merchant, and myself rambled about the town till three in the afternoon before we coud get anything for breakfast at length we found a little Dutch tippleing house and perswaded the Old woman to get us something to eat, it was a Stew of Pork bones and Cabbage so full of Garlick, nothing but necessity woud have compeled me to eat it my companion woud not taste a mouthful.

Nothing to be got here—all the inhabitants are mooved out. The town full of Soldiers. Viewing the town and Fortifications and contriveing meanes to efect my escape but despeare of it the Rivers are too well guard[ed].

This town is the best situated for trade of any p[l]ace I ever saw it is on a point of Land with warfs two thirds of the way round the town and very neare the Sea. The town is not so regular as Philadelphia nor so extensive neither has it so many good Buildings, but more Ellegant ones both Publick and private.

Here is three English Churches—the Old Trinity Church, St Paul's, and St Georges Chappel, Two Dutch Churches, Four Decenting Meeting houses, One

Quaker Meeting, and a Jews Synagog, And a French Church, A College and Hospital, two Ellegant Buildings.[55] There was a fine Equestrian statue of his Majesty but the Sleber has pulled it down and cast it into Bullets. The Statue of the Earl of Chatham is still standing unhurt in the attitude of an apple woman dresed like a Roman Orator. I am not a judge but dont think it clever.

The Liberty pole as they call it is covered with Iron bars. Streets fortifyed with small Batteries towards the River. My fellow traveler, Mr Cullens, and I shoud have lodged in the streets had we not luckeyly met one Godard, Post Master, who got us a sorry lodging at the Hull Tavern.[56] From the top of this house have a prospect of Long Island, Staten Island, Governors Island, Bedlows Island, and Gilbert Island—three last small ones. All the British Fleet and part of the Army, Make a fine appearance, but is utterly out of my Power to get to them. I never till now thought of it, But Honor forbids it as I am enabled to travel by the intrest of Mr Mason was I to make my escape, He might be reflected on.

Newark, New Jersey Sunday, Sept 8th 1776

Left New York early this morning. Crossed the North River to Poulershook. While we waited for the Stage viewed the Sleber Fortifications, here—they are made of earth but what number of Guns or what size I cannot tel, no admitance into the Fort. The Troops stationed here are Yankey men the nastiest Devils in the Creation. It would be impossible for any human Creature whose Organs of smelling was more dellicate then that of a Hog to live one day under the Lee of this Camp such a complication of Stinks. Saw a Yankey put a pint of Molasses into about a Gallon of Mutton Broth.

The Army here is numerous but raged Dirty, Sickly, and ill diciplined. If my country men are beat by these ragamuffins I shall be much surprised, their Fleet is large and it is said their Army is numerous.

New York must fall into their hands their Batteries on Long Island command the town. Heard a smart Cannonade crossing the Ferry this morning supposed to be at Hellgate. The Fleet is within 2 Miles of the town. Got to Newark by Diner. Great scarcity of provisions the roads full of Soldiers. Very uneasy must be obliged to go into Cannada or stay in this D--d Country.

Prince-town, New Jersey, Monday Sept 9th 76

Left Newark—breakfasted at Eliza town. Dined at Brunswick. Lodged at Prince-town. Great numbers of Soldiers on the road. Our Co chiefly Irishmen.
10th Left Prince-town. Breakfasted at Trenton. Dined at Bristol where we changed horses. Got to Philadelphia in the evening lodged at one Mrs. Stretches in second Street my old Lodging took up.

Spent the evening with the French Officers that are prisoners here, taken at St Johns. Very polite gentlemen but exceeding cautious. Town full of Soldiers.

Philadelphia, Wednesday, Sept 11th 1776

Dined at Mr Brewers. Spent the afternoon with Mr Buckhanhan. Lodged at Mrs

Stretches. My designs are frustrated spent a good deale of money to no sort of purpose. I must return to Virginia and endeavour to get to Cannada. 0 P. E.

12th Determined to set out to Virginia tomorrow. Dined at Mrs Stretches. Suped and Spent the evening at the Golden Fleece,[57] in Co with Marchington, Gresswold, Brewer, and Thornbur all, Sgnik Sdneirf, very merry. News that General Prescot and General McDonald were exchanged for G. Sullivan & G. Sterling—Sleber took at Long Island.

Christiana Bridge.[58] Friday Sep 13th 76
Left Philadelphia in Co with Messrs Marchington & Gresswold. Crossed Schuylkill at Greys Ferry—through Darby a little place. Dined at Chester a smart little town on the Delaware River, here Marchington and Greswold left me and I joined an Irish Taylor metamorphised into a Captn and an Irish Blacksmith his Lieutenant. Both going to Baltimore. Passed Brandywine Mills, here is 8 of them in a quarter of a mile so convenient that they can take the Grain out of the Vessels into the Mill. Wilmington a pretty town on the River then Newport a trifleing place. Lodged at Christiana Bridge a little town situated on a Creek of the same name.

Bushtown Maryland, Saturday Sept 14th 76
Breakfasted at the head of Elk, this River falls into Chessapeak Bay and is only 12 miles from Christianabridge. Fed our horses at Charlstown a small place at head of the Bay and seems to be on the decline. Crossed Susquehannah River at the Lower Ferry. Dined at the Ferry house. Lodged at Bushtown or Hartford which you please—this is a small and poor town.[59] Land poor in general all along the road. My companions rank Paddy's. The Captn talks as if he was able to take General Howe in two days with his Company.

Elkrige Landing Sunday Sept 15th 1776
Breakfasted at Skyers tavern. Dined at Baltimore, this is the princ[i]pal trading town in Maryland, it is regularly layd out and tollerably well Built, but the situation is exceedingly inconvenient. Ships cant come within a mile of the town to a place caled Fells point where they are sent up in Flats to town, about a mile below Fells Point is the Fort Lately built but I did not go to it. Saw the Buckskin Frigate of thirty six Guns just built. A fine Vessell. Lodged at Elkrige landing, a small Village. Great number of Iron works. Land poor in general. Very unwell excessive hot weather and uneasiness of mind has brought on a Fever.

Bladensburg Maryland, Monday Sept 16th 1776
Much better slept a little last night. Breakfasted at an indifferent house about 10 Miles from the Landing. Got to Bladensburg in the Afternoon. Lodged at Mr Wm Sidebothams. From Marple Bridg Road badly furnished with Inns and some of the poorest Land I have yet seen.

17th Fed my horse at Georgetown, this is a smart town on on [sic] the Potomeck River on the Maryland side. Crossed the River, 0 R. B. got to Alexandria spent the evening with Mr Wm Elzey and George Muir. Lodged at Mr. Flemings.
18th Left Alexandria in Co With Harry McCabe. Dined at the Falls Church. Got to Leesburg in the evening. Found my Old Friend P. Cavan ill of the fever and Ague. Lodged at Captn Taylors.

Cattail, Loudon County, Virginia Thursday September 19th 76
Mr Kirk insisted on me dining with him. Expected I was gone aboard the Fleet, am sorry it was not so. Lodged at the Cattail.
20th Dined at Mr Kirks—very unhappy.
21st At town. Mr Booker returned this evening.
22nd Sunday. Dined at Mr. Masons.
23rd Mr Kirk sent for me this morning to Assist him. Mr Cavan is sick of the Fever and Ague.
24th and 25th At Mr Kirks. News that Genl How had got possession of New York.[60] Lodged at the Cattail.
26th and 27th At home. Employed in doing nothing at all—very disagreeable business.

Cattail Loudon County Virginia Saturday Sept 28th 1776
Went to town in the morning. After Diner went to Hites Island. Spent the evening and Slept at Mr Cartwrights.
29th Sunday. At home if I have such a place.
30th At Cattail too much time for reflection. I am now disappointed in my favourite plan of geting home and it is reported that the Indians has begun to commit outrages on the back inhabitants so that my Canada Scheme is rendered abortive. I have nothing to trust to but Providence, and I have but little faith in that. However I am determined to rot in a jail rather than take up arms against my native Country

NOTES

1. Chambly, Canada, fell to the Americans on October 18, 1775. Enough supplys were captured to allow Montgomery to renew the siege of St. Johns. Mark M. Boatner, III, *Encyclopedia of the American Revolution* (New York: David McKay Company, Inc., 1974), 193.

2. Elizabeth Sorrell was the widow of Thomas Sorrell who had operated a tavern in Leesburg from at least October 27, 1766. Thomas Sorrell died in 1774 and Elizabeth continued to run the tavern. Loudoun County Court Order Book C, 1765-1767; Order Book F, 1773-1776, 480, All references to Virginia county court records hereafter are on microfilm at the Library of Virginia, Richmond.

3. This was Patrick Cavan who became a close friend of Cresswell. Patrick Cavan married Sarah Baker on March 1, 1798, in Loudoun County. Mary Alice Wertz, *Marriages of Loudoun County, Virginia, 1757-1853* (Baltimore, Md.: Genealogical Publishing Co., 1985), 25. In 1799 Patrick Cavan owned twenty lots in Leesburg. James C. Bradford, "Society and Government in Loudoun County, Virginia, 1790-1800" (PhD Dissertation, University of Virginia, 1976), 97.

4. James Booker was probably a member of the large Booker family in the Williamsburg area. He is listed among the tithables at Mann Pages's estate in Loudoun County in 1775-1777. Mann Page lived in Gloucester County, Virginia, not far from Williamsburg. Later Cresswell mentioned that Booker was going to Williamsburg to act as an overseer. See entry below for November 19, 1776. Ruth and Sam Sparacio, *Tithables Book: Loudoun County, Virginia, 1775-1781* (n. p. Antient Press, 1992), 15, 35.

5. On January 13, 1776, George Ancram was appointed third lieutenant of the artillery regiment raised in Virginia. H. R. McIlwaine, ed., *Journals of the Council of the State of Virginia*, vol. 1 (Richmond, Va.: Virginia State Library, 1931), 312-13.

6. George Johnston received his license to practice as an attorney in Loudoun County on March 12, 1770. He died in 1779. Loudoun Co. Order Book D, 1767-1770, 307. Loudoun County Court Will Book B, 1772-1782, 261-67.

7. St. John's fell to the Americans on October 11, 1775. John Connolly along with Allan Cameron and J. F. D. Smyth were captured in Frederick, Maryland after a servant informed on them. Boatner, *Encyclopedia of the American Revolution*, 262, 958-60.

8. On March 19, 1777, Joseph Speake was recommended to the governor to be appointed lieutenant of the Safeguard Galley. Navy Board Journal, 1776-1779, 192 (Library of Virginia).

9. Probably Alexander McIntyre who is listed as a tithable in Loudoun County in 1775. He was also mentioned as a tavern keeper. Loudoun County Tithables, 1758-1799. Microfilm in the Library of Virginia. Janice L. Abercrombie and Richard Slatten, *Virginia Revolutionary Publick Claims* (Athens, Ga.; Iberian Publishing Co., 1992), II, 78.

10. The rumor was incorrect. Quebec was attacked by the Americans on December 31, 1775, but was not taken. Boatner, *Encyclopedia of the American Revolution*, 906-909.

11. Philip Noland operated a ferry across the Potomac from at least 1756. In an act of the Virginia assembly in 1778, establishing ferries, it was noted that the ferry was run by Thomas Noland from his land in Loudoun County to the land of Arthur Nelson in Maryland. In March 1768 Philip Noland, Jr. was granted a licence to keep an ordinary at his ferry. Philip Noland, Sr. was his security. Loudoun County Court Order Book D, 1767-1770, 20. Harrison Williams, *Legends of Loudoun: An Account of the History and*

Homes of a Border County in Virginia's Northern Neck (Richmond, Va.: Garrett and Massie, Inc., 1938), 120-21. W. W. Hening, *Statutes at Large*, vol. 9 (Richmond, Va.: J. & G. Cockran, 1821), 585.

12. This was Alan Cameron and Dr. John F. D. Smyth. Cameron had been agent under John Stuart and received a lieutenant's commission from Dunmore to accompany Connolly. Dr. John J. F. Smyth was "intimately acquainted" with Maryland and Connolly wanted him as a guide and intended to make him surgeon of the regiment he intended to raise. John Connolly, "A Narrative of the Transactions, Imprisonment, and Sufferings of John Connolly, An American Loyalist and Lieut. Col. In His Majesty's Service," *Pennsylvania Magazine of History and Biography*, 12 (1888): 411-12. Loyalist Claim of John Ferdinand Dalziel Smith, Loyalist Claims, Series I – Evidence, Maryland 1783-1786, A. O. 12/6, 72-126, (Public Record Office, London). Treasury Board Papers-In letters 1784, T1/609 (Public Record Office, London). All references to records in the Public Record Office are on microfilm in John D. Rockefeller, Jr. Library, Colonial Williamsburg Foundation, Williamsburg, Virginia.

13. David Griffiths was born in New York in 1742. He was minister of Shelburne Parish in Loudoun County, Virginia, from 1771 to 1776 when he was appointed chaplain and surgeon to the third Virginia regiment. He was minister of Fairfax Parish, Fairfax County, Virginia, from 1780 until his death in 1789. E. L. Goodwin, *The Colonial Church in Virginia*, (Milwaukee, Wisc.: Morehouse Publishing Co., 1927) 275. McIlwaine, ed., *Journals of the Council of the State of Virginia*, 2: 409.

14. William Ellzey was appointed King's Attorney for Loudoun County in 1767. In 1774 he was appointed to the vestry of Cameron Parish. From 1761 until his death in 1795 Ellzey lived at what is now called Fleetwood Farm and then called Peggy's Green. The house is still standing. Loudoun County Court Order Book C, 1765-1767, 244; Loudoun County Court Order Book F, 1773-1776, 485. Calder Loth, ed., *The Virginia Landmarks Register*, 4th edition (Charlottesville: University Press of Virginia, 1999), 270.

15. Douglass named his home in Loudoun County after Garralland in Britain. Loudoun County Court Will Book C, 1783-1788, 13.

16. Cresswell later spells this man's name as "Campbell." Matthew Campbell died in Loudoun County in 1782. He appointed James Kirk and Patrick Cavan executors of his estate. Henry McCabe and James Willson proved the will in court. Loudoun County Court Order Book G, 1776-1783, 384.

17. This was likely John Harper who was a member of the Alexandria Committee of Correspondence. William J. Van Schreeven and Robert L. Scribner, eds., *Revolutionary Virginia: The Road to Independence,* vol. 2 (Charlottesville, Va.: University Press of Virginia, 1975), 88.

18. Dennis Ramsay (b. ca. 1756) was mayor of Alexandria from 1789 to 1790 and from 1793 to 1794. He was the son of William Ramsay. Political Graveyard, politicalgraveyard.com//geo/VA/al.html (accessed June 12, 2008). William Carlin, Account Book (Alexandria) 1750s-1770s, 70 (Privately owned). Microfilm copy in John D. Rockefeller, Jr. Library, Colonial Williamsburg Foundation, Williamsburg, Virginia.

19. For a discussion of Thomas Paine's "Common Sense" see Bernard Bailyn, "Common Sense," in *American Heritage* 26 (Dec. 1973): 36-40; 91-93.

20. This was probably Richard Conway of Alexandria owner of the sloop *Molly* or Thomas Conway, commander of the *Molly*. The *Betsey*, owned by Thomas and Richard Conway of Alexandria, was captured by the British at Sandy Hook on October 19, 1778. Donald Jackson, ed., *The Diaries of George Washington*, vol. 3 (Charlottesville, Va.: University Press of Virginia, 1978), 210. Naval Office Returns, South Potomac, Oct.

1774-Jan. 1775, T 1/512, f. 1. (Public Record Office, London.) High Court of Admiralty: Prize Papers, H. C. A. 32/286. (Public Record Office, London.)

21. Joseph Janney was a merchant in Leesburg. He was in business as early as 1765. In 1776 Janney's storekeeper in Leesburg was Strainge Backhouse, a Quaker. John Glassford & Co., Alexandria Ledger 1765-1766, f. 107 (Library of Congress) Microfilm in Rockefeller Library, Williamsburg, Virginia. Joseph Janney Account Book, 1773-1776, (Maryland Historical Society, Baltimore). Microfilm in Rockefeller Library, Williamsburg, Virginia.

22. This was likely Robert MacCrae who arrived in Virginia in 1775. He was a merchant and in 1780 was elected to the Common Council of Alexandria. James Donald Munson, "From Empire to Commonwealth: Alexandria, Virginia, 1749-1780," (PhD Dissertation, University of Maryland, 1984), 36-37.

23. This was probably John McGinnis who was listed as a tithable from 1775 through 1777 in Loudoun County. Dr. McNichols has not been identified. Margaret L. Hopkins, ed., *Index to the Tithables of Loudoun County, Virginia, and to Slaveholders and Slaves, 1758-1786* (Baltimore, Md.: Genealogical Publishing Co., Inc., 1991), 55.

24. Thomas Respess was recommended by the Loudoun County Court on January 13, 1777, as a proper person to serve as an officer in the militia. He received the appointment as captain. Loudoun County Court Order Book G, 1776-1783, 8. J. T. McAllister, *Virginia Militia in the Revolutionary War* (Hot Springs, Va.; McAllister Publishing Co., 1913), 212.

· 25. Saltpeter, potassium nitrate, was an important ingredient in making gunpowder as well as uses in medicine and meat preservation. On February the Continental Congress appointed a committee consisting of one member from each colony "to consider of further ways & means of promoting & encouraging the manufactures of salt petre sulphur & powder in these colonies." The Virginia Committee of Safety was already offering to buy saltpeter at six shillings per pound. A method of producing salt peter was published in the *Virginia Gazette* (Purdie) August 4, 1775 and January 12, 1776 and in the *Maryland Gazette* on August 24, 1775. Van Schreeven and Scribner, ed., *Revolutionary Virginia: The Road to Independence*, 6: 78. 128-29, 259-60.

26. Thomson Mason (1733-1785), younger brother of George Mason of Gunston Hall, lived at Raspberry Plain, a plantation he purchased in 1760. He completed his house at Raspberry Plain in 1771 He was elected, on June 14, 1774, to represent Loudoun County in the First Virginia Convention and at the same time appointed to the Loudoun County Committee of Correspondence. He probably did not attend the convention. He had previously represented Stafford County in the House of Burgesses from 1758 to 1761 and from 1765 to 1772. He represented Loudoun County in the house from 1772 to 1774 and in the House of Delegates from 1777 to 1778. In 1778 he was elected a judge of the general count of Virginia. He published a series of letters vigorously defending American liberties. Loudoun County Court Deed Book A, 1757-1760, 469. Robert L. Scribner and Brent Tarter, ed., *Revolutionary Virginia: The Road to Independence* (Charlottesville, Va.: University Press of Virginia, 1983) 7: 733-34. Dumas Malone, ed., *Dictionary of American Biography*, vol. 12 (New York: Charles Scribner's Sons, 1933), 376-77. Pamela C. Copeland and Richard K. MacMaster, *The Five George Masons: Patriots and Planters of Virginia and Maryland* (Charlottesville, Va.: University Press of Virginia, 1975), 114.

27. Esak Hopkins (1718-1802) was the first commander in chief of the Continental Navy. A native of Rhode Island, he was suspended as incompetent and for insubordination on January 2, 1778. Boatner, *Encyclopedia of the American Revolution*, 512.

28. On July 2, 1776, the Virginia Committee of Safety ordered Dr. William Pasteur, a Williamsburg physician, to "visit John Goodrich the Elder, now in the public Jail, Enquire into the state of his health, and report to the board." The report has not been found. In 1778 Goodrich announced he had escaped from "the rebels." McIlwaine, ed., *Journals of the Council of the State of Virginia*, 1: 58. For a discussion of the Goodrich family's exploits see George M. Curtis, III, "The Goodrich Family and the Revolution in Virginia, 1774-1776," *Virginia Magazine of History and Biography*, 84 (1976): 49-74. Kenneth Scott, *Rivington's New York Newspaper: Exerpts from a Loyalist Press, 1773-1783*, (New York: New-York Historical Society, 1973), 141.

29. On March 16, 1776, the Continental Congress resolved that on May 17, 1776, as "a day of humiliation, fasting, and prayer." Worthington Chauncey Ford, ed., *Journals of the Continental Congress, 1776-1789*, vol. 4 (Washington, D.C.: Government Printing Office, 1906), 207-209.

30. Cresswell probably got the news from the *Pennsylvania Gazette* which reported it in the June 26, 1776, issue. The report appeared in the *Virginia Gazette* on July 6, 1776.

31. The two letters were written by John Adams from Philadelphia and fell into British hands when the carrier was captured in Rhode Island. They were printed in Margaret Draper's *Massachusetts Gazette*. Lyman H. Butterfield, ed., *Adams Family Correspondence*, vol. 1 (Cambridge, Mass.; Harvard University Press, 1963), 255-58., L. II. Butterfield, ed., *Diary and Autobiography of John Adams*, vol. 2 (Cambridge, Mass.: Harvard University Press, 1961), 173-74.

32. On July 20, 1776, the *Roebuck*, with three other ships, headed up the Potomac River to obtain fresh water. On the 22nd the force dropped anchor near Sandy Point in Charles County, Maryland and did not proceed further up the river. Dean C. Allard, "The Potomac Navy of 1776," *Virginia Magazine of History and Biography*, 84 (1976): 422.

33. William Neilson was a landowner in Loudoun County. The "H. Nielson," mentioned on August 6, 1776, may have been Hugh Neilson, probably William's son. Loudoun County Court Order Book F, 1773-1776, 482.

34. A brother of George Washington, Samuel Washington lived in Berkeley County. He was one of the first justices of the peace of Berkeley, appointed in 1772. Benjamin J. Hillman, ed., *Executive Journals of the Council of Colonial Virginia*, vol. 6 (Richmond, Va.: Virginia State Library), 456.

35. Likely Francis Willis, Jr., the Fairfax agent, lived in Leesburg. W. W. Abbot and Dorothy Twohig, eds., *The Papers of George Washington, Colonial Series*, vol. 9 (Charlottesville, Va.: University Press of Virginia, 1994), 153.

36. Alexander Cooper is listed as a tithable in Loudoun County in 1775. Loudoun County Tithables, 1758-1799. Microfilm in the Library of Virginia, Richmond.

37. Thomas Stone (1743-1787) was a member of the Continental Congress from Maryland. Boatner, *Encyclopedia of the American Revolution*, 161-62. John Rogers also represented Maryland. He was elected on December 9, 1775. Paul H. Smith, ed., *Letters of Delegates to Congress, 1774-1789, September. – December 1775*, vol. 2 (Washington, D.C.: Library of Congress, 1977), xviii, 534. Francis Lightfoot Lee and Thomas Jefferson both represented Virginia in Congress.

38. In July 1791 George Washington said that Hanover was "commonly called McAlisters town." He described it as "a very pretty village with a number of good brick Houses & Mechanics in it. At this place, in a good Inn, we breakfasted." He noted that Yorktown was 18 miles from Hanover. Donald Jackson and Dorothy Twohig, eds., *The Diaries of George Washington*, vol. 6 (Charlottesville, Va.: University Press of Virginia, 1979), 168.

39. This was William Ross who operated a tavern from 1775-1778. William Frederick Worner, "Lancaster in 1776,"*Lancaster County Historical Journal*, 32 (1928): 148.

40. The Sign of the Wagon was in Chester County on "the provincial road leading from Philadelphia to Lancaster." It was described as a stone dwelling house 45 feet long and 30 feet wide, located about 41 miles from Philadelphia and 25 from Lancaster. *Pennsylvania Gazette*, July 21, 1773, December 14, 1774.

41. Cross Keys, operated by a Mr. Jacobs, was in Chester County and described as "very commodiously situated for any kind of public business." *Pennsylvania Packet*, December 12, 1778.

42. The Spread Eagle, operated by Jacob Hinkle, was on the Lancaster Road. *Pennsylvania Gazette*, May 29, 1776.

43. The Black Horse Tavern, on Market Street, was operated by William Graham. *Pennsylvania Gazette*, May 17, 1775.

44. Joseph Brewer, a loyalist, moved to Shelburne, Nova Scotia, and received grants of land. Lorenzo Sabine, *Biographical Sketches of Loyalists of the American Revolution*, vol. 2 (Boston, Mass.: Little, Brown & Co., 1864), 464.

45. Jeremiah Warder and Sons operated a store "in Third-street, opposite Church alley" in Philadelphia. *Pennsylvania Gazette*, February 27, 1772.

46. Philip Marchinton's store was on Market Street between Front and Second streets. *Pennsylvania Gazette*, May 3, 1775; June 14, 1775.

47. Gresswold was probably Joseph Greswold. City Tavern was on the west side of Second Street between Walnut and Chestnut streets. It was a gathering place for members of Congress. It was said to be "the most genteel place of its kind in all the colonies." Thomas R. Meehan, "Courts, Cases, and Counselors in Revolutionary and Post-Revolutionary Pennsylvania," *Pennsylvania Magazine of History and Biography*, 91 (1967): 31. David McCullough, *John Adams* (New York: Simon & Schuster, 2001), 81. It was sometimes called the New Tavern. Donald Jackson, ed., *The Diaries of George Washington*, 3: 275.

48. This was one of several clubs, or "fishing houses" near the Falls of the Schuykill. The collection was probably that of the Society of Fort St. David consisting mainly of Indian antiquities. Butterfield, ed., *Diary and Autobiography of John Adams*, 2: 133.

49. This was probably Thomas Mifflin (1744-1800). He was a Philadelphia merchant and a member of the provincial assembly and of the First Continental Congress. He was Washington's first aide-de-camp and later served as a general, quartermaster general, member of the Board of War, and president of the Continental Congress. He was later governor of Pennsylvania. *Pennsylvania Gazette*, May 18, 1776; Jackson, *Diaries of George Washington*, III, 277.

50. The Bettering House or Almshouse, built in 1767, was on Spruce Street between Tenth and Eleventh streets. John L. Cotter, Daniel G. Roberts, and Michael Parrington, *The Buried Past: An Archaeological History of Philadelphia* (Philadelphia, Pa.: University of Pennsylvania Press, 1992), 46-47.

51. Bristol, Pennsylvania, is about 20 miles northeast of Philadelphia and 3 miles northeast of Neshaminy Creek. Jackson, *Diaries of George Washington*, 3: 185.

52. This was the College of New Jersey, later Princeton University. Thomas Jefferson Wertenbaker, *Princeton, 1746-1896* (Princeton, N. J.: Princeton University Press, 1946), 372-73.

53. John Adams stayed in Princeton at the "Sign of Hudibrass" on August 27, 1774, when traveling to Philadelphia. He said it was "near Nassau Hall College." Butterfield, ed. *Diary and Autobiography of John Adams, Diary 1771-1781*, 2: 112.

54. Paulus Hook Ferry ran from New Jersey to New York. Wilbur C. Abbott, *New York in the American Revolution* (New York: Charles Scribner's Sons, 1929), 8.

55. The college was King's College, later Columbia University. David C. Humphrey, *From King's College to Columbia, 1746-1800* (New York: Columbia University Press, 1976), 270-78.

56. Hull's Tavern, the old "Province Arms" and later "Cape's Tavern," was on the northwest corner of Thames and Broadway. It survived the fire that consumed much of New York on September 21, 1776. John C. Fitzpatrick, ed., *The Diaries of George Washington, 1748-1779*, vol. 2 (New York: Houghton Mifflin Company, 1925), 112 note 9. *Virginia Gazette* (Dixon), October 11, 1776.

57. A tavern in Philadelphia on Second Street between Walnut and Chestnut streets. *Pennsylvania Gazette*, November 4, 1775. It was there from at least May 25, 1769, when the St. Andrew's Society met there. *Pennsylvania Gazette*, May 25, 1769.

58. Now called Christiana, the town was located on Christiana Creek which flowed into the Delaware. Robert G. Albion and Leonidas Dodson, eds., *Philip Vickers Fithian: Journal, 1775-1776* (Princeton, N. J.: Princeton University Press, 1934), 129.

59. Bushtown, now called Bush, was about a mile northeast of Abingdon, Maryland, in Harford County. James A. Bear, Jr. and Lucia C. Stanton, ed., *The Papers of Thomas Jefferson*, second series, *Jefferson's Memorandum Books, Accounts, with Legal Records and Miscellany, 1767-1826*, vol. 1 (Princeton, N. J.: Princeton University Press, 1997), 412, n. 70.

60. The British occupied New York City on September 15, 1776. Don Higginbotham, *The War of American Independence: Military Attitudes, Policies, and Practice, 1763-1789* (New York: The Macmillan Co., 1971), 160. Richard B. Morris, ed. *Encyclopedia of American History* (New York: Harper & Row, Publishers, 1976), 109-10.

Chapter 4
Retreat from the Future
September 30, 1776 to April 21, 1781

Journal, By Nicholas Cresswell, of Edale
near Chapelinlefrith, Derbyshire, in England
Continued from Vol 3rd September 30th 1776
To [April 21, 1781]

Cattail Loudoun County, Virginia, October 1st 1776
Went with Mr James Booker, to Mr Matthew Campbels. Spent the evening there, and got most Feloniously Drunk. This is a bad preface to my new book. D[r]unkenness the first remark.
2nd At home. Sick with my last nights Debauch. O! Temperance temperance, thou best of Virtues, what pains we take to ruin our Constitutions by these nocturnal excesses.
3rd 4th and 5th Employed I can't tell how, a worthless life indeed.
6th Sunday. Mr Booker and I went to the Quaker-meeting, but was too late, tho it was equally as well as if we had been sooner, for the Spirit did not moov any of them to speake. Can't conceive what service the people can receive by Grunting and Groaning for two or three hours without speaking a word. This is a Stupid Religeon indeed. Dined at Mrs Bakers[1] with A Sleber [Rebel] Officer. Got home in the evening.
7th At Leesburg returned in the evening. No News.
8th Went to Hites Island, on no good design. Lodged at Mr Cartwrights. Did not meet with success. The fruits of Idleness are, intemperance and a numbe[r]less train of eviles.

Cattail, Loudon County, Virginia, October 9th 1776
At home no Newspapers the last week. I suppose the Rascals has had bad luck of late and are affraid it should be known to the publick.
10th Went to town to assist Mr Kirk. Mr Cavan is sick.
The 6th Regmt of Virginians are Camped here, on their way to the Northward. A set of Dirty, Raged people badly Cloathed Badly Disciplined and badly Armed.[2] ! B. M.
11th Salt sels here at Forty Shillings Currency pr Bushel. This article usually sold for Four Shillings. If no Salt comes in there will be an insurrection in the Colony. ! B. M.
12th Spent part of the evening at Mr McCreys in Co with Messrs Kirk, Booker, McCabe, and Campbell. McCabe went with Kirk and me home where we entered into Political disputes and McCabe and I quarreled. Memd never to enter into political disputes for the future, if I can avoid it, especially with Slebers.

13th Mr Kirk, Messrs McCabe, Campbell, Dow, Dean,[3] and Cavan Dined and spent the evening with me at the Cattail. Mathematical disquisitions the chiefe subject of discourse this Afternoon. Far preferable to the cursed politics.

Cattail Loudon County, Virginia, October 14th 1776
15th 16th And 17th At home, intend to go to Alexandria tomorrow, as I am informed there is A Sloop bound for Bermudas, will endeavour to get a passage in her. There is no other method of geting out of this hatteful Country.

18th Dined at Mosses Ordinary. Got to Alexandria in the evening. Lodged at Mrs Haukins.

19th Saw the Master of the Sloop who informs me he is bound to Bermudas if he meets with none of the Kings Ships. He is in an Illicit trade, his port precarious, his passage extravagant, and appears to be an ill natured moross man. Am determined not to go with him. Dined at Mr John Muirs, A Merchant in town. This Gentleman is looked on as the pattern of Hospitallity and Generosity. But I am far from thinking him a good man. It is true he keeps an excellent table, A Glass of good Wine, punch & &, but he is an Epicure himself and likes a companion along with his Bottle. His humanity is not to be commended. He has five children by a Negro woman, Slave to a Gentleman in town they are all Slaves for life, he sees them dayly, wanting the common necessary's of life, without taking the least pitty or Compassion on their wretched condition. The man who can beare to see his own Flesh and Blood in this horrid situation without being most sensible affected, is lost to every feeling of humanity, and is a Degree worse than a brute.

Alexandria, Virginia, Sunday October 20th 1776
No service at Church today. Religeon is allmost forgot, or most basely neglected. In short the Parsons are not willing to expound the Gospel to people without being pay'd for it and there is no provision made for the Episcopal Clergy by these new Code of Laws, therefore Religeon as well as Commerce is at a stand.[4] Indeed the few that pretend to preach are meare retailers of politicks, sowers of Sedition and Rebellion, serve to blow the Cole of Discord and excite the people to arms. The Presbyterian Clergy are particularly active in supporting the measures of Congress from the Rostrum, gaining proselyte persecuting the unbelievers, preaching up the righteousness of their cause, and perswading the unthinking populace of the infallibillity of success. Some of these Religeous Rascals assert that the Lord will send his Angels to Assist the injured Americans. They gain great numbers of Converts and I am convinced if they establish their Independence that Presbyty will be the established Religeon on this Continent. Spent the evening with Mr Robert Muir & Mr Kirk.

21st This morning I am told that the Committee of this town will not permit me to depart this Colony as they look upon me to be a Spye. And that I must be obliged to give security or go to jail, wheather this is done to get me to enlist into their service or some Rascal has informed against me I cannot tell. Intended to have gone to Leesburg tonight but some Villain has stole my Surtout Coate. Spent the evening at Mr William Hartshorns.[5]

Cattail Loudon County, Virginia, October 22nd 1776

Mrs Haukins promised to pay for my Coate but dont believe her. Left Alexandria. Called at Goodwins Mill 0 L.J.B. Lodged at Mosses Ordinary.

23rd Got to the Cattail to Dinner. Mr Booker gone to Alexandria. I am housekeeper myselfe. 0.M.M.!.M.

24th 25th And 26th These three Days I have spent most disagreeably nothing to do, and all alone. When I reflect on my present situation it makes me misserable. I am now in an Enemy's Country forbid to depart. Little to subsist upon, and dare not do anything to get a liveing, for fear of geting myselfe ranked as an inhabitant and be Obliged to carry Arms against my Native Country, my Intrest and Inclination, unhappy alternative indeed, to turn Paricide or starve. Am determined to go amongst the Indians. I look upon them to be the more humane people of the two.

27th Sunday Went to town to a Methodist meeting.

28th General Muster of the County Malitia in Town, about 600 men appeared under Armed with Tobacco-sticks in general. Much rioting and confusion. Recruiting Officers for the Sleber Army offer Twelve Pounds bounty and 200 Acres of Land when the War is over, but get very few men. C.G.5.D.

29th At Town dined with Captn G. Johnston a Violent Sleber.

30th Dined at Mr Thomson Masons, who advises me to petition the Congress for permission to go home, promises to give me Letters of recommendation to some members of Congress.

31st Went to Mr Peeter Cars.[6] Droll adventure there dont know how it will terminate. Got some Silver Dollars at 6/6 pr Dollar.

Cattail Loudoun County, Virginia. November 1st 1776

Dined at Mr Kirks who perswades me to stay till Spring, but for what reason I cannot tell. Am in doubt wheather his advice proceeds from Friendship or Intrested motives. From him I have my present support, by his intrest I have been kept out of Jail, and without his approbation cannot go, and to stay and be dependent on him for bread and liberty is worse then Egyptian bondage. Determined to petition the Congress at all events.

2nd Dined at Mr Kirks, who is still harping on the Old string he now insists on me staying the Winter, endeavours to perswade me that there will be an end to these disputes this Fall. I see no probabillity of it therefore will not stay if I can help it.

3rd Sunday. At town, no Church. Mr Kirk uses every argument in his power to prevail on me to stay, indeed he is angry with me that I wont. I am resolved to persevere be the consequence what it will. I might as well be in the infernal regions as in this Country where my sentiments are known. Every rascal looks on me as an enemy to him and except I cou'd Tacitly submit to every insult or divest myself of the faculties of Sight, Speech, and Heareing must be misserable X.C.G.6.

4th Went to town and agree'd with Joseph Moffit to carry my Chest to Philadelphia.[7] He goes next week.

5th Mr Kirk promises to go with me into Berkley tomorrow. I am under sundry Obligations to Mr Nourse, it would be wrong to go and not acquaint him with it. As he, by me, has an opportunity of writeing to his Friends.

Piedmont, Berkley County, Virginia. November 6th 1776

Left Leesburg in Co with Mr Kirk. Dined at Keys Ferry. Lodged at Mr Nourses who was very glad to see us. My companion seems to have taken a great fancy to Miss Nourse. If there was a little more parrity in years it might do very well to make a match.

7th Got to Mr Gibbs in the afternoon. Mr Kirk seems to have taken particular notice of Miss Nourse. Hope it may amount to something in time. Spent an agreeable evening with two Irish Ladies, the Miss Reynolds, that was at Mr Gibbs'es.

8th Went to Winchester with Messrs Kirk and Gibbs. Dined there and spent the evening with Colnl Jacob Alligood, who is prisoner here.[8] Most of the Co. got drunk. Going to Mr Gibbs, Mr Kirk fell from his horse, and let him get away. At Mr Gibbs, Kirk and I got into a Political dispute which terminated in a quarrel, but made it up before we went to bed.

9th For the sake of the ride went to Winchester to enquire for Mr Kirks horse, but heard nothing of him. Breakfasted with Alligood who informs me I am suspected of being A Tory and Spye. Rat the Scoundrels. Dined and spent the afternoon at Mr John Reynolds, an Irish Gentleman who is settled as a Farmer here and is in a fine way to make a Fortune by it. Lodged at Mr Gibbs. No news of the horse, suppose somebody has stolen him. This is the pernicious efects of drunkenness.

Penneyroyal Hill, Frederick County Virginia, Novr 10th 1776

Mr Kirks uneasiness for the lose of his horse, disturbed me last night, and very ill became a man of his sense to make himselfe so exceedingly unhappy about such trifles tho I believe it is unavoidable in him, he is by nature fretfull. About Eight OClock the Boy came with his Beast and restored him to his usual good humour. Mrs Gibbs family Mr K and I dined at Mr Reynolds and spent an agreeable afternoon.

11th Left Mr Gibbs. Dined at Mr John Hites,[9] this Gentleman is falling a Victim to his Bachanalian excesses. Lodged at Mr Nourses.

12th Left Mr Nourses with some regret. He gave letters to my care for, Charles Fouace Esqr Admirallity Office,[10] Mr Hughs, linin Draper, York street Covent Garden and Mrs Seaman Honeton Devon. Dined at Keys Ferry. Mr Henry Peyton[11] was shot through the Body attempting to take a deserter from the Sleber Army got to the Cattail in the evening.

13th Employed in prepareing for my departure.

14th Mr Booker and I went to Mr William Neilsons a particular friend of mine an industrious man and a Sgnik Dneirf. [King's Friend] Lodged there.

15th Returned to the Cattail in the evening.

16th Went to town. Josiah Moffit tels me to have my things ready by next Saturday X.C.G.8.T [?].

Cattail Loudoun County, Virginia, Sunday, November 17th 1776
Went to Mr Campbels, from there to town, and Dined with Mr Cavan, Mr Kirk at Captn McCabes, sorry for it.

18th Mr Booker and I spent the evening at Mr Campbels very merryly. This Gentleman is falling a sacrifice to the sports of Venus.

19th Packing up my things. Mr Booker is going to live near Williamsburg. A very mad frolick this evening, set the house on fire three times, and broke Mr Dreans leg (a Gentleman that Mr Booker had brought to spend the evening with us) got drunk and committed a number of foolish actions.

20th Sick with my last nights intemperance. Went to town and took lodgings at Mrs Sorrels till I set out for Philadelphia will not live at Mr Kirks any longer.

21st Dined at Mr Thos Rispes and sold him my Salt peetre apparatus. Payed Mr Booker for my board and spent the evening with him at the Croked Billit.

22nd Prepareing for my journey. Hired a horse from Mr T. Rispe.

23rd News that General Howe was on his march to Philadelphia and drives the Sleber before him. Believe it to be true if I may be allowed to judge from the Countenance and Behaviour of the Fire-brands.

24th Sunday Spent the evening with Mr Booker and Mr Dean at the Crooked Billit. All the news-papers are stoped none are allowed to be give to the publick. A certain signe that the Rascals are defeated.

Leesburg Loudoun County Virginia. November 25th 1776
This morning took my farewell of Mr James Booker who is going to be Overseer to a Gentleman near Williamsburg. This Young-man is one of the most curious characters I have ever met with. he is Proud and Affable, Ostentatious and Niggardly. A Beau and a Sloven by turns, wheather the Moon has any influence over his passions, Or he was born under some capricious Planet, I cannot pretend to determine. Spent the evening at Mr Kirks who uses every means in his power to detain me here this Winter, but I am determined to go if there is a possibillity of geting a way.

26th Settleing my affairs. News that General Howe is at Brunswick in the Jerseys the Sleber Army flying towards Philadelphia and that the Congress had removed from Philadelphia to Baltimore. Brave news indeed.[12]

27th The Committee met to day am informed it is to search my papers if not to take me up and imprison me but will be prepared for them.

28th This morning three of the Committeemen waited on me and informs that the Committee did not think it prudent to let me go out of the Country at this time and hoped that I woud give my word of Honnor not to depart this Colony for three Months, otherways they wou'd confine me. I was obliged to do the first as the lesser evil of the two. They was polite enough not to search my Chest. Spent the evening at Mr Kirks, who seemed very glad that I was Obliged to stay. This affronted me, we both got Drunk and quarreled about State affairs.[13]

Alexandria, Virginia, November 29th 1776
Very sick with my last nights debauch, and very sorry for my last nights conduct. My present disagreeable confinement, the loss of three Years of the most Valuable part of life, the Disappointments and Misfortunes I have met with since I left my Native Country. And what is worst of all, the certainty of being Reproached with Obstinacy, and Extravagancy at my return. These bitter reflections will intrude themselves involuntary, and create a lowness of Spirit which too often is the cause of me drinking more then is of service. I must and will call my Resolution and Fortitude to my aid, or I shall insensibly sink into the Sot or the Drunkard. A Character so Despicable, aught to be avoided with the greatest care. Mr Kirk and I made up the quarrel this morning. Must not quarrel with him. He confesses that he did every thing in his power to intoxicate me, on purpose to raise my spirits. I will not borrow my spirits in that manner for the future. Left Leesburg. Dined at Mosses Ordinary. Got to Alexandria spent the evening with Mr McCrey.
30th This morning went to Mrs Hawkins expecting to get pay'd for my Coat suposeing that She was not informed that I was forbid to depart the Colony, but the Damd Jade tels me I am a Tory and she wont pay me a Farthing. This is provoking but I cannot help myselfe. Spent the evening with Mr McCrey.

Leesburg, Loudoun County, Virginia, Sunday, December 1st 1776
Left Alexandria. Dined at Mosses. Got to Leesburg at night. News that the English has taken Fort Washington and 2500 prisoners in it. This is the strongest Fortification they had, it is on the North end of New York Island. they have long boasted that all the forces belonging to Great Britain could not take it. What is it that Englishmen cannot do when ever they chuse to exert themselves. It is said they have deserted Fort Lee. If this be true I hope the Rascals will soon be Humbled.[14] !.C.
2nd Troubled with the Rheumatism in my Arms. 0.B.0.B.
3rd Abundance of Political puff's and lies told to amuse the publick, it is a matter of dispute with me wheather the Whigs or Tory's are the greatest propagaters of falshood [sic].
4th A Dutch mob of about 40 horsemen went through the town today, on their way to Alexandria to search for Salt if they find any they will take it by force. All of them armed with Swords or large Clubs. This article is exceeding scarce, if none comes in the people will revolt. They cannot possible subsist without a considerable quantity of this article, the people in general live on Saltmeat in the Summer. the excessive heat renders the keeping of Freshmeat very difficult, even for one day, and the thinness of inhabitants and markets prevents them kiling little els[e] but young hogs and fowls. They likewise give Salt to their

Horses, Cattle, Hoggs and Sheep allmost every day in the Summer. The cattle are exceedingly fond of it so much that they will follow you any where for lick of it. And it is so esentially necessary that they will not thrive without it.

Leesburg Loudoun County, Virginia, December 5th 1776
Exceedingly unhappy was it not for the Company of a few friends I shou'd be compleatly miserable.
6th This day the Dutchmen returned from Alexandria without doing the least mischief, the poor wretches has got about three Pints of Salt pr man, they are told that there will be plenty in a little time. But I hope his Majesty's Ships will prevent it comeing into the Bay. Spent the Evening at Mr Kirks in Co with Captn McCabe and Mr George West. J. K. had a scuffle with McCabe, it is true they were both in liquor, but wheather Mr Kirks anger was bent against McCabe or not, is a mistery to me. I kept perfectly Sober and left them as soon as I cou'd.
7th Mr Kirk is very uneasy concerning his conduct last night. Sobriety is a noble Virtue. 0. M. N.
8th Sunday. News, by private letters the publick papers are stoped, that General Howe was at Woodbridge in the Jerseys. God send him a safe, and speedy arival in Philadelphia. It is said the Sleber are flying before him.
9th This morning I was remarkably low spirit. About three OClock in the afternoon Mr Hugh Nielson came and insisted on my spending the evening at the Billit. I have spent it with a Vengence, with Flemming Patterson,[15] Cleone More,[16] Captn Wm Johnston[17] and H Neilson. Sent them all to bed Drunk and I am now going to bed myselfe at 9 in the morn as drunk as an honest man coud wish.

Leesburg Loudoun County Virginia, Decber 10th 1776
Got up at 2, in the afternoon. Got drunk before 10, with the same Co I was with yesterday. And am now going to bed at 2 in the morning most Princely drunk indeed. I saw all my Companions in bed before I left them, but most Damnable drunk, a fine Course of life truely, drunk every night this is Tempering [Tampering] with the Devil to it.
11th Much indisposed this morning. I heare my Past companions and Brothers in iniquity comeing up stairs. But am determined to keep sober to day.
12th Last night was the worst we have had since we first commenced the trade of Drunkards. Mr Kirk and P. Cavan joined us, we instituted a foolish society by the name of the Blackeey'd Club. I was President and Mr More Secretary. All of us got most intolerably drunk. This is the first day that I have had any time for reflection this week. Uneasiness of mind first engaged me in the last Debauch, Good company induced me to continue it, and now A Bitter reflection, an aching head, a sick stomach, a trembleing hand, and a number of disagreeab[l]e Concomitants that are anexed to this Detestable Vice cause me to quit the pursute. Drunkenness is certainly one of the most Odious Vices that mankind can possible be guilty of, the consequences are so exceedingly pernicious to our

Health, our Happiness, and Intrest, it is astonishing that any Being endowed with the faculty at thinking, shoud take such pains to Divest himselfe of Reason, that knowingly and willingly he will destroy his constitution and sink himselfe below the level of a Brute. Mr Kirk came and spent the evening at my lodgings.

Leesburg Loudoun County Virginia, December 14th 1776
News that General Howe is at Trenton in the Jerseys [blank] from Philadelphia. It is certain the Congress has left Philadelphia are now at Baltimore. Great numbers of Recruiting parties are out to raise men, but can scarcely get a man by any means, tho their Bounty is £12, none will enlist that can avoid it, they get some Servants & Convicts which are purchased from their Masters, these will desert the first opportunity. The violent Sleber are much dispirited. The Polititians (or rather Timid Whigs) give all up for lost. And the Torys begin to Exult. The time is out that the Flying Camp was enlisted for, and it is said that they refuse to serve any longer, tho they have been Solicited in the strongest terms. This will make a great deficiency in their Army the loss of Ten Thousand men. I am convinced that if General Howe will push to Philadelphia the day is his own. Find it will be best for me to remoove out of town for a little while or I may stand a chance of going to jail as I am too often abuseing these Rascals. Am determined to go into Berkley.

15th Sunday. Dined with Mr Kirk. After Dinner went to Mr Nielsons.

16th Left Mr Wm Nielsons, in Co with Mr Hugh Nielson who lent me a horse. Cross'd the Shanando River and got to Mr Francis Willis. Spent the Evening with Mr John Cook, Captn Throgmorton[18] and Doctor Armstrong son of General Armstrong.[19] All violent Sleber, but little discouraged.

Piedmont Berkeley County Virginia December 17th 1776
Went to Mr Nourse's, he was much surprized to see me supposd that I had been gone. Insists on me spending the Christmas with him.

18th Exceedingly unhappy, everyone here is industerously employed, and I am liveing for no use in the Creation, except it be to eat and drink. The pleasure that this numerous Family enjoys in the company and conversation of each other, The apparent harmony, Peace, and quietness that subsists amongst them calls thoughts of a very unpleasing nature to my mind, and makes me misserable— every one does their utmost to keep up my spirits and make the time pass agreeable. Miss Kitty Nourse, is not the most backward in this particular. She is one of the most Sensible, Agreeable and Wellbred Girls, that I have seen since I left England. Add to these, Industry, Economy (which, by the by, is a virtue very seldom to be met with in either Male or Female, in this cou[ntry]) Wit, Good nature and a Handsom person, Altogether renders her a valuable and agreeable companion. Was I fixed in my plan of life, and nothing at home, shou'd think myself happy. To prevent any disagreeable passion intruding am determined to leave the house tomorrow.

19th Went with Mr Nourse to A Sale of horses the property of the late Jacob Hite who was kiled by the Cherokee Indians last summer.[20] Sold amazeingly high. A Horse that I coud buy in England for £10 Woud sell here for £40. Went with Mr Gibbs home. Mr Nourse seems afronted, but he is not acquainted with my true reasons. Obliged to tel him [a] lie.

Pennyroyal Hill, Frederick County Virginia, December 20th 1776
Went to Mr Reynolds. Dined there. Returned to Mr Gibbs.
Mr Perry came here a Gentleman from Maryland that has purchased an Estate here.
22nd Sunday. Mr Gibbs, Mr Perry and I Dined at Doctor McDonalds. A very Polite gentleman.[21]
23rd Dined and Spent the Afternoon at Mr Reynolds.
24th At Mr Gibbs. Directing his workmen how to make a pump for his Still house.
25th Christmas Day but very little observed in this Country except it is amongst the Dutch.
26th The Snow fell last night Two Feet thick and Level, this is the greatest fall of Snow I have seen in this Country.
27th Dined at Mr Reynolds, in Co with Mr & Mrs Gibbs and Mr Perry. Spent an agreeable afternoon, what still adds to the pleasure, is, the Certain account of Genl Lees being taking taken [sic] prisoner. It is by a private letter and have not the least doubt of its being true.[22]
28th and 29th A Violent pain in my Breast and side affraid of a Pleuresy.
30th Much better went with Mr Gibbs to Winchester. News that General Howe had retreated to Brunswick. Washington had harrased his Reare, taken a many prisoners and play'd the devil.
31st This is the last day of the Old Year, Which I have spent in worse then Egyptian bondage. No prospect of altering my situation speedily. Spent the Day at Mr. Reynolds.

Penneyroyal Hill, Frederick County, Virginia, January 1st 1777
This is the first day of the New Year, which I am affraid will be spent, by me, to as little purpose as the two last have been. I am now in a Disagreeable and precarious, situation, I dare do nothing to get bread. Cannot return to my Native Country. The meanes of my support depends on the whim and Caprice of A Friend. In feare of going to Jail every day on account of my political principles. And no prospect of this unnatural Rebellion being suppresed this year. Am determined to make my escape the first opportunity. Spent the day very happy at Mr Gibbs with a few of his friends, Danceing and makeing ourselves as merry as Whiskey Toddy, and Good Company will afford.
2nd Spent the day at Mr Reynolds.
3rd At Mr Gibbs. Missfortunes and present Vagabond life causes great uneasiness of mind.
4th Left Mr Gibbs, who has treated me with the greatest kindness and hospitallity and insists on me returning back and spending a Month with him

before I leave the Country. Dined at Mr Francis Willis's. Crossed the Shanandoe River and the Blue Ridge got to Mr William Nielsons in the evening.

Scotland, Loudon County, Virginia, January 5th 1777
Sunday. This happens to be Mr Nielsons Birth-day, as well as mine. Wee spent it as happily as our situation wou'd admit we are both of the same opinion in political matters which makes it the more agreeable.

6th News that Washington had taken 760 Hessians prisoners at Trenton in the Jerseys.[23] Hope it is a lye. This afternoon heare he has likewise taken Six pieces of Brass Cannon.

7th The news is confirmed. The minds of the people are much altered. A few days ago they had given up the cause for lost. Their late successes have turned the Scale, and now they are all Liberty mad again. Their Recruiting parties coud not get a man (Except he bought him from his Master) no longer since then last week, and now the men are comeing in by companies. Confound the turncoate Scoundrels and the Cowardly Hessians together. This has given them new spirits. Got them fresh succours and will prolong the War perhaps for two Years, they have recovered their Panick, and it will not be an easy matter to through [throw?] them into that confusion again. Volunteer Companies are collecting in every County on the Continent and in a few months the Rascals will be stronger then ever. Even the Parsons some of them have tur[n]ed out as Volunteers, and Pulpit Drum or Thunder, which you please to call it, Summons all to Arms in this Cursed Bubble [Babble?]. Damn then all.

Scotland, Loudon County, Virginia, January 8th 1777
This is a most unhappy Country every necessary of Life is at an extravagan[t] price some of them indeed is not to be had for money. Poor people are allmost naked. Congress or Committee of Safety, or some of those infernal bodies have issued an Order that every one that is fortunate enough to be possesed of two Coats, is to give one to their Naked Soldiers. Grain now begins to beare a good price owing to such great quantities being Distilled and the small proportion that is in the ground. I am perswaded there will be A Famine very soon as well as A War.

9th 10th And 11th Very Cold weather, allmost stupid for want of employ.

12th Sunday. News that the Slebers Ships had taken 30,000 Sutes of Clothes that were intended to Cloath, our Army for the Winter believe it is a lye. However it serves the Rascals purpose to entice the people to enlist.

13th And 14th News, that Washington had entirely routed Our Army and the few that had escaped had been obliged to take refuge on Board the Ships. This must certainly be a lie.

15th I am exceeding kindly treated here, and am very happy in the Company of Mr Nielson. But the thoughts of receiving such unmerited kindness from an entire stranger, whom in all probabillity it will never be in my power to repay, makes me uneasy.

16th Intend to go to Leesburg tomorrow. I am unhappy every where the late news has increased my anxiety to be at home that I may have an Opportunity to be revenged of these miscreants.

Leesburg Loudon County, Virginia, January 17th 1777
Left Mr Nielsons. Got to Leesburg to my old Lodgings.

18th Dined and spent the evening at Mr Kirks who beggs me to make him the Model of a Machine for driveing Piles into the River, to build Warfs upon. Their late successes has made him believe that they will have a free and open trade to all parts of the World very soon. Such is the instabillity of human affairs. Six weeks ago this Gentleman was lamenting the unhappy situation of the Americans, And pittying the wretched condition of their much beloved Generall suposeing his want of Skill and Experience in Millitary matters, had brought them all to the Brink of Destruction. In Short, All was gone, all was lost. But now the Scale is turned and Washingtons name is extoled to the clouds. Alexander, Pompey and Hanibal were but pigmy Generals, in comparison with the Magnanimous Washington. Poor General Howe is rediculed in all companies and all my Country men abused. I am obliged to hear this dayly and dare not speake a word in their favor. It is the Damed Hessians that has caused this. Curse the scoundrel that first thought of sending them here.

19th Dined at Mr Kirks. I lead a most worthless Lazy life and cannot help it at present.

20th Sunday. Spent it as I do the rest of my time, doing nothing.

21st and 22nd Prepareing materials for the Model.

Leesburg Loudon County Virginia, January 23rd 1777
Curiosity and Company induced me to spend the evening at a place of no great credit. The various Scene's I saw may be of great service to me some time or other if I O.4.C.G.

24th Salt sold to the people at 6d pr Quart, by order of the great Committee of Safety—every tithable in the Family is allowed a Quart and no more. Even this seems to please the people. I believe they are all mad.

25th and 26th Employed in makeing the Model. Obliged to be Joiner and Smith myselfe.

27th Sunday. Dined with Mr Kirk. Eleven English prisoners arived and are to be stationed here all of them Soldiers. Have been summoned to mount Guard over them, but absolutly refused. I suppose this will be a Committee affair but I am determined to go to jail myselfe rather then guard an English prisoner.

28th Finished the Model, which answers exceeding well. It is an Inch to a Foot, Calculated for one man to raise a 1000 weight Twenty feet which falls on the head of the Pile. Summon'd again but refused to go.

29th The Captn of towns Malitia excused my appearing on Guard. To my great suprize find one of them to be Mr John Gee, He that married Miss Nancy Worthington.[24]

30th News that Fort Washington was retaken by the Yankeys.

31st News that New York was deserted by the English. But believe it is a lie. The Sleber has a surprizeing run of good luck if all be true. 0.6.C.G.

Leesburg, Loudon County, Virginia. February 1st 1777
Mr Gee & Mr Hugh Neilson Dined and spent the evening with me. Mr Gee tels me he was settled at New York as a Merchant, at the first of these troubles had mad[e] his sentiments known, which made him Obnoxtious to the populace. When it was known that General Howe intended to go to New York he was very industerous amongst the Kings Friends and had raised a company of Rangers, under the Famous Major Rodgers. This was known to the Committee before General Howe's Arival at New York. He was seized by the mob, carryed by them on a sharp rail through the town cut with knives, and much bruised with clubs. Afterwards put in a Dugeon or Dark prison, where they kept him three days without victuals. Then he was removed to Morristown in the Jerseys, from thence (on the approach of our Army) to Philadelphia. From Philadelphia to Baltimore where in their great confusion he got Amongs[t] the Soldiers and now passes for Clark to the 71st Regt. He is in a wretched condition, scarcely cloths sufficient to cover his nakedness, and very dirty. I have give him a Shirt, Hunting- Shirt, Jacket and Blanket, as they have only three Blankets in the whole Company. Mr Nielson has given him Leather to make him a pair of Breeches and I will get them made.

Leesburg, Loudon County, Virginia, February 2nd 1777
News that Washington and his Mermidons had defeated a large body of our troops, at Prince-town in Jersey.[25] This is very surprizeing that there shoud be any of our Army at Prince-town when it was affirmed for fact, that they were drove a Shipboard.
3rd And 4th My Landlady has got nothing to burn or any thing to Eat that is fit for a Christian, to pay 12 Shillings a week, is very hard, without I get the real necessaries of Life. Am determined to go to Captn Douglasse's.
5th Spent part of the evening with Mr Gee at the Crooked Billit. Affraid he is a Sot if that be the case he will be misserable. Mr Cavan came to my lodging on purpose to drink Ginn. I made him very merry before he went away. This is the first time I have seen him in Liquor.
6th Dined at Mr Kirks with Captn Wm Sandford a Cont'll Officer.[26] News that Fort Lee was retaken.
7th Left Leesburg and went to Captn Wm Douglasse's.
8th And 9th At Garralland.
10th Dined with Thomson Mason Esqr who is layed up in the Gout. No news these three days.
11th A Methodist Preaching here. In the evening the parson and I had a long discourse about the New Faith as he calls it. Find him a Sensible man, not so much biggoted as some of them are.

Garralland, Loudoun County, Virginia, February 12th 1777
13th 14th 15th 16th And 17th In the course of the last six days I have read more Religeous Authors and had more discourse about Religeon then in all my life before. Captn Douglass uses his utmost endeavours to make a Proselite of me. But I cannot find that Whitfields road to Heaven is one jot better, or nearer then Martin Luthers, therefore will continue in the opinion under which I was educated.
18th News that three of his Majesty's Ships are in the Bay determined to go on Board some of them if possible, as soon as I can meet with an opportunity.
19th 20th And 21st At Garralland. More Religeous discourse with the usual efect.
22nd Went to Leesburg. Dined at Mr Kirks. News that Washington was taken. This is too good news to be true returned to Garralland at night.
23rd News confirmed that Ships are in the Bay, my parole will be out soon and then I will give the Rascals the slip.
24th Went to town with Captn Douglass and his Family to a Methodist meeting. Lieut Ancram informs me that I am likely to brought into trouble for reporting that Washington was taken prisoner. Can give up my Authors. Dined at Mr Rispes.

Garralland, Loudon County, Virginia, February 25th 1777
Expected to have had a Methodist meeting here to day the Company, or Congregation, or Canting Whineing Hypocrites met but the Parson disappointed them. I am sorry that Captn Douglass shou'd be such a Dupe to these Religeous Quacks. He keeps a good table, is a good-natured man, easily led, and rather unsteady in his religeous principles allways glad to see or converse with these Faggend of the Scripture-mongers and as long as his house is open to them, they will haunt him as bad as they tell us the Devil haunts their meetings. They are a set of the Noisyest fellows I ever heard, instead of enforceing there arguments they only exalt their voice.
26th And 27th One of these Parsons has had a long Confab with me to day, he is one of the affected Biggoted little puppeys I ever met with. Out of his great kindness has made Old Pluto a Compliment of me.
28th This is a Fast day appointed by the Great Sanhedrim to return thanks for their late successes. And to beg a continuation of them. It is ordered to be kept sacred by all every one to go to Church or Meeting. I have not been it seems to be like Oliver Cromwells proceedings.

Garralland, Loudon County, Virginia March 1st 1777
Went with Captn Douglass and Mr Fleming Patterson to see Mr Josiah Clapham. He is an Assemblyman. Colonel of the County, and Justice of the Peace on the present establishment. He is an Englishman from Wakefield in Yorkshire, much in Debt at home, and in course a Violent Sleber here. Has made himselfe very popular by erecting a Manufactory of Guns, but it is poorly

carryed on. His Wife is the most notable woman in the County for Housewifery, but I shoud like her much better if she would keep a cleaner house. He has got a very good plantation, takes every mean Art to render himself popular amongst a set of ignorant Dutchmen that are settled in his neighbourhood. Dirty in Person and Principle. Returned to Garralland at night.

2nd Sunday. No news this week. Intend to go to Leesburg tomorrow. If I stay much longer here I may be the meanes of makeing a certain person in the Family unhappy, tho very inadvertently on my part, and I believe involuntaryly on theirs. This woud be an unpardonable as well as an ungratefull act in me, who has been so kindly treated in this agreeable family.

3rd Went to Leesburg. Saw a Revew [sic] of Captn Wm Johnstons Co a set of Rascally Servants & Convicts most of them just purchased from their masters. A Raged crew indeed. Captn Douglass is angry with me for leaving his house, but he is ignorant of the cause.

Leesburg Loudon County, Virginia, March 4th 1777

I have had the misfortune to affront one of the Committee men, by not giveing his Daughter a kiss, when I was introduced to her, this has offended the old man so much, that I am informed by my Friends he has several spyes to watch my actions, if anything treasonable is discovered (as he is pleased to term it) I am to be prosecuted to the utmost of the Law. Sorry I did not give the ugly, jade a Buss and have escaped the censure of this Ostentatious Blockhead. If I dont proceed with caution shall not get away this Summer.

5th And 6th Laying schemes how to get out of this hatefull place, something like building Castles in the Air. Intend to go to Alexandria to see if I can get any recompence for my Coat and collect some other small debts that are due to me, perhaps something may happen in my favor by & by.

7th Left Leesburg. Dined at Mosses ordinary. Got to Alexandria. Lodged at Mr Flemings.

8th This morning went to Mrs Haukins about my Coat much insulted by her son, an Adjutant in the Leber Army. Called an English Tory, and every bad name the puppey coud think of, And durst not resent it had I made the least quarrel the jail must have been my portion. However I got Ten Dollars for my Coat and think myselfe very well that I got any thing. Neither Law or Justice in this Country. Dined at Mr Fleming Pattersons an Honest Scotchman. Lodged at Mosses Ordinary.

Leesburg Loudon County, Virginia, Sunday, March 9th 1777

Much disturbed last night, by the groan's of a Methodist Parson who slept in the next room. Got to Leesburg to Dinner. A Company of Soldiers that had been raised in this County Marched out of town on their way to the Jerseys.

10th Court day. Several Recruiting parties but they get very few men, indeed the County, and Country in general is pritty well thined. Have avoided all Company to day as much as possible. In the afternoon Colonels Green and Greyson[27] came to my Lodgings with Mr Mason, told me they had seen my Model of the Pile

Machine, which pleased them so much that they made me an offer of an Engineers Captn Commission in their Army which with the perquisits belonging to it, is three Dollars pr Day. They paid me a great many Encomiums on my Mechanick abillities and did every thing in their power to perswade me to engage in the noble struggle for Liberty as they are pleased to call it. I excused myselfe with all the politness I was master of, or coud possible muster at this time, told them I coud not beare the thought of takeing up Arms against my native country was much obliged to them for the Honor they wou'd confer upon me, but as it is incompatible with my present sentiments must pardon my not accepting the offer. They was pleased to make me some genteel Compliments about my steadiness and resolution. At the same time blended with some bitter reflections on my Countrymen which rather nettled me.

Leesburg Loudon County, Virginia, March 11th 1777
News that the Sleber had killed 500 of the English near Brunswick, only with the loss of two men. This must certainly be a lie.

12th Dined at the Tavern with Captn Wm Johnston, for dinner and two bowls of Toddy paid 8/6 this I can verry ill afford, but it is necessary for me to keep up appearances.

13th Some thoughts of going amongst the Indians and either liveing among them till these disturbances are settled or to make my escape into Canada through the Indian Country this will be attended with a many disagreeable inconveniences. To go into Canada without hard money will answer no purpose without I enlist as a common Soldier, this I am not willing to do. Am determined to go to the Indians and live amongst them, very certain that I can live happy, and I am ashamed and affraid to return home in the situation that I came out, tho my misfortunes has been unavoidable, I know that I shall be sensured for Misconduct.

14th Went to Captn Douglasses. Saw them makeing Sugar out of the sap of the Sugar Maple. they boil it til the wattery particles evaporate and the sugar remains at the bottom of the pot. Four Gallons of the Water wil make a pound if it is early in the Spring. Something like Muscovado Sugar, I believe not quite so strong.

Leesburg Loudon County, Virginia, March 15th 1777
Dined with Mr Mason, who promises to give me every assistance in his power to return home. Proposes giveing me a Letter of Introduction and Recommendation to the Governour of Virginia by his permission to go on board the Men of War in the Bay, this is the most probable method of geting home, but will not attempt it till the next Month rather too cold to stay on Board the Ships without better and warmer Cloaths then I am master of at present.

16th Sunday. Heard a Sermon preached by the Revd David Griffith. A political discourse indeed there is nothing else to be expected now. Spent the evening at the Tavern with Mr Cleone More, Mr Kirk, and Captn McCabe, but left them as soon as I coud with deacency. Tavern charges extravagant.

17th Went with Mr Henry McCabe to dine at Mr William Elzey's, Senator for this District. Very Genteelly entertained by Mrs Elzey. Mr Elzey not at home.

18th Dined at Captn Douglasses. Spent the evening at the Tavern with Colonel Angus McDonald,[28] who inform's me that the Indians are broke out and killed several people about Fort Pitt. Must not go there this summer.

19th Left Leesburg and went to Mr Nielsons. Mr Griffith and his Lady are here and a most Violent Leber he is Doctor and Chaplain to one of their Regmt.

Scotland Loudon County, Virginia, March 20th 1777

21st And 22nd At Mr Nielsons. Great tumults and murmurings among the people. Caused by them pressing the Young men into the Army. The people now begin to feel the effets of an Independent Government and groan under it, but cannot help themselves, as they are allmost in general disarmed. May God continue and increase their confusion.

23rd Sunday. Left Mr Nielsons, got to town, found Mr Kirk layd up with the Gout. He desires me to direct the workmen how to make a pump to work by a Pendulum. I am under sundry obligations to this Gentleman that claim my warmest gratitude, promised to undertake it.

24th This morning begun to work at the pump, with a Prusian Carpenter and two Negroes. Went to the Saw-mill to get some wood proper for the work. Dined at Mr Elzeys. The Miss Elzeys very sensible but not kiling beauties.

25th Dined at Captn Douglasses and agreed with a man to furnish me with a pair of horses to Williamsburg, intend to set out the 10th of next month. I have no other method of geting any thing with me except it is on horse back.

Leesburg, Loudon County, Virginia, March 26th 1777

This morning got engaged in a terrible fray. Six Waggoners attacked Mr Dean in his Store all of them armed with Whips. He called to me for assistance. I got a good stick and had knocked two of them down when Mr Cavan came to our assistance, the battle then became general. Four to six, we had rather the advantag[e] of them in weapons, tho not in numbers and gave them a good drubing. Cavan has broke one the mens arms, and I have bared anothers Scull for about six Inches long, and hurt another very much. Have seized two of the ring leaders. Mr Dean is much hurt fainted several times with loss of Blood. The two men give security for his future good behaviour pay the Doctor and other expences which I believe has cost them about Six pound. Am very uneasy about the man that I hurt so very bad.

27th Find myselfe a little sore with the bruses I got yesterday. Mr Dean is much hurt and in bed. This is the happy fruits of Independanc[e], the populace are grown so insolent if you do not Tacitly submit to every insult or imposition they think proper, Immediately call you a Tory and think that if you have that Stigma upon your Character they have a right, Nay even take it a meritorious Act, to knock your brains out.

Leesburg, Loudon County, Virginia, March 28th 1777
Employed in directing the Workmen about the pump, find them profoundly ignorant. Memd. never to employ a Negro if White men is to be got. The people here are much biggoted to their own ways.

29th News that the English has left Brunswick, but I beli[e]ve it to be a lie. Washington who is Dictator for the present year has ordered Sixteen Battallions to be raised (in the States, as they call them) under the appellation of Guards or Washingtons Life Guards, which you please, these added to the Eighty Eight Battallions of Continental troops, will be a numerous Army. But I am perswaded they will find some difficulty in raising this number of men, if they, by pressing Drafting or other means collect this body of men together it will distress the Country exceedingly, and very probably bring a Famine on the Country.

30th Heard a good Sermon by the Revd Mr Griffiths.

31st A Great Riot in town betwixt the English prisoners and the Yankeys, some of the prisoners were ill used by a Scotch taylor now an Ensign in the Malitia. A Violent persecuting Scoundrell, one of the followers of Whitfield.

Leesburg, Loudon County, Virginia, April 1st 1777
2nd 3rd 4th And 5th Employed about the pump, which I have got Comp[l]eat this evening to entire satisfaction of Mr Kirk. This is the first piece of Mechanism of the kind in the Country, the people Gape and Stare at it with wonder and surprise, comeing in crowds to see it work. It gives me pleasure to find it answer so well as I have never seen one constructed in the same manner.

6th Sunday. Spent the evening with Mr Mason. Am informed by a Friend that there is two Spy's to watch all my proceedings. That my Chest is to be broke open, and my papers examined before I go. But will take care to disappoint the scoundrels in that particular.

7th Prepareing for my journey to Williamsburg. Mr William Elzey, the Senator, promises to give me a Letter to the Governour. This may be of service.

8th Left Leesburg. Dined at Mr Nourses, whose family is in the Small Pox. Got to Mr Gibbs in the evening.

9th Spent the afternoon at Mr Reynolds. Spining-wheels and Flax-breaks at every house they will make more coarse linin in these two counties then will be used in there families. Some few people makes very fine linin thirteen or fourteen hundred warp, but dont Bleach it well.

10th Dined and Lodged at Mr Reynolds.

Leesburg Loudon County, Virginia, April 11th 1777
Left Mr Reynolds. Breakfasted at Mr Gibbs whom I part from with regret, he is a Friendly, Hospitable, Honest man. Dined at Mr Nourses, who gave me letters to several of his friends in England, and one Directed to Lord Brownlow Berty.[29] Miss Nourse gave one to my care which she made me promise to deliver myselfe, if I go to London. I realy felt a sensible concern to bid farewell to this happy Family, so much good nature, affabillity, and harmony seems to subsist

amongst them that I am affraid I shall never see the like again. In short it is happiness after my own plan, if we may be allowed to judge from appearances. Mr James Nourse Junr came with me to town, spent the evening and lodged with me. He is very good-natured but not quite so sensible as his Sister, it is a pitty that this Family are Leber.

12th Prepareing for my departure. Mr George West proffered to lend me his Sulkey, got a small trunk for convenience of Carriage. News, that they had hanged a man at Philadelphia who had been employed by Lord Howe to hire Pilots for the Delaware River.

Leesburg Loudon County, Virginia, Sunday, April 13th 1777

Spent part of the day with Mr Mason, with whom I promised [to] correspond if I get home and these differences subside. I am happy, and unhappy, to leave this Country. This seems a Paradox, I am happy in leaveing a Country where allmost every one looks upon me with an Eye of jealousy and distrust and where I have lived for a long time in a miserable, and perpetual state of suspence, Spending money and the most valueable part of my Life in indolence, without an Object in view, or a probabillity of one, except, I quit the paths of Honor, Justice and Gratitude [and] Commence the Paricide, Rebel, Murderer, Plunderer, and an open Enemy to the Country that gave me Birth. This my Soul abhors, I will sooner Starve or Begg or Steal and be hanged for it, Then accept the most Lucretive or Honorary Post that is in their power to bestow upon me. On the other hand, I am unhappy to find my designs frustrated and prove Abortive, all my favourite and long concerted Schemes, Vanish like the Baseless Fabric of a Vision. And leaves me a Wreck behind. I think I may with propriety compare myselfe to a Wreck all my Ideal views of happiness and opulence are entirely quashed and rendered impracticable.

My present situation is next too wretchedness, and my prospect of extricateing myselfe exceeding precarious, entirely dependent on a Set of Urusping Rascals, accountable to none, (as they suppose[)] for their actions. The means for my present support entirely depends on the Whim and Caprice of one single person, whom I know is actuated by intrested principles, therefore cannot expect his assistance any longer than he supposes it Consonant with his intrest. All these, sum'd together, are not half so Grateing, as the thought of returning to my native Country in Poverty and Rags, and then obliged to beg like a Criminal to get my debts paid which I am now contracting, and in course must be obliged to contract before I get home. The bitter reflections Taunts and Sarcasm's my Friends will be subject to then upon my conduct, no matter wheather it be right or wrong. I have been unfortunate, therefore every one thinks they have a right to find fault with my proceedings. I believe their reproof's will be tinctured with a good deale of Acrimony, as I took this journey entirely against their consent. I must endeavour to Brave all these Rubs and Frowns of Fortune, with Fortitude and Patience, Submit myselfe to them, and follow their Councils and advice.

I have been brought up to no Trade therefore have no prospect of recruiting my fortune by Merchandizeing, not only that, but I want the meanes to pursue any sort of trade at present. Indeed I might turn Soldier and get a good Liveing by cuting the throats of my Friends and Countrymen. But this my Plaguy, Squemish conscience forbids and I must and will obey it's Dictates, or I am forever miserable.

I have this consolation, in the midst of all my troubles and difficulties. To be unfortunate, not guilty, of anything except it be acting contrary to the advice of my Parents. But I gave them sufficient reasons for the steps I took. Th'o I must confess I had more Cogent ones, which I did not chuse to mention to them or any one else. And I have the satisfaction to be well assured that my plan was well grounded. Admit times had continued as they were when I first came into this country. But this Cursed Rebellion has ruined all forever.

I am well convinced that I coud have lived much better and made more money, As a Farmer in this county, With Five Hundred Pound, then I can in England, with Two Thousand. Agriculture is in such an infant state, and the Value of Land so low that any one with the least spark of industry might make what money they please as a proof of it I will here subjoin a Plan I formed to myself in the Spring 1775. As times was then.

An Estimate of the Cost and Profit of an Estate containing 500 Acres, Supposeing it in Frederick or Barkley County, in Virginia.

		Vir Currency	
Cost		£ S.	D.
To the purchase of 500 Acres of Land at			
	40 s pr	1000 0	0
To 30 Breeding Mares a £30		900	
To one Stallion imported		100	
To 20 Cows and 10 Oxen @ £4/		120	
To 20 two Year Old Cattle @ 30/		30	
To 30 Ewes and 20 Weathers @ 12/		30	
To 5 Men Servants and two Women @ 20/		140	
To 20 Hogs at 10/		10	
To Poultry		2	
To Cloathing 5 Men and 2 Women @ 50/ Each		17 10	
To one Waggon		20	
To two Carts		20	
To 4 Plows @ 30/		6	
To two Harrows 40/		4	
To Gears for Waggon, Carts, Plows, and other Necessary implements of Husbandry		30	
Annual Quit Rent of 500 Acres at 2/6 pr 100 Acres		12	6
To Eight Tythables at 10/ pr Tythable		4	
		2434 2	6

Profits of an Estate of 500 Acres in Frederick or Barkley County Virginia

Profits		£	S	D
By 20 Year Old Colts at	£10	200		
By the Season of 50 Mares exclusive of My own @ £4/		200		
By 10 Fat Oxen out of my own Stock @ £10/		100		
By 20 Sheep Fed on Turnips and sold in Spring		20		
By 10 Oxen, purchased in the Fall, Fed on Turnips and sold in the Spring supposeing each of them to Clear £3/		30		
By produce of 30 Acres of Wheat at 12 Bushels to the Acre sold @ 2/6		45		
To 150 lb of Wool at 1/6		11	5	
		£606	5	0
Exchang at 25 pr Cent, the Sterling Cost is		£1947	6	2½
Sterling Profit		£485		

This calculation is made with ample allowance on the Costs. And a very moderate one on the Profits, on the Colts in particular, from Mares of £30 Value and the Horse imported, they very often sell at 2 Year Old for £30. And sometimes more if they are likely for the Course. The Cost of the Land is very high. The best Land, in such large track's, seldom averages more than 35/ pr Acre th'o perhaps one third of it is cleared from woods.

All Taxes are included under the Article Tythables Church, Poor, and Roads & &. Except the Quit Rents which are pay'd to Lord Fairfax as the Proprietor of the Northern Neck of Virginia. The value of Manure is not known here, if it is, they are too Lazy to make use of it, their method, is to clear a piece of Land from the woods, generally put it in Wheat the first year, Indian corn the next, and so alternately for Six or Seven Years together. By that time the strength of the Land is gone and they say it is wore out, through [throw?] it out to the Woods again, and set about clearing another piece. In a few Years it will recover it's Fertillity sufficient to bring Indian corn, which is of great use amongst them. Both for their Negroes Horses and all sorts of Cattle. It makes very indifferent Bread, and I look upon it as a troublesom and expensive thing to Cultivate. It is planted in hills about 1600 of them in an Acre, in the Month of April plowed, or rather Hoed every Fortnight till the Month of August, by that time it is fixed in the Ear they take no farther pains with it till November when they pluck the Blade of the staulk for fodder, for the Cattle in the Winter. The Ear remains on the Stalk till near Christmas to harden and dry. Indeed it woud keep their all Winter without takeing the least damage.

The Plant grows from four Feet to 12 Feet high and Produces from 12 to 30 Bushels the Acre. According to the Richness of the Land, and the attendance.

They seldom plant more than two Grains in one hill, if any extra ones shoots from the roots of these they are broke of before the Ear is formed.

Sometimes they sow Wheat amongst the Corn and get a Crop extraordinary. Wheat is sown in the Month of September they are obliged to sow it early or the severe Frosts in Winter woud kill it. Generally a Bushel to the Acre. Rye, Barley, Oats, Pease, Beans, Hemp, and Flax grows very well here, And would produce excellent Crops if they woud take any considerable pains in tilling the Land and make it fit to receive the seed. It is realy astonishing that it produces anything but weeds, as they seldom plow more then two Inches deep and leave one third of the Land undisturbed. I have seem Hemp 14 Feet high. I am not a judge in this Article) but I have been told by people that are, it is equal in goodness to the Riga Hemp. It is a pitty the cultivation of this usefull Plant is not more encouraged in this part of the world. It wou'd be a means of saveing large Sums we pay to Russians Annually for this Article. Among oursleves.

In short the Land will produce anything they will be at the pains to Cultivate. I do not know any reason why Crops of Wheat might not be produced here, equal in Quantity and Quality to the general Crops in England, if the People wou'd take the same method. I have seen Wheat weight 60 and 63 pound per Bushel very frequently.

The Cultivation of this Article is not alltogether Profitable. Because the Market is precarious. When Russia, Poland, and Germany are at Peace, Grain can be purchased cheaper there then in America. Consequently they must undersell the Americans at the Spanish, Portugal, and Mediterenian Markets. The West India are the only certain market they have, and in a Country allmost all are Farmers, the price must be low and very little demand, if their was no exportation.

But Beef, Pork and Horses will allways beare a good price while we have a trade with the West India Islands and the raising these things are not attended with any great expence. In the back parts of the Country their is no bounds to their outlet. When their is a plentifull Mast (What they call Mast, is Acorns, Wallnuts, Chesnuts and all Wild fruits) the Hogs will get Fat in the Woods with little, or no Corn. Great Quantities are kiled as soon as they are taken out of the Woods. Salted, Barreled and sent to the West Indies. Sells from 12 to 27 Shillings Currency per Hundred.

The Bacon cured here is not to be equaled in any part of the World, their Hams in particular. They first rub them over with Brown Sugar and let them lay all night. This extract's the wattery particles. They let them lie in Salt for 10 Days or a Fortnight, some rubs them with Hickory Ashes ins[t]ead of Salt Peetre, it makes them Red as the Saltpeetre and gives them a pleasant taste. Then they are hung up in the Smoke-house and a slow Smokey fire kept under them for three or four Weeks nothing but Hickory wood is burned in these Smoke-houses. This gives them an agreeable Flavor, far preferable to the Westphalia Hams, not only that, But it prevents them growing Rancid, and will preserve them for several Yeares by giveing them a fresh Smokeing now and

then. Beef cured in this manner is but very indifferent eating, indeed the Beef in
this Country is not equal in goodness to the English, it may be as fat, but not so
juicy. I think it is time to go to bed.

14th Disappointed by the Rascal who was to have gone with me to
Williamsburg, there is little dependence to be put in these Mercenary lazy
scoundrels. Spent the evening with Mr Mason who has extorted a promise from
me that entirely oversets all my intended schemes and will oblige me to do what
is very disagreeable.

Leesburg Loudon County Virginia April 15th 1777
Went to Captn Douglass's and engaged another man but I believe he like the
other will deceive me. Spent the evening at Leesburg with Mr Kirk, Mr Gibbs
and Captn McCabe.

16th This morning I have had my Chest searched for treasonable papers, by a
certain Mr Standhope[30] and Ensign McIntire,[31] by order of the Committee. Or
more properly the Court of Inquisition. The Scoundrels has plundered me of a
Shot pouch and powder horn which Captn White Eyes an Indian Chief gave me,
a Bearskin Blanket and several other articles of no very great value to me tho I
am very unwilling to part with them. I believe I might get them again, but the
remedy would be worse then disease. I think it the most prudent way to sit down
with the loss and say no more about it. I have very fortunately preserved my
Journal and the greatest part of my papers. Owing to the fidelity of my Boy who
suspected something of their business and found meanes to keep them below,
while I hid my papers in my Cardivine Case. My Diary excepted which had som
trifleing remarks in it. They seized it with the greatest Avidity and bore it off
with the rest of their plunder in great Triumph to the Committee room who have
been siting upon it all day—what will be the consequence I cant tell. Confusion
light upon them all.

Leesburg, Loudon County, Virginia, April 17th 1777
The Committee has puzzled themselves a long time but can find nothing that
amounts to treason against the States of America in my papers. I am Glad of it,
if they had my situation would have been dreadfull indeed, an imprisonment of
Five Years, or the Fine of Twenty Thousand pound would have been the
punishment. Neither of which I am willing to submit to the latter is utterly out of
my power. I must in course have submited to the first. The bare Idea of it makes
me shudder, the thought of a Prison even for debt is horrid. But these infernall
[penalties] for Tory's and Traytors, as the Rascals call them, make me tremble
with fear. I have hitherto escaped them, and may God of his goodness grant, that
I may allways escape them. If it is my fortune to become an inhabitant of those
horrid regions, may I bear my misfortune as becomes the character of an
Englishman and a Christian.

I am again disappointed of my horses. D—m the pittifull scoundrels
alltogether. I am determined to go by Water to Hampton.

Leesburg, Loudon County, Virginia, April 18th 1777
This morning I sent my Chest down to Alexandria and contrary to my
expectation, it went unmolested through the influence of my good Friend Mr
Mason. I invited Mr Kirk, Mr Cavan, Mr Deane, Captn McCabe and Mr Henry
McCabe to dine with me, as this is the last day I intend to spend in Leesburg,
they have all suped and spent the evening with me and got most heartily drunk.
And I am now going to bed at the Crooked Billet, as drunk as any honest man
aught to be.
19th Settled all my affairs and drew a Bill upon my my [sic] Father for
£69=10=2 in favor of Mr Kirk payable to Messrs Broomheads of Sheffield. This
is the Ballance I owe Mr Kirk if I escape now I shall not leave the Country one
penny in debt, and there is very few Europeans but what does, at this time,
except it is those who have had some trade in the Country and those are in
general Creditors. Left Leesburg but find no reluctance in parting with any one
but my good and worthy friend Mr Caven for whose Sincere friendship I have
the highest esteem. Lodged at Mosse's Ordinary with Mr Kirk. Drunk again.

Alexandria, Fairfax County, Virginia, Sunday, April 20th 1777
Got to Alexandria to Dinner. All the Towns people and a Regiment of Soldiers
that are quartered here all inoculated for the Smallpox, and I believe there is a
great number that has the great pox along with them. Such a pockefyed place I
never was in before. Spent the evening with Mr Kirk and Mr T. Crafts with
whom I lodge till I get a passage to Hampton.[32]
21st Tooke my passage in a Pilot Boat for Hampton, for which I am to pay £3
this is three Hundred pr Cent more then usual fare, so much is the paper
Currency depreciated in Value. Saw a Highlander (a Soldier in the 71st
Regiment now a prisoner of War here) whiped by his comrades for enlisting into
the Rebel service. He is the only one out of two Hundred and odd who has been
prisoners in this Colony that has enlisted into their service, his fellow prisoners
held a Court Martial over him, a Sergeant being the highest Officer present, and
condemned the poor wretch to receive 1500 lashes with a switch upon his bare
back, 100 every day till the number was complete. The man enlisted when drunk
and returned the money as soon as he was sober and absolutely refused to serve,
but this would not satisfy his enraged companions.

Alexandria, Fairfax County, Virginia, April 22nd 1777
This morning My worthy Friend Mr Kirk returned to Leesburg. This gentlemans
kindness I hope I shall allways remember with respect and gratitude, he has
allways behaved to me with great Friendship, Complaisan[ce], and Hospitality. I
have allways returned it to the utmost of my power. If my Father honors my
bills, I have this satisfaction, that he will be no looser by me, but a very
considerable gainer. A Certain Collin Keir a Young Scotch gentleman is to go
with me down to Hampton, he is a stranger to me, but appears to be a good
hearty joyous companion and a good Christian. News that nine English Men of

War are now in Delaware Bay. Saw a Scein drawn for Herrings and caught upwards of 40000 with about 300 Shad-fish. The Shad they use but the Herring are left upon the Shore useless for want of Salt. Such immence quantities of this fish is left upon the Shore to rot I am surprized it does not bring some epidemic disorder to the inhabitants, by the nauseous stench ariseing from shuch [sic] a Mass of putrefaction. Spent the evening with Mr Crafts at the Tavern.

Alexandria, Fairfax County, Virginia, April 23rd 1777
Waiting for a fair wind. Disagreeable thoughts will intrude themselves in spite of all I can do to avoid them. Spent the evening with Mr Robert Muir at Mr Crafts.
24th Sailed from Alexandria about noon. Mr Crafts gave me three Venison Hams. Called at Mr Marsdens to get a little stock, but he would not let us have so much as one Fowl, tho Mrs had often requested me to call at her house if ever I wanted stock for Sea and She would be glad to help me to some for the kindness I shewed her Son Mr Brook in our passage from the West Indies, but Mr Brook is dead. Mrs Marsden drunk and the Scoundrel her husband in an ill humour, therefore he is determined to keep his fowls and keep them he may for Nicholas. In the evening Ebb Tide and Wind a Head came to an Anchor off Sandy Point.
25th This morning parted our Cable in attempting to Weigh our Anchor. Obliged to run our Vessel aground in Nanjemoy Creek. Went to Nanjemoy to purchase another Anchor but cant meet with one. Dined at Mrs Leftwiches with my old Friend Mr Bayley. Lodged at Captn Knoxes with whom and Mr Wallace I spent an agreeable evening.

On Board the Pilot Boat, Sally, Potowmack River April 26th 1777
Parted with my good friends Mr Bailey, Captn B. Knox and Mr Wallace. To these gentlemen I am under infinite obligations for their great care of me in my sickness when I first arrived in this Country. These are all Scotchmen to which nation I had a particular dislike, owing to the prejudice of my education. I was taught to look upon them as a set of men divested of common humanity, ungenerous and unprincipled. I have allways found them the reverse of all this, and I most heartily condemn this pernicious system of education by which we are taught to look upon the inhabitants of a different Nation Language or Complection, as a set of beings far inferior to our own, this is a most iliberal and confined sentiment for human nature is invariable the same though the whole human species, from the Sootty African down to the fair European, allowances being made for their different customs manners and education. Proceeded down the River. Mr Keir had some business at Ceder Point, but the wind blew so hard he could not get a Shore or the Vessell Lay too till morning therfore we was obliged to bear away for Hampton.

Hampton, Virginia, Sunday April 27th 1777

Arrived here this Evening. Saw several Ships in the Bay but no Men of War. Lodged at the Sighn of the Bunch of Grapes kept by one Dames an Irishman.[33] This is a little port town but allmost ruined by the Soldiers who was quartered here last winter who made terrible havock by pulling the Wooden houses to pieces for fuel, all the Garden pails fences & & in the neighbourhood are entire burned up.

28th Hired a Horse to go to Williamsburg to wait upon the Governor and Council. This place is rather inconveniently situated for Trade, at the head of a small Creek, no Vessels of any considerable burthen can come to the town. Here is 4 of the [blank] Gallies here and a great number of row Boats for the use of the State. Here is a Company of Rifle-men stationed here, under the command of my old friend Captn John Lee, tho we are very friendly, I think he suspects me to be a Tory, he does not know that I am prisoner and I wont tell him.

Here is two Frenchmen at our Inn who have got Commissions in this Army. Tho I suspect one of them to be an Irishman who passes here for a Frenchman, for I hear him at this instant cursing the waiter in English, or rather Irish English.

Williamsburg the Capital of Virginia, April 29th 1777

Set out early this morning. Dined at York-town 24 Miles from Hampton. This is a pleasant town situated upon York River which is Navigable for the largest Ships Close to the town. Here is several very good Gentlemens houses built of Brick and some of their Gardens layd out with the greatest taste of any I have seen in America but now allmost ruined by the disorderly Soldiery, and what is more extrordinary, their own Soldiers, the guardians of the people and the defenders of their rights. Houses burned down, others puled to pieces for fewel, most of the Gardens thrown to the street, every thing in disorder and confusion and no appearance of trade. This melancholy scene fills the mind of the Itenerant traveler with gloomy, and horrid Ideas, here is a Battery consisting of 12 pieces of heavy Cannon, to command the River and a Company of Artillery stationed here, but they make a sorry appearance for so respectable a Corps, as the Artillery aught to be. Got here soon after dinner only 12 Miles from York-town, the road from Hampton is level and sandy through large pine Woods, interspersed with plantations and Gentlemens Houses, the land in general appears barren, the produce is Tobacco and Corn.

This is the finest town I have seen in Virginia it is situated between two Creeks, only navigable for Boats, the one falling into James and the other into York Rivers, it consists of one principal street about a Mile long, very wide and level, with a number of good buildings the Capitol at one end of the Street and the College at the other, towards endowing this College King Wm and Queen Mary gave £2000 and 2000 Acres of Land and a duty of one penny pr pound upon all Tobacco exported to the other Colonies towards the support of it, and there has been several donations to it since, but like all other publick Seminaries it is much abused. The Capitol is the place where all publick business is done. The Colonial Assemblies meet & &, they are both large and elegant Brick buildings. In the Capitol is a fine Marble Statue of the late Governor Botetourt,[34] as large as life, in the atitude of an Orator, a roll of parchment in one hand as an emblem of their Charter, and the Cap of Liberty in the other, it is mounted on a Pedestal and surrounded with Iron Balustrades on the Front of the Pedestal is his Excellncys arms and this inscription

The Right Honourable Norborne Berkley, Barron of Botetourt. His Majesty's late Lieutenant, and Governor General of the Colony and Dominion of Virginia.

On the right of pedestal is this inscription

Deeply impress'd with the warmest sense of Gratitude for his Excellence the Right Honourable Lord Botetourts prudent and wise administration, and that the remembrance of those many publick And Social Virtues which so eminently adorned his illustrious Character might be transmited to the latest posterity. The general Assembly of Virginia on the 20th of July Anno Domini 1771 Resolved with one united voice, to erect this Statue to his Lordships memory.

This underneath

Let wisdom and justice preside in any Country
    The people will rejoice and must be happy.

On the Left of the pedestal is the following inscription

America, B[e]hold Your Friend! who leaveing his native Country, declined those additional Honnours which she had there in store for him, that he might heal Your Wounds and restore Tranquility to this extensive Continent with what zeal and anxiety he pursued these glorious Objects Virginia thus bears her gratefull testimony.

On the back of the pedestal is the figure of Britania with her Spear and Shield, America with her Bow and Quiver, each holding an Olive Branch over an Alter with this Motto Concordia.

It is looked upon as a masterly piece of Statuary and what is very remarkable, not in the least defaced tho exposed to the publick such veneration had the people for this great man. The Governors Palace is a good Brick building but it does not make a grand appearance. Here is only one Church, none of the Grandest and I suppose here may be about 250 houses in town.

Lodged at Andersons Tavern.[35]

York-town Virginia. April 30th 1777

This morning I waited upon the Governor at the Palace delivered my Letters from Mr Mason & Mr Elzey and was most politely treated, had the honor of

Breakfasting with his Excellency who ordered me to meet him at the Council Chamber in the Capitol. I did so, and was examined very strictly about my sentiments some of which I thought proper to deny, and others, tho very impudently to avow.

All that I could say would not procure me permission to go on Board his Majesty's Ships in the Bay, however they have given me a permit to go in the Albion, A Ship that is to come round from N. Carolina to Nansymond River for 133 Scotch Gentlemen who are there waiting for her but I think she will never arrive there.[36] If she does come and I can't get a passage in her, they in their great Clemency will give me leave to go to France in one of their Vessels.

This is the highest Court in the Colony therefore I can have have no other redress. I am determined to risque a passage. Dined at Wmsburg with two Colonels 5 Majors 7 Captains and a number of inferior Officers. The Grace—G-d D-m the King of England by Colnl Innis,[37] for this Millitary diner I pay'd 27 s. D-m the Millitary and the times together. Got to York Town in the evening which I spent with Lieut Ancram and lodged at the Sign of the Swan.[38]

Hampton, Virginia. May 1st 1777
Left Yorktown. Got to Hampton in the afternoon. Mr Keir, who went to Norfolk [on] some business, is not yet returned. Great numbers of Frenchmen in Williamsburg, York-town and Hampton, indeed most of the Stores are kept by Frenchmen, every thing is at a most exorbitant price—at York-town I wanted a Single sheet of paper, but they refused to sell me one, unless I would take a Quire I must go without, for which they asked 9 Shillings. Salt at £3 pr Bushel, which I have seen sold at 2 s pr Bushel since I came into the Country. Linin Cloth at 30 S & 37 S pr Yard such as they usually sold at 3 s & 3s.6d pr yd. Woollen Cloth if Red, Green, Buff, or Blue, or any Colour fit for uniforms at £5 and £6 pr yd such as they usually sold at 18 s & 20 s pr yd. Buttons and trimings if suitable at what ever price they please to ask. Rum at 20 & 30 Shillings pr Gallon usually sold at 2 s pr Gallon, Loafe Sugar at 12 Shilling pr lb. usually sold at 1 Shilling, in short everything bears a great price, their imports in particular, owing to the little value of their paper Currency and the total want of Specie. Suped and spent the evening with some French-men.

Hampton, Virginia. May 2nd 1777
Mr Keir arrived in the night who informs me that the English prisoners have made their escape from Alexandria.[39] About noon my old worthy Friend Mr Cavan came to this place on purpose to see me. this is a very great proof of his respect to come allmost 300 Miles on purpose to bid me farewell. We have spent this evening, very happy together, but the probability of it being the last that we may ever spend together conveys a Gloomy Idea.

3rd This morning parted with my good and affectionate friend Mr Cavan for this Honest and Sincere Young Man I have the warmest friendship I ever yet had for man. May Heaven prosper all his undertakings and guard him in this land of misery. The concern at parting with him, and the thoughts what situation I may shortly be in myselfe requires all the fortitude I can muster to suport it with a tolerable grace. Mr Keir and I hired a passage Boat to carry us to Mopsack Bay,[40] to Colnl Lewis's an acquaintance of Mr Keirs providing things necessary for our passage.[41] Spent the evening with Commadore Tolliver who has the command of the Gallies here and some French Gentlemen.[42]

On Board the Passage Boat, Dorothy, Lynn haven Bay, Sunday May 4th 1777
Thank God for our good fortune so far. This morning got all our things on Board very early, thinking to give them the slip, that is to have got into the Bay before the Look-out Boats had been stiring. But I believe Commodore Tolliver had some suspition of our design, for he came to our lodgings very early and insisted upon us takaking [sic] a Julap with him which we repeated so often that all hands got very merry, my companion excepted, who was too angry with the
old Commodore for hindering us. I was well aware of the Commodor's intent, therefore drank plentifully with him helped him to abuse the King, Lord North, and all the British Ministry, this sort of behaviour puzzled the old man a little but made him very friendly and exceeding Complaisant, which complaisance we would very willingly have excused, for he would see us on Board as he said, to wish us a good passage, but in fact, to send a Guard along with us, as it has since proov'd. No sooner was we got on Board but he called the Master of the Boat a side, and had a long Confab with him.

He returned with the Boat-man, and beged that we would give, two young men that belonged to his Galley, a passage to Gloster Point. To this Mr Keir, in secret objected. But I with seeming cheerfullness, consented. tho in my heart, wished them both at the Devil, in a very short time they came with each of them a Bayonet at their side, which made my companion curse them very sincerely, but very privately. About 11 O:Clock we took our departure from Hampton with our two Galley-men the Master of the Boat and a Boy so that we had 4 to two, and to add to our misfortune a Boat with a Flag of Truce sailed out of the Harbour this morning for the Men of War and we had two Armed Look-out Boats to escape, which makes our situation very dangerous, however, I felt, and still feel, myselfe in good spirits. I am determined to effect my escape or perish in the attempt. Before we got out of the Creek I begun to ply our two Galley-men with Whiskey Grog which they took very freely, my companion in an ill humour allmost despareing of success, immagined the halter allready about his neck, and absolutly refused to drink one drop with the men.

Before we got out of Hampton Road, by acting the part of the drunken man and behaveing in a very free and familiar manner, I had ingratiated myselfe much into the good favor of our two unthinking Galley-men, and God forgive me, helped them to curse the King, Lord North, & & and tho it was Sunday, sung them some Rebel songs in short I said or did anything that I thought would please them or lull them into security. As soon as we had weathered Point Comfort the Wind came to to [sic] blow at S. E. the worst wind for us in the Compass, this caused a Rough Sea, and made me most horridly Sick. I went to

Caskade over the Bows Mr Keir followed me under a pretence to give me some assistance, or rather to make his diversion of me. But in fact to lay a scheme how to secure our Guard and the Boats hands, which we happily effected in the following manner. Mr Keir went into the hold and puled the Spile out of the water Cask and came upon Deck again. I as if by chance, saw the water runing out and called to the men to go and stop it, or we could have no more Grog. the thoughts of being deprived of this precious Liquor alarmed our two Galley-men, both equally desireous to preserve so valuable an article, jumped into the Hold together but could not find a Spile, I picked up a small piece of wood and gave it to the Boy who went down with it. When Mr Keir and I took the Hatch and shut them below we then had three of the fools secure. I most ingeniously confess that I did not like the fourth, who by this time had observed what we was about, and said he hoped we were only joking. I desired Mr Keir to fetch him to the others which he absolutely refused alledging that as he was the heavyer man, he could hold down the Hatch the better. I then went up to the man, put on the bigest look I could presented a Pistol to his head, and desired him to walk forward to his Companions. He seemed to hesitate a little, I begun [to] think that I should be under the necessity of giveing him his Quietus. But Mr Keir luckeyly called out, Dam his Soul, Blow his brains out, which frighted the poor fellow that he immediately fell upon his knees and begged his life. which I granted upon condition that he went to his companions without further resistance, which he, I believe with great reluctance consented to, we gave them a Bottle of Whiskey, a Venison Ham and left them to condole their misfortunes together, but we first took care to secure the Hatch. We had no sooner secured our prisoners, then their fell one of the thickest Fog's I ever saw, and the Wind continued at S. E. we have been beating about all afternoon in the greatest fear and anxiety, about Sun set the Fog cleared up, and we found ourselves at the mouth of this Bay, the wind falling away and flood Tide we stood inn Shore and are come to an Anchor about a Quarter of a Mile from shore. Mr Keir and I agree to keep Watch 2 hours at a Spell. We have seen no Ship Brig or Boat since we left Point Comfort, which is a great comfort to us, without we had seen some of his Majesty's Ships.

I write this upon Deck by Moonlight in my watch, our prisoners are all got drunk and Cursing each other as the author of their misfortune. I feel a pleasure I have long been a stranger to in the hopes of once more gaining my liberty. I am happy that we have secured these poor wretches without bloodshed. If we are retaken hanging will be our certain doom. But I am determined the Rascals shall never have the honor of hanging me. Collin is fast a sleep.

On Board the Bell & Mary, Chesapeak Bay, May 5th 1777

Last night, or rather this morning, Mr Keir fell asleep in his watch, which is such an instance of carelessness I cannot easily forgive. About 4 O Clock this morning the wind sprung up at N. W. Weighed and stood out of the Bay. Mr Keir and I was near quarreling about the Course we should stear. He was for standing out to Sea, in quest of some of his Majesty's Ships. I opposed this as a very desperate step we had not provision on Board for more then three days and little or no water, neither Quadrant, Log Glass, or Chart, four prisoners on Board, and a Crazy small Vessel with a very indifferent Compass. If we are blown out to Sea it is allmost impossible that we should ever make Land again, admit that we escape the dangers of the Sea, We must inevitable perish with hunger and fatigue. Or which is worse, perhaps be retaken by some of the Rebels Ships, without by mear accident we fall in with some of the Kings Ships. My opinion was for us to keep inn Shore and stand for New York which is about 100 Leagues we may possible get there in two or three days if we have favourable Winds, and we have a greater probabillity of meeting some of his Majesty's Ships that Course especially about Delawar Bay.

We disputed about this matter for some time. Mr Keir was at the Helm and stood out to Sea till we were almost out of sight of Land, when he jumped up in an extacy of joy, swore he saw the Pheonix Man of War a little upon our Starboard Bow about 4 Miles from us. And it realy prooved to be her in Company with a Ship, Brig, Sloop, and Schooner all prizes, we bore a down upon her, and in a little time her Cutter came a long side side [sic] of us and ordered us to go under the Phenix Stern. As soon as we got on Board the Phenix we told our situation to Captn Parker who behaved very Civilly to us, and understand[ing] that we wished to go to New York, he ordered us to go on Board this Ship who is bound ther as soon as we can get a Convoy. Captn Parker invited us to dinner with him and treated us very kindly and genteelly. And gave me the Epethet of the Englishman from the answer I gave to the Officer in the Cutter, when he first hailed us. As soon as we made the Ship our prisoners begged that we would get them at Liberty if possible, we immediately threw their Bayonets into the Sea and reported the Galley-men as inocent Country lads. And Captn Parker was kind enough to give them their liberty, all but the Boatman who is an Excellent Pilot, and he is put upon the Ships Books as Pilot at 9s pr Day.[43]

On Board the Bell and Mary off Cape Henry May 6th 1777

This Ship is the first that the Rebels took last Summer, then Called the Lady Julian, loaded with Rum and Sugar from Jamaica for London, Captn Steephens, and retaken on Saturday last, Bound to Bourdeaux laden with 468 Hhhd [sic] of Tobacco and some Flour.[44] Dined and Suped on Board the Phenix Captn Hyde Parker junr of 44 Guns and 280 men. I have had the pleasure of seeing them take one Sloop loaded with Salt and Rice from Carolina to Boston and drive two Schooners on Shore this day. The Second Lieutenant of the Phenix is Master of the Bell and Mary. This gentleman went round the World with Captn Wallace[45] and is a sensible well behaved friendly man. A Mr Wm Furneval a Cheshire man Midshipman belonging to the Phenix acts as his mate, appears to be a good natured man but quite a Sailor.[46] In the Evening his Majesty's Ship Thames of 32 Guns comanded by Captn Tyrringham How arrived from a Chase with a prize Sloop, this Ship is to be our Convoy to New York. I am a little Sea sick, but my mind is much at ease I have not the fear of a halter before my eyes. Wind Southerly.

On Board the Bell & Mary towards New York. May 7th 1777
Sailed for New York with his Majesty's Ship Thames for Convoy, in Company with a Prize Sloop and two Schooners. In the afternoon took a French Brig, supposed to be bound for Chesapeak Bay, but said she was bound for St Peeters in Newfoundland. Thick foggy weather, obliged to fire Guns and ring Bells for fear of Looseing Convoy. Wind light and Southerly.
8th Find Lieutenant Robinson a very cheerfull companion part of a Virtuosi but of the sensible sort. He has offered me a Passage in this Vessel Gratis if he goes in her to England. My companion and Brother Scape, begins to make a poor mouth, indeed we are both poor enough but it does no good talking about it. Foggy weather and Light Easterly winds. Our French Prize gave us the Slip last night and got clear off.
9th Pleasant weather but light winds. I understand provisions are very dear at New York. If I am obliged to stay there any time I shall be distressed in my finances.
10th Light Breezes and pleasant weather we pass our time very happily with Lieut Robinson and Mr Furneval whose drollery makes us all merry.

On Board the Bell & Mary towards New York. Sunday, May 11th 1777
My thoughts much confused, and a very great struggle in my mind. Honnor on one side, Revenge, Intrest, Inclination, and Necessity on the other. Which will get the better I cannot yet tell. Made the Jersey shore in the evening, the Land appears very low. Came to an Anchor close in with the Land the fleet in Co.
12th Weighed and came to Sail early this morning. About noon made the High Land of Mever Sink upon the Jersey shore. At 3 A. M. pass'd the Light House at Sandy Hook. It is about 100 Feet high built upon the Jersey Shore, here we found his Majesty's Ships, Syren, Emerald and the Preston of 50 Guns Commodore Hotham.[47]

Got a Pilot on Board. In the evening came to an Anchor. Long Island bearing East. Staten Island West.
13th Still at Anchor in sight of Sandy Hook and the Narrows. Wind at North blowing fresh, the Land appears to be hilly and stony some very pretty houses a long Shore but every thing about them seems to be going to ruin and destruction in consequence of this Rebellion.

On Board the Bell & Mary, New York, Harbour. May 14th 1777
This morning the Wind came round to South, Weighed, and got up to the Town about noon. Moored our Ship opposite the Navy Brewhouse which is on Long Island. Mr Robinson went a Shore, but wont permit Mr Keir and me to go, untill he has seen the Admiral. I must now determine what to do. Wheather to enter into the Army or return home. If I was at liberty to follow my own inclination I

would enter into the Army. But the Solemn promise I made Mr Mason on the 14th of April utterly forbids it, which was not to enter into any Army of 12 Months from that day. To this Gentleman I am under very great, and many obligations, had it not been for his kind interposition on the 20th of October 1775, and his offering to be Bound in a very large Sum, that I should not depart the Colony of Six Month from that time, I must have been draged to prison or have entered into their Army. What stamps the greater Value upon the obligation, he did it unsolicited and unknown to me. His giveing me letters of recommendatin to the Members of Congress, and the Governor and Council of Virginia, Nay I believe, he extorted this promise from me out of a principle of humanity extended to my Parents who he understood from my account are much averse to me entering into the Army.

I am certain Mr Mason can have no view of intrest in what he did for me, it is impossible that he should have any, only that ariseing from a generous mind helping a stranger in distress. Should I let my inclination or my necessity's get the better of my honnor, I shall forever detest myselfe, as a mean dirty rascal.

No! forbid it honor, forbid it Heaven, be the consequence what it will, I will not enter into the Army til the expiration of my promised time. But the thoughts of returning home a Beggar, is worse then death. I can bear to write upon this subject no longer.

15th Went a Shore with Lieutnt Robinson to the Secretary's Office, and had orders to wait upon the General Howe tomorrow morning at Nine O Clock. Dined at the Kings Head Tavern. Mr Keir and I took lodgings at a little dirty pot-house, the only one we can get at present, every thing here, is very dear provisions in particular. I believe Mr Keir intends entering into the Army. I heartily wish I was at liberty to go with him. Slept on Board this night.

New York. May 16th 1777

This morning waited upon General Howe, was indroduced to him by Major Cuyler.[48] His Excellency asked me about the affairs in Virginia and wheather I thought there was a great many friends to Government there. To both questions, I answered him with truth to the best of my knowledg. But I think his information has been bad and his expectations too Sanquine. I told him my own situation very Candidly, gave him my real reasons why I could not enter into the Army. He behaved to me with the greatest politness, seemed to aprove of my honourable resolution, as he was pleased to call it. And promised to do any thing for me that lay in his power in respect to my geting home, that is, if I meet with a Ship to my mind that is bound home he will give me a permit to go in her. I believe Mr Keir will enter into the Army and has some prospect of geting a Lieutenancy in Major Hollands Guides.[49] He is refered to Sir Wm Erskine[50] his Countryman therefore he needs not fear, for the Scotch will hang together. Lodged at one Captn Millar's a Scotch refugee from Norfolk in Virginia, it is a mean dirty nasty hole I am determined to leave it tomorrow.

New York May 17th 1777
Took lodgings at one John Titus, a Quaker in the Queen Street near the Navy Warf, at 28 Shillings pr Week and only to have two fresh Dinners in the week this is very high, but the cheapest I can get. I must get from New York as soon as possible. Mr Keir stays at the old place, it is such a nasty stinking Blackgaard [sic] place I cannot bear it.
18th Sunday. In the forenoon went to St Pauls Church and heard a Military Sermon by the Revd Mr O. Brien. This is a very neat Church, and some of the handsomest and Best Dress'd Ladys I have ever seen in America. I believe most of them are W—s. In the afternoon went to [blank] Church but I dont like the parson. Saw two boys kiled by the bursting of a Cannon. Drank Tea at Mr Gresswolds, Distiller.
19th and 20th I have spent these two days in enquireing about the Ships but I find there is no Fleet to Sail for England very soon. Exceeding uneasy. I see want and poverty comeing upon me very fast, and no means of avoiding them.

New York, May 21st 1777
Saw three Regiments of Hessians review'd by Generals De Heister and Knyphausen. Regiment De Denop Regiment De Losberg, Regiment De Knyphausen. They are fine troops but very slow in their motions when compared with the English. They fired several rounds with the greatest exactness. One of their Corporals run the Gantlet Eight times through the Regiment, he had upwards of 2000 lashes, which he bore with the greatest resolution and firmness, not a single Muscle of his face discomposed all the time. They appear to be a set of Cruel unfeeling people. They had a Train of Artillery consisting of Ten fine Brass Field pieces which they fired several rounds. Their Artillery-men seem to be the only Active men they have when they have a piece of Artillery to draw they moove very quick, at other times they seem to be half dead or quite stupid.
I live as cheap as I possible can and I find it will cost me 40 Shillings pr Week, York Currency, and there is no prospect of geting home soon, or to do any thing here to get a liveing. Patience, Patience.

New York, May 22nd 1777
This morning met with Mr Joseph Brewer, who has just made his escape from Philadelphia, this Gentleman has been obliged to leave his Wife behind him to the mercy of the Rebels, the persecution against the friends of Government was too violent, for a man of his warm temper to stay any longer amongst them with safety either of person or property. In the afternoon, very unexpectedly, but very agreeable, met with two old Cronie's, Captn Scot and Captn Buddecomb. I have been at the Play with Lieutn Robinson, to whom I gave a Ticket, my present circumstances will badly afford extravagancies of this kind, but this Gentleman has ofered me a passage home, if he goes master of the Bell & Mary, I think it only gratitude to oblige him if I can. I know him to be fond of plays and at the

same time fond of his money. We had the Honor of siting in the same Box with General Piggot before the General came to the house, a Centinal came and ofered to turn us out but the old Veteran swore he would not be Turnd a Drift with any one. The play was the Lyar, Polly Hunneycomb the entertainment, By the Officers of the Army, for the benefit of Soldiers Widows.[51]

New York. May 23rd 1777

Captn Buddecomb informs me that he has had several Letters from my friends, about me. The thoughts of returning to them a Beggar I cannot bear with patience my misfortunes have been unavoidable, And the common lot of Thousands besides myself, but that will be no excuse. I wish I could avoid going home.

24th Saw 800 of the Hessian Troops reviewed and their Train of Artillery. They are fine Healthy looking men but seem to be too heavy Cloathed for this hot Country.

25th Sunday. Mr Brewer and I crossed the East River and took a view of the Fortifications made by the Rebels upon Long Island. A Fort above the Ferry called Fort Sterling which commands the City of New York, appears to be a place of strength but we could not get admitance into it. About a Quarter of a Mile from Fort Sterling is another Fort called Cabble Hill, or Mutton Pye Battery by the Sailors. it is a small round Fort, but very strong, from its situation it commands the River and Country round as far as the Guns will reach subteranious Magazines for their Stores, Provisions and Water. the Barracks for the men are Bomb proof. It appears to me, (But I dont pretend to be a competent judge in Military affairs) that a small number of resolute men might have made a stand against the whole of the British Army. When the Rebels were defeated on this Island on the 28th of August last, great numbers of them were kiled in attempting to cross a Tide-mill dam, at low water to get to this Fort, they stuck fast in the mud and were either kiled by our people or drownded at High Water, saw the remains of them sticking up their knees and elbows in the mud. Here is great numbers of other Fortifications of different sorts which the Rascals in their Panick left as everlasting monuments of their great Labour, and great Cowardice. Dined at Flat Bush where the Rebels got their greatest drubing. this is a pretty Village a great number of Orchards about it and some very pritty houses about it. The Land is in general light and Sandy. Fences part stone part Wood, severall small hills and Stony. Got to town at Night.

New York. Monday. May 26th 1777

Some more Troops are arrived from Hallifax in Nova Scotia. I believe they are much wanted. Spent the day with Mr Brewer and Doctor Smith, who read us a narrative of his sufferings amongst the Rebels. This is the same Doctor Smith that I saw with Major Connoly at Frederick Town in Maryland, from which place he made his escape but was retaken. And made his escape a second time by the help of his Blankets from the top of the New Jail in Philadelphia.[52] Mr Keir has got a Lieutn in the Guides or rather Pioneers.

27th Last night it was so hot I could not bear a Sheet upon me in Bed and this morning it is so Cold I can bear to wear my great Coat. Dined with Captn Buddecomb on Board his Ship. There appears to be something misterious in Buddecomb's behaviour but I am at a loss to account for it. News that their has been an engagement at [sic] that the Rebels have lost a great number of men. But I believe there is as many lies in the papers here as amongst the Rebels.

New York. Wednesday. May 28th 1777

This day 14 Sail of Transports arrived with Troops from England. I have seen Mr Robinson but he cannot tell me when the Bell & Mary Sails for England, he seems to be in some doubt wheather she goes or not. I am determined to get a passage in the first Vessel that sails for England if I can. I cannot stay here much longer my money wont hold out more then another week. O! Poverty. Poverty, thou plague of my Life, when shall I get clear of thy troublesome company. If company is any consolation in Poverty, here is plenty of poor devils to keep me in countenance. I have not yet betrayed any signs of Poverty, only in my dress. I will let that be when I spend my last penny. To be poor and seem so is the devil.
29th I have taken my passage on Board a Brig belonging to Liverpool, but Bound for London. Called the Edward John Park Master. I have told my real situation to Captn Park who very kindly and humanely offers to supply me with what money I want till our arrival in London. He expects to Sail on Wednesday next with a Convoy.

New York. Friday. May 30th 1777

Exceedingly tired of my inactive situation. The house where I Lodge is kept by a Quaker, he and his Wife are two of the greatest Jews I ever knew and two of the greatest Hypocrites. These Religious hypocrites are of a deeper dye then the irreligious ones, because they make, what they call their Sacred Religion, a Cloke to cover the vilest of crimes. Some droll Cookery here. Molasses in every thing, even to Salt Pork. They are right Yankeys.
31st Troops arriveing. Others embarking. A great fuss and I believe there is very little done. Forty two Rebels came in to day to be whitewashed. Most heartily tired of this place nothing to do and live at a great expence. Suped and spent the evening with Captn Scot on Board the Brig Harriot in Company with Captains Buddecomb, Johnston, Powers & Grundy. Budecomb is a man of great low cuning, Powers low Wit, Johnston a Satyrist and Grundy a Sot but the best behaved man of the whole. Buddecombs behaviour is still a mistery that I cannot unriddle. he cannot bear to hear anything said in favor of Mr Kirk, he has not yet forgot his quarrel. Mem. be Cautious.

New York. Sunday. June 1st 1777

My present situation is far from being agreeable, tho much better then it was a Month ago. I now breath the air of Liberty and Freedom which I have been a stranger to since the 20th of October 1775. For very substantial reasons I have never mentioned this in my journal before.

As I have alwaws [sic] carryed it about with me, and have allways had a notion that I should be obliged to make my escape, something in the manner I at last effected it. if my own hand writeing had been produced as a witness against me (Supposeing that I had been taken in attempting to make my escape by people who did not personally know me I might have had some small chance of regaining my liberty, but had I allways carryd such a capital witness against me, in my pocket, and have been taken before I had time to destroy it, My life must undoubtedly have pay'd the forfiture of my Folly and Imprudence.

Instead of going to Church, I will rectify that mysterious part of my Journal, while it is fresh in my memory. Probably at some future period, when I have less time (for I have absolutely too much at present to do any thing as it aught to be done) but more inclination and my mind more at ease then it is at the present. I may Revise and Correct the many erors that frequent[ly] occur in it. I think I shall defer it till I am an Old man, for at present I have no thoughts of turning author.

In the Month of March 1775 I wrote to all my friends in England, and freely declared my sentiments upon the present Rebellion, indeed I then called it by no other name to my Friends. My letters I sent by a friend bound to Leghorn, but the Council of Safety's Boat, Boarded him in the Bay, and he was obliged to give up all the letters he had on Board, mine amongst the rest, which were read before the Council of Safety and sent express to the Committee at Alexandria with orders to secure my person, as one Inimical to the rights and liberties of America. But I was gone into the Back Country before the express arived at Alexandria, however, the Letters were lodged with the Chairman of the Committee till my return in October 1775. When a meeting of the Committee was immediately called and they thought proper in their great Wisdom and prudence to make a Resolve that the Body of Nicholas Cresswell should be commited to the care of the Jail Keeper untill he the said Nicholas Cresswell was fully convinced of his Political errors. In short, I was Arraign'd, Tryed, Condemned and the sentence nearly put in execution before I knew any thing about it. But by the kind interposition of Mr Thomson Mason immediately repriev'd, by his offering to be bound in any Sum they chose to mention that I should not depart the Colony of Six Months without their Consent.

I was utterly unacquainted with the whole proceeding till the day after the Committee had agree'd to send me to jail. When Mr Mason in a very polite letter let me know what he had done for me, hopeing that I would make myself as easy as possible in the Colony during the limited time, as he did not doubt but matters would be accomodated before the expiration of Six Months, as he trusted implicitly to my honnor, the fullfiling the contract he had made in my favour, at the same time made me an offer of His house and assistance in any thing that lay in his power. I then remooved to Leesburg and before the expiration of the Six Months was taken Sick and continued so till the latter end of July 1776 in this time I was not disturbed by the Committee I thought it a proper time to get a way. Accordingly I got letters of recommendation to some members of the Congress from my friend Mr Mason, by which meanes I got a pass from the Congress Dated Aust 29th 1776.

By virtue of this Pass I was permited to go to New York from which place I intended to make my escape to our Army then on Long Island. I got to New York on the 7th of September 1776 and had lay'd the plan for my escape to our Fleet or Long Island which ever I could get to. By means of a floating stage that was moored in the Old Slip, No other thing either Boat or Canoo was to be found. Just as I had found this out I unfortunately met with Mr Thomson a Presbyterian parson & Chaplain to one of the Virginia Regiments then at New York. With this gentleman I had quarreled about politics in November 1774. I believe he remembered it and suspected my design, but for that evening behaved with the greatest politeness only took care to put a guard over me. On the next morning he told me he knew my sentiments and if I did not chuse to return to Virginia with Lieutenant Moland I would be put in the provo immediately.

I assured him Curiosity was my only motive for comeing there I had no intention of going to the Enemy, this would not satisfy the Revd Sir. I must either return to Virginia or go to the provo. I had no other alternative. And to convince him that I had no intention of makeing my escape I would cherefully return with Mr Moland, but hoped he would not send me in the Character of a prisoner. He assured me Mr Moland would go with me in the character of a companion. I was under the necessity of submiting to this Puritanic Priest for fear of worse consequences. Mr Moland behaved very well to me all the way, allways willing to do as I did and had it not been for the thoughts of him being as a guard over me, would have been an excellent companion. Mr Thomson had wrote to the Committee of Leesburg concerning me by Mr Moland, who according[ly] met, and was for commiting me to prison but by the intrest of Mr Mason I was a second time reprieved. And they agree'd to take my own Parole for four Months from the 20th of September 1776 to the 20th of January 1777. In that time they used many threats and perswasions to get me into their Army. I had got Mullers Treatise upon Fortification and Gunnery, which some of their Military Officers had seen in my lodgings.[53] I had got some of the Technical terms belonging to the profession by heart, which I allways took care to use before the most Vain part of them, especially if I knew them to be ignorant. Such as those are allways the best Puffs with the Vulgar herd. When I hapened into company with those who understood it I allways took Care to give them evasive and ambiguous answers. By these meanes I became consequential amongst them and I believe it was the chief reason why they treated me with so much Civility, as they was pleased to call it.

My first Parole was no sooner expired but I was obliged to give a Second for three Months, from the Fifth of February to the Fifth of May. Which I broke with great reluctance only one day. But if such a breach of honor can be excused, I certainly may, in justice, claim some title [to] it. Because I suffered in consequence of a Law, made after the offence was commited, when I wrote my letters, Which was the original cause of my confinement, there was no Act, or Resolve made by the Colonial Convention, or the Congress, to imprison any one meerly for their sentiments. The Act, Resolve, Edict or what ever name it has, for imprisonment and confiscation of the efects of friends to Government, was made by the Congress in March 1776. After I had had a Ne Exit Colonia upon me for near Six Months. I think this is a sufficient and ample excuse for me breaking my parole a single day. I am weary with scribbleing therefore will give over.

New York. Monday. June 1st [sic] 1777

I have been here almost three weeks and I am as ignorant of the Motions or designs of our Army as if I had been in Virginia. Only this, the Soldiers seem very healthy and long to be in action. The Commander in Chief is either inactive, has no orders to Act, or he thinks that he has not force sufficient to oppose the Rebels. But which of these, or wheather any of them is the true reason I will not pretend to say. But this I am very certain off, if General Howe does nothing, the Rebels will avail themselves of his inactivity by collecting a very numerous Army to oppose him, whenever he shall think proper to leave Mrs Lorain and face them.

I have seen Captn Buddecomb to day and I observe he has a very different behaviour from what he used to profess in Virginia, But for what reason I cannot conceive. Wheather Mr Kirk told him anything to my prejudice in hopes to blow up a quarrel between him and me, in hopes to reape some advantage by it I can't tell. Or wheather he may think that I am in want of money, and is affraid I may ask him to lend I can't tell. If it is so, he may ease himselfe of those feares. I never will borrow money from such a mean spirited wretch. I have been deceiv'd in this fellow.

On Board the Brig Edward New York Harbour. June 2nd 1777

Captn Park invited me to come and live on Board the Brig and Mess with him, as it will be much cheaper then liveing on Shore. I was very glad of the ofer as I have only two Guineas left. Accordingly he sent the Boat for my Chest and Bed. I left my Jewish Quaker without regret. I have got two pair of Drill Trowsers made here the stuff cost me 12 Shilling and the Rogue of a Taylor has charged me 18 Shillings for makeing them. I am very confident that I could have had them made in England for half a Crown, everything is most extravagantly high in this place. Money is here in plenty and here is a set of people, who from the nature of their profession and their uncertainty of life, Spend it as fast as they can get it. But here is some who profit greatly by their extravagancy and are makeing fortunes very fast, by the Dissipation of the Soldiery. Captn Park dont expect to Sail this week.

On Board the Brig, Edward, New York Harbour. June 3rd 1777

Slinging my Cot and prepareing for the Voyage. I flatter myselfe with the prospect of an agreeable Passage along with Captn Park. Fourteen Sail of Transports are arrived with Hessian Soldiers on Board, from England. No News.

4th This being the Anniversary of his Majesty's Birth Day—at one O'clock, Fort George, The Men of War and Ships in the Harbour fired a Royal salute. In the evening Lord Howe gave a Ball to the Officers of the Navy and Army and their Ladies. At night the City was illuminated. I observ'd it was not generally illuminated.

A number of Hessian Chasseurs or Yaugers arrived. Green uniforms, and Boots, all Armed with Rifles. I am told they are as expert with them as the Virginians. But they appear to me to be too Clumsy for the Woods and too heavy Cloathed. I cant conceive why they weare Boots, they must be very inconvenient and troublesom in this hot and Wooddy Country. Spent the evening with Mr Furnival.

On Board the Brig, Edward, New York Harbour, June 5th 1777

This morning Captn Scot and I hired a Single Horse Chair amd took a Tour upon Long Island to Salisbury Plains through a little town Called Jamaica, but returned in the evening after a very pleasant and agreeable ride. our Noses was now and then regaled with the stink of a dead Rebel some of them have lain unburyed since last Augst.

This Island is about 150 Miles in length and where it is broadest about 22 in width. The land is in most parts rich with small hills and the West part of the Island stony, Produces Wheat and grain of all kinds and immence quantities of Apples. Their farms which are cultivated in the best manner of any I have seen in America, formerly abounded with Stock of all kinds. they are famous for breeding Horses and used to have annual Races upon Salisbury Plains, which are well calculated for that diversion. Agriculture has been at some degree of perfection upon this Island. The inhabitants are chiefly Dutch or the decendants of the Sweeds who first settled here.

On Board the Brig Edward New York Harbour. June 6th 1777

The Soldiers are very busy in shiping Millitary Stores and provisions as if some mighty expedition was on foot but where the storm is to burst, is a profound secret.

Saw the 16th or Queen Light Dragoons reviewed to day. they make a fine appearance. the Horses all seem in good condition. Commanded by Lieutenant [Colonel] Harcourt he that took Genl Lee prisoner.[54] The Regiment is to go on Board tomorrow, for I dont know where.

7th My Companion Mr Keir has this day got a Warrant for a Lieut Commission in Major Hollands Guides. I most Heartily wish him success. He is to embark for Brunswick tomorrow, the Millitary is all in motion certainly something will be done. We can hear them skirmishing with the Rebels every day but nothing of consequence sometimes they send in a few prisoners, and a number of our men Wounded in short the Hospitals are full of the Wounded and the prisons full of the Rebels.

On Board the Brig, Edward, New York Harbour. Sunday June 8th 1777
On Board all day, this evening a certain Colonel Cotton[55] came on board who is going passenger in this Vessel for London. He was a Colonel in the North Carolina Malitia but born at Boston in New England and is now a refugee haveing been obliged to leave his Wife and family in Carolina. I am surprised that he should be a Friend to Government for he appears to be a rigid Presbyterian, and if I mistake not, Like most of that order has a large share of hypocrisy about him. He talks so much about religeon and in such a Puritanic stile taging most of his sentences with some scrap of Scripture which gives me cause to think that [he] has no religeon at all in reality. I don't like your holy Cant's they are seldom what they would be thought to be.
9th No news in the papers to day we heard so much fireing last week expected something of consequence. Mr Furneval came and spent the evening with us on Board.

On Board the Brig Edward New York Harbour June 10th 1777
On Board all day. Nothing remarkable, I am quite tired of this inactive Lazy life.
11th Captn Banks a Master of one of the Transport Ships dined on Board our Vessel. A very sensible well behaved man. After Dinner, we took a walk upon Long Island, the fertility of this spot is worth observation. Asparagus grows in the open fields with very little cultivation. I suppose it has been planted some time or other, but does not appear to have had any manure about if for many Years, it is now in a flourishing state, and what is more remarkable the Land is gravelly and does not appear to be rich.
12th A Boy belonging to the Ship is broke out in the Smallpox. I am affraid this will be of bad consequence, as three of our hands has not had this disorder. I pitty the poor Boy am affraid he will want necessaries and attendance, indeed all the Crew seems to be affraid of comeing near him.

On Board the Brig, Edward, New York Harbour. June 13th 1777
Dined in town. Nothing in the papers today. this evening a Doctor, Blamire, who intends going passenger in this Vessel came on Board and stayed all night, he appears to be a good humoured man, and has seen a great deal of the World.
14th After Dinner Captn Park and I went upon Governours Island where the Rebels have made a great many Fortifications, they have taken great pains to let the world see that [they] can make Ditches and desert them. In the evening I went with Captn Park to the Butchers where he had a quarrel with some Gentlemen about a quarter of Mutton. I dont think Park behaved well did expect he would have got a good drubing, but he escaped it wonderfully.
15th Sunday. Captn Scot came and dined with us. He offers me any money that I want and wishes me to go with him to Newfoundland and Venice, and has made me some offers, but as I am circumstanced cannot accept them.

On Board the Brig, Edward, New York Harbour. June 16th 1777
On Board all day. Here is now the greatest number of Ships in this Harbour I ever saw together before, or perhaps may ever see again. It is supposed that here is 600 Square Rigg'd Vessels exclusive of small Craft and four Sail of the Line.
17th Dined with Mr Furneval on Board the Bell & Mary. Furneval and I went a Shore and spent the evening at the Hull Tavern. In our return to the Boat comeing by some houses there were Burned down we hear the Cryes of a Woman, we searched about and soon, to our great surprise, found a poor Woman in Labour, and all alone. She told us she was a Soldiers widdow and begged we would help her to some assistance. We immediately carryed her to the house of a Sadler in the Broadway whom we raised from his pillow and told him the poor Womans situation. But he absolutely refused to let her stay in his house, declareing that he woud not keep a Lying-in Hospital for our W-r, however with threats, promises and the poor Woman declareing that it was impossible for her to be remooved. He at length consented that she might lye in a back Shop he had. we immediately removed her thither and made her a very poor Bed of a Bearshin, a packsheet and an old Blanket. Furnival went with a negro Boy to see for a Midwife while I stayd with the woman for fear of the Sadler turning her out of doors. The poor woman cryed out lustily and I was confoundedly affraid of the Young one comeing before the midwife arrived. The Irish rogue of a Sadler nor the unfeeling jade his Wife would come near us, or offer the poor creature the least assistance, tho she begg'd for help in the [most] pitifull tone I ever heard. I was much affraid that I must have been under the disagreeable necessity to trying my skill in the Obstetric way. But in the critical minute Furnival arrived with an old Drunken W— he had picked up somewher [sic] or other and she refused to perform the office without we would give her two Dollars. Furneval gave her one and I another.

She immediately fell to work. I am sure the pains of Labour must be violent for the poor woman roared out most horridly, I think I heare the sound yet in my ears, however in about ten minutes she produced a Girl which was wraped in the Mothers apron with the addition of Furnevals handkerchief and mine for she had not one single rag prepared for the occation. We then got some Wine Rum Nutmeg, Bread & & to the amount of two Dollars more, and got the good wife a Caudle which she took with out much invitation. In about half an hour she was able to sit up in her miserable bed and returned us her thanks for saveing her life as she said, in the most sincere and mooving manner. The D—d unnatural B—h of a Sadlers wife never came near us all the time but lay in Bed cursing the poor woman with the most horrid imprecations about 12 O Clock we left her in good spirits considering her situation, when we came a way I gave her One Dollar and a quarter which is the last and all I have in the world.

The poor woman is heartily welcome to it and I am happy that I had it in my power to relieve such real distress. Furneval gave her two Dollars and swears he will stand Godfather to the Child. I have no intention of doing myself that honor.

Am in hopes it will be dead before morning, we promised to go and see her in the morning and make her Case known to some of the Officers.

I wish the drunken jade of a Midwife dont rob her before morning I dont like her looks. Captn Park is very merry at our adventure and declares he will be at the Christening he says we must keep the Child between us which part of the ceremony I dont like. This is the first Birth I have ever been concerned with, And I hope it will be the last time that I shall meet with such a complication of distress. She told us a long story about her virtue and sufferings, but she is an Irish woman, and I dont believe half of it. I am confounded tired with scribbleing about the Girl in the Straw therefore will give over.

On Board the Brig, Edward, New York Harbour. June 18th 1777

The Agent Victualer has informed Captain Park that we are not to Sail for England this fortnight. As this time will be very tedious to us Colnl Cotton, Colnl Reid (another Refugee from North Carolina) and I intend to take a trip to Brunswick to see the Army, agree to set out tomorrow. Furneval and I wont visit the Girl in the Straw this two or three days.

19th Went a Shore this morning to take our passage for Brunswick in one of the Suttleing Sloops, but none goes til tomorrow. This afternoon I met with John Dodd, one of the people that escaped out of Alexandria Jail. By the Assistance of Mr Keir. He informs me that they all got off safe, but Davis, the guide, and a Scotch Sergeant who was so much dispirited, at not finding us at Ceder Point agreeable to our promise that they immediately returned, and delivered themselves to the mercy of the Rebels.[56]

The rest of the company seized a Sloop in the River which they left for a Pilot Boat. But for fear of meeting with some of the Rebel Look-out Boats, they quited her and took to the Land. By traveling in the night and through the Woods they got to the Delaware-Bay, where they seized a Boat and got a Board the Roebuck Man of War. They all arrived here last night, except Mr Rodgers who belongs to the Roebuck, and Captn Parker, one of [the] company has got a Virginia paper of the second Inst. which informs that, Davis has impeached Mr Wales that is, Mr Keir's Uncle, Mr. George Muir Mr Chisum Mr Kilpatrick, Mr Heppurn and Mr Murdo, that they was all sent to Williamsburg jail and had their Trials on the 30th of May. Wales, Chisum, Davis and Murdo was condemned to be hanged on the Friday following. Muir, Kilpatrick and Heppurn to be imprisoned for Five years and all their property to be apropriated to the use of the State of Virginia.[57]

They likewise of ofer [sic] a reward of 200 Dollars for takeing Collin Keir, and Nicholas Cresswell, as the two Villains that contrived aided and assisted, the Torys, Sailors and Soldiers that were confined in Alexandria jail to make their escape. they give us every scandalous Epithet that scurrility Malice and reveng can invent. But what surprises me (tho very agreeable) they never mention one word about me breaking my Parole.[58] I hope they think it was fullfiled. I petitioned Captn Parker to give me the paper but he refused. Indeed none of them (Goodrich excepted) has had the good manners to thank us for the risque we run in assisting them to Arms and amunition in Alexandria, not to mention the expence we was at in procureing them, and provisions for them when they should have come on Board the pilot Boat in the Potowmac River. They are a set of ungratefull Scoundrels. Such is the folly of Risqueing Life, Character or Fortune in doing friendly acts for strangers. I am determined never to be guilty of it again. They are too often repayd with ingratitude.

Brunswick New Jersey. June 20th 1777
This morning left New York in Co with Collnl Cotton and Colnl Reid, on Board a Suttleing Sloop for this place.

When we got through the Narrows we was entertained with one of the most pleaseing and delightfull scenes I ever saw before. Four Hundred Sail of Ship's, Brig's Schooners, and Sloops with five Sail of the Line all under-way and upon a Wind at once, in the Compass of two Miles. A gentle Breese and fine cleare day, aded greatly to the beauty of this delightfull view. They are all bound to Perth Amboy, it is said to take the Troops on Board. About noon we got into the mouth Rareaton River with flood tide. This River is very crooked and very narrow. We often saw scouting parties of the Rebels and just as we passed a Row Galley that lay in the River, some of the Rebel Rifle-men fired upon her from amongst the Weeds, she returned it with two or three great Guns which soon drove the Rascals out of their lurking places and made them seek for safety in their heels.

A little before we got up to the Town we met several Sloops loaded with provisions House-hold furniture and Camp Equipage which informed us that the Royal Army was defeated by the Rebels and most part of them cut to pieces, we had heard a heavy Cannonade all day and at that instant heard them very busy with small arms which served to put us in a very great Panic, the two Colonels and two of the Boats hands were for returning immediately. But the Master of the Boat and myself absolutely refused to return till we had been at Brunswick which we was then in sight of. I dont know wheather we should have been able to have prevailed with the two Warlike Colonels to have come up to town, had it not hapened that while we were disputing about it, a party of the Rebels and a party of our Army begun to fire upon each other a cross the River about two miles below us, this was a weighty reason for us to get these two Heroic Colonels up to town where we arrived about 8 O Clock, and to our great joy found the report we had heard to be false. The man we heard it from was a Suttler and had a Sloop comeing up the River with Calves & Sheep, the one we was in was loaded with those articles and were the only ones that was expected to arrive for some time with fresh stock. Could he have frighted us back again he would have engrossed the whole Market to himself. This I believe was his only motive for teling us the abominable lie. Colonel Cotton soon found some of his old acquaintance a Captn Beaumont Waggon Master General at whose Tent we were very kindly entertained and lodged. This gentleman informs us that the Army intends to evacuate this place tomorrow and March to Amboy. He does not know what is the meaning of the Cannonade to day or where it has been. I am convinced both my Colnls are Rank Cowards from the great tripidation so visible when we heard the false report. But now they have got a glass of Wine in their heads, are as bold and courageous as Mars himselfe.

Bonum Town, New Jersey, June 21st 1777

Spent the forenoon with my old Friend Lieut Keir in viewing the different encampments, which is certainly one of the finest sights in the World everything is conducted with so much order and regularity. I wish much to be a Soldier, more particularly at this time that I might have an opportunity of revenging myselfe upon these ungratefull Scoundrels. Mr Keir resents the ungratefull and dishonest behaviour of Parker and his companions, they refuse to pay him for the Arms he purchased for their use. About 4 O Clock this afternoon the

advance Guard of the Army with about 500 Waggons loaded with amunition and Baggage Marched from Brunswick and Camped at this place. Colnls Read and Cotton and me rode in a Baggage Waggon and made ourselves very merry with the different scenes that we saw amongst the Soldiery and their Ladies. Our Camp is within a quarter of a Mile of the enemies Picket guard, we have a good force with us. I dont Care if they pay us a visit.

Staten Island. June 22nd 1777

Last night I had most uncomfortable lodging along with Colonel Reid upon a Tent only spread upon the ground in which [we] wraped ourselves, almost bit to death with Musquitoes and poisoned with the stink of some Rebels who have been buryed about three weeks in such a slighty manner that Waggons have cut up part of the half corrupted carcases and made them stink most horrible. By 5 O Clock this morning all the Tents were struck and the Army ready to March. About 8 the Main Body of the Army came up, at that instant some of the Rebel Scouting parties fired upon our Centinals which brought on a smart Skirmish. I happened to see them in the Bushes before they fired but mistook them for some of our Rangers they was about 300 Yards from me. When the engagement began I got upon a little hillock to see them the better but an Honest Highlander advised me to retire into a small Breast work just by, without I had a mind to stick up myselfe as a mark for the Rebels to shoot at.

I thought proper to take his advice and retired to the place he directed me to where I had a very good view of their proceedings. I observed a party of our men go through a Rye field I suppose with an intent to get into the Rear of the Rebels and by that meanes surround them, but was met as soon as they got out of the field by about the same number of the Rebels when they was about 100 Yards from each other, both parties fired but I did not observe any fall. they still advanced to the distance of 40 Yards or less, and fired again. I then saw a good number fall on both sides. Our people then rushed upon them with their Bayonets and the others took to their heels. I heard one of them call out murder lustily, this is laughable if the consequence was not serious. A Fresh party immediately fired upon our people but was dispersed and pursued into the Woods by a Company of the 15th Regmt.

A Brisk fire then began from Six field pieces the Rebels had screted [sic] in the Woods which did some mischief to our men. The engagement lasted about thirty five minutes. Our people took the Field pieces about 40 prisoners and kiled about 150 of the Scoundrels with the loss of 39 Kiled and 27 Wounded. I went to the place where I saw the two parties fire upon each other first before the Wounded was removed, but I never before saw such a shocking scene. Some dead others dieing. Death in different shapes, some of the wounded making the most pittifull lamentations, others that were of different parties curseing each other as the author of their misfortunes. One old veteran I observ'd (that was shot through both legs and not able to walk) very coolly and deliberately loading his piece and cleaneing it from the blood. I was surprised at the sight and asked him his reasons for it. He with a look of contempt, said, To be ready in case any of the Yankeys came that way again.

About 10 O'Clock the whole Army was in motion it is said our Army burned Brunswick when they left others contradict the report and say it was left without damage. But all the Country houses is in flames as far as we can see, the Soldiers are so much enraged they will set them on fire, in spite of all the Officers can do to prevent it. They seem to leave the Jerseys with reluctance. The Train of Artillery and Waggons extends about Nine Miles and is upwards of 1000 in number. Some people say there is 20,000 Men but I am affraid there is not so many the real numbers are for very good reasons kept secret. About 2 OClock the Van arrived at the City of Perth Amboy, 14 Miles from Brunswick the road is through [woods?] and plantations, but pretty good. The Rebels kept skirmishing with our Rear all the way but little loss on either side.

This City (for it is called a City) tho it does not contain more then 200 Houses mostly built of wood, Is the Capital of East New Jersey, and was called Perth Amboy from it's first founder, the Earl of Perth, who was, once proprietor of East New Jersey, but surrendered his right to the Crown in 1737. I believe it never was a place of any trade tho very conveniently situatioed for it. here is a fine safe and commodious harbour and within sight of the Sea. But very few Rivers of any consequence empty themselves into it which perhaps may be the reason why they had no trade here. The City is very handsomly lay'd out in Hundred Acres of land and contains 150 Lots or Squares for building upon. Here is one Church, A meeting house. The Court-house is a good Brick building. And the Governor's house is an Ellegant stone building said to have cost £4000

Here we found some of the Hessian Light-horse who are just arrived, that is the Men and Horses. But the wise conductors of these matters sent the Saddles in another Ship which is not arrived so that they are of no use at present. These troops are Cloathed in Green, and armed with most enormous long crooked Swords. Here is a good Barracks in this town for about 2000 men. We crossed the sound to Staten Island and Dined at a public house with Colonel Rodgers, the famous Major Rodgers [of the] last War, he is a New Englander by birth but a mear Savage from his education. Then we walked about 4 Miles and lodged at a farm house, an acquaintance of Colonel Cottons. Every one is surprised at our Army quiting the Jerseys, where they are bound too is a profound secret, the people on this Island begins to be very uneasy, they apprehend a visit from the Rebels very soon. I am confoundedly tired with scribling.

On Board the Brig Edward New York Harbour June 23rd 1777

This morning we hired a Waggon to carry us to the Ferry with some pig's we had bought for our Sea store, at the unreasonable price of 8d pr lb. Staten-Island is about 12 Miles long and about 9 Broad, the produce chiefly live Stock, of which in times of peace they raised immence quantities, it abounds with salt Marshes or Salt Meadows which breed vasts swarms of Musquetoes, very troublesom insects. Arrived at New York in the evening found Captn Park making ready for Sea as fast as possible. Furneval informs me that our Child died before morning and that some of the Officers had taken the woman away which I am very glad of. Here is various conjectures concerning the late proceedings of our Army, some say that they are going to Philadelphia by Sea, others say it is only a Feint to get Washington out of his strong hold. What is the meaning I cannot guess.

On Board the Brig, Edward, New York Harbour, June 24th 1777

On Board all day. When I see this once flourishing opulent and happy City, one third part of it now in ruins, It brings a sadness and melancholly upon my mind, to think that a set of people Who three Years ago, were doing everything they could for the mutual assistance of each other, and both party's equally gainers, Should now be cuting the throats of each other and destroying their property whenever they have an opportunity and all this mischief done by a set of designing Villains. The reflection is too severe to bear with patience. This City is an unhappy instance of the strange madness and folly that reigns amongst them. When the Rebels were drove out of it in September last by the Royal Army, They formed a hellish design [to] burn it down to the ground, and then lay the blame upon our Troops they so far succeeded as to burn about one third, the most beautifull and valueable part of the City. If one was to judge from appearances they would suppose the Rebels had intended to dispute every Inch of ground with our troops, in every Street they have made Ditches and Barricadoes every little eminence about the town is Fortifyed, but they basely and Cowardly deserted them all as soon as ever our people got ashore. Now all these Ditches and Fortifyed places are full of stagnate water, damaged Sour Crout and filth of every kind. the noisom vapours arriseing from the mud left in the Docks and Slips at Low-water, the unwholsome smells occationed by such a number of people being crowded together in so small a compass almost like herrings in a Barrel, most of them very dirty and not a small number sick of some disease the Itch, Pox, Fever or Flux, so that alltogether here is a Complication of stinks enough to drive a person whose sense of smelling was very delicate and his Lungs of the finest contexture, into a consumption in the space of twenty-four hours. If any author had an inclination to write a treatise upon stinks and Ill smells, he never could meet with more subject matter, then in New York. Or any one who had abilities and inclination to expose the viscious and unfeeling part of human nature or the various arts, ways, and meanes that are used to pick up a liveing in this World, I recommend New York as a proper place to collect his Characters. Most of former inhabitants that possessed this once happy spot are utterly ruined and from opulence reduced to the greatest indigenes some in the Rebel jails by force others by inclination in their Armies.

On Board the Brig Edward New York Harbour June 25th 1777
Went a Shore in the morning and saw Mr Goodrich who gave me a kind invitation to dine with him but I decline his invitation. I wont dine with such a set of ungratefull scoundrels. All the City in a Political ferment concerning the motions of our Army. Colnl Cotton has taken a ride upon Long Island with a pretence to buy stock but I rather suppose he is gone for a very different purpose. I know him to be a hypocrite.
26th This morning the Agent Victualler came on Board and told us to prepare for Sea to be ready at a moments warning. I immediately got a horse & Chair and went in quest of Colnl Cotton found him at a Farm house about 6 Miles beyond Jamaica upon Long Island, where we Lodged. There has been a Heavy Cannonade since one O Clock this morning without intermission, and still continues.

On Board the Brig Brig [sic] Edward New York Harbour June 27th 1777
Got on Board to breakfast but we did not need to have been in such a violent hurry. The fleet is not to leave New York this three days. Went a Shore in the afternoon. News that our Army had intirely routed the Rebels. Kiled 2000 and taken 4700 prisoners, with the loss of 800. I am affraid this is too good news to be true.
     This affair should have happened at Amboy.
28th Yesterdays News is contradicted to day, it is said that there is only 50 Kiled and 70 taken prisoners, with the loss of 8 Kiled on our side. Here is as many lies in circu[l]ation here, as there is in Virginia. The lie of the day is, that Washington is taken prisoner.
29th And 30th On Board where I intend to stay as much as possible. I have no money but what I borrow and I can't go a Shore But it will be some extra expence to me. O! Poverty Poverty thou worst of Curses. Tho an old companion, I hate thee.

On Board the Brig Edward, New York Harbour, July 1st 1777
On Board all day, a very good reason for it, want of money. Captn Park suspects my reason for being low spirited, and very kindly offers to assist me to what money I want while we stay here. I am determined to accept it let the want come at the last.

2nd Went on Board his Majesty's Ship Centurion of Fifty Guns commanded by Robert Brathwait Esqr[59] with Colnl Cotton, Colnl Reid and an Irish Captain. Saw General Lee who is prisoner on Board this Ship who understanding that I came from Virginia, invited me to drink Tea with him and had a good deal of Chat with me about his plantation in Berkley County, Virginia. He is a tall, thin, Ill looking man and appears to be about 50 Years of age. He has been particularly active in this Rebellion, he is very sensible but rash and violent in his sentiments as well as actions.

News that our troops had left Amboy and are Camped upon Staten Island. Colnl Cotton informs me we are to have a Young Lady passenger. I think she is an amunition Wife of his.

On Board the Brig Edward New York Harbour, July 3rd 1777

On Board all day. No news from the Army we heare them exchange a few shots now and then.

4th Mr Furneval, Captn Jolly of the Ellis, and Capt Nailor of the Valliant (two Letters of Marque) dined with us on Board to day, all hands very merry. I even forgot my poverty in a cherefull Glass and good Company. Colnl Cotton is a little disappointed about his little Girl. O! the religious old hypocrite.

5th This day arrived three Men of War with General Clinton on Board, likewise a fleet with provision from Cork. I hope they have brought something better then Sour-Crout. Our Army still inactive.

6th Sunday. Dined on Board the Valliant Captn Nailor, a Letter of Marque belonging to Liverpool carries 14 Guns besides Swivles. Very merry.

On Board the Brig Edward, New York Harbour, July 7th 1777

This morning we had orders to get our Water on Board with every thing ready for Sea, and proceed to Hell-Gate[60] tomorrow the place appointed for the fleet to rendevous.

About 4 O Clock Furneval came on Board and insisted upon me going with him to spend the evening along with some gentlemen of the Navy and Army, at the Hull Tavern where we stay'd till about 12 O Clock. I thought it too late to go on Board, went to my old Lodgings in Queen-Street. As I went down St Johns Street I heard something floundering in the Ditch. I stoped and by the light of the moon could perceive something like a human being stir the mud a little. I plunged in and found it to be a man whom I hauled to the Shore quite insensible. I puled the dirt out of his mouth with my fingers and in a little time I could perceive him make a noise. I then went to the next Centry which happened to be a Hessian. I told him the situation of the man below in the Street but he did not understand English.

After we had sputtered at one another for some time, the Sergeant of the Guard came who could speak English who very civilly called a light and went with me to the man who by this time could speake. And told us that he had been insulted by a Girl of the Town and had been imprudent enough to treat her rather indelicately, one of her Bullies had Cut him in several places in the head knocked him down and draged him into the Ditch. Desired that we would help him to his lodgings in Queen-Street which the Hessian Sergeant and me did. the Bruises he had received and the muddy stinking water he had swallowed made him very ill, I went as soon as we had got him to bed and called Doctor Smith to him who immediately let him blood. He appears to be a Genteel well Behaved man returned me thanks in the most polite terms for saveing his life. I am happy that I have been an instrument of preserving it.

On Board the Brig Edward, Hell-gate, July 8th 1777
This morning I called to see the man I found in the ditch last night, but found him a sleep and did not chuse to wake him. I understand his name is Leydum an English gentleman, who has lately made his escape from Philadelphia jail where he had been confined several months for his atachment to Government. I have heard of this gentleman in Maryland. Breakfasted and Dined with Furneval on Board the Bell & Mary, in the afternoon got underway with the first of the Flood-tide and at 5 in the evening at Hellgate 6 miles from New York. Here the River or Sound, passes among some Rocks. the East River and New-England tides meets and causes the water to whirl round the Rocks with amazeing velocity the violent commotion occationed by the meeting of the tides causes the water to rise to a great height and flow over the Rock in some places it seems to fall perpendicularly down, which makes the Navigation very dangerous. the Channel is about 20 yd wide. if you miss it, you are Certainly lost, which has been the case with Many vessels attempting to pass it at improper times.

On Board the Brig Edward, Hellgate, July 9th 1777
Went to New York in the Boat with Colnl Cotton to purchase Stores for the Voyage. Dined with Captn Scot on Board the Brig Harriet. Drunk Tea at Mrs Bennets with Major L—s Lady and several other ladies, after Tea I waited upon Mrs L—s to her lodgings. she insisted upon me staying to sup and spend the evening with her. I did not need much solicitation to spend an evening with a handsome and polite Young lady. After supper and a Chearfull Glass of good Wine we entered into a verry agreeable Tete-a-tete and then O! Matrimony matrimony, thou coverest more Female frailties then Charity does sins. Thou most necessary of all contracts under thy auspicious sanction the wanton Girl may satisfy all her natural craveing Desires and escape with impunity if she is not taken in actual Car Cop. Thou was originally hatched betwixt the W. and the P.t. to answer the pecuniary purposes of the one, and serve as a Cloak for all the Wanton Slips and Backfallings of the other in this great Contract (which is oftener made to serve pecuniary purposes, then where there is a real union of hearts) the advantage is manifestly in favor of the woman she may—with the greater freedom and less fear for if she should happen to propagate in consequence of any of her promiscuous amours, the convenient husband must father the Brat toil and sweat to rear it, while the — secretly laughs him to scorn, for credulously believing the spurious Bantling to be part of his own flesh and

blood. O! Ignorance, how materially necessary thou art to the happiness of mortals in general, But married men in perticular. Was it not for thy friendly aid, Thousands would be miserable. Nicholas if ever thou sined religeously in thy life, it has been this time. This kind affable and most obligeing Lady in publick was most rigidly religious. At Mrs Bennets she had treated the character of a poor Lady in the neighbourhood who had made a slip and unfortunately been caught in the fact in a most barbarous and cruel manner. She run over the Scriptures from Genesis to Revelations, for sentences to proov the Heinous crime of fornication. In that strain she continued till after supper and then I soon found she was made of warm flesh and blood. In short she is the greatest medly I ever knew. In publick she has all the apparent religion of the most rigid and Hypocritical Presbyterian Parson, the neatness and temperance of a Quaker with the Modesty of a Vestal. In private the Air and behaviour of a professed courtezan, And in Bed the Lechery of a Guinea Pig. Nicholas Nicholas if ever thou marry a woman who pretends to so much religion, has no charity for the common and natural frailties of her sex, May thou have the dreadfull word Cockold wrote in large characters upon thy forehead, for thou most assuredly will be one of the horned tribe recommend me to the Girl who has compassion upon those who in an unguarded moment may have given way to the weakness of human nature, with honesty enough in her composition to confess that she has all her natural feelings, But Philosophy enough to deny improper requests with good-humour, With little Levity or Wantonness in her disposition. (Perfection I do not expect to find in a human being.) Such a one I think would make me very happy. But rather then I would marry one who over acts the part of religion pretends to so much chastity and is in appearance, a stiff, prudish, formal lump of mortality. I would go into Lapland and be dry nurse to a Bear.

But stop Nicholas dont treat the Lady so unmercifully her husband is gone to War, she remembers the old saying that all Cuckold's go to heaven, therefore if he should happen to die in the Bed of Honour and not have time to prepare himself properly for a future state his dear wife, Believing faithfully in this doctrine has prudendly and dutifully taken care to secure him a Birth in the happy mantions above, But sorry and affraid to part with so kind a husband, and willing to contribute everything in her power to prevent so capital a misfortune, and sensible by her Millitary knowledge that a little defensive armour is of service. Like a good tender, carefull and loveing Wife, to my certain knowledge has taken care to fortify his head with a Horn Work.

Rare Doctrine for a tender Conscience, the Ablest Casuist could not have done it better. Schools may teach Divines may preach, Laws may inflict punishments But natural causes will produce natural effects in spite of all they can do or say against it the desire of propagating our species is so exquisitely pleaseing to us and nature has wove it so firmly in our composition, while instinct so powerfully prompts us to it. It is in vain for all Laws human or Devine to attempt to hinder it.

On Board the Brig Edward. Hell-Gate July 10th 1777
This morning returned to the Ship. Ruminating upon my last nights adventure most of this day, It will not bear reflection—understand we are to have the Niger Frigate for our Convoy. Went A Shore with Colnls Reid and Cotton, But returned on board in the evening. This has been one of the hotest days we have had this Summer.

11th A note, or rather Billet Dex [Doux] from Mrs L— I am convinced that Women, as well as Ships, Birds and Fish, are steered by the tail. Can the poor Girl get no one in Town to relieve her Concupiscence but she must be under a necessity of sending for me. I am determined to go at all events, it would be ungratefull to refuse so kind an offer. My Ship-mates begin to smell a Rat I am rated by them confoundedly, but let them go on, While I fare well at no expence to myself I care not, and somebody must do the poor Lady's drudgery it is work she must and will have done. Should like her better if she was not such a religious— [sic].

On Board the Brig Edward. Hell-Gate. July 12th 1777
I think I have taken my farewell of New York, tho I promised to pay one visit more but never intend to perform. Cannot beare the abominable hypocrite.

I wish to be at Sea but hear nothing of our Sailing this week. I wish to be at home, and Yet dread the thought of returning to my native Country a Beggar, the word sounds disagreeable in my ears. But Yet it is more pleasing and creditable than the Epithet of Rascal and Villain, even if a large and opulent fortune was annexed to them, though one of the latter sort is in general better receiv'd, then an indigent honest man. I am poor as Job, but not quite so patient. Will hope for better days, if I am at present, plagued with poverty my conscience does not accuse me of any Extravagance or neglect of sufficient magniitude to bring me into such indigent circumstances. However I have Credit, Health, Friends, and good Spirits which is some consolation in the midst of all my distress. Better days may come.

[On Board the] Brig Edward. Hell-Gate July 13th 1777
News that our Army has surprised Washington and taken him prisoner. Affraid it is too good to be authentic, his great caution will allways prevent him being made a prisoner to our inactive General.

Washington is certainly a most surpriseing man, one of Natures geniuses, a Heaven-born General, if there is any of that sort. That a Negro-driver should with a ragged Banditty of undesciplined people, the Scum and refuse of all Nations on earth, so long keep a British General at Bay, Nay, even oblige him, with as fine an Army of Veteran Soldiers as ever England had on the American Continent, to retreat, It is astonishing. It is too much by Heaven's, there must be double-dealeing somewhere. General How, A man brought up to War from his youth, To be puzzled and plagued for two yeares together, with a Virginia

Tobacco-planter. O! Britain how thy Laurels tarnish in the hands of such a Lubber.

The life of General Washington will be a most copious subject for some able Biographer to exercise his pen upon. Nature did not make me one of the Biographic order, however I will make some remarks conserning this great and wonderfull man.

George Washington, the American Hero, was second son of a creditable Virginia Tobacco Planter, (which I suppose may in point of Rank, be equal to the better sort of Yeomanry in England) I believe his Mother is still liveing and two of his Brothers. One of them lives in Berkley County in Virginia, the other in Faquire County in Virginia. Both able Planters and men of good character. In the early part of his life he was surveyor of Farefax County in Virginia it was then a Frontier County, and his Office was attended with much trouble, but not any considerable profit this business accustomed him to the Woods and gained him the character of the best Woods-man in the Colony. His older brother, Mr Lawrence [marked out and "Jno Augustine" written above] Washington was a Captain in the American Troops raised for the expedition against Carthagena, but afterwards incorporated with the regulars, he died in the service, And our Hero, George, came to the patrimonial Estate. In the Year 1753 he was chosen by the Assembly of Virginia to go to the French Forts on the Ohio, to know the reason why they made encroachments on the Back parts of Virginia which office he performed to the entire satisfaction of his employers. On his return he published his journal which did him great credit, and first made him popular amongst his countrymen. In the Year 1754 the Governor of Virginia gave him the command of about 1000 troops (all Virginians) with orders to drive the French from their encroachments in the Back settlements.

In this expedition he prooved unsuccessfull, on the 3rd of July 1754 he suffered himself to be surrounded by the French and Indians, at the Big Meadows in the Alligany Mountain, and was obliged to capitulate but upon what terms I do not recollect. He by some meanes or other got from the French very soon and had the command of a Regiment of Virginians, and was with the unfortunate General Braddock when he was defeated by the French and Indians on the Banks of the Moningahaley River July 9th 1755, prior to which, He, with a part of his Regiment, fell in with a scouting party of his own in the woods, an engagment began and a number of men was killed before the mistake was discovered. He continued in the Army most of the War but never performed any action to render himself conspicuous. Before the expiration of the War he married a Mrs Custis, a Widow Lady with whom he had a very good fortune, by her entreaties he left the Army in which he never gained any great esteem by his own country Officers or men. By all accounts it was his frugality that lost him the good will of his Officers, and the strict decipline he allways observed, the love of his men. Indeed any kind of order or subordination illy agrees with his countrymen, in general. After he quit the Army he was made a member of the Virginia House of Burgesses in which he was much respected for his good private character, but allways looked upon as too bashfull and timid for an

Orator. He lived as a Country Gentleman, much noted for his Hospitality, Great knowledg in agriculture, and industry in carrying his various manufactories of Linen and Woollen to greater perfection then any man in the Colony.

On the breaking out of these troubles he was chosen in Company with Messrs Peyton Randolph, Richard Henry Lee, Patrick Henry, Richard Bland, Benjamin Harrison, and Edmund Randolph Esqrs to act as Deputies or Delegates for the Colony of Virginia in the First Congress or Sanhedrim held at Philadelphia September 5th 1774, and appointed General and Commander in Chief of all the Rebel forces (by Congress) June 17th 1775. I believe he acccepted this post with reluctance but the great, and almost unexpected success he has had, may now sooth, and become agreeable to his natural ambitious temper.

He undoubtedly pants for military fame and considering the little military knowledg and experience he had, before he was made a General he has performed wonders he was generally unfortunate (indeed I may with propriety say allways) in every action where he was immediately concerned, untill the affair at Trenton in the Jerseys. Since that unluckey period (for us) he has only been too successful.

His education is not very great nor his parts shining, his disposition is rather heavy, then Volatile, much given to silence, in short he is but a poor speaker but shines in the Epistolary way. His person is tall and genteel, Age betwixt Forty and Fifty, his behaviour and deportment is easy genteel and obliging with a certain something about him, which pleases every one, who has anything to do with him. There cannot be a greater proof of his particular address, and good Conduct, than his keeping such a number of refractory, headstrong people together in any tolerable degree of decorum his house is at a place called Mount Vernon about 12 Miles below Alexandria on the Banks of the Potowmeck River in Virginia, where he has a very fine Plantation and Farm,But by the best accounts I could get his Estate alltogether, before these troubles did not amount to more than £800 pr An. Vir. Currency, but Estates in this Country are seldom valued by the Year, it is some difficulty to know exactly what they are worth where they keep great numbers of negroes and make large Crops of Tobacco. His friends and acquaintances reckon him a just man, exceedingly honest, but not very generous, perhaps they may give him this character, because he manages his Estate with industry and economy, very seldom enters into those Foolish, Giddy, and Expensive frolicks, natural to a Virginian. He keeps an excellent Table and a stranger, let him be of what Country or Nation he will, allways met with a most Hospitable reception at it. His entertainments were allways conducted with the most regularity, and in the genteelest manner, of any I ever was at on the Continent (and I have been at several of them, that is, before he was made a General) temperance he allways observed was allways cool-headed and exceeding cautious himself. But took great pleasure in seeing his friends entertained in the way most agreeable to themselves. His Lady is of a Hospitable disposition, allways good-humoured and chearfull, and seems to be actuated by the same motives with himself, but she is rather of a more lively disposition, they are, to all appearance, a happy pair.

He has no Children by his Wife, but she had two by her first Husband, a Son and Daughter, the Daughter died unmarried, the Son, Mr John Custis, a very worthy Young Gentleman, is lately married, and lives with his Mother at Mount Vernon. He lives entirely as a Country Gentleman, has no post Civil or Military. The General seems by nature calculated, for the post he is in, he has a manner and behaviour peculiar to himself, and particularly adapted to his present station and rank in life. It is said (and I believe with great truth) that he never had an intimate particular bosome friend, or an open profess'd enemy, in his life. By this method of behaviour, he in a great measure, prevents all parties and factions, and raises a spirit of emulation amongst his Officers and men, As there is no favorite to pay their court too, and pave their way to preferment. And the General, I believe is proof against bribery, they have no way to advance themselves but by merit alone. His private character is amiable he is much beloved and respected by all his acquaintance. From my personal acquaintance with him, and from every thing that I have been able to learn of him, I believe him to be a Worthy Honest-man, guilty of no bad vice, except, we reckon ambition amongst the number and here, we ought to judge charitably. The temptation was very great, to a mind naturally ambitious, nature made him too weak to resist it. As an Officer, he is quite popular almost Idolized by the Southern provinces, but I think he is not so great a favourite with the Northern ones. The ignorant and deluded part of the people, look up to him as the Saviour and protector of their Country, and have implicit confidence in every thing he does. The Artfull and designing part of the people, that is, the Congress and those at the head of affairs, look upon him as a necessary tool to compass their Diabolical purposes. He certainly deserves some merit as a General, that he with his Banditty, can keep General How, Danceing from one town to another for two years together with such an Army as he has. Confound the great Churcclehead he will not unmuzzle the mastiff's or they would eat him and his raged crew in a little time was they properly conducted with a man of resolution and spirit. Washington my Enemy as he is, I should be sorry if he should be brought to an ignominious death.

The Devil is certainly got on Board the Newmarket they are fighting like furies.

On Board the Brig Edward, Hell-Gate. July 14th 1777
Went a Shore on Long-Island. Drank Tea with some very agreeable Young Lady's. These people, before these unhappy disputes, lived in ease and affluence but are now obliged to wash and sew for bread. The manner in which these unfortunate people bear this great reverse of circumstances, is worthy [of] imitation. Got on Board late in the evening.
15th This afternoon Captn Park and I went in the Boat to Fort Knyphausen,[61] it is about 12 Miles above New York, Was built by the Rebels and taken from them by Lieutnt General De Knyphausen and all the Rebel Garrison made

prisoners of War, about 8 Months ago. Situated on an advantageous eminence, it is a regular Fortification surrounded with a deep and broad dry Ditch and strong Abbatis. The Magazine is said to be Bomb proof, with Ambriziers for 35 Gunns

But at present, they have not so many Guns mounted. There is a small Battery of some heavy Guns to the West of the Fort close to the North River, likewise another small Battery to the Northward about a Musket-shot from the Fort, which cut off a great number of the Hessians when they made their attack. It seems to be a place of great strength, both by nature and art, Capable of makeing a virgourous defence, if it had been garrisoned with veteran troops. I think it woud scarcely have been possible to have taken it by storm.

It is an ugly disagreeable country, Full of large Rocks and Woods, and seems entirely calculated for the Rebels to excerise their Sculking Cowardly manner of fighting to the greatest advantage. The North River is allmost straight as a line for several miles here, but wide and good navigation. Great Rocks on both sides, some almost perpendicular and a prodigious height something like Matlock in Derbyshire. Hessian Garrison at the Fort.

On Board the Brig Edward, Flushing Bay, Long Island. July 16th 1777

This morning had orders to Weigh, proceeded to this place. General De Heister came on Board the Niger, understand he is going passenger for England. News that General Prescot is taken prisoner at Rhrode [sic] Island and that Ticonderoga is taken from the Rebels.

17th This morning General Pigot came on Board the Niger, he is Bound to Rhode Island to succeed General Prescot, who was taken by the Rebels in Bed with a Farmers daughter near Newport. This is the second time the General has been prisoner with the Rebels.

A. M. A light wind, got up to the City Island. The Lady Gage an armed Ship, belonging to Lord and General How is appointed our Rear Guard.

18th At M. Weighed Light Breeze and pleasant weather. The sound is now about 6 Leagues over. Marks of ruin and Devastation on both Shores. Calm in the Evening, at Anchor.

On Board the Brig, Edward, Long-Island Sound. July 19th 1777

Most part of this forenoon at Anchor quite Calm. At M. a light Breeze, got under way. All this afternoon we have kept close inn with the Connecticut Shore, the Country seems as if it had been populous. But this cursed Rebellion, has totally ruined this part of it, almost every house seems to be deserted and the Major part of them in Ashes. Strange that the artifices of a few designing Villains should have it in their power, to ruin such a number of honest well meaning people, that they should so far infatuate them, by their horrid lies and meane pittifull arts, to give up the invaluable blessing of Peace, the sweet enjoyment of real, and happy Liberty. In exchange for all the dreadfull horrors of War poverty and Wretchedness. All this is done (as the poor deluded wretches are taught to believe) with a view to secure to themselves, and posterity, what they have long been in possession of in the greatest Lattitude of any people on earth. But unfortunately never Yet knew the intrinsick value of it. In short, they are like the Dog in the Fable, quit the substance for an empty shadow. If we have good luck we shall not be long before we leave sight of this unhappy Country, This Country turn'd Topsy Turvy changed from an Earthly Paradice, to a Hell, upon Terra Firma. I have seen this a happy County and I have seen it miserable, in the the [sic] short space of three Years. The Villainous arts of a few and the obstinacy of a many, on this side the Water added to the complicated Blunders, Cowardice, and Knavery of some of our blind <u>Guides</u> in England, has totally ruined this Country. I wish the Devil had them. These unhappy wretches have substituted, Tyranny, Oppression and Slavery for Liberty and Freedom. The Whims, Cruelty, and Caprice of a Vile Congress gives them Law's. And a set of Puritanic Rascals retails the Scriptures, and gives them the little religion they have, but for the good it does them, they might as well be without these unhappy wretches are as much divided as it is possible to be without actually drawing the sword against one another (I meane in political opinion) but the strict and Tyrannical laws, made by the Congress, and executed with the utmost rigor by their Committee's, Deters the more sensible part of the people from declareing their real sentiments. The Congress, under the fallacious pretence of nursing the Tender Plant Liberty, which was said to thrive so well in American soil, have actually tore it up by the very root. In short, these people's Pride, Obstinacy, and Folly have brought more calamities on their own heads, then ever Pharoah, did by his Obstinacy, bring upon the Egyptians. A man suspected of Loyalty (which in this place is more heinous Crime then sining against the Holy Goast [sic]) is in more danger, by far, than an Old Woman and her Tabby Cat, was formerly in England and Scotland, if she was suspected of witchcraft. To cheat him is lawfull; to steal from him is serving the Cause and Country if he is imprudent enough openly to avow his sentiments, Taring and Feathering was the punishment, they at first underwent. But now they are proscribed in the publick papers by order of that Diabolical, Infernal set of miscreants the Congress. Confiscation of their whole property, imprisoning and hanging, nay, even firing their house or poisoning him, is thought a sweet smelling favour before the Most High. As the Rascally Presbyterian Clergy have all along been the chief Instigators and Supporters of this unnatural Rebellion, they commonly honor the Loyalists with the title of Tory, Atheist, Deist, or the most approbious name that the most inveterate malice, aided by that cursed enthusiastic, uncharitable bloody-minded, and cruel persecuting spirit, which in general constitutes a considerable part of the character of these <u>Fanatic</u> brawlers, or rather <u>Bellows</u> of Sedition and Rebellion. Divine teachers, or Godly teachers, I cannot call them. Without a vile prostitution of that Sacred function these Religious scoundrels have a wonderfull knack of reconciling the greatest opposites, and uniting the most jaring differences, when they have an opportunity to turn those things to their advantage. For instance, A Papist, that a few Years ago was a more reproachfull name than a murderer (amongst the New-Englanders) is now become a friendly appellation, when applyed to any of their friends. At the same time they Excerate his Majesty for allowing the Cannadians liberty of conscience or a free use of their religious cerremonies. They endeavour to perswade the people that he is actually turned Papist, that his Subjects are all going to revolt and cut of his head, every thing is done to make the ignorant multitude believe, that the Kings of France and Spain, the Pope, Pretender, King of Prussia and the Grand-Turk will invade England with innumerable hosts; in support of their glorious cause. The Empress of Russia, Prince of Hesse, and others who have given any assistance to Great Britain are all to be Deposed their Dominions divided amongst the other European powers, who are friendly disposed towards the <u>Virtuous</u> Americans. The <u>Happy United</u> and Blessed Independent States, as a reward for their glorious struggle, are to be put in Possession of the Brazils.

Notwithstanding these rediculous assertions and extravagant bravadoes, vast numbers of the people awake from their delirium. Yet are unwillingly compeled to submit to the arbitrary proceeding of Congress, with seeming patience and with apparent reverance kiss the rod that so tyrannically strikes them, But secretly curse the hand that unjustly enslaves them under the specious mask of Guardians of their liberties. France is freedom's self, compared with America. Freedom of speech is what they formerly enjoyed but is now a stranger in the Land. The boasted Liberty of the Press, is as a tale that was told many people have been confined in Jail for several months, without comeing to a trial, or ever knowing the crimes of which they are accused, and at last discharged without a word. But if they can proov that they are well wishers to his Majesty's Arms—Dreadfull is their situation indeed. If they are fortunate enough to escape with life, all their property is conficated and their persons forced into the army. To render their misery complete their Magistrates are chosen from the most violent part of the people, in general very fond of useing their usurped authority without mercy, whose notions of politics, Law, Justice, and Equity are such as make them truely contemptible, but of this, no one dare complain. Their military Officers, are in general, people of desperate fortune and violent dispositions, who wish to establish their beloved <u>Independence,</u> that they may avoid paying the debts they owe to their Mother Country.

Before I bid farewell to this, once, Happy Country, I will mention the remarks, and observations I have made of the Country and people while I have been amongst them. New-England I know little about, Except it be the trade and people. They have more Naval Craft then all the Continent beside great numbers of which are employed in the Fisheries. Their exports are Fish, Salt Provisions, Horses, Cattle and Lumber, Imports are Rum, Sugar, Molasses, Corn and European goods, they import large quantities of Molasses from the West Indies which they Distill and sell in Affrica, and the other Colonies which goes by the name of Yankey-Rum or Stink-e-buss, they generally exchange this Article with the Southern Colonies for Corn and Flour, as they do not grow Corn sufficient to serve themselves. They are very industrious people, and in general very sober, but naturall addicted to all kind of meaneness, that will any way serve their intrest and the greatest Hypocrites on Earth. as to their religion, Hudibras describes it to a tittle.

> Tis Presbyterian true Blue
> For they are of what stubborn Crew
> Of Errant Saints, whom all men grant
> To be the true Church Militant:
> Such as do build their Faith upon
> The holy Text of Pike and Gun;
> Decide all Controversie by
> Infallible Artillery;
> And prove their Doctrine Orthodox
> By Apostolick Blows and Knocks;
> Call Fire and Sword, and Desolation
> A godly, thorough, Reformation.[62]

Their Cruelty to the innocent Quakers that setled amongst them, about Seventy Years ago will allways be remembered, not only by the Quakers, but by every humane person, with the utmost Destestation, their present behaviour sufficiently shews, that they are willing to act over-again those Tragic Scenes in which their Oliverian Ancestors took so much delight, but enough of these Scoundrels. The province of New-York was pretty much the same as New-England, that is, the Exports and Imports nearly alike. But the Nature and Disposition of the people more Hospitable, Honest and Generous—the face of the Country, as far as I have seen of it, is Hilly and Rockey, but well cultivated, they have large Orchards of Apple-trees from which they make excellent Cyder and Export large Quantities of Apples to the other Colony's. A great deale of Peltry, Pot-Ashes and Naval Stores, was Annually sent to England from New-York, before the Rebellion. Most of which came down the North River from Albany. Here is a great number of very genteel houses in the Neighbourhood of New-York, Chiefly built by Officers who served in America the last War, and liked the Country too well to return to England at the Peace. Great numbers of Dutch settled in the Back parts of this Colony.

The Jerseys are Hilly in most parts but very small hills, with a good deal of stony land, the general part of the Land that I have seen in the Jerseys is light and Sandy but well Cultivated, much after the English method. They grow great quantity's of Grain of all kinds and Export great deal of Wheate and Flour to the Eastern Markets. They are famous for Ham's, which go under the name of Burlington Hams, and are esteemed the best in the World, the greatest part of their Exports are Salt-Pork, Live Cattle and Grain with some Lumber.

Few large Towns in the Jerseys, it is chiefly in large Farms and small Villages, here is a great many Stone Houses, Barns, Granaries, Mills and likewise stone fences—the Country is well cleared of Wood, the Roads and Fields tolerable regularly lay'd out, with a great number of Publick-houses for the accomodation of travelers at a very small expence.

Pennsylvania, one of the most flourishing Provinces on the American Continent. Philadelphia is the Capital, but I have before described it. Tis a Proprietary Province belonging to the Family of the Pen. The face of the Country is much the same as the Jersey's, and likewise the produce. Great numbers of beautifull Ships have been built at Philadelphia, it was a considerable branch of their Trade, the back parts of the Province amply supply them with Timber for that purpose. With Iron in plenty and Hemp for Rigging. The Inhabitants of this Province are strange mixture of English, Scotch, Irish, Dutch and Germans with a considerable number of Jews. There Religion is as various as their Country, but the Quakers are the most numerous. It was a piece of sound policy in the Propretor [sic], to tolerate all kinds of Religion no matter what Sect, or profession they are of. If they acknowledge one Supreme God it is enough. They had the free liberty to pay their Devotions in what manner they pleased.

Before this unhappy Rebellion, these people, so very different in respect to Country, Language and Religious Tenet's lived together in the greatest Peace and Harmony. Each profession mantains [sic] their own Teachers, no established Religion amongst them. The inhabitants, in general are remarkable industrious and have established some Manufactorys amongst them. One at Germantown about six miles from Philadelphia for Woollen Stockings. Another at Lancaster Sixty Miles West of Philadelphia for Guns, Axes, Hoes, and various kinds of hardware of that sort. These are the only Manufacturing Towns, of any note, that I know on the Continent. There is several Snuff-mils and Paper-mills in Philadelphia and it's neighbourhood. In the Town there is some very large Distilleries for Rum, and a Large Brewhouse for Ale and Porter. I have drank Ale and Porter Brewed here, from malt made in the Country, as Good as we generally meet with in England.

Maryland is (or with greater propriety) I may say (was) a Proprietary Government or Province, Belonging to Lord Baltimore. The face of the Country is delightfully pleaseing, but not so full of inhabitants, or so well Cultivated as the Northern Provinces. The principart [sic] part of their exports is Tobacco, likewise Wheat, Flour, Provisions, Lumber and great quantities of Iron. The Land is in general level, and in some places very rich and might have been purchased upon very moderate terms. Their Taxes are pay'd in Tobacco, likewise their Church benefices are collected in Tobacco, but there is allways some Glebe Lands annexed to the Liveing. There is a great number of Roman-Catholick in this province, But not such a Spirit of Trade as there is in the Northern provinces. They can procure a good livelyhood with very little industry and have such numbers of Slaves, it makes them quite Indolent. Annapolis is the Capital.

Virginia is the Finest Country I ever was in. It is said by some people to extend from the Atlantic, Westward to the Missisippi River. In such an amazeing extent of Country there is all sorts of Land. From the Sea to the Blue-Mountains it is pretty level, and in general rich, but thinly inhabited and badly

Cultivated. The chief produce Tobacco and Indian-Corn. The Blue-Mountains Intersect the Colony in S. W. Direction, in North-Carolina they are lost in the Appalachian Mountains. They are a Ridge of Barren hills for the most part, though there is some very fertile and pleasant Vallies interspersed amongst them.

From the Blue-Mountains, Westward, to the Appalachian Mountain is about 150 Miles. Is one of the pleasantest Countries I ever beheld. The Land is Rich beyond conception, the face of the Country beautifull and the Air and situation healthy. But very thinly peopled. The produce Wheat, Hemp and Tobacco. Great numbers of Hogg's and Cattle of all sorts are Bred and Fed here.

If the Potowmeck River was made Navigable to the Mouth of the Shanando River, this would be one of the most Desireable Country's that my Ideas are capable of forming. Indeed they have attempted it, and have had a Nephew of the Famous Mr Brindley's to view it, actually begun to work upon it, and got a considerable subscription for defraying the expence. But they have entrusted the management of the Work to such an unsteady worthless sort of a man with the distraction of the times, I am affraid will render it abortive. The Country Westward, of the Applachian Mountains, I think I have before described. The chief and staple Produce of Virginia is Tobacco, of which they export great quantities—more then all the other Colonies put together, likewise great quantities of Wheat, Flour, Provisions, Lumber and Tar with som little Hemp and Indigo, the last Article, does not thrive very well here.

Here is people of all Kinds of Religion, but the Protestant is the Established one.

This Colony abounds with large Navigable Rivers more than any other Colony on the Continent. All discharge themselves into Chesapeak-Bay, the Finest Bay in the World. But the people, in general, seem insensible of the great advantages of these fine Rivers. Very few Virginians apply themselves to Trade, but trust wholly to their Plantations. The great number of Negroes they have, the warmth of the Climate, and the very easy manner in which a comfortable subsistence is procured in this plentifull Country all conspire to make the inhabitants exceedingly indolent. A very considerable part of this Colony belongs to Lord Fairfax, Chesapeak-Bay on the East, Potowmeck River on the North, Rappahannock River on the South and the Applachian Mountains on the West, are his Lordships Boundries, But any lands that are not taken up or allready possessed are easily procured. Any person who finds a piece of Land unoccupyed he apply's to the Surveyor of the County, who Surveys it and sends a plat of it to the General Office, a Grant is immediate made (if no other person Claims by a prior Survey) without any other expence then paying for the Survey, and a Chief or Quit-rent of Two Shillings and Sixpence Sterling, Annually, for every Hundred Acres neither is the Quitrent payed untill they have had it in possession three Years. Government Lands gives Ten-Years. North Carolina, I never have been in, only the uninhabited parts of it, But I believe it is much like Virginia, only fewer inhabitants, and a greater number of Negroes. They grow more Indigo some Rice, but not so much Tobacco as Virginia, the other produce is much the same as Virginia, Wheat excepted, more Tar, and Pork is exported from Carolina then Virginia. Very little Naval Craft belongs to North Carolina.

South Carolina, I have only been in the uninhabited parts of it. But I believe it is much the Same as North Carolina only warmer and thiner inhabited with greater numbers of Slaves. Their produce is Chiefly Rice and Indigo. Georgia, East and West Florida I know little about. I believe they are very thinly Inhabited, are very Hot disagreeable and unhealthy Country's to live in. Great numbers of Cattle are Bred on the Frontiers of Georgia South and North Carolina, which in the latter end of the Year, they drive into the Northern Colonies to sell. The Land is remarkable Rich and affords good Pasture, in back parts of those Colonies. Along the Coast the Inhabitants are in general Wealthy, but Indolent to an extreme.

The Continent of America, take it, All in All, is undoubtedly one of the finest Country's in the World. It plentifully abounds with every necessry of life. And allmost every luxury that the most Voluptious Epicure could desire may be procured with little trouble or expence.

Every part of the Continent abounds with large Navigable Rivers all of them plentifully stored with Fish of varous sorts. I have seen upwards of 50,000 Herrings caught at one Haule in the Sein, with several Hundred Shad-Fish. In the Winter incredible numbers of Swans, Geese and Ducks come down from the Lakes and frequent these Rivers. The face of the Country is in general Delightfully pleaseing, the Air Good and mostly Clear and Serene. But subject to very sudden transitions from Heat to Cold. If the Wind comes from the N. or N. W. it is very Cold Summer or Winter. The first of a N. W. Wind in the Summer, is generally attended with severe Gusts, Thunder, Lightening and Rain. And in the Winter with very severe Frosts, much harder than any we have in England. These sudden alterations and the disagreeable Vapours that are Exhaled by the heat of the Sun, from the Marshey Lands, occation Fevers and Agues, which with the Flux, I believe are the only disorders that predominate in this Country.

The inhabitants, particularly in the Southern Colonies (What I mean by the Southern Colonies, is all South of New York) are—or rather was, for these unhappy times have positively made a great alteration in their Disposition as well as circumstances—the most Hospitable people on Earth if a Stranger went amongst them—no matter of what Country—if he behaved deacently, had a good Face, a Good Coat, and a tolerable share of Good-nature, Would Dance with the Women and Drink with the Men, with a little necessary Adulation, of which, By the Way, they are very fond. With these qualifications he would be entertained amongst them with the greatest Friendship, as long as he pleased to stay. If he is a Traveler he is recommended from one Gentlemans House to another to his journey. I believe it possible to travel though both Carolina's, Virginia and Maryland without a single Shilling, the Ferryages excepted. In short there would no fear of anything but the Constitution, which probably might suffer from the excess of good chere[sic].

They are rather Volatile then otherways. But in general very good natural Capacities. If they have any Genius tis not cramped in their infancy, by being over-awed by their Parents. There is very little subordination observed in their Youth. Implicit obedience to Old Age, is not among their qualifications. Their persons are in general Tall and Genteel particularly the Women, they are remarkable well shaped, I think I have not seen three Crooked Women in the Country. Few, or none of them weares Stays in the Summer, and there is but few, that weares them constantly in the Winter, which may be a principal reason, why they have such good shapes. But to counterballance this great perfection, they have very bad Teeth, very few of them has a good Mouth at Twenty-Five. It is said, that eating so much Hot Bread (for they in general Bake every meal) and Fruit, is the reason why their teeth decay so early. They are Good-natured, Familiar and Agreeable upon the whole. But Confoundedly indolent.

The men are universal Mechanics Carpenter, Sadler and Cooper, but very indifferent Husbandmen. Though the inhabitants of this Country are composed of different Nations and different Languages, Yet is is [sic] very remarkable that they in general speak better English then the English do—no County or Colonial Dialect is to be distinguished here. Except it be the New-Englanders, who have a sort of Whineing Cadence, that I cannot describe. The great population of this Country is amazeing, the Emigrations from Europe added to the natural population, is supposed to double their numbers every 20 Years. Some will say every Sixteen Years. It is certain that they increase much faster then they do in England, Indeed they Marry much sooner. Perhaps one reason may be, in England they cannot mantain a family with so much ease as they do in America which I believe deters many from marrying very early in life. None in England, but those who have not the fear of Want and Poverty before their Eyes, will marry till they have a sufficiency to mantain and provide for a family.

But here there is no fears of that sort, with the least spark of industry they may support a family of small Children, when they grow to manhood, they can provide for themselves. That great Curiosity, an <u>Old Maid</u> is seldom seen in this Country, they generally Marry before they are Twenty-Two—often before they are Sixteen.

In short, this was a Paradise on Earth, for Women the Epicures Elysium, and the very Center of Freedom and Hospitality. But in the short space of three Years—Tis become the Theater of War, the Country of Distraction and the Seat of Slavery, Confusion and Lawless Oppression. May the Allmighty of his infinite goodness and mercy Reunite and Reestablish them in their former happy and flourishing situation. I am allmost tired with scribbleing, But these hints may be of service if ever I correct my Journal. Heard several Guns Fired suppose them to be signals made by the Rebels.

On Board the Brig Edward, Long-Island Sound July 20th 1777
The first part of these 24 Hours Light Breeses. Evening the Fleet Becalmed. The Land on the Connecticut Shore appears Good. Long-Island Sandy and Barren.

21st This afternoon a fine Breese from the Westward. A Rebel Privateer Doged us, the Swan Sloop gave Chace drove her into New-London Harbour. She fired several Shots at the Privateer but at too great a distance to do any execution. At 10 P. M. the East end of Long-Island caled Montock Point, Bore West of two Leagues from whence we take our Departure Lattd 41°° 18" N. Lond 70°° 20" W. I now probably may bid a long farewell to America.

22nd A Heavy Gale of Wind came on last Night, and still continues. The Sea a Roaring—the Ship a Roleing—the Riging breaking—the Mast's a Bending—the Sails a Rattleing—the Captain Swearing—the Sailors Grumbling—the Boys a Crying—the Hogs a Grunting—the Dog a Barking—the Pots and Glasses Breaking—the Colonel Ill of the C—p in Bed. All from the Top-Gallant-Truck to the Keel, from the Jibb Boom to the Tafferel in the utmost confusion. Few of the Fleet in sight. I am confoundedly sick.

On Board the Brig Edward At Sea, towards England. July 23rd 1777

The Gale has continued Violent till this morning. Shiped several heavy Sea's in at the Cabin Windows. More moderate this evening. We have four of the Fleet missing. Several has carried away Top-Gallant-Masts, Yards, & &.

24th A high an Short Sea—suppose ourselves to be in the Gulph-Stream. Weather moderate. The Missing Vessels are the Lady-Gage, a Tobacco Ship, and two Brigs.

25th Contrary, but light Winds. Very Sick.

26th Fine Wind and pleasant weather. The Hypocritical Colnl Cotton, Sick of a certain fashionable disorder, that one would scarcely expect to find in so rigid a Presbyterian. But I find, all men, be their Religion what it will are made of Flesh and Blood. I do not pitty him.

27th Sunday. Fine Wind and pleasant. At M. Saw a Sail from the Mast-head to Windward of us.

28th Good Wind and pleasant. Caught a Dolphin the flesh is remarkable white but very dry. Sick, Sick, Sick.

29th And 30th Fine Wind and pleasant weather this day one of the missing Vessels joined the Fleet, a Brig with Tobacco.

31st Pleasant weather and a good Wind. I hope I have pretty well over this confounded Sea Sickness.

On Board the Brig Edward at Sea towards England August 1st 1777

Pleasant weather and a fine Wind. The good humour and honest behaviour of Captn Park is very agreeable.

2nd Cloudy weather. Wind come round to the Eastward.

3rd Light Breeses in the morning from the Eastward. Evening Calm. Saw a very uncommon Sea Monster, along side, But cannot pretend to give a particular description of it. Captain Park and I sunk an empty Bottle well Corked into the Sea about 100 Fathom deep. We tied a piece of Leather over the Cork But upon our drawing it up again we found the Cork forced into the Bottle, and the Bottle filled with water but could not perceive any difference in the taste of the common Sea Watter from that in the Bottle. I suppose the extreme Cold at that Depth Condences the Air in the Bottle, and the great weight of the Water above Forces in the Cork.

4th Hazy Weather and an Easterly Wind.

5th The Wind is come round to W.S.W. Blows hard. Comodore gave Chace to a Sail, to Windward of us, but without Success.

6th Wind Westwardly. With Rain and Hazy Cold weather.

7th Fine Cleare weather and Good Wind.

8th Pleasant weather but a Heavy Rolling Sea from the Nwd.

9th Thick Foggy Blowing weather. Wind from the Eastward.

On Board the Brig Edward, towards England. August 10th 1777

Sunday. Very pleasant weather and a fine Wind. Kild one of our pigs.

11th 12th And 13th Fine weather and good Wind—nothing remarkable.

14th Pleasant and Fair Wind. The Commodore spoke A French Brig.

15th Saw three Ships standing to the Eastward. I cannot write my Journal, But I must be overlooked by this Hypocritical Colnl Cotton, a pimping Dog. Yr Hbl Servant Sir—this has drove him upon Deck in a violent passion but he does not own it. Pleasant Weather. Fair Wind.

16th Light Airs and Pleasant Weather. At M. His Majesty's Ship Resolution 64 Guns commanded by Sir Chalonel Ogle came into the Fleet. at 4 P. M. Hove the Lead and got Ground in 95 Fathom Water. Fine White sand and black Specks with small Shells. Scilly Island Beares N. 11°° 39" E. Dist 60 Leagues. At 7 P. M. The Lieut of the Resolution came on Board and pressed one of our men.

17th Sunday. General De Heister Dined on Board the Resolution on his going over the Side was saluted by the Resolution with 13 Guns. at M Hove the Lead. Ground in 60 Fathom Fine Brown and Black Sand. At 5 P. M. the Niger made Signall for all Masters. Orders to proceed to Portsmouth.

On Board the Brig Edward towards England. August 18th 1777

Pleasant Weather. This evening a Strange Sloop came into the Fleet and spread an Allarm. The Comodore Fired at Her and Brought Her Too. Can't learn what she is.

19th Fair Wind and Pleasant Weather. Caught a Small Blue Shark.

20th At 6 P. M. St Agnew's Light-House, on the Island of Scilly Bore N. N. E. Dist about 6 Leagues. Find an error of 4 Degrees Longd in my Reckoning, owing to our Log-Line being too Short. Fine Wind and Pleasant.

21st At M. the Start Bore N. N. E. Distance 4 Leagues very pleasant weather.

22nd This morning Saw the West End of the Isle of Wight. this gives an universall joy to all on Board, myself excep[t]ed. the thoughts of returning to my Native Country a Beggar is more than I can support with becomeing fortitude. it casts such an unusual Damp upon my Spirits that I am more Dead then Alive. At 11 A. M. Came to an A[n]chor at Spit-Head, all the Fleet in Company. We have had an agreeable passage of 33 Days from our Departure from the East End of

Long-Island. And an Absience of Three Years, Four Months and Thirteen Days from England. Colnl Cotton and Captn Park will Hurry me on Shore—had rather stay on Board.

On Board the Brig Edward. *Spit-head, Portsmouth August 23rd 1777*
Last night Colnl Cotton, the Captn and I, went a Shore—the Wind blew so hard that we was obliged to make the first land we could, was several times very near oversetting. The Hector Man of War, Carried away her Main-Top Mast Turning up to Spithead, while we was in the Boat. Landed near the South-Sea-Castle on Portsmouth Common. Hauled our Boat a shore. Suped and Lodged at the Blue Posts. This morning, By the intrest of Mr Furnival, saw the Dock-Yard. The great quantities of Naval Stores of all kinds, and the very great conveniences for Building and refiting Ships of War are very well worth seeing. Afternoon went to see the Hospital for Invalids. A Noble Building indeed.

Very accidentally met with Mr John Legdum, the person I helped out of the Ditch in New-York. This Gentn has been imprisoned and ruined in America is now in very-great distress, but has too much pride to return to his Friends in his present situation. they are people of property near Coventry. His Gratitude caused me to spend every penny I had with him. My very imprudent Conduct and very narrow escape in this place will will [sic] not bear reflection. Got on Board late in the Night.

On Board the Brig Edward, *From Portsmouth towards London. Aus 24th 1777*
My last nights adventure needs not be mentioned here. I shall allways remember it. This morning had orders to proceed to Depford, His Majesties Ship Kent is appointed our Convoy to the Nore, At A. M. Got underway at 6 P. M. the Swan-Cliff on the Isle of Wight Bore N. E. B [13?]. N. Distance 4 Leagues. Pleasant Weather.

25th At 4 P. M. A Breast of Dover. Got a Pilot from there. 6 P. M. Came to an Anchor Off Deal in the Downs. Bought some things here. Borrow the money from the Captn.

26th A Fine Gentle Breese and pleasant weather. We have kept close Inn Shore all day, and had a most Delightfull View of the Country. At Anchor in Westcoat Bay.

27th We have had a Very fair Wind all Day and pleasant weather. If it had shifted as we could have wished it could not have been better. Came to an Anchor at Depford at 6 P. M. We have a Pilot who is upwards of 60 tho has been in this trade all his life and never had a Wind to bring him up the River Thames in one Day before.

The prospect has been beyond discription pleaseing all day. Mr Abby, the Mate, has got a bad wound on his foot with the Anchor. Thames a narrow crooked River.

On Board the Brig Edward. Depford August 28th 1777

This morning the Captn and me, went to London, by Water. Found Mrs Dixon and Mr John Ellis of whom I have borrowed Twenty Pound upon my own Credit. I was in very great want of money. Wrote to my Father and Spoke for some new Cloaths. I have great occation for them—for I am a Ragged, Shabby Weather-beaten mortal. Got on Board at Night.

29th Went up to Town. Dined with Mr John Ellis. Spent the Evening at the Tavern with Tim Dixon and Furnival. I believe half the People in this bustling place are Rebels in their Hearts. Lodged at Mrs Dixons where I shall make my home for the time I stay here.

30th I have been under a necessity of geting Ten Pound more from Mr Ellis. God knows when or how I shall be able to repay him.

31st Sunday. Went to St Dunstan's Church in the Forenoon. St James's Park in the Evening.[63]

London September 1st 1777

Went to Mrs Hughes, and Delivered all Mr Nourses Letters to her.

2nd Dined with Mrs Hughes. Spent the Evening with Mr John Green, my Old School fellow.

3rd Saw Mr Robert Needham Junr,[64] he informs me that my Uncle Tym is Dead. Some other very disagreeable news, concerning the Family. Went with him to Drapers Hall. And to see the Lord Mayor proclaim Barthemew Fair, in Smithfield.

4th Went with Sam Dixon and some other Company to see Vauxhall Gardens. This is the last night that they are kept open for the Season there has been some Lamps broken by the Mob, and other Riotous proceeding.[65]

5th Went to the Theatre in the Hay-Market, with Miss Dixon. Henry the Eigth [sic] and the Fary.

6th Got my Chest A Shore, Seeing the Humours of the Town in the Evening.

7th Sunday. Went to St Dunstans Church in the forenoon. Spent the Evening at the Dog and Duck[66] with J. Dixon and Captn Deacon.

London, September 8th 1777

This day I have received a very kind Letter from my Father. I have returned him an answer. I am utterly at a loss what to do. Stay at home I cannot, without things are altered for the better since I left it. I am determined to wait upon Lord Dunmore when he returns to Town, and endeavour to get a Commission in the Marine service. In the Evening went with Miss Dixon to Danbury Tea Gardens.

9th Very uneasy in mind. I dread the thoughts of going home. In the evening went to Baggnige Wells[67] with J Dixon and Furneval.

10th This morning settled my account with Captn Park and Colnl Cotton this has reduced me to Beggary again. I am still in Debt to Captn Park £2/15S. He has behaved to me with the greatest kindness, honour and good-nature.

11th Went to Visit Miss Astley this morning. Afterwards waited upon Doctor Solander[68] by Mr Robinsons introduction and at his request. The Doctor very politely shewed me the Brittish Museum. Such an amazeing Collection of Curiosities I cant describe it. In the Evening at a Conversation Club in Bread-Street with S. Dixon.

London, September 12th 1777
Went with Mrs Dixon to the Old-Bailey to hear the Trials. But could not get admission under a Crown a piece—this is more money than I can at present spare. After Dinner Sam Dixon went with me to see New-Gate Prison. Such another place I never wish to see—in stead of punishing Vice, tis a Nursery for it—those that have been confined here, and afterwards are acquited, may justly say, that they have studied in the Thieves Accademy. Tis a New Strong and Good Building.
13th This morning went to Westminster-Abby with Mr Wommersley. This is the Largest building I ever saw, the monuments numerous and Grand. But I cannot pretend to give any description of them. In the Evening went with Sam Dixon to Sadlers Wells, saw the Tumblers Rope-Dancers & & &.[69]
14th Sunday. Dined at Charles Fouace's Esqr at Chelsey. Here is a Noble Hospital for Disabled and superanuated Soldiers.[70] I cannot learn that Lord Dunmore will return to Town this Month.

London September 15th 1777
I want to be at home, Yet I am affraid of going. but my money is allmost done. What a Curse it is to be continually poor. Drank Tea at Mr Browns. Spent the Evening with Furneval seeing the Humours of this overgrown Town. Some scenes that I have this night seen are allmost increditable.
16th I am under the disagreeable necessity of borrowing Five Guineas from Sam Dixon. Confound this poverty it has been my constant attendant for a long time but I am not yet reconciled to it. Spent the evening with Miss Astley!
17th I am determined to wait no longer upon his Lordship—have taken my passage for Ashbourn in the Coach which is to Sail on Sunday Evening. Saw the Tower with Mr Wommersley and some Lady's of his acquaintance.
18th Wrote to my Father to meet me with horses at Ashbourn. Saw Ellis Barber. Who informs me that my Brother Richd is married And that they felt the Shock of an Earth-quake in Edale last Sunday.

London September 19th 1777
Went with Mr Hugh's to Levers Museum. An amazeing large Collection of the Rarest Curiosities and arranged in the greatest order. But to extensive for me to pretend to describe.[71] Dined with Mr Hugh's. Spent the Evening with Furneval.
20th Prepareing for my journey home. No news of Lord Dunmore. My Spirits are very low allmost as low as my pocket. Got my Chest to the Waggon.
21st Sunday. Dined at Mrs Dixons with Sam Dixon and his Wife. I am much obliged to this good family. Furneval and Sam Dixon accompanied me to the Coach. Sorry to part with the Honest and Generous Furneval. Six inside

passengers in the Coach. Outside covered like a Pidgeon-house. Suped and changed Horses at St Albans. Changed horses again at Dunstable, Woburn, and Newport- Pagnel.

22nd Breakfasted and changed Horses at Northampton, again at Market harbro. Dined at Leicester. Changed horses at Loughb'ro. Lodged at the Bell in Derby. Very Low Spirited and very ill.

23rd Got to Ashbourn to breakfast. No horse arrived for me very Ill and low Spirited. Obliged to go to Bed at 3 O'Clock in the afternoon.

Edale September 24th 1777

Hired a horse of the Landlord at the Blackamores Head. Dined at the Forrest. Got home in the evening. My Parents seem very glad to see me—particularly my poor Mother. She is much Aged since I left England. My Father set out for Chesterfield Fair soon after I arrived—but remembered to order me to Sheare or Bind Corn, tomorrow. I think this rather hard. I am so weak with a violent Lax that I can scarcely walk a Hundred Yards without being much fatigued—my Mother is overjoyed at my arrival. My Spirits are very low but I endevour to keep them up as well as I can. All my Brothers that are at home, are much grown. Dick I understand has been a bad Boy.

25th This forenoon I have been binding Corn. It is very disagreeable exercise in my present weak condition. Afternoon Mr Champion my worthy Friend came to see me. The Old Gentleman looks well. I am happy to see it. He condoles my misfortunes more like a parent then a friend. Mr Lingard[72] came to see me in the Evening.

Edale September 26th 1777

I have been Binding Corn all Day. So much fatigued that I can scarcely get up stairs to bed. It is very hard, but I am determined to beare it without murmuring, if I possible can.

27th Went to the New-Smithy to Robert Kirks—the old man is very happy to hear from his son.[73] I am confoundedly stark weary and low spirited.

28th Sunday. Went to the Chapel, the people stare at me as if they would Devour me. I could hear some of them say—What a poor Dun looking Man he is. My old friend Mr Bray came to see me, and Mr Lingard, who is as inquisitive and absent as usual.

29th Shearing all Day hard Labour indeed but I must bear it with patience—If I can—I am much better in health then I was, but Low Spirited.

30th My excessive fatigue prevents me sleeping, but I still go to the field and do the best I can without grumbleing, at leaste, in appearance. O! Patience Patience.

Edale October 1st 1777

Employed in Shearing. But dont like it a bit better then I did. Resolution and Patience come to my Aid.

2nd And 3rd. Employed as above, but it is far from being agreeable exercise. I am under a necessity of submiting to it.

4th This envening my Brother Richard and his Wife came to see my Father for the first time since his marriage. I understand he has been a very wild obstinate Youth. Tis no more then I expected. His marriage has been against the consent of his friends. His Wife seems to be a young inocent Girl but appeares good-natured and modest. I am affraid he will make but a poor Husband he has the look of a Rake.

There is no provision made for them either by her friends or his own that I can learn. What strange infatuation can induce people to be so cursed foolish to marry without knowing how they are to subsist afterward.

Edale October 5th 1777 Sunday

This day my Brother Richard and his Wife made their appearance at Edale Chappel. Miss Thomason his Wifes Sister (a perfect Original By Heaven's) and her Brother (an awkward Country Lad) was with them. Mrs Charington Mr Lingard and some other Company Dined with them at my Fathers. All appear to be in High spirits, Except myself, however I have affected a cherefullness, but in fact am very uneasy. I greatly pitty these two unthinking mortals.

6th And 7th At Home. Sheareing as my strength increases this exercise is not so disagreeable. I be[g]in to have an uncommon voratious appetite.

8th Went to Hassop. Dined with Mr Needham at Rowdale. I am rather surprised to find all his Daughters unmarried. I know of no Young Lady's that are more likely to make good wifes.

Edale October 9th 1777

At home employed in shearing. It is still very disagreeable business—but it will be over shortly.

10th When I was in London I acquainted my Father that I had borrowed £30 of Mr John Ellis which I had promised to pay on the 11th prnt. He has kindly given me the Cash.

Dined at Sheffield—find little alteration here. Only the people are in general (here and every where else) prejudiced in favour of the Rebels. Got to Chapeltown in the evening, where I found Mr John Ellis.

11th Paid Mr John Ellis Junr the money which I borrowed from him in London. Left Chapelton and got to Middop where I found all my friends well.

12th Sunday. Dined with Mr Perkin at Ughill whose family I find just as I left it. Got home in the evening. I am tired with answering very silly questions—they appear such to me—though some of them are asked with great simplicity.

Edale October 13th 1777

There is such a sameness in my life at present it is not worth while to keep a Journal. I am affraid it is likely to continue longer than I could wish it.

As no proposals have been Yet made to me concerning my future way of life I immagin my Father expects I shall stay at home in my present Dependent situation. I cannot bear it. Though at present his behaviour is very kind and in some respects indulgent, but that Morossness he observes to some of family is very disagreeable to me. I expect something of the same sort so soon as the first Gust of Paternal Affection subsides. But I am determined to stay with seeming patience till April next, and behave in such a manner as not to give any just offence. I call this waiting the Chapter of accidents - something fortunate may hapen [sic]. Memd. Never to have anything to doo with my Relations. I know their disposition only too well. Some of them begins to hint at my Poverty allready. I must be patient and if <u>possible</u> Silent.

Saturday Aprill 21st 1781. Nicholas Cresswell was married at Wirks worth in Derbyshire to Mary Mellor the youngest daughter of Mr Samuel Mellor of Idridgehay in the parish of Wirksworth, By the Revd Mr Bennet. Mr Robt Poole stood Father, Mr Sml Mellor Junr and Miss Hannah Dawson; present at the ceremony.[74]

My rambling in now at an end!

Notes

1. The widow of Nathan Baker (d. 1775) Mrs. Elizabeth Baker operated a tavern in Leesburg. The ordinary license obtained by her husband in 1773 identified the tavern as being in Leesburg at the house of Samuel Canby. The Bakers were Quakers. Loudoun County Court Order Book F, 1773-1776, 70, 440, 466, 532 and Will Book B, 1772-1782, 104. All Virginia county court records cited hereafter are on microfilm at the Library of Virginia, Richmond.

2. The Sixth Virginia Regiment was authorized by the fourth Virginia convention on December 1, 1775 and taken into Continental service in February 1776. It was part of General Stephen's brigade at Trenton. E. M. Sanchez-Saaedra, *A Guide to Virginia Military Organizations in the American Revolution, 1774-1787* (Richmond, Va.: Virginia State Library, 1978), 48-50.

3. A Samuel Dean appears as a tithable in Loudoun County in 1776. Loudoun County Tithables, 1758-1799 (Library of Virginia).

4. At its October 1776 session the Virginia legislature suspended the "An Act for the support of the clergy" passed during the reign of George II, which provided for the public support of the clergy. W. W. Hening, *Statutes at Large*, vol. 10 (Richmond, Va.: George Cochron, 1822), 111.

5. William Hartshorne was a merchant in Alexandria. He moved there from Philadelphia with his partner John Harper. W. W. Abbot and Dorothy Twohig, eds., *The Papers of George Washington, Colonial Series*, vol. 9 (Charlottesville, Va.: University Press of Virginia, 1994), 238-39.

6. This may have been the Peter Carr who married Mary Minner on July 23, 1796 in Loudoun County. Mary Alice Wertz, complier, *Marriages of Loudoun County, Virginia, 1757-1853* (Baltimore, Md.: Genealogical Publishing Co., Inc., 1985), 23.

7. This was probably Josiah Moffit. He served in the Loudoun County militia when he was identified as "Gent." See entry for November 28, 1774. J. T. McAllister, *Virginia Militia in the Revolutionary War* (Hot Springs, Va.: McAllister Publishing Co., 1913), 211.

8. Jacob Ellegood was lieutenant colonel of the "Queen's Loyal Virginia Regiment" raised by Governor Dunmore. He was captured in 1775 and transferred to Winchester in 1776. Treasury Board In Letters, 1775-1783, T 1/583, pp. 160-161; Treasury Minute Book LIII, 1782-1783, T 29/53, p. 58. Public Record Office, London. All citations to records in the Public Records office are on microfilm at the John D. Rockefeller, Jr. Library, Colonial Williamsburg Foundation, Williamsburg, Virginia. Virginia Committee of Safety Ledger, 1775-1776, f. 107, (Library of Virginia).

9. John Hite, son of Jost Hite who settled in the Shenandoah Valley in 1732, lived just south of Winchester at his plantation called Springdale. Robert G. Albion and Leonidas Dodson, eds., *Philip Vickers Fithian: Journal, 1775-1776* (Princeton, N. J.: Princeton University Press, 1934), 29.

10. Charles Fouace was probably a relative of Mrs. Nourse who was formerly Sarah Fouace. Donald Jackson, ed., *The Diaries of George Washington*, vol. 3 (Charlottesville, Va.: University Press of Virginia, 1978), 13.

11. This may have been Henry Peyton, Jr., who was recommended by the Frederick County Justices on September, 6, 1774, as a proper person to be examined for a licence to practice as an attorney. He was described "as a person of Probity, honesty and good de-

meanor. Frederick County Court Order Book 16, 1772-1778, 369.

12. The Continental Congress did not resolve to move to Baltimore until December 12th where they were to meet on December 20th. Worthington Chauncey Ford, ed., *Journals of the Continental Congress*, vol. 4 (Washington, D.C.: Government Printing Office, 1906), 1027.

13. On this day, Cresswell witnessed a deed between James Kirk and Septimus Levering for lot 49 in Leesburg. Patrick Cavan and William Smith also witnessed the deed. Loudoun County Court Deeds L, 1775-1778, 236-38.

14. The British captured Fort Washington on November 16th and Fort Lee four days later. Fort Lee was on the New Jersey side of the Hudson River opposite Fort Washington. Bernard A. Uhlendorf, ed., *Revolution in America: Confidential Letters and Journals 1776-1784 of Adjutant General Major Baurmeister of the Hessian Forces* (New Brunswick, N. J.: Rutgers University Press, 1957), 67-71. Mark M. Boatner, III, *Encyclopedia of the American Revolution* (New York: David McKay Co., Inc., 1974), 386-88.

15. Fleming Patterson was a merchant in Leesburg at least as early as 1765. John Glassford & Co. Alexandria Ledger 1765-1766, f. 37 (Library of Congress). Microfilm in John D. Rockefeller Jr., Library, Colonial Williamsburg Foundation, Williamsburg, Virginia.

16. Cleone Moore was a merchant in Colchester, Virginia. He was appointed captain in Colonel Grayson's Additional Continental Regiment of Infantry on Jaunary 29, 1777. Robert A. Rutland, ed., *Papers of George Mason*, vol. 1 (Chapel Hill, N. C.: University of North Carolina Press, 1970), lxxxi. Sanchez-Saavedra, ed., *A Guide to Virginia Military Organizations*, 74.

17. This may have been William Johnson, who was appointed captain in the Prince William District Battalion in October 1775. Sanchez-Saavedra, *A Guide to Virginia Military Organizations*, 22.

18. John Cooke and John Throckmorton were justices of the peace for Berkeley County. They were appointed on April 14, 1773. Benjamin J. Hillman, ed., *Executive Journals of the Council of Colonial Virginia*, vol. 6 (Richmond, Va.: Virginia State Library, 1966) 522-23.

19. Dr. James Armstrong was the son of General John Armstrong. James graduated from the University of Pennsylvania in 1769 and practiced medicine in Winchester, Virginia. He was a medical officer in the Revolution and later settled in Carlisle, Pennsylvania where he continued his medical practice. He died on May 6, 1828, in Carlisle. Lawrence F. Kennedy, compiler, *Biographical Directory of the American Congress, 1774-1971* (Washington, D. C.: United States Government Printing Office, 1971).

20. Hite's death was reported in the *Virginia Gazette* on August 30, 1776: "Mr. Harrison likewise informs, that Mr. Jacob Hite, who lately removed from Berkeley county to the neighbourhood of the Cherokee country with his family, and a large parcel of negroes, was murdered at his own house by those savages, with most of his slaves, and his wife and children carried off prisoners; his son, who was in the Cherokee country, was likeside murdered." *Virginia Gazette* (Purdie), August 30, 1776.

21. Probably Dr. John McDonald who was permitted to practice "innoculation" for smallpox in Frederick County in 1771. J. E. Norris, ed., *History of the Lower Shenandoah Valley counties of Frederick, Berkeley, Jefferson and Clarke, their Early Settlement and Progress to the Present Time*, (Chicago: A. Wagner & Co., 1890), 123.

22. The letter writer was correct. General Charles Lee was captured near Basking Ridge, New Jersey, on December 13th by a detachment of British cavalry. Edward G. Lengel, *General George Washington: A Military Life* (New York: Random House, 2005), 177-78.

23. Washington actually captured 893 German officers and enlisted men at Trenton. The battle began on December 26, 1776. Lengel, *General George Washington*, 185, 188.

24. John Gee married Ann Worthington on February 14, 1768, in Stockport, England. FamilySearch.com

25. The Battle of Princeton was fought on January 3, 1777. Lengel, *General George Washington*, 201-206.

26. William Sanford was appointed to the rank of captain in the Second Virginia Regiment of Foot on December 25, 1776. Sanchez-Saavedra, *A Guide to Virginia Military Organizations*, 36.

27. William Grayson was Captain of the Independent Company of Prince William County from 1774-1775. On June 21, 1776, he was named assistant secretary to General Washington. He was one of the first pair of senators Virginia sent to the United States Congress. Sanchez-Saavedra, *Guide to Virginia Military Organizations*, 9, 22. Joseph Horrell, ed., "New Light on William Grayson: His Guardian's Account," *Virginia Magazine of History and Biography*. 92 (1984): 423-43.

28. Angus McDonald (c. 1726-1778) immigrated to America from Scotland after the Battle of Culloden in 1746. In the 1760s he built his home, Glengary, near Winchester in Frederick County, where he was rent collector for Lord Fairfax and in 1774 performed a similar service for George Washington. He was noted for his strong personality and as a rigid disciplinarian. Jackson, *Diaries of George Washington*, 3: 322. Nicholas B. Wainwright, ed., "Turmoil at Pittsburgh: Diary of Augustine Prevost, 1774," *Pennsylvania Magazine of History and Biography*, 85 (1961): 127 n. 56.

29. The letter to Lord Brownlow Berty (1729-1809), Duke of Ancaster and Kesteven, may have been regarding Nourse's son William who was a prisoner of the British. William returned home in 1783. "Diary of Mrs. James Nourse," *The Magazine of the Jefferson County Historical Society*, 24 (1958): 21, 27. Vicary Gibbs, ed., *The Complete Peerage of England Scotland Ireland Great Britain and the United Kingdom*, vol. 1 (London: The St. Catherine Press, Ltd, 1910), 128-29.

30. In 1773 William Stanhope was evidently employed by Ellsey and Blackburn in Leesburg. In 1774 he was foreman of the grand jury for Loudoun County and in 1779 was named a justice of the peace. Loudoun County Court Order Book F, 1773-1776, 511; Order Book G, 1776-1783, 141. Loudoun County Tithables 1769-1779, 198.

31. This was likely Alexander McIntyre who was granted a license to keep an ordinary at his house in Leesburg in 1778. He died in 1788. Loudoun County Court Order Book G, 1772-1783, 129; Loudoun County Court Will Book D, 1788-1793, 24.

32. Thomas Crafts supplied tents for the Virginia military in 1776. H. R. McIlwaine, ed., *Journals of the Council of the State of Virginia*, vol. 1 (Richmond, Va.: Virginia State Library, 1931), 65.

33. The Bunch of Grapes was in operation from at least 1766. It was described as "the best accustomed house" in Hampton. At this time it was operated by John Dames. He died in 1784. *Virginia Gazette* (Purdie & Dixon), April 16, 1767; Blance A. Chapman, *Wills and Administrations of Elizabeth City County, Virginia, 1688-1800*, (Baltimore, Md.: Genealogical Publishing Co., 1980), 130.

34. The statute of Lord Botetourt is now in the Earl G. Swem Library at the College of William and Mary, Williamsburg, Virginia.

35. On Duke of Gloucester Street, Anderson's Tavern still stands in Williamsburg, but is now called Wetherburn's Tavern after an earlier owner. At the time Cresswell was there it was operated by Robert Anderson and was a center of Revolutionary activity. The Virginia Committee of Safety met there. Harold B. Gill, Jr., "Governing from a Tavern," *Colonial Williamsburg Journal*, 18, no. 4, (1996): 60-62.

36. British citizens in Virginia were allowed to engage the *Albion* "for the purpose of transporting themselves to their native country" by the Virginia council on February 7, 1777. By May 30, 1777, the *Albion* had not left Virginia waters. H. R. McIlwaine, ed., *Official Letters of the Governors of the State of Virginia*, vol. 1 (Richmond, Va.: Virginia State Library, 1926), 101; McIlawine, ed., *Journals of the Council of the State of Virginia*, 1: 404, 420.

37. Col. James Innes. For an account of his career see Jane Carson, *James Innes and His Brothers of the F. H. C.* (Charlottesville, Va.: University Press of Virginia, 1965).

38. At this time Lt. George Ancram was attached to a Continental Army artillery unit stationed at Yorktown. He was assumed dead by January 6, 1778. *Virginia Gazette* (Pinckney) May 16, 1777; McIlwaine, ed. *Journals of the Council of the State of Virginia*, 2: 59-60.

39. A one hundred dollar reward was offered for the following prisoners who escaped from the Alexandria jail on April 25, 1777: Bartlett Goodrich, James Parker, George Blair, John Cunningham, John Rothery, Josiah Rogers, John Todd, William Nicholls, and John Duncan. *Maryland Gazette*, May 1, 1777.

40. Mobjack Bay in present day Gloucester and Matthews counties.

41. This was probably Warner Lewis, county lieutenant of Gloucester County. Robert L. Scribner and Brent Tartar, eds., *Revolutionary Virginia: The Road to Independence*, vol. 4 (Charlottesville, Va.: University Press of Virginia, 1978), 106.

42. Charles Taliaferro was in charge of the state's flat boats. Navy Board Journal, July 23, 1776 – Feb. 27, 1779, 213 (Library of Virginia).

43. There is no mention of the encounter in the Captain's Log or the Master's Log of HMS *Phoenix*. Both Cresswell and Colin Kerr are noted as being sent to New York in a prize in the "List of Men Borne as Supernumeraries for Victuals only For Protection." The list indicates they were picked up on May 5th. Admiralty, Captains' Logs, 1776 July – 1778 July, Adm 51/694. Admiralty, Masters' Logs, 1775-1778, Adm 52/1909. Admiralty, Muster Books, Adm 36/8407. (Public Record Office, London.).

44. The *Bell and Mary* was called the *Lady Juliana* when captured by the Americans who renamed her *Billy and Mary*. When she was recaptured by the British they named her *Bell and Mary*. It was a 300 ton ship manned with fifteen men. High Court of Admiralty. Ships' Papers 1777, HCA 32/280. (Public Record Office, London.)

45. Cresswell refers to Samuel Wallis (1728-1795) who made a voyage round the world in 1766-1768. Peter Kemp, ed. *The Oxford Companion to Ships and the Sea* (Oxford: Oxford University Press, 1988), 923-24.

46. William Furnivall was later commander of the Sloop Haerlem. He lost the use of his right arm from a wound received during a battle in Virginia. During the war he claimed that he was "twice shipwrecked, and twice made a prisoner." Secretary's Department, Orders in Council, 1783. Adm. 1/5176. (Public Records Office, London.)

47. The *Syren* was 28 gun ship. The *Preston* was a fourth rate ship and the *Emeral* was a fifth rate. William Hotham (1736-1813) as commodore on the *Preston* joined Admiral Howe in 1776 for service in America. He supported the landing at Kip's Bay, New York, in September 1776. During the Philadelphia campaign he remained in New York as senior officer. Robert Beatson, *Naval and Military Memoirs of Great Britain from 1727 to 1783*, vol. 6 (London: Longman, Hurst, Rees and Orme, 1804). 48, 92. Boatner, *Encyclopedia of the American Revolution*, 518-19.

48. Major Cornelius Cuyler was an aide de camp to General Sir William Howe. *A list of the General and Staff Officers and of the Officers in the several Regiments serving in North-America* (New York: MacDonald & Cameron, 1777), 3.

49. Major Samuel Holland was surveyor-general of the colonies north of Virginia.

On March 30, 1777, Sir William Howe ordered Major Holland's Corps of Guides and Axmen to be augmented. In May 1777 Holland ordered "All persons who are engaged in Major Holland's corps of guides and pioneers" to report for duty. Lorenzo Sabine, *Biographical Sketches of Loyalists of the American Revolution*, vol. 1 (Boston: Little, Brown & Co., 1864), 536-37. *New York Gazette and Weekly Mercury*, May 19, 1777.

50. General William Erskine (1728-1795) was Sir Henry Clinton's Quarter Master General. He took part in the Monmouth Campaign and from 1778-1779 was in command of the eastern district of Long Island. He returned to England in 1779. Boatner, *Encyclopedia of the American Revolution*, 348-49.

51. This was the John Street Theater which opened on the December 7, 1767. The theater was refitted by the British for amateur plays acted by "gentlemen of the army and navy." It opened the season in January 1777 with the receipts for the first season donated to widows and orphans of soldiers and sailors who had lost their lives in the war. The play, "The Lyar," was written by Samuel Foote in 1764. The satire, "Polly Honeycombe" was written by George Colman in 1760. William Dunlap, *A History of the American Theatre* (New York: J. J. Harper, 1832), 28, 49-50. Thomas Jefferson Wertenbaker, *Father Knickerbocker Rebels: New York City during the Revolution* (New York: Charles Scribner's Sons, 1948), 121. Martin Banham, ed., *The Cambridge Guide to World Theatre* (Cambridge, England: Cambridge University Press, 1988), 215-16. "The Dramatic Work of Samuel Foote," http://www/questia.com/PM.qst?a=o&d=5376579 (Accessed September 9, 2008)

52. This is Dr. J. F. D. Smythe.

53. The book was probably John Muller, *A Treatise containing the practical part of Fortification* (London, 1774). This popular work went through many editions.

54. General Charles Lee was taken prisoner at Basking Ridge, New Jersey, on December 13, 1776. He was exchanged in April 1778. Boatner, *Encyclopedia of the American Revolution*, 62, 63; 606. *Virginia Gazette* (Dixon) January 3, 1777.

55. James Cotton of North Carolina was a colonel in the militia. In 1776 he was on the Royal side at Moore's Creek Bridge, but fled "at the first fire." In 1779 he was attainted and his estate confiscated. Sabine, *Loyalists*, 1: 337.

56. An advertisement dated "Alexandria, April 10, 1777," in the *Maryland Gazette* on May 1, 1777, for the escaped prisoners did not mention Dodd but did list John Todd. In the manuscript journal the name is clearly "Dodd." The advertisment also named Bartlett Goodrich, James Parker, George Blair, John Cunningham, John Rothery, Josiah Rogers, John Todd, William Nicholls, and John Duncan as escapees. Perhaps Cresswell made an error in transcribing his notes.

57. The *Virginia Gazette* reported on May 30, 1777, that "Thomas Davis (late Adjutant Davis) and six other Tories and traitors, mounted a waggon, under a proper guard, making a very *decent* appearance, passed down the street on their way to the public gaol, from Alexandria, where they are to remain for trial." On August 8, the *Gazette* reported that Davis was convicted for treason "but discharged on a motion in arrest of judgment." *Virginia Gazette* (Purdie), August 8, 1777.

58. There was no newspaper published in Virginia on June 2, 1777, and Cresswell's name does not appear in any extant copy of the *Virginia Gazette*. Cresswell must be referring to some other document.

59. Capt. Robert Braithwaite was given command of HMS Centurion in July 1775. *Virginia Gazette* (Dixon), October 7, 1775.

60. Hell Gate is the narrow channel at the north end of the East River where the Harlem River and Long Island Sound converge. James A. Bear, Jr. and Lucia C. Stanton, eds., *The Papers of Thomas Jefferson. Second Series. Jefferson's Memorandum Books,*

Accountsm, with Legal Records and Miscellany, 1767-1826, vol. 1 (Princeton, N. J.: Princeton University Press, 1997), 760; John A. Tilley, *The British Navy and the American Revolution* (Columbia, S. C.: University of South Carolina Press, 1987), 90.

61. This was the former Fort Washington captured by the British on November 16, 1776, and renamed Fort Knyphausen in honor of the Baron von Knyphausen who led the main attack. Boatner, *Encylopedia of the American Revolution*, 386-388, 588-589.

62. These are lines 191-202 of Part 1, Canto 1, of Samuel Butler's *Hudibras.* The book first published in London in 1663 has gone through many editions. Whether Cresswell was writing from memory or had the book with him is unknown. If he was writing from memory, he made a few errors. The actual lines read:

Twas Presbyterian true Blue;
For he was of that stubborn Crew
Of Errant Saints, whom all men grant
To be the true Church militant:
Such as do built their Faith upon
The holy Text of Pike and Gun;
Decide all Controversies by
Infallible Artillery;
And prove their Doctrine Orthodox
By Apostolick Blows and Knocks;
Call Fire and Sword, and Desolation
A godly, thorough, Reformation.

63. There were two churches in London at this time known as St. Dunstan. One, St. Dunstan in the East, was near the Tower of London. The other, St. Dunstan in the West, was on Fleet Street. The latter was likely the church Cresswell visited because it was not far from St. James Park. It was demolished in 1830. Ben Weinreb and Christopher Hibbert, eds., *The London Encyclopaedia* (New York: St. Martin's Press, 1983), 703-704.

64. This may have been the Robert Needham who died in Wirksworth Parish, Derbyshire, September 1819 at age 77. Wirksworth Parish Records 1608-1899. Web site: www.wirksworth.org.uk/PRO65.htm (Accessed on June 14, 2008).

65. Probably opened just before the Restoration in 1660, Vauxhall Gardens was known as New Spring Gardens. In 1732, Jonathan Tyers took over and transformed it into one of the popular amusements in London. It was usually opened from May to August. Closed in 1859, it was not until 1785 that it was officially called Vauxhall Gardens. It was just across the Thames from Chelsea Hospital. Weinreb and Hibbert, eds., *The London Encyclopaedia*, 910-12. Liza Picard, *Dr. Johnson's London* (New York: St. Martin's Press, 2001), 245-46. Dan Cruickshank, *The Royal Hospital Chelsea: The Place and the People* (London: Third Millennium Publishing, 2004), 88.

66. In St. George's Fields, Lambeth, the tavern was established in 1642 at a medicinal spring. It was first advertised in 1731 and in 1769 a bowling green and swimming bath were added. It closed in 1799. Weinreb and Hibbert, eds., *The London Encyclopaedia*, 231.

67. Located on King's Cross Road, Bagnigge Wells was a popular area for outings. It contained a bowling-green, flower gardens, fish ponds, fountains, and other amusements. It closed in 1841. Roy Porter, *London: A Social History* (Cambridge, Mass.: Harvard University Press, 1994), 173. Weinreb and Hibbert, eds., *The London Encyclopaedia*, 32.

68. Daniel Charles Solander (1736-1782), a native of Sweden, moved to England in 1760. In 1768 he accompanied Joseph Banks on Cook's voyage in the Endeavour. In

1773 he was made keeper of the printed books at the British Museum. Sidney Lee, ed., *Dictionary of National Biography*, vol. 53 (London: Smith, Elder & Co., 1898), 212-13.

69. The first music house was built on Rosebery Avenue in 1683 by Thomas Sadler as a side attraction to a medicinal well. In 1746 the theater was restored and a regular company was engaged in 1753. Weinreb and Hibbert, eds., *The London Encyclopaedia*, p. 687.

70. Chelsea Hospital was founded in 1682 by Charles II. The building, designed by Sir Christopher Wren, was completed in 1692. It served military veterans disabled in war. The central building remains almost unchanged to the present. Weinreb and Hibbert, eds., *The London Encyclopaedia*, 145-46. Cruickshank, *The Royal Hospital Chelsea*, passim.

71. Sir Ashton Lever (1729-1788) was a noted collector of vairous objects but later concentrated his collection efforts in shells and fossils. In 1774 he moved his collection to London where he purchased Leicester House in Leicester Square. He filled sixteen rooms and passageways with his collection. The museum was open each day from ten to four for admission of 5 shillings 3 pence per person. Lee, ed., *Dictionary of National Biography*, 33: 137.

72. This is probably John Lingard who was born in Chapel-in-le-Frith and became a sizar at St. Catherine's College at Cambridge in 1763. University of Cambridge, *Alumni Cantabrigienses*, J. A. Venn, compl., vol. 4, part 2 (1752-1900), 175.

73. Robert Kirk was the father of James Kirk of Virginia. See the christening record of James Kirk. FamilySearch.com.

74. The marriage was recorded in the Wirksworth Parish records with Hannah Dawson and Samuel Mellor as witnesses. Cresswell was noted "Gentleman." Wirksworth Parish Records 1608-1899. Web site: www.wirksworth.org.uk/PR21.htm#538. (Accessed June 14, 2008.)

AFTERWORD

[The following material was added at a later date and we do not treat it as part of the journal proper.]

Friday January 10th 1783 My Wife was delivered of a boy, which was baptized the same evening by the name of Hannibal. The child died the sunday following and was buryed in the Family burying place in Edale Chapel. This was a premature Birth, and the third my Wife has had since our marriage.

Robert the Son of Nicholas and Mary Cresswell was Born Sunday December 14th 1783 about 9 O'Clock in the morning.

Mary Mellor—The Daughter of Nicholas and Mary Cresswell was Born Wednesday April 19th 1786 about 7 O Clock in the morning.

Samuel—The Son of Nicholas & Mary Cresswell was Born the Monday the 2nd of January 1797 - 8 in the morning. Baptized Sunday the 5th Feby 1797 Christened 12 June Died 26 July 1797

Hannah—The Daughter of Nicholas and Mary Cresswell was Born Thursday the 18th of September 1788 about half past Six O Clock in the morning.

Eliza Cresswell The Daughter of Nicholas and Mary Cresswell Born Monday October 18th 1790 about 8 Minuets past 9 O Clock at night.

Thomas Cresswell The Son of Nicholas and Mary Cresswell was Born Sunday the 2nd September 1792 about 6 O Clock in the Morning. Died the 20th of October 1795.

Sarah Cresswell The Daughter of Nicholas and Mary Cresswell was Born June the 1st 1795 about 10 O Clock in the morning.

Ellin Daughter of N & M Cresswell Born 28th August 1799 about half past 3 in the afternoon Baptised 29th Sept 99 Cx 14 July 1800.

[Inverted and Reversed]
The Royal Arms borne by the King of England
Mars hales quarterley, in the first grand quarter Mars three lions passant-guardant in pale, Sol, the imperial ensigns of England: these are impaled with the royal arms of Scotland, consisting of Sol, a lion rampant within a double tressure flowered and counter flowered, with fleurs de lis Mars, The second quarter contains the arms of France namely, Jupiter, three fleurs de lis, Sol. The third for Ireland, exhibits, Jupiter, an harp, Sol, stringed, Luna, In the fourth grand quarter is represented his present majesty's own coat of arms, being Mars, two lions passant-quardant, Sol, for Brunswick, impaled with Lunenburg, giving Sol, semie of hearts, proper, a lion rampant, Jupiter, haveing for antient Saxony, Mars, a horse current, Luna, grafted in base; and in a shield surtout, Mars, the

diadem or a crown of Charlemagne; the whole surrounded with a garter, as sovereign of that order. Above the helmet, as the emblem of soverign jurisdiction, is an imperial crown; the crest, a lion passant-quardant crowned with the like; the supporters, a lion rampant-quardant, Sol, crowned as the former, and an Unicorn Luna, gorged with a crown, and chained. The royal motto is Dieu et mon droit implying "that the King of England holds his crown of God only. The table of the compartment is adorned with the rose and thistle intermingled, as the emblem of the union of England and Scotland.

The Prince of Wales, bears the Kings arms, with the addition of a label of three points, charged with nine torteaux, his device being a coronet beautifyed with three Ostrich feathers inscribed Ich dien, signifying in the German language "I serve."

An Account of the number of Souls, in the undermentioned Colonies. Was taken by a Special order from his Majesty, to the Several Governors, and by them Directed to the Sheriff's, Constables & & within their several Districts in 1763.

New Hampshire	150,000
Massachusets Bay	400,000
Rhode Island	59,678
Connecticut	192,000
New York	250,000
New Jersey	130,000
Pennsylvania, includeing the Delawar Counties	350,000
Maryland	320,000
Virginia	650,000
North Carolina	300,000
South Carolina	225,000
Total	3,026,678

N.B. Slaves are included in this account.

Bibliography

Newspapers

England
Liverpool
Williamson's Liverpool Advertiser, And Mercantile Chronicle.

Maryland
Annapolis
Maryland Gazette.

New York
New York City
New York Gazette and Weekly Mercury.

Pennsylvania
Philadelphia
Pennsylvania Gazette.
Pennsylvania Packet.

Virginia
Alexandria
Virginia Gazette & Alexandria Advertiser.

Williamsburg
Virginia Gazette (Dixon).
Virginia Gazette (Pinkney).
Virginia Gazette (Purdie).
Virginia Gazette (Purdie & Dixon).
Virginia Gazette (Rind).

Web Sites

Access to Archives. http://www.a2a.org.uk.
Dramatic Work of Samuel Foote. http://www.questia.com/PM.qst?a=o&d=5376579
FamilySearch International Genealogical Index. FamilySearch.com
Parish Register of Peak Forest Chapel. Transcribed by Rosemary Lockie. April 1996.
    http://www.genuki.org.uk/big/eng/DBY/PeakForest/pftext2.html.
Hope Parish Marriage Register.
    http://freepages.genealogy.rootsweb.com/~dusk/hope_marriages.html#top
Political Graveyard. http://politicalgraveyard.com/VA/ofc?alexandria.html.
Wirksworth Parish Records 1608-1899. http://www.wirksworth.org.uk/PR21.htm.

Maps

Henry, John. *A New and Accurate Map of Virginia*. London, 1770.

Books

Abbott, Wilbur C. *New York in the American Revolution*. New York: Charles Scribner's Sons. 1929.

Abercrombie, Janice L. and Richard Slatten. *Virginia Revolutionary Publick Claims*. 3 vols. Athens, Ga.: Iberian Publishing Co., 1992.

Abernethy, Thomas Perkins. *Western Lands and the American Revolution*. New York: Russell & Russell, Inc., 1959.

Adams, John. *Diary and Autobiography of John Adams*. L. H. Butterfield, ed. 3 vols. Cambridge: Harvard University Press, 1961.

Alden, John Richard. *General Charles Lee: Traitor or Patriot?* Baton Rouge: Louisiana University Press, 1951.

Allen, R. C. *The Rigging of Ships in the Days of the Spritsail Topmast, 1600-1720*. New York: Dover Publications, Inc., 1994.

Bailey, Kenneth P. *The Ohio Company of Virginia and the Westward Movement, 1748-1792*. Glendale, California: The Arthur H. Clark Co., 1939.

Bakeless, John. *Background to Glory: The Life of George Rogers Clark*. Baton Rouge: Louisiana State University Press, 1957.

Banham, Martin, ed. *The Cambridge Guide to World Theatre*. Cambridge: Cambridge University Press, 1988.

Baurmeister, Carl Leopold. *Revolution in America: Confidential Letters and Journals 1776-1784 of Adjutant General Major Baumeister of the Hessian Forces*. Translated and Annotated by Bernhard A. Uhlendorf. New Brunswick, N. J.: Rutgers University Press, 1957.

Beatson, Robert. *Naval and Military Memoirs of Great Britain from 1727-1783*. 6 vols. London: Longman, Hurst, Rees and Orme, 1804.

Blanton, Wyndham B. *Medicine in Virginia in the Eighteenth Century*. Richmond, Va.: Garrett and Massie, 1931.

Boatner, Mark M., III. *Encyclopedia of the American Revolution*. New York: David McKay & Co., 1974.

Bond, Beverly W., Jr., ed. *The Courses of the Ohio River taken by Lt. T. Hutchins Anno 1766 and Two Accompanying Maps*. Cincinnati: Historical and Philosophical Society of Ohio, 1942.

Booth, Russell H., Jr. *Tuscarawas Valley in Indian Days, 1750-1797*. Cambridge, Ohio: Gomber House Press, 1997.

Bradford, James Chapin. "Society and Government in Loudoun County, Virginia, 1790-1800." Ph.D. Dissertation. University of Virginia, 1976.

Brandow, James C. *Genealogies of Barbados Families*. Baltimore, Md.: Genealogical Publishing Co., 2001.

Buck, Solon J. and Elizabeth Hawthorn Buck. *The Planting of Civilization in Western Pennsylvania*. Pittsburgh: University of Pittsburgh Press, 1979.

Burton, Clarence M. *Ephraim Douglass and his Times: A Fragment of History*. New York: William Abbatt, 1910.

Butler, Samuel. *Hudibras*. 2 vols. Baltimore, Md.: F. Lucas Jr. and P. H. Nicklin, 1812.

Butterfield, C. W., ed. Washington-Crawford Letters. Being the Correspondence between George Washington and William Crawford, from 1767 to 1781, concerning Western Lands. Cincinnati: R. Clarke & Co., 1877.

Butterfield, Lyman H., et al., eds. *Adams Family Correspondence*. 8 vols. Cambridge, Mass.; Harvard University Press, 1963-2007.

Calloway, Colin G. *The American Revolution in Indian Country: Crisis and Diversity in Native American Communities*. Cambridge: Cambridge University Press, 1995.

Carothers, Bettie Stirling. *1776 Census of Maryland*. Westminster, Md.: Family Line Publications, 1992.

Carson, Jane. *James Innes and His Brothers of the F. H. C.* Charlottesville: University of Virginia Press, 1965.

Chapman, Blanch A. *Wills and Administrations of Elizabeth City County, Virginia, 1688-1800*. Baltimore, Md.: Genealogical Publishing Co., 1980.

Cleland, Hugh. *George Washington in the Ohio Valley*. Pittsburgh, Pa.: University of Pittsburgh Press, 1955.

Copeland, Pamela C. and Richard K. MacMaster. *The Five George Masons: Patriots and Planters of Virginia and Maryland*. Charlottesville: University Press of Virginia, 1975.

Cotter, John L., et al. *The Buried Past: An Archaeological History of Philadelphia*. Philadelphia: University of Pennsylvania Press, 1992.

Cruickshank, Dan. *The Royal Hospital Chelsea: The Place and the People*. London: Third Millennium Publishing, 2004.

Crumrine, Boyd. *History of Washington County, Pennsylvania, with Biographical Sketches of Many of its Pioneers and Prominent Men*. Philadelphia: L. H. Everts & Co., 1882.

———, ed. *Virginia Court Records in Southwestern Pennsylvania: Records of the District of West Augusta and Ohio and Yohogania Counties, Virginia, 1775-1780*. Baltimore: Genealogical Publishing Co., Inc., 1974.

Dandridge, Danske. *Historic Shepherdstown*. Charlottesville: The Michie Co., 1910.

Davies, D. P. *A New Historical and Descriptive View of Derbyshire*. Belper, Derbyshire, England: S. Mason, 1811.

Directory of Sheffield; Including the Manufacturers of the adjacent Villages. Sheffield: Gales & Martin, 1787. Reprint: New York: Da Capo Press, 1969.

Dunlap, William. *A History of the American Theatre*. New York: J. J. Harper, 1832.

Eby, Jerrilynn. *Laying the Hoe: A Century of Iron Manufacturing in Stafford County, Virginia*. With a transcript of *The Accokeek Iron Works Business Ledger, 1749-1760* on CD. Westminister, Md.: Willow Bend Books, 2003.

Eckert, Allan W. *That Dark and Bloody River*. New York: Bantam Books, 1996.

Eddis, William. *Letters from America*. Edited by Aubrey C. Land. Cambridge, Mass.: Harvard University Press, 1969.

Filson, John. *The Discovery, Settlement and Present State of Kentucke*. New York: Corinth Books, 1962. Reprint of 1784 edition.

Fithian, Philip Vickers. *The Journal and Letters of Philip Vickers Fithian: A Plantation Tutor of the Old Dominion 1773-1774*. Edited by Hunter Dickinson Farish. Williamsburg, Va.: Colonial Williamsburg, Inc., 1957.

———. *Philip Vickers Fithian: Journal, 1775-1776*. Edited by Robert G. Albion and Leonidas Dodson. Princeton, N. J.: Princeton University Press, 1934.

Flexner, James Thomas. *George Washington: Anguish and Farewell (1793-1799)*. Boston: Little, Brown & Co., 1972.

Ford, W. C., et al., eds. *Journals of the Continental Congress, 1774-1789.* 34 vols. Washington, D.C.: Government Printing Office, 1904-1937.

Gibbs, Vicary, ed. *The Complete Peerage of England Scotland Ireland Great Britain and the United Kingdom.* 13 volumes in 14. London: The St. Catherine Press, Ltd, 1910.

Goodwin, Edward Lewis. *The Colonial Church in Virginia.* Milwaukee, Wisc.: More house Publishing Co., [c. 1927].

Gore, John. *Gore's Liverpool Directory For the Year 1774.* Liverpool, J. Gore, 1774.

Hammon, Neal O. and Richard Taylor. *Virginia's Western War: 1775-1786.* Mechanicsburg, Pa.: Stackpole Books, 2002.

Hassler, Edgar W. *A History of Western Pennsylvania during the Revolution.* Pittsburgh, Pa.: J. R. Weldin & Co., 1900.

Heitman, Francis B. *Historical Register of Officers of the Continental Army during the War of the Revolution.* Reprint of the 1932 edition. Baltimore, Md.: Genealogical Publishing Co., Inc. 1982.

Hening, W. W., ed. *Statutes at Large.* 13 vols. New York, Richmond, and Philadelphia: Various imprints, 1809-1823.

Herndon, G. Melvin. *William Tatham and the Culture of Tobacco.* Coral Gables, Fla.: University Of Miami Press, 1969.

Higginbotham, Don. *The War of American Independence: Military Attitudes, Policies, and Practice, 1763-1789.* New York: The Macmillan Co., 1971.

Hinshaw, William W. *Encyclopedia of American Quaker Genealogy.* 7 vols. Ann Arbor, Mich.: Edwards Brothers, Inc., 1936-1950.

Hodge, Frederick Webb., ed. *Handbook of American Indians North of Mexico.* 2 vols. New York: Pageant Books, Inc., 1959.

Holton, Woody. *Forced Founders: Indians, Debtors, Slaves, & the Making of the American Revolution in Virginia.* Chapel Hill: University of North Carolina Press, 1999.

Hopkins, Margaret Lail, compiler and editor. *Index to the Tithables of Loudoun County, Virginia and to Slaveholders and Slaves, 1858-1786.* Baltimore, Md.: Genealogical Publishing Co., Inc., 1991.

Hurt, R. Douglas. *The Ohio Frontier: Crucible of the Old Northwest, 1720-1830.* Bloomington: Indiana University Press, 1998.

Humphreys, David C. *From King's College to Columbia, 1746-1800.* New York: Columbia University Press, 1976.

Hutchins, Thomas. *A Topographical Description of Virginia, Pennsylvania, Maryland, and North Carolina.* London: J. Almon, 1778.

Jefferson, Thomas. *The Papers of Thomas Jefferson. Second series. Jefferson's Memorandum Books, Accounts, with Legal Records and Miscellany, 1767-1826.* 2 vols. James A. Bear, Jr. and Lucia C. Stanton, eds. Princeton, N. J.: Princeton University Press, 1997.

Johnson, Allen and Dumas Malone, eds. *Dictionary of American Biography.* 22 vols. New York: Charles Scribner's Sons, 1928-1944.

Jones, David. *A Journal of Two Visits Made to Some Nations of Indians on the West Side of the River Ohio in the Years 1772 and 1773.* New York: Arno Press, 1971. Reprint of the 1774 edition.

Kemp, Peter. *The Oxford Companion to Ships and the Sea.* Oxford: Oxford University Press, 1988.

Kennedy, Lawrence F., compiler. *Biographical Dictionary of the American Congress, 1774-1791.* Washington, D.C.,: Government Printing Office, 1971.

King, George H. S. *The Register of Overwharton Parish, Stafford County, Virginia, 1723-1758.* Fredericksburg, Va.: G. H. S. King, 1961.

Kleber, John E. *The Kentucky Encyclopedia*. Lexington, Ky.: The University Press of Kentucky, 1992.

Kneebone, John T., et al., eds. *Dictionary of Virginia Biography*. 3 vols. Richmond, Va.: Library of Virginia, 1998-2006.

Lee, Charles. *Lee Papers*. 3 vols. *Collections of the New-York Historical Society for the Year 1873*. New York: New-York Historical Society, 1874.

Lee, Jean B. *The Price of Nationhood: The American Revolution in Charles County*. New York: W. W. Norton & Co., 1994.

Lee, Sidney, ed. *Dictionary of National Biography*. 63 vols. London: Smith, Elder & Co., 1885-1901.

Lengel, Edward G. *General George Washington: A Military Life*. New York: Random House, 2005.

List of the General and Staff Officers and the Officers in the several Regiments serving in North America. New York: MacDonald & Cameron, 1777.

Livermore, Shaw. *Early American Land Companies: Their Influence on Corporate Development*. New York: Octagon Books, 1968.

Loth, Calder, ed. *The Virginia Landmarks Register*. 4th edition. Charlottesville, Va.: University Press of Virginia, 1999.

Lyle, Maria Catharine. *James Nourse and his Descendants*. Lexington, Ky.: Transylvania Printing Co., 1879.

McAllister, J. T. *Virginia Militia in the Revolutionary War*. Hot Springs, Va.: McAllister Publishing Co., 1913.

McConnell, Michael N. *A Country Between: The Upper Ohio Valley and its Peoples, 1724-1774*. Lincoln: University of Nebraska Press, 1997.

McCullough, David. *John Adams*. New York: Simon & Schuster, 2001.

McIlwaine, Henry R., Wilmer L. Hall, and Benjamin J. Hillman, eds. *Executive Journals of the Council of Colonial Virginia, 1680-1775*. 6 vols. Richmond, Va.: Virginia State Library, 1925-1966.

————, et al, eds. *Journals of the Council of the State of Virginia*. 5 vols. Richmond, Va.: Virginia State Library, 1931-1982.

————, ed. *Official Letters of the Governors of the State of Virginia*. 3 vols. Richmond, Va.: Virginia State Library, 1926-1929.

Malone, Dumas, ed. *Dictionary of American Biography*. 22 vols. New York: Charles Scribner's Sons, 1928-1958.

Martin, James Kirby. *The Human Dimensions of Nation Making: Essays on Colonial and Revolutionary America*. Madison, Wisc.: The State Historical Society of Wisconsin, 1976.

Maryland Historical Trust. *Inventory of Historic Sites in Calvert County, Charles County and St. Mary's County*. Annapolis, Md.: Maryland Historical Trust, 1980.

Mason, George. *The Papers of George Mason, 1725-1792*. Edited by Robert A. Rutland. 3 vols. Chapel Hill, N. C.: University of North Carolina Press, 1970.

Merrell, James H. *Into the American Woods: Negotiators on the Pennsylvania Frontier*. New York: W. W. Norton & Co., 1999.

Morris, Richard B. *Encyclopedia of American History*. New York: Harper & Row, Publishers, 1976.

Mulkearn, Lois, ed. *George Mercer Papers Relating to the Ohio Company of Virginia*. Pittsburgh, Pa.: University of Pittsburgh Press, 1954.

Munson, James Donald. "From Empire to Commonwealth: Alexandria, Virginia, 1749-1780." PhD Dissertation. University of Maryland, 1984.

Nelson, Paul David. *General Horatio Gates: A Biography.* Baton Rouge: Louisana State University Press, 1976.

Norris, J. E., ed. *History of the Lower Shenandoah Valley Counties of Frederick, Berkeley, Jefferson and Clarke, their Early Settlement and Progress to the Present Time.* Chicago: A. Warner & Co., 1890.

Olmstead, Earl P. *David Zeisberger: A Life among the Indians.* Kent, Ohio: Kent State University Press, 1997.

Pendleton, Edmund. *The Letters and Papers of Edmund Pendleton, 1734-1803.* Edited by David J. Mays. 2 vols. Charlottesville, Va.: University Press of Virginia, 1967.

Picard, Liza. *Dr. Johnson's London.* New York: St. Martin's Press, 2001.

Porter, Roy. *London: A Social History.* Cambridge, Mass.: Harvard University Press, 1994.

Porter, W. S. *Notes from a Peakland Parish.* Sheffield, England: J. W. Northend, 1923.

Pownall, Thomas. *A Topographical Description . . . of the Middle British Colonies, &c., in North America.* London, 1776.

Rice, Otis K. *The Allegheny Frontier: West Virginia Beginnings, 1730-1830.* Lexington, Ky.: University Press of Kentucky, 1970.

Rouse, Park Jr. *The Great Wagon Road.* Richmond, Va.: Dietz Press: 1995.

Sabine, Lorenzo. *Biographical Sketches of Loyalists of the American Revolution, with an Historical Essay.* 2 vols. Boston: Little, Brown and Co., 1864.

Salmon, Emily J., ed. *Hornbook of Virginia History.* Third edition. Richmond, Va.: Viginia State Library, 1983.

Sanchez-Saavedra, E. M. *A Guide to Virginia Military Organizations in the American Revolution, 1774-1787.* Richmond: Virginia State Library, 1978.

Sanders, Joanne McRee, ed. *Barbados Records. Baptisms, 1637-1800.* Baltimore, Md.: Genealogical Publishing Co., 1984.

Schomburgk, Robert H. *The History of Barbados.* London: Frank Cass & Co., 1971. Reprint of the 1848 edition.

Scott, Kenneth, compiler. *Rivington's New York Newspaper: Excerpts from a Loyalist Press, 1773-1783.* New York: New-York Historical Society, 1973.

Selby, John E. *The Revolution in Virginia: 1775-1783.* Williamsburg, Va.: The Colonial Williamsburg Foundation, 1989.

Smith, Paul N., et al., eds. *Letters of Delegates to Congress, 1774-1789.* 22 vols. Washington, D.C.: Library of Congress, 1976-2000.

Sparacio, Ruth and Sam Sparacio. *Tithables Book: Looudoun County, Virginia 1770-1774.* N. p. The Ancient Press, 1992.

———. *Tithables Book: Looudoun County, Virginia 1775-1781.* N. p. The Ancient Press, 1992.

Staudt, John G. "Suffolk County," in *The Other New York: The American beyond New York City,* Joseph S. Tiedemann and Eugene R. Fingernut, eds. Albany, N. Y.: State University of New York Press, 2005.

Stetson, Charles W. *Washington and His Neighbors.* Richmond, Va.: Garrett and Massie, Inc., 1956.

Syrett, David. *The Royal Navy in American Waters, 1775-1783.* Hants, England: Scolar Press, 1989.

Thwaites, Reuben Gold and Louise Phelps Kellogg, eds. *Documentary History of Dunmore's War.* Madison, Wisc.: Wisconsin Historical Society, 1905.

———, eds. *Frontier Defense on the Upper Ohio, 1777-1778.* Madison, Wisc.: Wiscosin Historical Society, 1912.

————, eds. *The Revolution on the Upper Ohio, 1775-1777*. Madison, Wisc.: Wisconsin Historical Society, 1908.

Tiedemann, Joseph S. and Eugene R. Fingerhut, eds. *The Other New York: The American Revolution beyond New York City, 1763-1787*. Albany, N. Y.: State University of New York Press, 2005.

Tilley, John A. *The British Navy and the American Revolution*. Columbia, S. C.: University of South Carolina Press, 1987.

Van Schreeven, William J., Robert L. Scribner, and Brent Tartar, eds. *Revolutionary Virginia: The Road to Independence*. 7 vols. Charlottesville, Va.: University Press of Virginia, 1973-1983.

Venn, John, ed. *Alumni Cantabrigienses: A Biographical List of all known Students, graduates and Holders of Office at the University of Cambridge, from the earliest times to 1900*. 10 vols. Cambridge: Cambridge University Press, 1922.

Washington, George. *The Diaries of George Washington*. John C. Fitzpatrick, ed. 4 vols. Boston, Mass.: Houghton Mifflin Co., 1925.

————. *The Diaries of George Washington*. Donald Jackson and Dorothy Twohig, eds. 6 vols. Charlottesville, Va.: University Press of Virginia, 1976-1979.

Washington, George. *The Papers of George Washington, Colonial Series*. W. W. Abbot et al., eds. 10 vols. Charlottesville, Va.: University Press of Virginia, 1994-1995.

Weinreb, Ben and Christopher Hibbert, eds. *The London Encyclopaedia*. New York: St. Martin's Press, 1983.

Wertenbaker, Thomas Jefferson. *Father Knickerbocker Rebels: New York City During the Revolution*. New York: Charles Scribner's Sons, 1948.

————. *Princeton, 1746-1896*. Princeton, N. J.: Princeton University Press, 1946.

Wertz, Mary Alice. *Marriages of Loudoun County, Virginia, 1757-1853*. Baltimore, Md.: Genealogical Publishing Co., 1985.

White, Richard. *The Middle Ground: Indians, Empires, and Republics in the Great Lakes Region, 1650-1815*. Cambridge: Cambridge University Press, 1991.

Williams, Robert A., Jr. *The American Indian in Western Legal Thought: The Discourses of Conquest*. New York, Oxford University Press, 1990.

Withers, Alexander Scott. *Chronicles of Border Warfare*. Edited by Reuben Gold Thwaites. Cincinnati, Ohio: The Robert Clarke Co., 1908.

Williams, Harrison. *Legends of Loudoun: An Account of the History and Homes of a Border County of Virginia's Northern Neck*. Richmond, Va.: Garrett and Massie, Inc., 1938.

Zeisberger, David. *The Moravian Mission Diaries of David Zeisberger, 1772-1781*. Edited by Heran Wellenreuther and Carola Wessel. Translated by Julie Tomberlin Weber. University Park, Pa.: Pennsylvania State University Press, 2005.

Articles

Abbot, W. W., ed. "General Edward Braddock in Alexandria: John Carlyle to George Carlyle, 15 August 1755." *Virginia Magazine of History and Biography*. 97 (1989): 204-14.

Allard, Dean C. "The Potomac Navy of 1776." *Virginia Magazine of History and Biography*. 84 (1976): 411-30.

Bailyn, Bernard. "Common Sense." *American Heritage*. 26 (1973), 36-40; 91-93.

Bailey, Kenneth P. "George Mason: Westerner." *William and Mary Quarterly*. Second series. 23 (1943): 409-17.

Beckner, Lucien. "John Findley: The First Pathfinder of Kentucky." *The Filson Club History Quarterly*. 43 (1969): 206-215.

Bowman, Larry. "The Virginia County Committees of Safety, 1774-1776." *Virginia Magazine of History and Biography*. 79 (1971); 322-37.

Bray, William. "Observations on the Indian Method of Picture-Writing." *Archaeologia: or Miscellaneous Tracts Relating to Antiquity*. 6 (1782); 159-62.

———. "A Sketch of a tour into Derbyshire and Yorkshire, including part of Buckingham, Warwick, Leicester, Nottingham, Bedford, and Hertford-shires." In John Pinkerton, *A General Collection of the Best and Most interesting Voyages and Travels in all parts of the World*. Vol. 2. London, 1808.

Connolly, John. "A Narrative of the Transactions, Imprisonment, and Sufferings of John Connolly, An American Loyalist and Lieut. Col. In His Majesty's Service." *Pennsylvania Magazine of History and Biography*. 12 (1888): 310-24, 407-20; 13 (1889): 61-70, 153-67, 281-91.

Curtis, George M., III. "The Goodrich Family and the Revolution in Virginia, 1774-1776." *Virginia Magazine of History and Biography*. 84 (1976): 49-74.

"Diary of Mrs. James Nourse." *The Magazine of the Jefferson County Historical Society*. 24, (1958): 21-28.

"Extracts from 'The Barbados Mercury'." *The Journal of the Barbados Museum and Historical Society*. 17 (1950): 110.

Foster, James W. "Potomac River Maps of 1737 by Robert Brooke and Others." *William and Mary Quarterly*. Second series, 18 (1938): 406-18.

Gill, Harold B., Jr. "Governing from a Tavern," *Colonial Williamsburg Journal*, 18 (1996): 60-62.

———. "Wheat Culture in Colonial Virginia." *Agricultural History*. 52 (1978): 380-93.

Horrell, Joseph, ed. "New Light on William Grayson: His Guardian's Account." *Virginia Magazine of History and Biography*. 92 (1984): 423-43.

Matley, Charles Alfred. "The Geology of Bardsey Island." *Quarterly Journal of the Geological Society*. 69 (1913): 514-27.

Meehan, Thomas R. "Courts, Cases, and Counselors in Revolutionary and Post-Revolutionary Pennsylvania." *Pennsylvania Magazine of History and Biography*. 91 (1967): 3-34.

Nelson, Larry L. "Cultural Mediation, Cultural Exchange, and the Invention of the Ohio Frontier." *Ohio History*. 105 (1996): 72-91.

Nourse, James. "Journey to Kentucky in 1775." *Journal of American History*. 29. (1925): 121-39, 251-60, 351-64.

Schaukirk, Ewald Gustav. "Occupation of New York by the British." *Pennsylvania Magazine of History and Biography*. 10 (1886): 418-45.

Sosin, Jack M. "The British Indian Department and Dunmore's War." *Virginia Magazine of History and Biography*. 74 (1966): 54-50.

Wainwright, Nicholas B. ed. "Turmoil at Pittsburgh: Diary of Augustine Prevost, 1774." *Pennsylvania Magazine of History and Biography*. 85 (1961): 111-62.

White, William E. "The Independent Companies of Virginia, 1774-1775." *Virginia Magazine of History and Biography*. 86 (1978): 149-62.

Williams, Edward G., ed. "The Journal of Richard Butler, 1775: Continental Congress' Envoy to the Western Indians." *Western Pennsylvania Historical Magazine*. 46 (1963): 381-395; 47 (1964): 31-45, 141-56.

Worner, William Frederick. "Lancaster in 1776." *Lancaster County Historical Journal.* 32 (1928): 148-49.

Unpublished Primary Sources

Allason, William. Business Records. Library of Virginia. Richmond, Virginia.
American Loyalist Claims—Special Agents' Reports on Claims, 1784-1803. T. 79-73. Public Record Office. London.
Baynton, Wharton, and Morgan. Correspondence, 1763-1783. Pennsylvania Historical and Museum Commission. Harrisburg, Pennsylvania.
Captains' Logs. Adm 51/694. Public Record Office. London, England
Carlin, William. Account Book, 1750s-1770s (Alexandria, Virginia). Privately owned. Microfilm in John D. Rockefeller, Jr. Library. Colonial Williamsburg Foundation. Williamsburg, Virginia.
Carter-Keith Papers. Virginia Historical Society. Richmond, Virginia.
Charles County Maryland. Court Records. Hall of Records, Annapolis, Maryland.
Frederick County Virginia Court Records. Frederick County Courthouse. Winchester, Virginia.
Glassford, John & Co. Alexandria Ledger 1765-1766. Library of Congress. Washington, D.C.
High Court of Admiralty. Ships' Papers, 1777. HCA 32/280. Public Record Office. London, England.
High Court of Admiralty. Prize Papers, 1778. HCA 32/286. Public Record Office. London, England.
Janney, Joseph. Account Book 1773-1776. Maryland Historical Society. Baltimore, Maryland.
Letters to the Secretary of State from the Governor, Lord Dunmore, with enclosures and replies. CO 5/1352. Public Record Office London, England.
Letters to the Secretary of State from the Governor, Lord Dunmore, with enclosures and replies. CO 5/1353. Public Record Office London, England.
Loudoun County Virginia Court Records. Loudoun County Courthouse. Leesburg, Virginia.
Loyalist Claims, Series I – Evidence, Maryland 1783-1786. A. O. 12/6. Public Record Office. London, England.
Masters' Logs. Adm 52/1909. Public Record Office. London, England.
Mellish of Hodstock. Nottingham University, England.
Miscellaneous Manuscripts. Chicago Historical Society. Chicago, Ill.
Naval Office Returns. Barbados. T 64/48. Public Record Office. London, England.
———. South Potomac. T 1/498. Public Record Office. London, England.
Navy Board (Virginia). Journal, July 23, 1776 – Feb. 27, 1779. Library of Virginia. Richmond, Virginia.
Noland, Pierce. Bounty Warrant. Library of Virginia. Richmond, Virginia.
Register of Passes, 1772-1774. Adm 7/98. Public Record Office. London, England.
Repton Priory deed transcripts; Tymm family of Edale; Nicholas Cresswell of Edale, and miscellanea. Derbyshire Record Office, Derby, England.
Secretary's Department, Orders in Council, 1783. Adm 1/5176. Public Record Office. London, England.

Shepard, David. Papers. Draper Manuscripts. State Historical Society of Wisconsin. Madison, Wisconsin.

Treasury Board – In Letters 1784. T1/609. Public Record Office, London, England.

Treasury Board – Out Letters (General) XXXIV, 1781-1783. T 27/34. Public Record Office. London, England.

Treasury: General Accounts, Auditor's Declarations. T 31/287. Public Record Office. London, England.

Treasury: General Accounts, Quarterly. T 33/161. Public Record Office. London, England.

Treasury Minute Book LIII, 1782-1783. T 29/53, Public Record Office. London, England.

Virginia Committee of Safety Ledger, 1775-1776. Library of Virginia. Richmond, Virginia.

Virginia. Treasurer's Office Receipt Books. Library of Virginia. Richmond, Virginia.

Washington, George. Cash Memorandum Book 1774-1775. Library of Congress. Washington, D.C.

Index

Hartford, 119
Hartshorn, William, 129
Harwood, Capt., 59
Harwoods Landing, 56, 59
Haukins, Mrs., 128, 129, 140
Hawkins, Mrs., 132
Hay-Market, 192
Hayrick, 113
Hazelwood, Mr., 21
Head of Elk, 119
Hell Gate, 118, 174, 175, 177
Henly, Mr., 36
Henry, Governor Patrick, 112, 179
Hepburn, Mr., 168
Herbert, Miles, 18
Hite, Jacob, 29, 134
    John, 130
Hites Island, 120
Hole Town, 21
Holland, Major, 158, 165
Holy Head, 7
Honeton, Mrs. Seaman, 130
Hope, 3, 4
Hopewell, 29
Hopkins, Esak, 108
Horner, William, 27, 34
Horse stealer, 105
Hospital, Chelsey, 193
Hostages, 30
Hotham, Commodore, 157
How, Capt. Tyrringham, 156
Howe, General, 101, 119, 120, 131, 133,
    158, 181
    Lord, 112, 144, 165, 181
Hudibras, 184
Hughes, Mrs., 192
Hughs, Mr., 130, 193
Hunneycomb, Polly, 160
Hurricane, 21

Iffil, Mr., 22
Illinois, 31, 32, 40
Illinois Company, xv-xvi
Independent Companies
    Formed, 26
    Exercised, 28, 31, 34
    Gentlemen's, 35
    Mechanics, 35
Indian, Cabins, 74
    Cherokee, 134

Culture, 82-85
Dance, Described, 75-76
Delaware, 76, 80
Description, 30
Dress, 72, 84
Houses, 85
Language, 84
Mingo, 75
Mohawk, 75
Ottawa, 80
Shawnee, xvi, 30, 53, 79, 80
Tribes, 85
Warmarks, 76
Indian Affairs, Superintendent of, 51
Indian Corn, Cultivation, 146-147
Indian, Trader, 69, 70, 79
Innis, Capt., 33
    Col., 153
Intolerable Acts, ix
Island, Big Tree, 53
Isle of Wight, 190

Jackson, Dr., 89
    Samuel, 2, 5, 21
Jamaica, New York, 165, 173
Janney, Joseph, 105, 106, 113
Jefferson, Thomas, 114, 115
Jew Fish, 18
Johns, Mr., 104
Johnston, B., 71
    Benjamin, 41
    Capt., 161
    Capt. G., 129
    Capt. William, 133, 140, 141
    George, 101, 106
    Mr., 41, 55, 57, 58, 59, 60, 101
    William, 103
Jolly, Capt., 174
Journal, Preserved, 148
    Rectified, 162

Kanaughtonhead, 74, 77, 79
Kaskasky, 35
Keir, Collin, 150, 155, 168
    Lt., 170
    Mr., 150, 154, 157, 159, 160, 168
Kentucky, Harrodsburg, x
Keys, Mr., 87
Keys Ferry, 29, 130
Kid, Mr., 21